JUBILEES
INSIGHTS

S.N.Strutt

ISBN 978-1-78222-793-9

Book design, layout and production management by Into Print
www.intoprint.net
+44 (0)1604 832149

CONTENTS

INTRODUCTION		7
Chapter 1	THE TEN COMMANDMENTS	12
Chapter 2	CREATION	21
Chapter 3	EVE IS CREATED	31
Chapter 4	BIRTH OF CAIN & ABLE	41
Chapter 5	THE FALLEN ANGELS	53
Chapter 6	NOAH	68
Chapter 7	CANAAN CURSED	79
Chapter 8	WRITINGS OF THE WICKED WATCHERS	89
Chapter 9	SONS OF NOAH DIVIDE THE LAND	101
Chapter 10	DEMONS AND THE TOWER OF BABEL	106
Chapter 11	POST-FLOOD WARS BEGIN	125
Chapter 12	ABRAHAM	132
Chapter 13	SHECHEM	138
Chapter 14	GOD CALLS ABRAHAM	147
Chapter 15	GOD'S COVENANT WITH ABRAHAM	152
Chapter 16	ISAAC PROMISED	158
Chapter 17	HAGAR CAST OUT	163
Chapter 18	ISAAC TO BE A SACRIFICE	167
Chapter 19	SARAH DIES: DOUBLE CAVE	170
Chapter 20	CIRCUMCISION	178
Chapter 21	ABRAHAM BLESSES ISAAC	183
Chapter 22	JACOB BLESSED	190

Chapter 23	DEATH OF ABRAHAM	199
Chapter 24	JACOB STEALS THE BIRTHRIGHT	208
Chapter 25	LABAN	217
Chapter 26	ISAAC DECEIVED BY JACOB	222
Chapter 27	JACOB FLEES FROM ESAU	227
Chapter 28	RACHEL	231
Chapter 29	JACOB FLEES FROM LABAN	236
Chapter 30	DINAH & SHECHEM	239
Chapter 31	BETHEL	248
Chapter 32	VISIONS	254
Chapter 33	BILHAH	259
Chapter 34	SHECHEM	266
Chapter 35	REBEKKA DIES	271
Chapter 36	ISAAC, RACHEL & LEAH - ALL DIE	276
Chapter 37	ESAU SEEKS REVENGE	281
Chapter 38	JACOB SLAYS ESAU	285
Chapter 39	JOSEPH IN EGYPT	288
Chapter 40	PHARAOH'S DREAMS	294
Chapter 41	TAMAR	299
Chapter 42	JOSEPH & THE FAMINE	304
Chapter 43	BENJAMIN'S SACK	310
Chapter 44	JACOB HEARS GOD'S VOICE	315
Chapter 45	JACOB GOES TO EGYPT	319
Chapter 46	JACOB DIES	323
Chapter 47	MOSES	327
Chapter 48	10 PLAGUES ON EGYPT	330

| Chapter 49 | THE PASSOVER | 342 |
| Chapter 50 | SABBATHS | 348 |

Appendix

I STORY OF THE SERPENT

II DOES THE EARTH HAVE A SPIRIT?

III THE ABYSS

IV BACKGROUND INFO INTO BOOK OF JUBILEES

V WAS THE BOOK OF JUBILEES PART OF THE CANON?

VI VERSIONS AND ORIGINAL LANGUAGE

VII WHAT DOES THE YEAR OF THE JUBILEE MEAN?

VIII ASTRONOMICAL *'TIME'* FAKERY

IX BACKGROUND OF DIFFERENT WAYS OF MEASURING THE LENGTH OF THE YEAR

X HOW THE SCIENTISTS ALTERED TIME

XI LIES IN SCIENCE

XII THE BIG BANG

XIII THERE IS NO CHAOS & RANDOMNESS TO THE UNIVERSE

XIV WHERE DID THE CONCEPT OF TIME COME FROM?

XV THE 360 DAY PROPHETIC YEAR OF THE BIBLE

XVI THE BOOK OF REMEDIES

XVII COMPARISON KJV OF THE BIBLE AND THE SEPTUAGINT

XVIII TIMEFRAME OF 7000 YEARS OF WORLD HISTORY

XIX AGE OF THE EARTH

XX NEPHILIM

XXI ORIGIN OF THE HYBRID CREATURES & CHIMERAS KNOWN

AS THE GIANTS & THE MONSTERS IN THE BOOK OF THE GI-
ANTS

XXII IDOL WORSHIPPING & SORCERY LEADS TO THE 'MARK OF
THE BEAST'

XXIII DEVOURING BEASTS & MONSTERS

XXIV ZION

XXV THE KING JAMES VERSION OF THE 'OLD TESTAMENT' WAS
WRITTEN IN 1611 COMPARED WITH 'THE SEPTUAGINT' WHICH
WAS WRITTEN AROUND 200-300 BCE

XXVI MY SIX BOOKS & USEFUL WEBSITE LINKS:

CREDITS: I would especially like to give many thanks to my wife
for our discussions into what to include in this book & her editorial
help. I would also like to thank all those who have encouraged me to
write this book of *JUBILEES INSIGHTS*
Front cover artwork by Suzanne Strutt: www.instagram.com/suzan-
nestruttartist & www.facebook.com/suzannestruttartist

INTRODUCTION

This is the history of the division of the days of the law and of the testimony, of the events of the years, of their (year) weeks, of their Jubilees throughout all the years of the world, as the Lord spoke to Moses on Mount Sinai when he went up to receive the tables of the law and of the commandment, according to the voice of God as he said unto him, 'Go up to the top of the Mount.'

QUESTION: "WHAT IS THE YEAR OF JUBILEE?"

Answer: The word "jubilee"—literally means "ram's horn" in Hebrew—and is defined in **Leviticus 25:9** as **the sabbatical year after seven cycles of seven years (49 years).** The fiftieth year was to be a time of celebration and rejoicing for the Israelites. The ram's horn was blown on the tenth day of the seventh month to start the fiftieth year of universal redemption. The **Year of the** Jubilee involved a year of **release from indebtedness** (**Leviticus 25:23-38**) and all types of bondage (vv. 39-55). **All prisoners and captives were set free**, all slaves were released, **all debts were forgiven**, and all property was returned to its original owners. In addition, all labour was to cease for one year, and those bound by labour contracts were released from them. **One of the benefits of the Jubilee was that both the land and the people were able to rest. (See: APPENDIX for more on this)**

'JUBILEES INSIGHTS' 'SYNOPSIS' OF THE CHAPTERS: NOTE: THIS SYNOPSIS MENTIONS ONLY THE MAIN TOPICS COVERED:

CH.1 Moses and the Burning bush. The 'Angels of the Presence' speak to him. He is taught the whole 'History of the World' from the beginning of Creation to the end. God warns Moses that Israel will go astray and worship idols. He predicts that Israel will be taken captive by other nations. He also predicts that Israel will only finally become righteous after the Messiah has returned in the time of Jacob's Trouble and Israel has learned to confess her sins.

CH.2 Sabbath instituted. Creation story. Sea monsters mentioned.

CH.3 Creation of Adam and Eve: History of 'The Serpent': 'speech' is taken away from the animals.

Adam and Eve are 7 years in the garden before Temptation enters.

CH.4 Cain marries his sister: Eve had 9 sons & many daughters: Enoch is the first person to write things down. Enoch spends 6 Jubilees with the angels and is brought to the Garden of Eden: 4 Holy locations on earth.

CH.5 Fallen angels: Giants: Heavenly Tablets: Jubilees = 49 years: 7 floodgates of heaven

CH 6 Noah: Atonement: Festival of First Fruits: 7 abysses: Solar year: Canaan cursed

CH.7 Names of 3 types of giants. Each type a different size. Demons appear after the flood: Nephilim writings on rocks. (megaliths?)

CH.8 Noah divided the earth to his 3 sons. Centre of the 'naval' of the earth. (hollow earth)

CH.9 Mastema is another name for Satan: Dangerous demons blinding and killing mankind: Malignant fallen angels: Book of Herbs and Medicines: Tower of Babel: Canaan is double-cursed and steals Shem's lands.

CH.10 Details of the Tower of Babel in the days of Peleg and Reu. Cyclopean structures: Portals

CH.11 Graven Images- Idol worship: Abraham drives away the ravens of Mastema: Abraham invents a modern plough:

CH.12 Abraham the Idol Smasher: God's promise to Abraham. Hebrew is the 'tongue' of Creation

CH.13 Shechem: God promises the lands to Abraham: Abraham makes an altar to God: Nimrod = Amraphel.

CH.14 'Sacrifice of a lamb' instituted: Abraham has a vision of 'Light and Darkness'

CH.15 Eternal 'Covenant of Peace' between God and Abraham: 'Covenant of Circumcision'

CH.16 Plant of Righteousness = the Messiah

CH.17 Mastema (Satan) tries to tempt Abraham

CH.18 Courts in heaven. Satan the prosecuting attorney.

CH.19 Abraham chooses Jacob to be Isaac's successor

CH.20 Severe Laws with very severe punishments.

CH.21 Abraham is 175 years old when he dies.

CH.22 Abraham anoints Jacob to continue the family line

CH.23 Abraham dies: Double cave: Was it a Portal? Man's age to be reduced to 70: End Days: a child will look like an old man.

CH.24 Isaac curses the Philistines

CH.25 Rebecca tells her son not to take a Canaanite wife

CH.26 Isaac calls Esau to make venison before he dies. Jacob the deceiver

CH.27 Esau's evil intentions revealed in a dream to Rebecca: Jacob dreams of a ladder up to heaven: A portal?

CH.28 Jacob marries 4 wives.

CH.29 Land of Rephaim = land of the giants.

CH.30 Dinah and Shechem: Shechem slaughtered 'in torment'.

CH.31 Rachel gives her father's idols to Jacob to be burned.

CH.32 Tithing initiated. God changes Jacob's name to Israel.

CH.33 Reuben takes advantage of father's concubine Bilhah

CH.34 Wars because of the slaughter at Shechem.

CH 35 Potiphar the eunuch?

CH.36 Eternal execration: Rachel dies young in childbirth.

CH.37 Esau full of malice

CH 38 Esau slain by Jacob

CH.39 Potiphar's wife tries to entice Joseph

CH.40 Pharaoh's dreams

CH.41 Tamar and Judah

CH.42 Jacob's sons accused of being 'spies' by Joseph down in Egypt

CH.43 Joseph reveals himself to his brothers.

CH.44 God appears to Jacob in a vison and tells him not to fear to go down to Egypt

CH.45 Seven Years of Famine in Egypt. Jacob goes down to Egypt

CH.46 Joseph dies at 110 years old.

CH.47 Birth of Moses

CH.48 Mastema tries to kill Moses.

CH.49 Passover instituted: Pascal Lamb: Moses at Shechem

CH.50 End of Satan

THE BOOK OF JUBILEES IS QUOTED IN FULL IN THIS BOOK OF 'JUBILEES INSIGHTS.'

THE FORMAT OF THIS BOOK

i) The original text from the **Book of Jubilees** will be surrounded by boxes to make it easier to notice the original text.

ii) I decided to give **each chapter** a title to make it easier for the reader and also a **synopsis of each chapter** and the **APPENDIX** to make it much easier to find specific topics.

iii) I have typed a chapter of the **Book of Jubilees**, and included in each chapter my commentaries, which are just that: my opinions, speculations and theories, which are gleaned from much study of the subject matter. Most, if not all of which, could prove to be true, and are written with the express intention to motivate the reader to do a more thorough investigation for him or herself, to prove whether correct or not, as I am sure that some of the ideas, speculations and conjecture will be quite far out there, to some people.

iv) I have also put cross-references to the Bible, and other Apocryphal books where appropriate.

v) **Details:**

The first '**comment'** in each chapter, will be noted as being '**Comment:1**' & then **C.2, C.3**, etc. The original Text from the **Book of Jubilees** is in slightly larger text than either the 'comments' or '**Bible verses**. Three different types of writing are used. One for the original text, and another type of writing for my comments, and yet another for the Bible verses.

vi) The longest commentaries and conclusions are in the '**APPENDICES'** of this book of which there are around 30.

Stephen Nigel Strutt (August 2020)

JUBILEES INSIGHTS
by S N Strutt 2020

Chapter 1: THE TEN COMMANDMENTS

> 1 And it came to pass in the first year of the Exodus of the children of Israel (coming) out of Egypt, in the third month, on the sixteenth day of the month, [2450 Anno Mundi] that God spoke to Moses, saying: 'Come up to Me on the Mount, and I will give thee two tables of stone of the law and of the commandment, which I have written, that thou mayst teach them.'

Comment:1: '**Anno Mundi**' is Latin and means 'years of the world' or 'years since the creation of the world'. [**2450 Anno Mundi**] = approx. 1550 BCE.

EXO.19:3 And Moses went up unto God, and the LORD called unto him out of the mountain, saying, 'Thus shalt thou say to the house of Jacob, and tell the children of Israel'.

> 2 And Moses went up into the mount of God, and the glory of the Lord abode on Mount Sinai, and a cloud overshadowed it six days.

EXO.19:9 And the LORD said unto Moses, Lo, I come unto thee in a thick cloud, that the people may hear when I speak with thee and believe thee for ever. And Moses told the words of the people unto the LORD.

> 3 And He called to Moses on the seventh day out of the midst of the cloud, and the appearance of the glory of the Lord was like a flaming fire on the top of the mount.

EXO.19:16 And it came to pass on the third day in the morning, that there were thunders and lightnings, and a thick cloud upon the mount, and the voice of the trumpet exceeding loud; so that all the people that was in the camp trembled.

> 4 And Moses was on the Mount forty days and forty nights, and God taught him the earlier and the later history of the division of all the days of the law and of the testimony.

C.2 '*taught him the earlier and the later history*' – God was telling Moses about the laws that He had passed down to Moses from the Beginning of time to the End. What God had taught Enoch before the Great Flood and Noah right after the Flood, and then to Abraham, Isaac and Jacob and now unto Moses and then after Him to Joshua.

5 And He said: 'Incline thine heart to every word which I shall speak to thee on this mount, and write them in a book in order that their generations may see how I have not forsaken them for all the evil which they have wrought in transgressing the covenant which I establish between Me and thee for their generations this day on Mount Sinai.

6 And thus it will come to pass when all these things come upon them, that they will recognise that I am more righteous than they in all their judgments and in all their actions, and they will recognise that I have been truly with them.

C.3 What does this mean '*I have been truly with them*'? This should read '*I have been honest and faithful with them.*'

7 And do thou write for thyself all these words which I declare unto, thee this day, for I know their rebellion and their stiff neck, before I bring them into the land of which I swore to their fathers, to Abraham and to Isaac and to Jacob, saying: 'Unto your seed will I give a land flowing with milk and honey'.

EXO.33:3 Unto a land flowing with milk and honey: for I will not go up in the midst of thee; for thou art a stiff-necked people: lest I consume thee in the way.

8 And they will eat and be satisfied, and they will turn to strange gods, to (gods) which cannot deliver them from aught of their tribulation: and this witness shall be heard for a witness against them.

EXO.34:17 Thou shalt make thee no molten gods.

9 For they will forget all My commandments, (even) all that I command them, and they will walk after the Gentiles, and after their uncleanness, and after their shame, and will serve their gods, and these will prove unto them an offence and a tribulation and an affliction and a snare.

10 And many will perish and they will be taken captive, and will fall into the hands of the enemy, because they have forsaken My ordinances and My commandments, and the festivals of My covenant, and My sabbaths, and My holy place which I have hallowed for Myself in their midst, and My tabernacle, and My sanctuary, which I have hallowed for Myself in the midst of the land, that I should set my name upon it, and that it should dwell (there).

13

> 11 And they will make to themselves high places and groves and graven images, and they will worship, each his own (graven image), so as to go astray, and they will sacrifice their children to demons, and to all the works of the error of their hearts.

C.4 Can we imagine that man has stopped doing what it says in this verse 11 *'worship, each his own (graven image), 'sacrifice their children to demons'?* There is evidence abounding in the scriptures that these things are still going on today on an even bigger scale. When it comes to God's Final Judgements in the Book of Revelations at the very end of chapter 9 it states:

REV.9:20 And the rest of the men which were not killed by these plagues yet repented not of the works of their hands, that they should *not worship devils,* and *idols* of gold, and silver, and brass, and stone, and of wood: which neither can see, nor hear, nor walk:

REV.9:21 Neither repented they of their *murders,* nor of their *sorceries,* nor of their *fornication,* nor of their *thefts.*

C.5 Today, we hear all the time of *children being kidnapped* and used in some sort of *witchcraft/sorcery ritual* along with sexual perversions & cursed paedophilia as a sacrifice unto Satan or one of his Fallen angels to get their favour or 'blessing.' This is especially true of the so-called 'Elite' of today and very rich trying to 'curry the favour' of Satan and do his bidding, and is the exact description that God gives to the Merchants of the earth who have enslaved mankind through murder, sorcery & theft:

REV.18:15 The merchants of these things, which were made rich by her, shall stand afar off for the fear of her torment, weeping and wailing,

REV.18:24 And in her was found the *blood of prophets,* and of *saints,* and of *all* that were *slain upon the earth.*

> 12 And I will send witnesses unto them, that I may witness against them, but they will not hear, and will slay the witnesses also, and they will persecute those who seek the law, and they will abrogate and change everything so as to work evil before My eyes.

II EZDRAS 2.1 Thus says the Lord, 'I brought this people out of bondage, and I gave them commandments through my servants the prophets, but they would not listen to them and made my counsels void.

PSALM 78.21-22 Therefore the Lord heard this and was wroth; so a fire was kindled against Jacob and anger also came against Israel. Because they believed not in God, and trusted not in his **SALVATION**

C.6 This is an amazing statement by Almighty God Himself. Here God is stating that although God Himself has indeed chosen Israel as His special nation, who were supposed to be both a *witness to the nations* and an *example of God's presence* among mankind, that God was prophesying that Israel would go astray and worship Idols. He also stated that even though He would send prophets unto Israel, that they would not listen to them, but would slay them. This is reflected in the **New Testament** by the **Messiah Jesus himself, the Son of God, in Matthew Chapter 23** in His exhortation to the Pharisees:

MAT.23:31 Wherefore ye be witnesses unto yourselves, that ye are the children of them which *killed the prophets.*

MAT.23:34 Wherefore, behold, *I send unto you prophets*, and wise men, and scribes: and some of them ye shall kill and crucify; and some of them shall ye scourge in your synagogues, and persecute them from city to city:

MAT.23:35 That upon you may come all the righteous blood shed upon the earth, from the blood of righteous Abel unto the blood of Zacharias son of Barachias, whom ye slew between the temple and the altar.

MAT.23:37 O Jerusalem, Jerusalem, thou that kills the prophets, and stones them which are sent unto thee, how often would I have gathered thy children together, even as a hen gathers her chickens under her wings, and ye would not!

C.7 This verse is mirrored in the Apocryphal book of II Ezdras.

II EZDRAS 1.16 I gathered you as a hen gathers her brood under her wings. But now, what shall I do to you? I will cast you out of My presence. When, you offer oblations to me, I will turn my face from you, for I have rejected your feast days, and new moons, and circumcisions of the flesh

II EZDRAS 1.17 I sent you my servants the prophets, but you have taken and slain them and torn their bodies in pieces. Their blood will I require of you says the Lord

MAT.23:38 Behold, your house is left unto you desolate.

II EZDRAS 1.18a Thus says the Almighty, your house is desolate.

II EZDRAS 1.18b I will drive you out as the wind drives straw and your sons will have no children, because with you they have neglected my commandments and have done evil in my sight. (See: My book '**EZDRAS INSIGHTS**')

C.8 These last verses given by Moses in 1500 BC, King David in the year 1000, Ezra in 500 BC & the Messiah in 30 A.D were fulfilled many times throughout history. Israel was attacked and raided by the Philistines around 1200 BC, & God finally raised up Samson to destroy the Lords of the Philistines. In the year 1000 BC. God raised up King David to throw off the scourge of the Philistines and their giant Goliath. King David was a godly king; but even he had to fight many wars to subjugate all the enemies of Israel. The Northern Tribes were conquered in around 722 BC by the Assyrian empire. In around 589 Nebuchadnezzar the king of the Babylonian empire captured Jerusalem and took them all away as slaves.

15

C.9 Finally, when they killed their own Messiah Jesus Christ in 30 AD, they were themselves totally *slaughtered and driven out of Israel by the Romans in 70 AD,* even as Jesus Himself had prophesied would happen to them because of *their rejection of Himself as their own Messiah.* So, the prophecy by Jesus Himself was fulfilled 40 years later.

C.10 See the Appendix for 7000 - year Time Frame of Biblical World History

> 13 And I will hide My face from them, and I will deliver them into the hand of the Gentiles for captivity, and for a prey, and for devouring, and I will remove them from the midst of the land, and I will scatter them amongst the Gentiles.

C.11 Why is the word 'devouring' used? That is a word one normally associates with a wild ravenous beast doing the devouring. It reminds me of a verse in the Book of Revelations:

REV.6:8 ONE OF THE FOUR HORSEMEN: THE 4ᵀᴴ 'HORSEMAN OF DEATH'

'And I looked and behold a pale horse: and his name that sat on him was Death, and Hell followed with him. And power was given unto them over the fourth part of the earth, to **kill** with sword, and with hunger, and with death, and with the **beasts** of the earth'.

C.12 Scripture is stating here that an entity called **DEATH** causes some people to be **DEVOURED** by the **BEASTS** of the earth. What is this really talking about? This is a mystery that most people do not understand.

What could be prowling our planet waiting to devour people?

I will speak more of this in the **APPENDIX XXV 'DEVOURING BEASTS & MONSTERS'**

> 14 And they will forget all My law and all My commandments and all My judgments, and will go astray as to new moons, and sabbaths, and festivals, and jubilees, and ordinances.
>
> 15 And after this they will turn to Me from amongst the Gentiles with all their heart and with all their soul and with all their strength, and I will gather them from amongst all the Gentiles, and they will seek me, so that I shall be found of them, when they seek me with all their heart and with all their soul.

C.13 This is stating that sometime after Israel has come together again as a nation that the time will come when finally, Israel becomes a godly nation once more. When will this happen according to scripture? According to the above verse, this will only happen when Jesus returns to the earth in His victorious 2nd Coming to both destroy the Anti-Christ & his world empire with its capital in Jerusalem, and to 'rescue the remnant' of the faithful in Israel. According to **Ezekiel 38-39** Israel will be attacked by Russia in the future, and two thirds of the population will be decimated. Timeframe: It is called the **'Time of Jacob's Trouble'.**

JER.30:7 Alas! for that day is great, so that none is like it: it is even the time of Jacob's trouble, but he shall be saved out of it.

JER.30:3 For, lo, the days come, saith the LORD, that I will bring again the captivity of my people Israel and Judah, saith the LORD: and I will cause them to return to the land that I gave to their fathers, and they shall possess it.

JER.30:11 For I am with thee, saith the LORD, to save thee: though I make a full end of all nations whither I have scattered thee, yet I will not make a full end of thee: but I will correct thee in measure, and will not leave thee altogether unpunished.

> 16 And I will disclose to them abounding peace with righteousness, and I will remove them the plant of uprightness, with all My heart and with all My soul, and they shall be for a blessing and not for a curse, and they shall be the head and not the tail.

C.14 This verse doesn't make sense and seems to have some words omitted 'I will remove them the plant of uprightness' should say something like 'bring them the 'plant of uprightness'

C.15 *'Plant of uprightness'*. This exact expression was also used in the **Book of Enoch** and seemed to prophecy about the coming of Abraham at least 1000-1500 years before Abraham was even born.

Book of Enoch Chapter 93.1,5. 1. 'Concerning the children of righteousness and concerning the elect of the world,
And concerning the '**plant of uprightness**', I will speak these things,
Yea, I Enoch will declare (them) unto you, my sons: 5. 'And after that in the third week at its close A man shall be elected as the plant of righteous judgement, And his posterity shall become the plant of righteousness for evermore'.

C.16 The '**plant of uprightness**' mentioned here is referring to Abraham who he prophesied about 1500 years before he was even born in Enoch's 'vision' for the whole spectrum of Time itself.

'His posterity shall become the plant of righteousness for evermore' This is clearly talking about the descendants of Abraham.

EZE.34:29 And I will raise up for them a 'plant of renown', and they shall be no more consumed with hunger in the land, neither bear the shame of the heathen anymore.

C.17 Jesus was also known as the 'Plant of Uprightness' or 'Plant of Renown'. He also said of Himself:

JOHN.15:1 I am the true vine, and my Father is the husbandman.

JOHN.15:5 I am the vine, ye are the branches: He that abides in me, and I in him, the same bringeth forth much fruit: for without me ye can do nothing.

> 17 And I will build My sanctuary in their midst, and I will dwell with them, and I will be their God and they shall be My people in truth and righteousness.

C.18 God will finally start to rule the earth in the form of His Son the **Messiah** from Jerusalem, after having taken out the **Anti-Christ** and having locked up Satan (the power behind the Anti-Christ) for 1000 years in the **Bottomless Pit**. Then finally will start the **1000-year Golden Age** of the **Millennium** with **Jesus Christ** as the ruler of the earth, together with all of his saints of all ages from Adam to Enoch to Noah to Abraham to Moses to all of the Old Testament prophets and godly kings such as king David up to the present time. Millions will be there together with Christ to rule the earth in the Golden Age to come!

REV.19:19 And I saw the beast, and the kings of the earth, and their armies, gathered together to make war against him that sat on the horse, and against his army.

REV.19:20 And the *beast was taken*, and with him the *false prophet* that wrought miracles before him, with which he deceived them that had received the *mark of the beast*, and them that worshipped his image. These both were cast alive into a lake of fire burning with brimstone.

REV.19:21 And the remnant were slain with the sword of him that sat upon the horse *(Jesus)*, which sword proceeded out of his mouth: and all the fowls were filled with their flesh.

REV.20:2 And he laid hold on the dragon, that old serpent, which is the Devil, and Satan, and bound him a thousand years,

REV.20:3 And cast him into the bottomless pit, and shut him up, and set a seal upon him, that he should deceive the nations no more, till the thousand years should be fulfilled: and after that he must be loosed a little season.

> 18 And I will not forsake them nor fail them; for I am the Lord their God.'

ISA.2:2 And it shall come to pass in the last days, that the mountain of the LORD's house shall be established in the top of the mountains and shall be exalted above the hills; and all nations shall flow unto it.

ISA.2:3 And many people shall go and say, Come ye, and let us go up to the mountain of the LORD, to the house of the God of Jacob; and he will teach us of his ways, and we will walk in his paths: for out of Zion shall go forth the law, and the word of the LORD from Jerusalem.

ISA.2:4 And he shall judge among the nations and shall rebuke many people: and they shall beat their swords into ploughshares, and their spears into pruninghooks: nation shall not lift up sword against nation, neither shall they learn war anymore.

---

19 And Moses fell on his face and prayed and said, 'O Lord my God, do not forsake Thy people and Thy inheritance, so that they should wander in the error of their hearts, and do not deliver them into the hands of their enemies, the Gentiles, lest they should rule over them and cause them to sin against Thee.

20 Let thy mercy, O Lord, be lifted up upon Thy people, and create in them an upright spirit, and let not the spirit of Beliar rule over them to accuse them before Thee, and to ensnare them from all the paths of righteousness, so that they may perish from before Thy face.

21 But they are Thy people and Thy inheritance, which thou hast delivered with thy great power from the hands of the Egyptians: create in them a clean heart and a holy spirit and let them not be ensnared in their sins from henceforth until eternity.'

PSA.51:10 Create in me a **clean heart**, O God; and renew a right spirit within me.

---

22 And the Lord said unto Moses: 'I know their contrariness and their thoughts and their stiff-neckedness, and they will not be obedient till they confess their own sin and the sin of their fathers.

C.19 'And they will not be obedient till *they* **confess their own sin** **and the sin of their fathers.**' What has been the sin of Israel throughout history? God mentioned it many times through all the prophets including the Messiah Jesus: 'Rebellion against God' & 'unwillingness to listen' to the voice of God and His Holy Spirit:

JER.2:13 For my people have committed two evils; they have *forsaken Me the fountain of living waters*, and *hewed them out cisterns, broken cisterns, that can hold no water.*

1SA.15:22 And Samuel said, Hath the LORD as great delight in burnt offerings and sacrifices, as in *obeying the voice of the LORD*? Behold, *to obey is better than sacrifice*, and to hearken than the fat of rams.

1SA.15:23 For *rebellion is as the sin of witchcraft*, and stubbornness is as *iniquity and idolatry*. Because thou hast *rejected the word of the LORD*, he hath also rejected *thee* from being king.

1JN.1:9 If we confess our sins, he is faithful and just to forgive us our sins, and to cleanse us from all unrighteousness.

> 23 And after this they will turn to Me in all uprightness and with all (their) heart and with all (their) soul, and I will circumcise the foreskin of their heart and the foreskin of the heart of their seed, and I will create in them a holy spirit, and I will cleanse them so that they shall not turn away from Me from that day unto eternity.

II EZDRAS 1.16 For I have rejected … the circumcisions of the flesh

C.20 God is mentioning that the circumcision of the flesh means nothing without the circumcision of the heart.

> 24 And their souls will cleave to Me and to all My commandments, and they will fulfil My commandments, and I will be their Father and they shall be My children.
>
> 25 And they all shall be called children of the living God, and every angel and every spirit shall know, yea, they shall know that these are My children, and that I am their Father in uprightness and righteousness, and that I love them.

C.21 'Israel' whether physical or spiritually interpreted does have a special place in the heart of God for many reasons '*Children of the living God'* There is a very interesting verse in the New Testament like verse 25:

ROM.9:26 And it shall come to pass, that in the place where it was said unto them, 'Ye are not my people'; there shall they be called the *Children of the Living God.*

> 26 And do thou write down for thyself all these words which I declare unto thee on this mountain, the first and the last, which shall come to pass in all the divisions of the days in the law and in the testimony and in the weeks and the jubilees unto eternity, until I descend and dwell with them throughout eternity.'
>
> 27 And He said to the angel of the presence: Write for Moses from the beginning of creation till My sanctuary has been built among them for all eternity.
>
> 28 And the Lord will appear to the eyes of all, and all shall know that

> I am the God of Israel and the Father of all the children of Jacob, and King on Mount Zion for all eternity. And Zion and Jerusalem shall be holy.'

C.22 Here God is clearly stating that in spite of all of Israel's sins and iniquities that the days will come when Israel shall be purified, and all will come to know the Messiah Jesus Christ. There are already many **Messianic Jews in Israel** today, so things are changing, but slowly. The following four verses sounds like the **Messiah Jesus** talking to his prophets in the **Old testament**. These **Old testament verses were indeed perfectly fulfilled in the New Testament, as you can see below:**

PROPHECY: ZEC.12:10 And I will pour upon the house of David, and upon the inhabitants of **Jerusalem,** the **spirit of grace** and of **supplications**: and they shall **look upon me whom they have pierced, and they shall mourn for him, as one mourns for his only son, and shall be in bitterness for him, as one that is in bitterness for his firstborn.**

PSA.22:16 For dogs have compassed me: the assembly of the wicked have enclosed me: they *pierced my hands and my feet.**

FULFILLED PROPHECY: MAT.27:31 And after that they had mocked him, they took the robe off from him, and put his own raiment on him, and led him away to *crucify him.**

PROPHECY:PSA.22:17 I may *tell (count) all my bones: they *look and stare upon me.**

FULFILLED PROPHECY: JOH.19:33 But when they came to Jesus, and saw that he was dead already, they *brake not his legs:**

JOH.19:36 For these things were done, that the scripture should be fulfilled, **A bone of him shall not be broken.**

JOH.19:37 And again another scripture saith, They shall *look on him whom they pierced.**

PROPHECY: PSA.22:18 They *part my garments among them, and *cast lots upon my vesture.**

FULFILLED PROPHECY: MAT.27:35 And they *crucified him, and *parted his garments, *casting lots: that it might be fulfilled which was spoken by the prophet, They parted my garments among them, and upon my vesture did they cast lots.**

> 29 And the angel of the presence who went before the camp of Israel took the tables of the divisions of the years - from the time of the creation - of the law and of the testimony of the weeks of the jubilees,

according to the individual years, according to all the number of the jubilees (according, to the individual years), from the day of the (new) creation when the heavens and the earth shall be renewed and all their creation according to the powers of the heaven, and according to all the creation of the earth, until the sanctuary of the Lord shall be made in Jerusalem on Mount Zion, and all the luminaries be renewed for healing and for peace and for blessing for all the elect of Israel, and that thus it may be from that day and unto all the days of the earth.

C.23 What are the Luminaries? Enoch also mentions them in the **Book of Enoch**. Sometimes they are **stars**, and sometimes stars are referring to **angels**. Quite a mystery.

Enoch 71.4 And He showed me all the secrets of the ends of the heaven, And all the chambers of all the stars and all the luminaries, whence they proceed before the face of the holy ones

C.24 'From the day of the (new) creation when the *heavens and the earth shall be renewed* and all their creation according to the powers of the heaven, and according to all the creation of the earth, until the *sanctuary of the Lord shall be made in Jerusalem on Mount Zion'*

REV.21:1 And I saw a **new heaven and a new earth**: for the first heaven and the first earth were passed away; and there was no more sea.

REV.21:2 And I John saw the holy city, **new Jerusalem**, coming down from God out of heaven, prepared as a bride adorned for her husband.

REV.21:3 And I heard a great voice out of heaven saying, Behold, the tabernacle of God is with men, and he will dwell with them, and they shall be his people, and God himself shall be with them, and be their God.

REV.14:1 And I looked, and, lo, a Lamb (Jesus, the Messiah) stood on the mount Zion, and with him an hundred forty and four thousand, having his Father's name written in their foreheads.

REV.7:4 And I heard the number of them which were sealed: and there were sealed an hundred and forty and four thousand of all the tribes of the children of Israel.

Chapter 2: CREATION.

1 And the angel of the presence spoke to Moses according to the word of the Lord, saying: 'Write the complete history of the creation, how in six days the Lord God finished all His works and all that He created, and kept Sabbath on the seventh day and hallowed it for all ages, and appointed it as a sign for all His works'.

Comment:1: *'Kept Sabbath on the seventh day and hallowed it for all ages and appointed it as a sign for all His works.'* This would seem to state that God rested the 7th Day. God honoured the 7th day or the Sabbath as He wants us all to *rest* the 7th day and *spend the day devoting our time to being with God in both Prayer and reading God's Word as well as in communicating and receiving from Him.*

All those spiritual exercises keep us spiritually well nourished.

JOHN.7:38 He that believeth on me, as the scripture hath said, out of his belly shall flow rivers of living water.

C.2 Many say that the 7th day is a symbol of the 7th Millennium which will be the Golden Age of Rest & Peace with No More War! i.e. 1 Day of Creation = 1000 years. Total Timeframe for the earth = 7 Days= 7 X 1000= 7000 years of World History from The Creation until the New Heaven & New Earth.

2 For on the first day He created the heavens which are above and the earth and the waters and all the spirits which serve before him - the angels of the presence, and the angels of sanctification, and the angels (of the spirit of fire and the angels) of the spirit of the winds, and the angels of the spirit of the clouds, and of darkness, and of snow and of hail and of hoar frost, and the angels of the voices and of the thunder and of the lightning, and the angels of the spirits of cold and of heat, and of winter and of spring and of autumn and of summer and of all the spirits of his creatures which are in the heavens and on the earth, (He created) the **abysses** and the darkness, eventide (and night), and the light, dawn and day, which He hath prepared in the knowledge of his heart.

ENOCH 18.11 And I saw a deep *abyss* with columns of heavenly fire, ..columns of fire fall which were beyond measure..

ENOCH 77.3 .. and the 2nd contains seas of water, and the *abysses* and forests and rivers, and darkness and clouds…

C.3 ABYSS: definition: "bottomless, unfathomable, (as noun) bottomless gulf,"
SOURCE: https://www.merriam-webster.com/dictionary/abyss

FOR MORE ON THE 'ABYSS': See APPENDIX: XXXI: THE 'ABYSS'

C.4 All of these spirits and angels seem to refer directly to the 'physical creation', so that it is natural that they could have been specifically created by God Himself for the exact purpose of taking care of the earth: the angels of the presence, and the angels of sanctification, and the angels of the spirit of fire and the angels of the spirit of the winds, and the angels of the spirit of the clouds, and of darkness, and of snow and of hail and of hoar frost, and the angels of the voices and of the thunder and of the lightning, and the angels of the spirits of cold and of heat, and of winter and of spring and of autumn and of summer and of all the spirits of his creatures which are in the heavens and on the earth. Even the more spiritual definitions: 1) The angels of the presence. 2) The angels of sanctification could be interpreted as helping mankind to communicate with God, by humbly coming into His presence. Certain angels have been appointed since creation to take care of mankind and were specifically designed for this exact purpose. These angels have taught mankind both before the great Flood in Enoch's time, & after the Flood through the Laws of Moses about what is written on the Heavenly Tablets. These were laws, as to *how to keep 'clean and pure' both physically and spiritually*. Sanctified: just means 'cleansed and set aside for further use' Thus the name 'Kosher' food in Jewish, meaning that which is 'pure' and 'sanctified by God'.

C.5 It is very important to point out that many Christians are taught that all the angels were created at the time of the physical creation. This can easily be disproved by the story of the 'Watcher class of angels. They were apparently created to understand mankind and his thinking processes. According to the Book of Enoch (See my book 'Enoch Insights' for the details about this subject), originally 200 Watchers (A specific class of angels) were in Rebellion, against God even before the Creation. When they got the opportunity, they fled from the spiritual realm of heaven to the physical realm in order to escape being in the direct presence of God Himself.

C.6 The Spirit world was apparently in existence, long before the physical realm was brought into being'. There were angels and archangels, as well as peoples in Heaven and the Spirit world, long before the creation of the physical world. Just to further state for now, that there was a *greater importance to God creating the physical realm than just creating planet earth.* God in creating the physical realm was creating 'A Greater Choice'. Why would He do that, unless He had a very important reason? I explained in my other books that God *created the physical realm because of Satan's 'Rebellion in the Heavenly Realm'* some time *before* the actual *creation of the physical realm* by God. Cutting a long story short on this occasion: From what I have read, *God thought that if His right hand man or Archangel Lucifer could not be trusted, then whom could God trust, if people were given both total choice* *to do good or evil, when they could no longer see God as in the spiritual realm*. Thus, the Garden of Eden was created in the original Creation. The big question: But why did God allow a deceitful slimy snake to be in the garden? Apparently, it is all about Choice.

<SEE my books '**Enoch Insights**' and '**Ezdras Insights**' for a much more thorough answer to this question.>

---

3 And thereupon we saw His works, and praised Him, and lauded before Him on account of all His works; for seven great works did He create on the first day.

4 And on the second day He created the firmament in the midst of the waters, and the waters were divided on that day - half of them went up above and half of them went down below the firmament (that was) in the midst over the face of the whole earth.

5 And this was the only work (God) created on the second day.

6 And on the third day He commanded the waters to pass from off the face of the whole earth into one place, and the dry land to appear.

7 And the waters did so as He commanded them, and they retired from off the face of the earth into one place outside of this firmament and the dry land appeared. And on that day He created for them all the seas according to their separate gathering-places, and all the rivers, and the gatherings of the waters in the mountains and on all the earth, and all the lakes, and all the dew of the earth, and the seed which is sown, and all sprouting things, and fruit-bearing trees, and trees of the wood, and the garden of Eden, in Eden and all.

C.7 Notice that the Lord God created the *earth* on the *3rd day*, but the *sun, the moon and the stars on the 4th day*. The earth is therefore de-facto the *centre of the universe* according to God's Word. The Bible states the exact same thing, & so do also the Apocryphal books and also ancient books such as the Book of Enoch. In other words, the universe is Geo-Centric and not Helio-CentriC. (See my website: **GEO-CENTRIC UNIVERSE:** http://www. outofthebottomlesspit.co.uk/418830180)

---

8 These four great works God created on the third day. And on the fourth day He created the sun and the moon and the stars, and set them in the firmament of the heaven, to give light upon all the earth, and to rule over the day and the night, and divide the light from the darkness.

> 9 And God appointed the sun to be a great sign on the earth for days and for sabbaths and for months and for feasts and for years and for sabbaths of years and for jubilees and for all seasons of the years.

C.8 God created the sun, the moon and stars for signs and seasons, & thus the birth of Astrology.

GEN.1:14 And God said, 'Let there be lights in the firmament of the heaven to divide the day from the night; and let them be *for signs*, and *for seasons*, and for *days*, and *years*'.

> 10 And it divides the light from the darkness [and] for prosperity, that all things may prosper which shoot and grow on the earth. These three kinds He made on the fourth day.
>
> 11 And on the fifth day He created great sea monsters in the depths of the waters, for these were the first things of flesh that were created by his hands, the fish and everything that moves in the waters, and everything that flies, the birds and all their kind.

GEN.1:21 And God created great whales, and every living creature that moves, which the waters brought forth abundantly, after their kind, and every winged fowl after his kind: and God saw that it was good.

C.9 See the whole chapter of **Job 41** for an amazing description of a very large **sea monster** called **Leviathan**:

JOB.41:21 His breath kindles coals, and a flame goes out of his mouth.

JOB.41:33 Upon earth *there is not his like*, who is made without fear.

JOB.41:34 He beholds all high things: he is a *king over all the children of pride*.

C.10 Here it specifically states that God created large *sea monsters* & not just whales or giant squids. There is plenty of evidence to show that there are indeed monsters in both the oceans and even large lochs and lakes, such as the infamous Loch Ness Monster. Scientists tell us that the Loch Ness Monster is some sort of pre-historic 'Plesiosaurus Sea monster'. How could a Plesiosaurus quoted by Evolutionists as having become extinct millions of years ago, still be alive? The sea monsters really poke a big hole in the Evolutionary theory and the time sequence. According to the Bible time charts, the earth is *only* just over 6000 years old and not millions or billions of years old. (**See my website: THE BIG LIE OF EVOLUTION: http://www.outofthebottomlesspit.co.uk/443228701**). **See also**: **THERE ARE ABSOLUTES:** http://www.peopleofthekeys.com/docs/library/There+Are+Absolutes

12 And the sun rose above them to prosper (them), and above everything that was on the earth, everything that shoots out of the earth, and all fruit-bearing trees, and all flesh.

13 These three kinds He created on the fifth day. And on the sixth day He created all the animals of the earth, and all cattle, and everything that moves on the earth.

14 And after all this He created man, a man and a woman created He them, and gave him dominion over all that is upon the earth, and in the seas, and over everything that flies, and over beasts and over cattle, and over everything that moves on the earth, and over the whole earth, and over all this He gave him dominion.

15 And these four kinds He created on the sixth day. And there were altogether two and twenty kinds.

16 And He finished all his work on the sixth day -all that is in the heavens and on the earth, and in the seas and in the abysses, and in the light and in the darkness, and in everything.

17 And He gave us a great sign, the Sabbath day, that we should work six days, but keep Sabbath on the seventh day from all work.

18 And all the angels of the presence, and all the angels of sanctification, these two great classes -He hath bidden us to keep the Sabbath with Him in heaven and on earth.

19 And He said unto us: 'Behold, I will separate unto Myself a people from among all the peoples, and these shall keep the Sabbath day, and I will sanctify them unto Myself as My people, and will bless them; as I have sanctified the Sabbath day and do sanctify (it) unto Myself, even so will I bless them, and they shall be My people and I will be their God.

C.11 This verse above shows us when God first chose for Himself a nation to dwell in and this verse from Revelations shows its complete fulfilment.

REV.21:3 And I heard a great voice out of heaven saying, Behold, the tabernacle of God is with men, and he will dwell with them, and they shall be his people, and God himself shall be with them, and **be their God**.

20 And I have chosen the seed of Jacob from amongst all that I have seen, and have written him down as My first-born son, and have sanctified him unto Myself for ever and ever; and I will teach them the Sabbath day, that they may keep Sabbath thereon from all work.'

21 And thus He created therein a sign in accordance with which they should keep Sabbath with us on the seventh day, to eat and to drink, and to bless Him who has created all things as He has blessed and sanctified unto Himself a peculiar people above all peoples, and that they should keep Sabbath together with us.

1PE.2:9 But ye are a chosen generation, a royal priesthood, an holy nation, a **peculiar people**; that ye should shew forth the praises of him who hath called you out of darkness into his marvellous light;

1PE.2:10 Which in time past were not a people, but are now the people of God: which had not obtained mercy, but now have obtained mercy.

22 And He caused His commands to ascend as a sweet savour acceptable before Him all the days . . .

23 There (were) two and twenty heads of mankind from Adam to Jacob, and two and twenty kinds of work were made until the seventh day; this is blessed and holy; and the former also is blessed and holy; and this one serves with that one for sanctification and blessing.

C.12. Here God is making a point that there were exactly **22** generations from Adam to Jacob. Why is he making this point? These 22 generations is what established God's **Chosen Race** of people. It took this long until God had His own chosen race of people on earth. Before that time God had individuals who obeyed Him, but not a race of people It was God Himself who created Israel for Himself and it took Him waiting patiently for 22 generations from Adam until Jacob. **Jacob** himself was finally renamed by God Himself as Israel, after he had become a 'new man' and was no longer 'Jacob the deceiver', but **Israel – Prince of God and man.**'

C.13 It also states that there were **22** kinds of work made until the seventh day when God rested. Why is this important? God is simply stating that it took Him 6 days to make the main 22 works of Creation, but it took 22 Generations of mankind until He could actually find a people that He could chose as His special nation - Israel.

Israel was created by God Himself over 22 generations, slowly but surely. It is also showing very clearly how that God is in perfect control of both the times and seasons and as to when something important will happen, such as **the**

birth of the nation of Israel through Jacob the **22nd Patriarch**.

C.14 Is it just a coincidence, but there are **22** chapters in the **Book of Revelations**, which Book also ends up in its two last chapters including **21 and 22** talking about the **NEW HEAVEN AND EARTH or the NEW CREATION**. It took God 20 chapters talking about the **destruction of the wicked**, the **Rescue of the Righteous** and the **Devil being locked up for good,** before God could finally realise what He has desired to do since the beginning of Creation itself and that is to **create a New Heaven and New Earth** wherein dwelleth righteousness with no more sin and iniquity, and thank God - no more Satan and evil.

2PE.3:13 Nevertheless we, according to his promise, look for **new heavens and a new earth**, wherein **dwelleth righteousness**.

C.15 Biblical Numerology: From the above **verse 23**, of this chapter, which I will place here again as it is **so important to our study**:

2.23 'There (were) two and twenty heads of mankind from Adam to Jacob, and two and twenty kinds of work were made until the seventh day; this is blessed and holy; and the former also is blessed and holy; and this one serves with that one for sanctification and blessing'.

C.16 Another very important observation is that God Himself is connecting His own 22 original works of Creation in the very first 6 days, with His own creating of the nation of Israel unto Himself, which took Him 22 generations of the righteous. Why does He do that?

C.17 Here we find some interesting facts: the whole verse is talking about some sort of **CREATION**. Why the number 22? Let's have a closer look:

From the days of **Adam** until **Noah** were **10 generations**. From **Noah** to **Abraham** were **10 generations**. From Abraham to Jacob were **2 generations**. The numbers are really **10 + 10 + 2 = 22**

The number **10** represents **LEADERSHIP** in the Bible, as in the case of both Noah and Abraham.

C.18 Noah essentially brought mankind into a **new world** or **new creation**, after the **old world had been destroyed in the Great Flood**.

C.19 Unto Abraham was given the promise by God that **through his seed** would come a **HOLY NATION**, God's own nation. He was also promised that the Messiah and Saviour of all Mankind would come through 'his seed'

C.20 Think how fantastic it is that in only two generations that against all odds and great difficulties God did fulfil His great promises in Jacob/Israel.

How many men on earth have had 4 wives and 12 sons? Well perhaps some Muslims today, but generally that was not the case back in Abraham's time. Jacob only wanted Rachel as a his wife, but God had other ideas, and he ended up with 4 wives. Why? Because God wanted to bring forth the literal 'Birth of a whole nation' in Jacob who became Israel and had 12 sons who became the 12 Tribes of Israel.

C.21 Notice how in the New Testament in the Book of Revelations in chapters 21-22, how that **the Gates of the New Heavenly city are named after the 12 Tribes of Israel** or Jacob's 12 sons. The Foundations of the New Jerusalem are made with the names of the 12 Apostles of the Messiah. Here we see the perfect coming together of both the Old and New Testament in fulfilling God's promises, which he actually originally gave to Enoch before the Great Flood and then to Noah and his family and then to Abraham.

C.22 So then what is the significance of the number 2 here? Let's look it up: This is what I found and the source of the information:

The number 2 conveys the meaning of a union, **division** or the verification of facts by witnesses. **A man and woman**, though two in number, are made one in **marriage** (Genesis 2:23 - 24). There is also the **union between Christ and the church** (see 1Corinthians 12). The testimony of God is divided into Old and New Testaments. Source: https://www.biblestudy.org/bibleref/meaning-of-numbers-in-bible/2.html

C.23 In studying Jacob's life the **number 2** does show up many times. 1) Jacob had a **twin brother,** with whom he was always at odds. 2) He had to take 2 wives instead of 1 initially who were sisters. Later he had to take 2 more wives in order for God to bring forth the total of 12 sons needed for the original 12 tribes of Israel. Two of Jacobs sons were singled out by God Himself: **Judah** as the **Tribe of the Kings** and from which Tribe would come the Messiah. **Levi** was to become the **Tribe of the Priests**.

---

24 And to this (Jacob and his seed) it was granted that they should always be the blessed and holy ones of the first testimony and law, even as He had sanctified and blessed the Sabbath day on the seventh day.

25 He created heaven and earth and everything that He created in six days, and God made the seventh day holy, for all His works; therefore, He commanded on its behalf that, whoever does any work thereon shall die, and that he who defiles it shall surely die.

26 Wherefore do thou command the children of Israel to observe this day that they may keep it holy and not do thereon any work, and not to defile it, as it is holier than all other days.

27 And whoever profanes it shall surely die, and whoever does thereon any work shall surely die eternally, that the children of Israel may observe this day throughout their generations, and not be rooted out of the land; for it is a holy day and a blessed day.

C.24 I realise that to us in modern times, it is very hard to understand how

God could be so severe to His people. To slay them if they did anything on the Sabbath day? This is a very valid question, which I have covered in detail later in this book. Just to summarize for now what Jesus Himself said in the New Testament: 'Moses because of the hardness of your hearts gave you these laws, but from the beginning it was not so...

MAT.19:8 He saith unto them, Moses because of the hardness of your hearts suffered you to put away your wives: but from the beginning it was not so.

JOH.1:17 For the law was given by Moses, but grace and truth came by Jesus Christ.

---

28 And everyone who observes it and keeps Sabbath thereon from all his work, will be holy and blessed throughout all days like unto us.

29 Declare and say to the children of Israel the law of this day both that they should keep Sabbath thereon, and that they should not forsake it in the error of their hearts; (and) that it is not lawful to do any work thereon which is unseemly, to do thereon their own pleasure, and that they should not prepare thereon anything to be eaten or drunk, and (that it is not lawful) to draw water, or bring in or take out thereon through their gates any burden, which they had not prepared for themselves on the sixth day in their dwellings.

C.25 Why was God so strict with His own people? Firstly because He expected a better sample of His own people, so He had to set the standard high from the birth of the nation of Israel.

Secondly, how does one get a whole nation to stop what they normally do and to rest in the Lord? One must take away all the obvious distractions that could possibly get in the way, so that's exactly what God did. So that as a nation Israel could learn to honour God and give Him the time that He deserved -the Seventh Day or the Sabbath. God made this very clear in both the Old Testament and the New testament spoken by the Messiah Himself:

MAT.22:37 Jesus said unto him, **Thou shalt love the Lord thy God with all thy heart, and with all thy soul, and with all thy mind.**

MAT.22:38 This is the first and great commandment.

MAT.22:39 And the second is like unto it, Thou shalt love thy neighbour as thyself.

MAT.22:40 On these two commandments **hang all the law and the prophets.**

C.26 The **Sabbath** was created as a day to **REST** and a day to **PRAY** and to read **God's Word** by God Himself in the **Old Testament**.

However God did not mean for Israel to get 'under the letter of the law' by observing the Sabbath. There could be some **rare exceptions** to '**doing no** work' on the Sabbath. In the **New Testament** the **Messiah** makes it very clear concerning the Sabbath:

MAR.2:27 And he said unto them, **The sabbath was made for man**, and **not man for the sabbath:**

MAR.2:28 Therefore the **Son of man is Lord also of the sabbath.**

MAR.3:4 And he saith unto them, Is it **lawful to do good on the sabbath days**, or to do **evil**? to save life, or to kill?

C.27 The **7th Day** as the **Sabbath** or the **Holy Day** is reflected in the **7th Millennium** or the **Golden Age of 1000 years** of REST and PEACE on earth, where there will be **no more war** and when the **Lord and His Saints** will teach the peoples of the earth how to be godly and how to both **love and honour God** but taking the time **to listen to Him**. <**LINK** to my website: http://www.outofthebottomlesspit.co.uk/443225279>

---

30 And they shall not bring in nor take out from house to house on that day; for that day is more holy and blessed than any jubilee day of the jubilees; on this we kept Sabbath in the heavens before it was made known to any flesh to keep Sabbath thereon on the earth.

31 And the Creator of all things blessed it, but he did not sanctify all peoples and nations to keep Sabbath thereon, but Israel alone: them alone he permitted to eat and drink and to keep Sabbath thereon on the earth.

32 And the Creator of all things blessed this day which He had created for blessing and holiness and glory above all days.

33 This law and testimony was given to the children of Israel as a law for ever unto their generations.

Chapter 3: EVE IS CREATED

1 And on the six day of the second week we brought, according to the word of God, unto Adam all the beasts, and all the cattle, and all the birds, and everything that moves on the earth, and everything that moves in the water, according to their kinds, and according to their types: the beasts on the first day; the cattle on the second day; the birds on the third day; and all that which moves on the earth on the fourth day; and that which moves in the water on the fifth day.

Comment:1: In this particular chapter I have put many Bible verses, which mirror the story of the Garden of Eden, although upon occasion the verses are slightly different, but obviously from the same source. I have done this so that you can directly compare this Book of Jubilees with the Bible. The 'Book of Jubilees' is referred to in Israel as 'Little Genesis'

GEN.2:19 And out of the ground the LORD God formed every beast of the field, and every fowl of the air; and brought them unto Adam to see what he would call them: and whatsoever Adam called every living creature, that was the name thereof.

2 And Adam named them all by their respective names, and as he called them, so was their name.

GEN.2:20a And Adam gave names to all cattle, and to the fowl of the air, and to every beast of the field;

3 And on these five days Adam saw all these, male and female, according to every kind that was on the earth, but he was alone and found no helpmeet for him.

GEN.2:20b But for Adam there was not found an helpmeet for him.

4 And the Lord said unto us: 'It is not good that the man should be alone: let us make a helpmeet for him.'

GEN.2:18 And the LORD God said, It is not good that the man should be alone; I will make him an help meet for him.

5 And the Lord our God caused a deep sleep to fall upon him, and he slept, and He took for the woman one rib from amongst his ribs, and this rib was the origin of the woman from amongst his ribs, and He built up the flesh in its stead, and built the woman.

GEN.2:21 And the LORD God caused a deep sleep to fall upon Adam, and he slept: and he took one of his ribs, and closed up the flesh instead thereof;

GEN.2:22 And the rib, which the LORD God had taken from man, made he a woman, and brought her unto the man.

C.2 Why did God create the woman out of a rib of Adam's and not just 'out of the dust of the earth' in same the way that He had created Adam? I suppose that if God had created Eve of dust like Adam, then Adam could have thought that she was exactly the same as him. Alternatively, if God had created Eve out of a bone of his head, she could have thought that she must be superior to Adam. Or, if God had created Eve from a bone in Adams' foot, then maybe Adam might think that he could simply 'lord it' over Eve. Instead, therefore, God used 'a rib close to the heart of Adam' and 'enclosed the flesh therefore' and created a woman: to be 'Close to Adam's heart' in flesh and spirit. Neither one to 'lord it' over each other, but for both to work together in loving harmony.

> 6 And He awaked Adam out of his sleep and on awaking he rose on the sixth day, and He brought her to him, and he knew her, and said unto her: 'This is now bone of my bones and flesh of my flesh; she shall be called [my] wife; because she was taken from her husband.'

C.3 Notice how it mentions how Adam awoke from his sleep to see a very beautiful naked woman standing before him and probably smiling at him favourably. How did he react? Like any normal healthy man would react. Wow! What was this beautiful naked woman doing here in front of him? So, he immediately 'knew her' which simply means that he made love with her.

C.4 I will never forget the reaction of one of our very inquisitive daughters, when she was young and I was reading in Genesis about Adam meeting Eve for the first time, and my little daughter exclaimed upon reading '**and he knew her**', 'Oh My goodness 'Couldn't Adam at least have said hello first and shook her hand? I said to her 'Well he probably did say hello first.' We couldn't stop laughing at her reaction.

C.5 God with the Story of Adam and Eve in their original nakedness, was probably trying to teach people that sex was created to be beautiful between a man and woman and was also for the purpose of pro-creation.

C.6 Why did God bring the woman to the man naked, unless it was for him to see the importance of the woman in her nakedness. Perhaps so that he wouldn't get tripped off on something else?

C.7 It is sad to see that in modern times many people are practically sexless, more interested in devices than even in relationships, which is ungodly, and against God's original plan for humans to have sex and to procreate.

C.8 Sex is not a sin in the right relationships and was not the original sin that caused the downfall of mankind. That is a religious idea from the churches,

34

from the 'traditions of man' and a LIE of Satan, used to control the church people.

C.9 I have even heard of Catholic priests telling woman that if their husbands didn't come to church, then they should withhold sex from them – which is strictly forbidden in the New Testament in talking about marriage which states 'withhold not yourselves from each other, except for prayer and fasting for a season, but then come together again, lest Satan tempt you for your incontinence (lack of doing it)

1CO.7:5 Defraud ye not one the other, except it be with consent for a time, that ye may give yourselves to fasting and prayer; and come together again, that Satan tempt you not for your incontinency.

C.10 Notice how the Book of Jubilees is quite a religious book at times, and likes to adhere to the *'letter of the law'*, and has to make things seem proper - by calling the woman a wife and the man a husband, before they even got married, which was totally unnecessary. Eve was created as a woman before she was actually a wife, and likewise Adam was created as a man before he became a husband. As I mentioned above, I cover all this in greater detail, later in this book, about the war of 'Grace versus the letter of the Law'. Satan likes to use the 'letter of the Law' to get people all mixed up. The Bible gets the last verse more accurate:

GEN.2:23 And Adam said, 'This is now bone of my bones, and flesh of my flesh: she shall be called Woman, because she was taken out of Man'.

> 7 Therefore shall man and wife be one and therefore shall a man leave his father and his mother, and cleave unto his wife, and they shall be one flesh.

GEN.2:24 Therefore shall a man leave his father and his mother and shall cleave unto his wife: and they shall be one flesh.

GEN.2:25 And they were *both naked, the man and his wife*, and were not ashamed.

C.11 Is it true that Adam and Eve were completely naked *or* were they originally wearing 'Robes of Light' which vanished when they fell and ate the forbidden fruit? (See: 'CORRUPTING THE IMAGE'- by Douglas Hemp)

> 8 In the first week was Adam created, and the rib-his wife: in the second week He showed her unto him: and for this reason, the commandment was given to keep in their defilement, for a male seven days, and for a female twice seven days.

C.12 I don't know if my wife would like me to refer to her as *'the rib'*. That sounds a bit demeaning, but of course - that is not intended.

> 9 And after Adam had completed forty days in the land where he had

> been created, we brought him into the garden of Eden to till and keep it, but his wife they brought in on the eightieth day, and after this she entered into the garden of Eden.

C.13 Here is some interesting information that you won't find anywhere else including the Bible. It is stating that Adam and Eve were created outside of the Garden of Eden and then God put them into the Garden of Eden after 40 days and 80 days respectively.

GEN.2:15 And the LORD God took the man and put him into the garden of Eden to dress it and to keep it.

> 10 And for this reason the commandment is written on the heavenly tablets in regard to her that gives birth: 'if she bears a male, she shall remain in her uncleanness seven days according to the first week of days, and thirty and three days shall she remain in the blood of her purifying, and she shall not touch any hallowed thing, nor enter into the sanctuary, until she accomplishes these days which (are enjoined) in the case of a male child.

C.14 Here it mentions the *'heavenly tablets'* which is an interesting concept. This is stating that before anything actually happened on earth or was actually written down on tablets on the earth that it had already been written down in heaven on heavenly tablets. We find the same thing exactly mentioned in the book of Enoch from Pre-Flood times or around 1500 years before Moses.

BOOK OF ENOCH 81.1-2 And he said unto me: 'Observe, Enoch, these **heavenly tablets**, And read what is written thereon, And mark every individual fact.' And I observed the heavenly tablets, and read everything which was written (thereon) and understood everything, and read the book of all the deeds of mankind, and of all the children of flesh that shall be upon the earth to the remotest generations.

LEV.12:1 And the LORD spoke unto Moses, saying:

LEV.12:2 'Speak unto the children of Israel, saying, If a woman have conceived seed, and born a man child: then she shall be unclean seven days; according to the days of the separation for her infirmity shall she be unclean.'

C.15 The fact that the 'exact same statement' is made in the Bible and specifically told to Moses by God Himself proves that the text of this Book of Jubilees was also originally written by Moses, even if the book of Jubilees was compiled at a later date than the original manuscripts actually written to record events at the time of Moses.

> 11 But in the case of a female child she shall remain in her uncleanness two weeks of days, according to the first two weeks, and sixty-six days in

the blood of her purification, and they will be in all eighty days.'

LEV.12:5 But if she bear a maid child, then she shall be unclean two weeks, as in her separation: and she shall continue in the blood of her purifying threescore and six days (66 days).

C.16 Why were these laws made? Most of the time the laws had to do with what was good for your health or in the case of food – in Jewish, *Kosher*. Sadly in modern times people's health is not protected like it should be.

12 And when she had completed these eighty days we brought her into the garden of Eden, for it is holier than all the earth besides and every tree that is planted in it is holy.

13 Therefore, there was ordained regarding her who bears a male or a female child the statute of those days that she should touch no hallowed thing, nor enter into the sanctuary until these days for the male or female child are accomplished.

14 This is the law and testimony which was written down for Israel, in order that they should observe (it) all the days.

15 And in the first week of the first jubilee, [1-7 A.M.= Anno Mundi' = years of the world] Adam and his wife were in the garden of Eden for seven years tilling and keeping it, and we gave him work and we instructed him to do everything that is suitable for tillage.

16 And he tilled (the garden), and was naked and knew it not, and was not ashamed, and he protected the garden from the birds and beasts and cattle, and gathered its fruit, and eat, and put aside the residue for himself and for his wife [and put aside that which was being kept].

GEN.2:25 And they were both naked, the man and his wife, and were not ashamed.

17 And after the completion of the seven years, which he had completed there, seven years exactly, [8 A.M.] and in the second month, on the seventeenth day (of the month), the serpent* came and approached the woman, and the serpent said to the woman, 'Hath God commanded you, saying,

GEN.3:1 Now the serpent was more subtle than any beast of the field which the LORD God had made. And he said unto the woman, Yea, hath God said, Ye shall not

37

eat of every tree of the garden?

C.17 (*See the **APPENDIX: THE HISTORY OF THE SERPENT ON EARTH**)

> 18 'Ye shall not eat of every tree of the garden' And she said to it, 'Of all the fruit of the trees of the garden God hath said unto us, Eat; but of the fruit of the tree which is in the midst of the garden God hath said unto us, Ye shall not eat thereof, neither shall ye touch it, lest ye die.'

GEN.3:3 But of the fruit of the tree which is in the midst of the garden, God hath said, Ye shall not eat of it, neither shall ye touch it, lest ye die.

> 19 And the serpent said unto the woman, 'Ye shall not surely die: for God doth know that on the day ye shall eat thereof, your eyes will be opened, and ye will be as gods, and ye will know good and evil.

GEN.3:4 And the serpent said unto the woman, Ye shall not surely die:

GEN.3:5 For God doth know that in the day ye eat thereof, then your eyes shall be opened, and ye shall be as gods, knowing good and evil.

> 20 And the woman saw the tree that it was agreeable and pleasant to the eye, and that its fruit was good for food, and she took thereof and did eat.

GEN.3:6 And when the woman saw that the tree was good for food, and that it was pleasant to the eyes, and a tree to be desired to make one wise, she took of the fruit thereof, and did eat, and gave also unto her husband with her; and he did eat.

> 21 And when she had first covered her shame with fig leaves, she gave thereof to Adam and he eat, and his eyes were opened, and he saw that he was naked.
>
> 22 And he took fig leaves and sewed (them) together, and made an apron for himself, and covered his shame.

GEN.3:7 And the eyes of them both were opened, and they knew that they were naked; and they sewed fig leaves together and made themselves aprons.

C.18 Before Adam and Eve sinned, they had pure, sinless hearts and a heavenly outlook. They only became ashamed of nudity after they fell and had sin in their hearts – the wrong sinful view of things.

> 23 And God cursed the serpent, and was wroth with it for ever . . .

GEN.3:14 And the LORD God said unto the serpent, 'Because thou hast done this, thou art cursed above all cattle, and above every beast of the field; upon thy belly shalt thou go, and dust shalt thou eat all the days of thy life':

> 24 And He was wroth with the woman, because she harkened to the voice of the serpent, and did eat; and He said unto her: 'I will greatly multiply thy sorrow and thy pains: in sorrow thou shalt bring forth children, and thy return shall be unto thy husband, and he will rule over thee.'

GEN.3:16 Unto the woman he said, I will greatly multiply thy sorrow and thy conception; in sorrow thou shalt bring forth children; and thy desire shall be to thy husband, and he shall rule over thee.

> 25 And to Adam also he said, ' Because thou hast harkened unto the voice of thy wife, and hast eaten of the tree of which I commanded thee that thou should not eat thereof, cursed be the ground for thy sake: thorns and thistles shall it bring forth to thee, and thou shalt eat thy bread in the sweat of thy face, till thou return to the earth from whence thou was taken; for earth thou art, and unto earth shalt thou return.'

GEN.3:17 And unto Adam he said, 'Because thou hast hearkened unto the voice of thy wife, and hast eaten of the tree, of which I commanded thee, saying, 'Thou shalt not eat of it: cursed is the ground for thy sake; in sorrow shalt thou eat of it all the days of thy life.

GEN.3:18 Thorns also and thistles shall it bring forth to thee; and thou shalt eat the herb of the field;

GEN.3:19 In the sweat of thy face shalt thou eat bread, till thou return unto the ground; for out of it was thou taken: for dust thou art, and unto dust shalt thou return.'

> 26 And He made for them coats of skin, and clothed them, and sent them forth from the Garden of Eden.

GEN.3:21 Unto Adam also and to his wife did the LORD God make coats of skins and clothed them.

GEN.3:22 And the LORD God said, Behold, the man is become as one of us, to know good and evil: and now, lest he put forth his hand, and take also of the tree of life, and eat, and live for ever:

GEN.3:23 Therefore the LORD God sent him forth from the garden of Eden, to till the ground from whence he was taken.

GEN.3:24 So he drove out the man; and he placed at the east of the garden of Eden Cherubim, and a flaming sword which turned every way, to keep the way of the tree of life.

> 27 And on that day on which Adam went forth from the Garden, he offered as a sweet savour an offering, frankincense, galbanum, and stacte, and spices in the morning with the rising of the sun from the day when he covered his shame.

C.19 What are these spices of **'frankincense, galbanum, and stacte'**

Here is the definition: Stacte (Greek: στακτή, stakté or Hebrew: נָטָף, nataf) is one of the ingredients of the most sacred temple incense, the HaKetoret, discussed in Exodus 30:34. It was to be mixed in equal parts with onycha (labdanum), galbanum and mixed with pure frankincense and made into an incense for burning on the altar of the... My research has led me to the conclusion that stacte is indeed myrrh and most probably myrrh and benzoin mixed. [Source: https://curtisdward.wordpress.com/2010/02/02/what-is-stacte/]

Book of Enoch 29.2 And there I saw aromatic trees exhaling the fragrance of frankincense and myrrh, and the trees were similar to the almond tree.

Book of Enoch 31.2 Whereon were aloe trees, and all the trees were full of stacte, being like almond trees, 3 And when one burnt it, it smelt sweeter than any fragrant odour.

> 28 And on that day was closed the mouth of all beasts, and of cattle, and of birds, and of whatever walks, and of whatever moves, so that they could no longer speak: for they had all spoken one with another with one lip and with one tongue.

C.20 '*closed the mouth of all beasts, and of cattle, and of birds, and of whatever walks, and of whatever moves, so that they could no longer speak*'. Here, we are told that at one time all the animals could talk with Adam and Eve. In the Book of Jasher, it makes the point that God created man '*able to speak*', as though that was a 'new thing' special to the physical creation. They obviously communicate in a different way in the spirit world, and from all accounts it, is likely to be telepathy.

JASHER 1.2 And God formed man from the ground, and he blew into his nostrils the breath of life, and man became a living soul 'endowed with speech'.

> 29 And He sent out of the Garden of Eden all flesh that was in the Garden of Eden, and all flesh was scattered according to its kinds, and according to its types unto the places which had been created for them.

30 And to Adam alone did He give (the wherewithal) to cover his shame, of all the beasts and cattle.

31 On this account, it is prescribed on the heavenly tablets as touching all those who know the judgment of the law, that they should cover their shame, and should not uncover themselves as the Gentiles uncover themselves.

32 And on the new moon of the fourth month, Adam and his wife went forth from the Garden of Eden, and they dwelt in the land of Elda in the land of their creation.

C.21 In the Book of Jasher it gives more details as to what happened to Adam and Eve when they left the Garden of Eden:

Book of Jasher 1.2 'And the Lord God drove them that day from the garden of Eden, to till the ground from which they were taken, and they went and dwelt at the **east** of the garden of Eden; and Adam knew his wife Eve and she bore two sons and three daughters.'

33 And Adam called the name of his wife Eve.

34 And they had no son till the first jubilee, [8 A.M. .= 'Anno Mundi' = years of the world] and after this he knew her.

C.22 Presumably this would mean that the first Jubilee did not start until Adam and Eve had left of the Garden of Eden where they had lived for exactly 7 years.

35 Now he tilled the land as he had been instructed in the Garden of Eden.

41

CHAPTER 4: THE BIRTH OF CAIN & ABLE

> 1 And in the third week in the second jubilee she gave birth to Cain, and in the fourth she gave birth to Abel, and in the fifth she gave birth to her daughter Awan.

Comment:1: From reading this verse it would seem to state that Cain was born in one Jubilee and Abel in the next, or 50 years later. The time-sequence does not appear to match here, as Abel was not born 50 years later than Cain. Abel and Cain were apparently around the same age. Also the very next verse states that in the first (year) of the third jubilee Cain slew Abel so there is a contradiction in the time sequence between verses one and two. Perhaps it should have read in verse 1: and in the fourth (week). and in the fifth (week) [Def: A jubilee = 49 years: A week equals 7 years]

> 2 And in the first (year) of the third jubilee, Cain slew Abel because (God) accepted the sacrifice of Abel and did not accept the offering of Cain.

GEN.4:3 And in process of time it came to pass, that Cain brought of the fruit of the ground an offering unto the LORD.

GEN.4:4 And Abel, he also brought of the firstlings of his flock and of the fat thereof. And the LORD had respect unto Abel and to his offering:

> 3 And he slew him in the field: and his blood cried from the ground to heaven, complaining because he had slain him.

GEN.4:8 And Cain talked with Abel his brother: and it came to pass, when they were in the field, that Cain rose up against Abel his brother, and slew him.

C.2 Why does it state 'his blood' cried from the ground. How can something dead like blood that has been spilled out of a human body, and has 'gone cold' have a voice?

Of course we all assume that this is just a very old expression just meaning 'his spirit' cried from the ground. Is that all it means?

Jesus stated that indeed the life of the physical body is in the blood. It is also stated that without our spirit our bodies would die. There are therefore two things that are important for us to stay alive: Physically our blood gives life to every cell of our physical bodies. Spiritually speaking our eternal spirit gives life and energy to our bodies and our eternal spirit is who we really are. We are two beings in one. A spirit body inside a physical body that merely houses it for a season.

When the physical body dies, such as in the case of Abel being murdered by Cain, Abel's blood was soaking into the ground and was **still warm,** meaning he was still **in the process of being killed**, whilst **his spirit was leaving his body** at the **exact same time**.

It was obviously **Abel's spirit that was crying out to God for vengeance** against Cain. It is indeed interesting that the writer did not make the distinction between the blood and the spirit.

It is as though the writers are thinking 'Because the blood is spilled and causes the death of the martyrs, with Abel being the very first martyr, therefore **it is their blood that is calling out for vengeance as it is still warm and they are just passing from life to death**: All that to say that the ancient writers described things accurately as they wanted to convey the idea that the spirits of the first martyr Abel was crying out to God '*as he died',* and not sometime later after death.

In the following verses it is also similar. It does not say '**avenge our souls**, but **blood**' Quite a mystery! What do you make of this expression?

REV.6:9 And when he had opened the fifth seal, I saw under the altar the **souls of them that were slain for the word of God,** and for the testimony which they held:

REV.6:10 And they cried with a loud voice, saying, How long, O Lord, holy and true, dost thou not judge and **avenge** our **blood** on them that dwell on the earth?

REV.6:11 And white robes were given unto every one of them; and it was said unto them, that they should rest yet for a little season, until their fellow servants also and their brethren, that should be **killed** as they were, should be fulfilled.

> 4 And the Lord reproved Cain because of Abel, because he had slain him, and he made him a fugitive on the earth because of the blood of his brother, and he cursed him upon the earth.

GEN.4:11 And now art thou cursed from the earth, which hath opened her mouth to receive thy brother's blood from thy hand; **(See APPENDIX II) for more on this topic)**

GEN.4:12 When thou till the ground, it shall not henceforth yield unto thee her strength; a fugitive and a vagabond shalt thou be in the earth.

1JN.3:12 Not as Cain, who was of that wicked one, and slew his brother. And wherefore slew he him? Because his own works were evil, and his brother's righteous

C.3 Notice that the Bible verse above suggests something very strong. 'Not as Cain, who was of that wicked one'. Is John implying that Cain was used by the Devil, or much worse, that he was actually born/fathered by the Devil? How did that happen, if true? What evidence do we have for assuming this? Look at the following from the Jewish Encyclopaedias: 'Cain was also viewed as a type of 'utter perverseness', an 'offspring of Satan', "a son of wrath", 'a lawless rebel' who said, "There is neither a divine judgment nor a judge", whose words of repentance were insincere whose fleeing from God was a denial of His omnipresence (and all his generations must be exterminated "the desire of the spirit of sin" He is the first of those who have no share in the world to come.' [Source: http://www.jewishencyclopedia.com/articles/3904-cain]

C.4 See my book '**JASHER INSIGHTS'** for a lot more details concerning Cain, and why he was a '**compulsive murderer'** and of an evil bent.

C.5 It was indeed the **licentious daughters** of Cain that attracted the evil **fallen angels** to make love with them centuries later. I will cover that, in this book in more detail in the next chapter.

> 5 And on this account, it is written on the heavenly tables, 'Cursed is he who smites his neighbour treacherously, and let all who have seen and heard say, 'So be it'; and the man who has seen and not declared (it), let him be accursed as the other.'

C.6 It is very interesting that this very old expression stating '*So Be it*' was the exact expression as used by Pharaoh in the old movie THE TEN COMMANDMENTS which also happens to be from the same timeframe as this book of Jubilees. The maker of that movie obviously had done his homework well - Cecil B DeMille.

> 6 And for this reason we announce when we come before the Lord our God all the sin which is committed in heaven and on earth, and in light and in darkness, and everywhere.
>
> 7 And Adam and his wife mourned for Abel four weeks of years, [99-127 A.M.= Anno Mundi' =years of the world] and in the fourth year of the fifth week [130 A.M.] they became joyful, and Adam knew his wife again, and she bare him a son, and he called his name Seth; for he said 'GOD has raised up a second seed unto us on the earth instead of Abel; for Cain slew him.'
>
> 8 And in the sixth week [134-140 A.M.] he begat his daughter Azura.
>
> 9 And Cain took Awan his sister to be his wife and she bare him Enoch at the close of the fourth jubilee. [190-196 A.M.]
>
> 10 And in the first year of the first week of the fifth jubilee, [197 A.M.] houses were built on the earth, and Cain built a city, and called its name

after the name of his son Enoch.

GEN.4:17 And Cain knew his wife; and she conceived, and bare Enoch: and he built a city, and called the name of the city, after the name of his son, Enoch.

11 And Adam knew Eve his wife and she bare yet nine sons.

C.7 Here is a detail not found in the Bible, that Eve bore 9 more sons after that she had born Cain, Abel and Seth, which means 12 sons in total, not to mention all her many daughters. Adam and Eve could have had at least 24 children, or even more, considering that they lived to be over 900 years long.

12 And in the fifth week of the fifth jubilee [225-31 A.M.] Seth took Azura his sister to be his wife, and in the fourth (year of the sixth 12,13 week) [235 A.M.] she bare him Enos.

C.8 This [235 **A.M.**] date is exactly the same as the date given in the biblical Timeframe Chart. I will be pointing out with each date mentioned in this book of Jubilees which dates concur with the biblical Timeframe Charts and which ones do not. I will then make a conclusion as to why some dates are not the same. (See **APPENDIX** for the Biblical Timeframe Chart)

13 He began to call on the name of the Lord on the earth.

14 And in the seventh jubilee in the third week [309-315 A.M.] Enos took Noemi his sister to be his wife, and she bare him a son in the third year of the fifth week, and he called his name Kenan.

C.9 Why did the early humans often marry their sisters? Something that is abhorrent to us in modern times. Is it just possible that something was genetically different well before the Great flood when the very first humans were living on the earth? One reason one is not supposed to marry one's sister is that any offspring could be still-born or even a cretin as the blood grouping and DNA are too similar.

C.10 It was very different in the early days after the Creation. There is even evidence that mankind used to have what is called a triple helix in their D.N.A before the Great Flood. After the Great flood somehow God altered man's DNA to the double helix. In other words God down-graded mankind because of his former wickedness before the Great flood and God knew that mankind could no longer be trusted with certain powers generally afforded by the extra strand of DNA of what is known as the Triple Helix.

C.11 What difference did the Triple Helix make to mankind before the Great Flood? Well, that is largely unknown to us today, except one famous scientist and writer has suggested that the 3rd strand of the DNA Helix gave man more powers of perception. (See: '**CORRUPTING THE IMAGE**'- by Douglas Hemp.)

15 And at the close of the eighth jubilee [325, 386-399 A.M.] Kenan took Mualeleth his sister to be his wife, and she bare him a son in the ninth jubilee, in the first week in the third year of this week, [395 A.M] and he called his name Mahalalel.

16 And in the second week of the tenth jubilee [449-55 A.M.] Mahalalel took unto him to wife Dinah, the daughter of Barakiel the daughter of his father's brother, and she bare him a son in the third week in the sixth year, [461 A.M.] and he called his name Jared, for in his days the angels of the Lord descended on the earth, those who are named the Watchers, that they should instruct the children of men, and that they should do judgment and uprightness on the earth.

C.12 The above dates are exactly the same as the dates given in the biblical Timeframe Chart. (See the **APPENDIX** for the Biblical Timeframe Chart)

C.13 'And he called his name Jared, for in his days the 'angels of the Lord' descended on the earth, those who are named the 'Watchers'. Watchers were a special class of angels, who were originally assigned to mankind to both read his thoughts, and to be ideal for both communicating with mankind and instructing him in the ways of righteousness. However, there was a 'Rebellion in Heaven' and Satan and his Fallen angels rebelled, & in Jared's time 200 of these Fallen angels came down to earth according to the Bible and the Apocryphal books of Enoch, Jasher & Jubilees, and took the beautiful women as their wives and *begat giants*.

17 And in the eleventh jubilee [512-18 A.M.] Jared took to himself a wife, and her name was Baraka, the daughter of Rasujal, a daughter of his father's brother, in the fourth week of this jubilee, [522 A.M.] and she bare him a son in the fifth week, in the fourth year of the jubilee, and he called his name Enoch.

C.14 This date [522 A.M.] is incorrect according to the Bible and is off by 100 years and should read [622 A.M.] According to the biblical Timeframe Chart Jared was 162 when he begat Enoch. The Book of Jubilees puts Jared as 62. Why the difference. We will discuss that later on. This is the first date so far that does not agree with the biblical Timeframe Chart.

C.15 This was the Enoch who wrote about the Fallen Angels and the Giants, and about his many trips to heaven, and all that God revealed to him about the future of the planet from the beginning to the very end. In fact the whole panorama of the 7000+ years of World History was revealed to Enoch by God Himself. (See my book **'Enoch Insights'**)

18 And he was the first among men that are born on earth who learnt

46

writing and knowledge and wisdom and who wrote down the signs of heaven according to the order of their months in a book, that men might know the seasons of the years according to the order of their separate months.

C.16 *'First among men that are born on earth who learnt writing and knowledge and wisdom and who wrote down the signs of heaven'.*
Enoch was the first man to learn to write, as stated in this Book of Jubilees.

C.17 To read an in-depth study on this topic of **ENOCH** see my other books 'JASHER INSIGHTS' & 'ENOCH INSIGHTS'.

19 And he was the first to write a testimony and he testified to the sons of men among the generations of the earth, and recounted the weeks of the jubilees, and made known to them the days of the years and set in order the months and recounted the Sabbaths of the years as we made (them), known to him.

20 And what was and what will be he saw in a vision of his sleep, as it will happen to the children of men throughout their generations until the day of judgment; he saw and understood everything, and wrote his testimony, and placed the testimony on earth for all the children of men and for their generations.

C.18 Here it is categorically stating *'Enoch saw in a vision of his sleep, as it will happen to the children of men throughout their generations until the day of judgment; he saw and understood everything.'*

JASHER 3.2 And the soul of Enoch was *wrapped up in the instruction of the Lord, in knowledge and in understanding*; and he wisely retired from the sons of men and secreted himself from them for many days.

21 And in the twelfth jubilee, [582-88] in the seventh week thereof, he took to himself a wife, and her name was Edna, the daughter of Danel, the daughter of his father's brother, and in the sixth year in this week [587 A.M.] she bare him a son and he called his name Methuselah.

C.19 This date [587 A.M.] is incorrect according to the Bible and should read [687 A.M.] The timeframe is still off by 100 years.

JASHER 3.13 And these are the generations of Enoch, Methuselah, Elisha, and Elimelech, three sons; and their sisters were Melca and Nahmah, and Methuselah lived eighty-seven years and he begat Lamech.

22 And he was moreover with the angels of God these six jubilees of

years, and they showed him everything which is on earth and in the heavens, the rule of the sun, and he wrote down everything.

23 And he testified to the Watchers, who had sinned with the daughters of men; for these had begun to unite themselves, so as to be defiled, with the daughters of men, and Enoch testified against (them) all.

ENOCH 13.7 'And I recounted before them all the visions which I had seen in sleep, and I began to speak the words of righteousness, and to reprimand the heavenly *Watchers*.'

24 And he was taken from amongst the children of men, and we conducted him into the Garden of Eden in majesty and honour and behold there he writes down the condemnation and judgment of the world, and all the wickedness of the children of men.

C.20 This is a unique verse in that it states that Enoch was 'translated' for a specific purpose and was taken to a specific place (The Garden of Eden) which still existed, although Adam and Eve had been banned from it many centuries before Enoch was translated. It was in the Garden of Eden that Enoch wrote down the entire history of the world as shown to him by God and His angels.

ENOCH 39.3) "And in those days a whirlwind carried me off from the earth and set me down at the end of the heavens".)

25 And on account of it (God) brought the waters of the flood upon all the land of Eden; for there he was set as a sign and that he should testify against all the children of men, that he should recount all the deeds of the generations until the day of condemnation.

26 And he burnt the incense of the sanctuary, (even) sweet spices acceptable before the Lord on the Mount.

27 For the Lord has four places on the earth, the Garden of Eden, and the Mount of the East, and this mountain on which thou art this day, Mount Sinai, and Mount Zion (which) will be sanctified in the new creation for a sanctification of the earth; through it will the earth be sanctified from all (its) guilt and its uncleanness throughout the generations of the world.

C.21 This *last verse* is obviously very important and speaks of the great importance of the following locations as in regards to the New Heaven and the New Earth, when things will be perfectly righteous and Evil will no longer exist: '¹*Garden of Eden, and the ²Mount of the East) and this mountain on which thou art this day = ³Mount Sinai, and ⁴Mount Zion (which) will be sanctified in the new creation for a sanctification of the earth'- will be sanctified in the new creation for a sanctification of the earth*

¹Garden of Eden: Where God originally placed Adam and Eve when things were *perfectly good*. At a time when mankind could actually see God and communicate with Him directly.

GEN.3:8 And they heard the voice of the LORD God walking in the garden in the cool of the day.

² **Mount of the East** =Mount of Olives, East of Jerusalem, where Jesus was in the garden of Gethsemane just before He was crucified and subsequently gave His live that all humanity might have Eternal life.

MAT.26:30 And when they had sung an hymn, they went out into the mount of Olives.

MAT.26:36 Then cometh Jesus with them unto a place called Gethsemane.

³ **Mount Sinai**: The mountain on which Moses received the 10 Commandments, and more importantly spoke to God 'Face to Face' **Mount Sinai**, also known as **Mount** Moses or **Mount Horeb**, is a mountain in the South **Sinai** region of Egypt. Standing 7497ft (2285m) tall, the peak is best known as the possible location of the biblical **Mount Sinai**, where according to the both the Bible and the Quran, God told Moses the Ten Commandments.

II EZDRAS 2. 21 'I, Ezra, received a command from the Lord on Mount Horeb to go to Israel. When I came to them, they rejected me and refused the Lord's commandment'. (See my book '**EZDRAS INSIGHTS**')

⁴ **Mount Zion**: This is the mountain on which Jesus will land when He returns to conquer the earth and take it away from Satan the usurper of God's Creation.

REV.14:1 And I looked, and, lo, a **Lamb** stood on the mount Sion (or Zion), and with him an hundred forty and four thousand, having his Father's name written in their foreheads.

REV.7:4 And I heard the number of them which were sealed: and there were sealed an hundred and forty and four thousand of all the tribes of the children of Israel.

JOHN 1.29 ' The next day John seeth Jesus coming unto him, and saith, Behold the **Lamb** of God, which taketh away the sin of the world.

C.22 Psalm 87: 2-3 states: "The Lord loves the gates of Zion / more than all the other dwellings of Jacob. / Glorious things are said of you, / city of God."

According to this verse, *Zion* is synonymous with *city of God*, and it is a place that God loves. Zion is Jerusalem. Mount Zion is the high hill on which David built a citadel. It is on the southeast side of the city.

The word Zion occurs over 150 times in the Bible. It essentially means "fortification" and has the idea of being "raised up" as a "monument." Zion is described both as the city of David and the city of God. As the Bible progresses, the word *Zion* expands in scope and takes on an additional, spiritual meaning.

C.23 In Summary: As you can see, all of these 4 locations are very Holy and sacred to God as well as very important & significant locations for Eternity. These specific locations will serve as reminders of obedience, submission & dedication to God and Salvation through the Messiah.

---

28 And in the fourteenth jubilee [652 A.M. .= Anno Mundi' =years of the world] Methuselah took unto himself a wife, Edna the daughter of Azrial, the daughter of his father's brother, in the third week, in the first year of this week, [701-7 A.M.] and he begat a son and called his name Lamech.

C.24 According to the Bible these dates [652 A.M.] & [701-7 A.M.] are really off the mark by quite some distance in time? According to the Bible Methuselah wasn't even born until [687 A.M] Lamech wasn't born until [874 A.M.] according to the Bible. This now shows a discrepancy in time of 173 years. Why is there this discrepancy? We will summarize and make conclusions about this later.

GEN.5:25 And Methuselah lived an hundred eighty and seven years, and begat Lamech.

---

29 And in the fifteenth jubilee in the third week Lamech took to himself a wife, and her name was Betenos the daughter of Baraki'il, the daughter of his father's brother, and in this week she bare him a son and he called his name Noah, saying, 'This one will comfort me for my trouble and all my work, and for the ground which the Lord hath cursed.'

C.25 Here it states that Lamech took a wife in the fifteenth Jubilee. A Jubilee is 50 years, so 15 Jubilees is 750 years. If we look at the Bible Time Chart at the year 750, Lamech had not even been born yet and was not to be born until 874 A.M. According to the Bible, Noah wasn't born until 1056 [A.M.]

JASHER 4.14 And Methuselah called his name Noah, saying, 'The earth was in his days at rest and free from corruption', and Lamech his father called his name Menachem, saying, 'This one shall comfort us in our works and miserable toil in the earth, which God had cursed'.

30 And at the close of the nineteenth jubilee, in the seventh week in the sixth year [930 A.M.] thereof, Adam died, and all his sons buried him in the land of his creation, and he was the first to be buried in the earth.

GENESIS 5.5 And all the years of Adam were 930 years and he died

31 And he lacked seventy years of one thousand years; for one thousand years are as one day in the testimony of the heavens and therefore was it written concerning the tree of knowledge: 'On the day that ye eat thereof ye shall die.' For this reason, he did not complete the years of this day; for he died during it.

C.26 The following expression in the above verse is also mentioned in the Bible: *'for one thousand years are as one day'*

2PE.3:8 But, beloved, be not ignorant of this one thing, that one day is with the Lord as a thousand years, and a thousand years as one day.

C.27 Incidentally these two above verses, could also be stating something very important. That is, that every day of Creation represents 1000-years of man's available time on earth. So, for the full '7 days of the week' of the Original Creation by God Himself, this would equal 7000 years of World History until the Final Great Judgment of God, followed by the Eternal Age of the New Heaven and the New Earth.

32 At the close of this jubilee Cain was killed after him in the same year; for his house fell upon him and he died in the midst of his house, and he was killed by its stones; for with a stone he had killed Abel, and by a stone was he killed in righteous judgment.

33 For this reason it was ordained on the heavenly tablets: With the instrument with which a man kills his neighbour with the same shall he be killed; after the manner that he wounded him; in like manner shall they deal with him.'

34 And in the twenty-fifth [1205 A.M. .= 'Anno Mundi' = years of the world] jubilee Noah took to himself a wife, and her name was Emzara, the daughter of Rake'el, the daughter of his father's brother, in the first year in the fifth week [1207 A.M.]: and in the third year thereof she bare him Shem, in the fifth year thereof [1209 A.M.] she bare him Ham, and in the first year in the sixth week [1212 A.M.] she bare him Japheth.

C.28 This date of [1205 A.M.] is very different than the date given in the Bible. Here is states that Shem was born in the year [1209 A.M.] In the Bible it states that Shem was born in the year [1558] Here now showing a difference in time of 347 years.

Why the discrepancy in time? Now that is a very good question.

Chapter 5: THE FALLEN ANGELS

> 1 And it came to pass when the children of men began to multiply on the face of the earth and daughters were born unto them, that the angels of God saw them on a certain year of this jubilee, that they were beautiful to look upon; and they took themselves wives of all whom they chose, and they bare unto them sons and they were giants.

SEPTUAGINT LXX: Genesis 6.2,5. And it came to pass when men began to be numerous upon the earth, and daughters were born unto them, that the sons of God (Fallen Angels) having seen the daughters of men that they were beautiful, took to themselves wives of all whom they chose. Now the giants were upon the earth in those days.; and after that when the sons of God were wont to go into the daughters of men, they bore children to them who were the giants of old, the men of renown.

Comment:1: The **Fallen Angels**, and how they fell and their coming to earth to co-habit with women, and their resultant sons the Giants, is a very big topic that is well covered in the books of **Enoch** and **Jasher, Jubilees** and is also mentioned in the Bible.

GEN.6:2 That the '*sons of God*' saw the daughters of men that they were fair; and they took them wives of all which they chose.

GEN.6:4 There were *giants* in the earth in those days; and also after that, when the sons of God came in unto the daughters of men, and they bare children to them, the same became mighty men which were of old, men of renown.

ENOCH 6.2 And the *angels*, the *children of heaven*, saw and lusted after them, and said to one another "Come, let us choose us wives from among the children of men and beget us children".

C.2 It is very important to point out that it was **not all the beautiful woman** on the earth that seduced the Angels of God to come and mate with them. What kind of women were these particular beautiful women? Apparently, they were in fact the descendants of the infamous **licentious daughters** of Cain, who used to perform orgies in public that attracted the evil **fallen angels** to mate with them centuries later. Remember that Cain their forefather was of the Devil himself, so it is not really surprising to learn about these things as reported by Josephus in the first century A.D

C.3 GENERATIONS OF CAIN

The seven generations of Cain, as the brood of Satan, are accordingly represented as types of rebels. While, the pious men all descended from Seth, there sprang from Cain all the wicked ones who rebelled against God and whose perverseness and corruption brought on the Flood: they committed abominations and incestuous crimes in public without shame. The daughters of Cain were those "fair daughters of men" who by their lasciviousness caused the fall of the "sons of God"., but were attracted by the gay and sensuous mode of life in which the children of Cain indulged; the latter spending their days at the foot of the mountain, in wild orgies, accompanied by the music of instruments invented by Jubal, and by women, in gorgeous attire, seducing the men to commit the most abominable practises. Also speaks of the excessive wickedness of the posterity of Cain, which grew in vehemence with every generation; while the posterity of Seth remained virtuous during seven generations, after which the fall of the angels ensued who produced gigantic offspring in making love with the women on earth. [**SOURCE:** http://www.jewishencyclopedia.com/articles/3904-cain

> 2 And lawlessness increased on the earth and all flesh corrupted its way, alike men and cattle and beasts and birds and everything that walks on the earth - all of them corrupted their ways and their orders, and they began to devour each other, and lawlessness increased on the earth and every imagination of the thoughts of all men (was) thus evil continually.

C.4 The book of Enoch gives an *allegorical* story involving the animals in chapters **86** and **87**. Here is an excerpt from my book '**ENOCH INSIGHTS**':

[**ENOCH 86 1.** 1 And again I saw with mine eyes as I slept, and I saw heaven above, and behold a star fell from heaven, and it arose and ate and pastured amongst those oxen. And after that I saw the large and the black oxen, and behold they all changed their stalls and pastures, and their cattle, and began to live with each other.

LUK.10:18 And he said unto them, I beheld Satan as lightning fall from heaven

REV.12:4 And his tail drew the third part of the stars of heaven, and did cast them to the earth

ENOCH 86.2 And again I saw in the vision, and looked towards the heaven, and behold I saw many stars descend and cast themselves down from heaven to that first star, and they became bulls amongst those cattle and pastured with them amongst them.

C.5 This story shows how the angels of God came down from heaven following that first fallen star, and they started to corrupt mankind by mating with the women and fathering strange children, which turned out to be giants. Illustrated well here in this story as the progeny no longer merely being white (good) bulls, but now elephants, camels and asses. These new creatures were generally much bigger.

ENOCH 87.1 1 And again I saw how they began to gore each other and to devour each other, and the earth began to cry aloud.] [End of excerpt from '*ENOCH INSIGHTS*']

C.6 How is such a thing even possible that '*all flesh corrupted its way, alike men and cattle and beasts and birds and everything that walks on the earth-all of them corrupted their ways' and 'their orders',* and they began to '*devour each other'.* How is it even possible that animals, birds as well as humans could *'corrupt their orders'*?

ENOCH 7.2 And they became pregnant, and they bare *great giants*, whose height was **three thousand ells***, who consumed all the acquisitions of men; and when men could no longer sustain them, the *giants* turned against them and *devoured mankind.*

C.7 How high was **3000 ells***? The staggering answer to that is as high as 450 feet - according to the expert on Giants Steve Quayle. [www.stevequayle.com]

BARUCH 3.26-28 There were giants famous from the beginning that were of so great stature and so expert in war. Those did not the Lord choose, neither gave he the way of knowledge to them: But they were destroyed, because they had no wisdom, and perished in their own foolishness

> 3 And God looked upon the earth, and behold it was corrupt, and all flesh had corrupted its orders, and all that were upon the earth had wrought all manner of evil before His eyes.

C.8 'Corrupted its orders'. Here it is saying that somehow the Fallen Angels managed to corrupt the 'species barrier' put in place by God himself. The first Fallen angels cohabitated with woman and 200 of those original angels that fell were locked up. However, later in time, many more angels fell, & not being content to barely breed with women as they degenerated, they eventually during the latter years prior to the Great Flood, managed to somehow procreate with all kind of creatures and beasts and thus creating the chimeras of all types including mermaids, centaurs, minotaur, harpies, and countless others. (See my books **'Enoch Insights'** & **'Jasher Insights'**, for a lot more details on this subject)

Jasher 4.16,18. And all the sons of men departed from the ways of the Lord in those days, as they multiplied upon the face of the earth with sons and daughters, and they taught one another their evil practices, and they continued sinning against the Lord.

And their **judges and rulers** went to the daughters of men and took their wives by force from their husbands according to their choice and the sons of men (Sons of God =Fallen angels), in those days took from the cattle of the earth, the beasts of the field and the fowls of the air, and *taught the mixture of animals of one species with another*, in order to therewith provoke the Lord; and God saw the whole earth and it was corrupt, for all flesh had corrupted its ways upon earth, all men and all animals.

C.9 Is it just possible that the '**Sons of God'(Fallen angels)** & their sons the Giants were the 'judges and rulers' over mankind in those days, as mentioned in this last verse of Jasher 4.16-18? It was the golden Age of the Giants and Demi-gods in the 500 years before the Great Flood of Noah.

> 4 And He said that He would destroy man and all flesh upon the face of the earth, which He had created.

GEN.6:4 There were *giants* in the earth in those days; and also after that, when the sons of God came in unto the daughters of men, and they bare children to them, the same became *mighty men* which were of old, men of renown.

GEN.6:5 And God saw that the wickedness of man was great in the earth, and that every *imagination of the thoughts of his heart was only evil continually.*

GEN.6:6 And it repented the LORD that he had made man on the earth, and it *grieved him at his heart.*

GEN.6:7 And the LORD said, I will *destroy man whom I have created from the face of the earth*; both man, and beast, and the creeping thing, and the fowls of the air; for it repents me that I have made them.

JASHER 4.19 And the Lord said, I will blot out man that I created from the face of the earth, yea from man to the birds of the air, together with cattle and beasts that are in the field for I repent that I made them.

SEPTUAGINT LXX Genesis 6.6,13, & 8. And the Lord God having seen that the wicked actions of men were multiplied upon the earth and that everyone in his heart was intently brooding over evil continually. And the Lord God saw the earth and it was corrupted; because all flesh had corrupted its ways upon the earth. And God said, I will blot out man whom I have made from the face of the earth, even man with cattle, and reptiles and flying creatures of the sky, for I am grieved that I have made them.

C.10 I can see why God was upset with the Fallen angels and even mankind in general, but what about the animals? There must be a valid reason why God destroyed the animals also? Adam and Eve ate fruits and vegetables and nuts and seeds and not animals or the beasts of the earth. The key in answering this question is 'because **all flesh** had **corrupted its ways** upon the earth.' How is it possible that the animals had also corrupted their ways?

C.11 One thing we know from studying the Book of Enoch is that the Fallen angels first started by mating with human woman, but later on they became more and more **depraved and demonic** in nature and started to **pervert the DNA of animals by mating with them.**

C.12 Fallen angels mated with animals in their depraved state. We might say how is that even possible? The Fallen angels had the power to be **shape-shifters** and could **literally turn themselves into the shape of any animal.** Thus, they would take on the form of different animals and mate with them until they got pregnant.

ENOCH 19.1-2 [EXCERPT FROM 'ENOCH INSIGHTS'] 1 And Uriel said to me, "Here shall stand the angels who have connected themselves with women, and their spirits assuming many different forms are defiling mankind and shall lead them astray into sacrificing to demons as gods, (here shall they stand) till the day of the great judgment in which they shall be judged till they are made an end of."

C.13 Here it clearly shows that angels are able to be *shape-shifters*. All

56

through history sacrificing to Demons as gods has been very commonplace, though it *still exists in modern times*, it is mostly camouflaged.

2 And the **women** also of the angels who went astray shall become **sirens**, and I, Enoch alone saw the vision, the ends of all things, and no man shall see as I have seen. [End of excerpt from '*ENOCH INSIGHTS*']

C.14 The offspring would be a hybrid of both angel DNA and animal DNA, and thus came the chimeras of ancient mythology into being.

C.15 Human and animal **chimeras** came into being as well as the **Giants and monsters in the times before the Great Flood. (See the Book of the Giants)**

C.16 With this knowledge, we find the corruption of most of God's original creation. So, it is not surprising that God was grieved at his heart and decided to destroy all of His creation, that is all but Noah and his wife and three sons and their wives.

C.17 How did the flesh-eating omnivore monsters like T-Rex come into existence?

The fact is that God had originally created a vegetarian world for mankind and the animals. I believe it very likely that the Fallen angels in their rebellion against God tinkered around with the DNA of reptiles and peaceful dinosaurs like the brontosaurus and produced horrific hybrids such as T-REX and things like velociraptors and pterodactyls, which were non-stop meat eaters just like the giants born of angels and women.

C.18 Those MONSTER creatures did not live millions of years ago as taught by evolutionists and science falsely so-called, but they did exist some 5000 years ago before the Great Flood. They certainly were not created by God Himself, as God had originally created all the animals to be herbivores and not carnivores.

C.19 Why did God decide to destroy all of the animals, with the exception of the sea monsters, other sea creatures and the fish. Why were the creatures of the sea not slain? If we think about it logically, God needed some creatures of the sea to devour all the dead bodies from the millions of people and animals who drowned in the Great Flood.

C.20 When God destroys the world again in the Wrath of God as predicted in Revelation 16 and at the Final battle of 'Good versus Evil' called Armageddon, it states the following: Revelation 19.

REV.19:17 And I saw an angel standing in the sun; and he cried with a loud voice, saying to all the fowls that fly in the midst of heaven, Come and gather yourselves together unto the supper of the great God;

REV.19:18 That ye may **eat the flesh of kings**, and the **flesh of captains**, and the flesh of mighty men, and the **flesh of horses**, and of them that sit on them, and the flesh of all men, both free and bond, both small and great.

C.21 God many times in scripture pointed out that if people were wicked and disobedient against Him then they would be '**DEVOURED'**.

[**Jubilees 1.13** And I will hide My face from them, and I will deliver them into the hand of the Gentiles for captivity, and **for a prey, and for devouring**, and I will remove them from the midst of the land, and I will scatter them amongst the Gentiles.]

C.22 'Devoured' by what, we might question? Look also at this strange verse in The **Book** of **Revelations Chapter 6:**

REV.6:8 And I looked and behold a pale horse: and his name that sat on him was Death, and Hell followed with him. And power was given unto them over the fourth part of the earth, to kill with sword, and with hunger, and with death, and with the beasts of the earth.

C.23 What beasts of the earth? I believe that when the Wrath of God comes, it won't be normal birds that come to **devour** the bodies of **200,000,000 slaughtered soldiers** at Armageddon, but some of the ancient massive hybrid birds such as the pterodactyls and other flying monsters. Normal birds would have a very hard time devouring so many corpses! Where are the ancient meat-eating dinosaurs? Were they all killed off at the time of the Great flood, or do some in fact still exist and are they presently in hiding from mankind?

C.24 If you read the stories of Admiral Byrd from the 2nd world War, you will find that he ventured inside the earth and discovered a 'New land' or the Inner World, where he stated that there were massive creatures roaming around, which were like mammoths and dinosaurs and massive birds like the ptero- dactyls. [Admiral Richard Byrd]: **Source:**

https://www.bibliotecapleyades.net/tierra_hueca/esp_tierra_hueca_2d.htm

5 But Noah found grace before the eyes of the Lord.

GEN.6:8 But Noah found grace in the eyes of the LORD.

SEPTUAGINT Genesis 6.10 Noah was a just man being *'perfect in his generation'*. Noah was well pleasing to the God.

C.25 What is the full meaning of this enigmatic expression 'perfect in his generation'

According to the amazing and insightful book by **Douglas Kemp** '**Corrupting the Image'** this above expression is talking about a whole lot more than just Noah being an 'upright man' in spirit.

Douglas claims in his amazing book that it actually means that the 'seed of Noah' had not been corrupted with Satan's seed from the word '**semion**' from the original Greek.

It is important to understand that one of Satan's main purposes was to corrupt the 'righteous seed' from the beginning of Creation in an attempt to stop the **MESSIAH** from being '**born of a woman**' and defeating Satan's whole purpose of first enslaving mankind and then finally both destroying mankind physically and spiritually along with the rest of God's Creation.

Conclusion: Satan apparently, in his 'deluded way of thinking', thought that if he could corrupt all of the 'seed of the woman' then the Messiah would never be born - and thus mankind could not be saved – end of mankind! Fortunately for us, God did find one righteous man and his wife – Noah and his wife to continue on the seed of mankind.

GEN.3:15 And I will put enmity between thee and the woman, and between thy *seed (semion)* and her *seed*; it shall bruise thy head, and thou shalt bruise his heel

The Messiah was prophecied to come can crush Satan's head and to deliver mankind by giving his life for a ransom for the souls of all mankind who would receive His gift of **Salvation**: http://www.outofthebottomlesspit.co.uk/418605189

ENOCH 10.1 Then said the Most High, the Holy and Great One spoke, and sent Uriel to the son of Lamech, and said to him: "Go tell *Noah* and tell him in my name 'Hide thyself!' and reveal to him the end that is approaching, that *the whole earth will be destroyed,* and a *deluge is about to come upon the whole earth, and I will destroy all that is upon it."*

JASHER 4. 21 And Noah found grace in the sight of the Lord, and the Lord chose him and his children to raise up seed from them upon the face of the whole earth.

> 6 And against the angels whom He had sent upon the earth, He was exceedingly wroth, and He gave commandment to root them out of all their dominion, and He bade us to bind them in the depths of the earth, and behold they are bound in the midst of them and are (kept) separate.

C.26 *'against the angels whom He had sent upon the earth, He was exceedingly wroth, and He gave commandment to root them out of all their dominion'.* This verse is mirrored in the New Testament:

JUD.1:6 And the angels which kept not their first estate, but left their own habitation, he hath reserved in everlasting chains under darkness unto the judgment of the great day.

> 7 And against their sons went forth a command from before His face that they should be smitten with the sword and be removed from under heaven.

C.27 We can see a very similar verse in the **Book of Enoch:**

ENOCH 10.9 And to Gabriel said the Lord "Proceed against the bastards and the reprobates, and against the children of fornication, and destroy the children of fornication, the children of the Watchers (The Giants) from amongst men and cause them to go forth. Send them one against the other that they may destroy each other in battle. For length of days they shall not have."

> 8 And He said, 'My spirit shall not always abide on man; for they also are flesh and their days shall be one hundred and twenty years'.

GEN.6:3 And the LORD said, My spirit shall not always strive with man, for that he also is flesh: yet his days shall be an hundred and twenty years.

C.28 Here we can clearly see that God severely reduced man's time on earth from before the Great Flood, when many people lived up to 900 years old. At the time of the Great Flood, God said he would reduce man's age to 120 years old. If we look at biblical Time Charts, we find that it actually took until the time of Joseph who died at 110 years old before this curse of reduction in the years of man was fully realized. His 11 brothers died at ages between 120-138 years old. Joseph lived circa 550 years after the Great Flood. Man actually continued to degenerate until by 800 after Joseph in the time of King David or around 3000 years ago, man lived to be only 70 years old.

PSA.90:10 The days of our years are threescore years and ten (70); and if by reason of strength they be fourscore years yet is their strength labour and sorrow; for it is soon cut off, and we fly away.

C.29 In modern times the average age for humans to die is still around 70 years old.

> 9 And He sent His sword into their midst that each should slay his neighbour, and they began to slay each other till they all fell by the sword and were destroyed from the earth.

C.30 *'till they all fell by the sword and were destroyed from the earth'.* It is stating here that all the Giants were 'incited' by God's 'good' angels to 'do battle the one against the other', until they were finally 'all consumed from the earth' in the 500-year time period leading up to the Great Flood of [1150 A.M. -1650 A.M.= **'Anno Mundi' = years of the world**]

ENOCH 10.11 And the Lord said unto Michael "Go bind Semjaza and his associates (Fallen angels) who have united themselves with women so as to have been defiled with them in all their uncleanness. And *their sons (the Giants) have slain one another*, and they have seen the destruction of their beloved ones, bind them *(200 Fallen Angels)* fast for seventy generations in the valleys of the earth till the day of their judgement and the consummation till the judgement that is for ever is consummated."

> 10 And their fathers(The Fallen angels) were witnesses (of their destruction), and after this they were bound in the depths of the earth for ever, until the day of the great condemnation, when judgment is executed

on all those who have corrupted their ways and their works before the Lord.

C.31 In this Book of Jubilees it states *'until the day of the great condem-nation*, *when judgment is executed'*; and also in the Book of Enoch as mentioned in the two verses above, the sons of the Giants and the Fallen angels would be judged at the Great White Throne Judgement. From Enoch's time the first '200 Fallen angels' were bound for 70 generations or until the 7000 years of World History is finished. (**See APPENDIX** for more on **TIME CHARTS**)

C.32 Here it makes it clear that it is talking about the Fallen Watchers and their reprobate sons the Giants:

ENOCH 10. 9 And destroy all the spirits of the reprobate and the children of the Watchers, because they have wronged mankind. Destroy all wrong from the face of the earth, and let every evil work come to an end, and let the Plant of Righteousness appear.

11 And He destroyed all from their places, and there was not left one of them whom He judged not according to all their wickedness.

12 And he made for all his works a new and righteous nature, so that they should not sin in their whole nature for ever but should be all righteous each in his kind alway.

C.33 Here God is looking far ahead from Moses's time to the 'End of all things', or the end of the '7000 years of mankind upon the earth'. In fact to the end of the Golden Age of 1000 years when God's Final Judgement occurs. After that will come the New Heaven and New Earth wherein dwelleth only righteousness and no evil at all.

ISA.66:22 For as the New Heavens and the New Earth, which I will make, shall remain before me, saith the LORD, so shall your seed and your name remain.

ISA.66:23 And it shall come to pass, that from one new moon to another, and from one sabbath to another, shall all flesh come to worship before me, saith the LORD.

13 And the judgment of all is ordained and written on the heavenly tablets in righteousness - even (the judgment of) all who depart from the path which is ordained for them to walk in; and if they walk not therein, judgment is written down for every creature and for every kind.

C.34 What can this strange expression actually mean? *'judgment is written down for every creature and for every kind'*. This is implying that there are other creatures than simply human as they would have to be able to be 'held accountable for their actions' if they are to be judged, and not merely dumb beasts.

Could it also be talking about Fallen Angels and creatures created by them as their strange progeny? Such as the chimeras of many types, who were intelligent as they were half angelic and half human in some cases. The fact is that before the Great Flood there were many types of human and bestial chimeras due to the Fallen Angels interference with both the human races and the animal races. It is even reported that they also interfered with the insects and birds making very strange hybrids.

REV.20:11 And I saw a great white throne, and him that sat on it, from whose face the earth and the heaven fled away; and there was found no place for them.

REV.20:12 And I saw the dead, small and great, stand before God; and the books were opened: and another book was opened, which is the book of life: and the dead were judged out of those things which were written in the books, according to their works.

> 14 And there is nothing in heaven or on earth, or in light or in darkness, or in Sheol or in the depth, or in the place of darkness (which is not judged); and all their judgments are ordained and written and engraved.
>
> **REV.20:13** And the sea gave up the dead which were in it; and death and hell delivered up the dead which were in them: and they were judged every man according to their works.

REV.20:14 And death and hell were cast into the lake of fire. This is the second death.

ECC.12:14 For God shall bring *every work into judgment*, with every *secret thing*, whether it be good, or whether it be evil.

> 15 In regard to all He will judge the great according to his greatness, and the small according to his smallness, and each according to his way.
>
> 16 And He is not one who will regard the person (of any), nor is He one who will receive gifts, if He says that He will execute judgment on each: if one gave everything that is on the earth, He will not regard the gifts or the person (of any), nor accept anything at his hands, for He is a righteous judge.

REV.20:15 And whosoever was not found written in the Book of life was cast into the lake of fire.

17 And of the children of Israel it has been written and ordained: If they turn to him in righteousness He will forgive all their transgressions and pardon all their sins.

18 It is written and ordained that He will show mercy to all who turn from all their guilt once each year.

19 And as for all those who corrupted their ways and their thoughts before the flood, no man's person was accepted save that of Noah alone; for his person was accepted in behalf of his sons, whom (God) saved from the waters of the flood on his account; for his heart was righteous in all his ways, according as it was commanded regarding him, and he had not departed from aught that was ordained for him.

ENOCH 10.1 Then said the Most High, the Holy and Great One spoke, and sent Uriel to the son of Lamech, and said to him: "Go tell *Noah* and tell him in my name 'Hide thyself!' and reveal to him the end that is approaching, that the whole earth will be destroyed, and a deluge is about to come upon the whole earth, and I will destroy all that is upon it."

20 And the Lord said that he would destroy everything which was upon the earth, both men and cattle, and beasts, and fowls of the air, and that which moves on the earth.

21 And He commanded Noah to make him an ark, that he might save himself from the waters of the flood.

GEN.6:14 Make thee an ark of gopher wood; rooms shalt thou make in the ark, and shalt pitch it within and without with pitch.

SEPTUAGINT LXX Genesis 6.18 'And behold I bring a flood of water upon the earth, to destroy all flesh in which is the breath of life under heaven, and whatsoever things are upon the earth shall die.

JASHER 5.26 And do thou take unto thee gopher wood and go to a certain place and make a large ark and place it in that spot.

22 And Noah made the ark in all respects as He commanded him, in the twenty-seventh jubilee of years, in the fifth week in the fifth year (on the new moon of the first month). [1307 A.M.]

C.35 According to Biblical Time Charts the above-mentioned date of 1307 A.M. is incorrect. The date given in the K.J.V of the Bible is 1658 A.M which shows a discrepancy of 351 years.

GEN.6:14 Make thee an ark of gopher wood; rooms shalt thou make in the ark, and shalt pitch it within and without with pitch.

GEN.6:15 And this is the fashion which thou shalt make it of: The length of the ark shall be three hundred cubits, the breadth of it fifty cubits, and the height of it thirty cubits.

GEN.6:16 A window shalt thou make to the ark, and in a cubit shalt thou finish it above; and the door of the ark shalt thou set in the side thereof; with lower, second, and third stories shalt thou make it.

JASHER 6.26-28 And do thou take unto thee gopher wood and go to a certain place and make a large ark and place it in that spot.

C.36 God gave many instructions to Noah and apparently one of the unusual things that Noah used on the Ark were **DROGUE STONES**: These were massive rocks about 2-3 meters high and around 14 in number that acted as ballast around Noah's Ark and would cause it to face into the wind and also gave great stability in a stormy sea: https://www.youtube.com/watch?v=1O8wGjwyS7o

C.37 There was also another ingenious invention supposedly used on Noah's Ark, and that was probably invented by God Himself. That invention given to Noah was: that of putting a 'hole in the bottom of the boat which also had a chimney'.

This hole apparently had a 'chimney like hole' as do submarines where the 'air-pressure' keeps the sea water out of the submarine.

Divers can readily get quickly out of the submarine through that hole.

These holes were apparently very useful in the case of Noah's Ark - as with the movement of the waves the waters in the 'chimney hole' would go up and down, thus forcing much 'needed **air**' into the bottom section of the boat where incidentally all the animals were located. This hole apparently also served for **garbage disposal**.

I heard about that many years ago on one of Kent Hovind 'Creation Science' videos.

---

27 And thus shalt thou make it; three hundred cubits its length, fifty cubits broad and thirty cubits high.

28 And thou shalt make unto thee a door, open at its side, and to a cubit thou shalt finish above, and cover it within and without with pitch.

SEPTUAGINT LXX Genesis 6 .19-20 And I will establish my covenant with thee, and thou shalt enter into the ark, and thy sons and thy wife, and thy sons' wives with thee. And all the cattle, and all the reptiles and all the wild beasts, even of all flesh, thou shalt bring in pairs into the ark, that thou mayest feed them; male and female shall they be.

---

23 And he entered in the sixth (year) thereof, [1308 A.M.] in the second month, on the new moon of the second month, till the sixteenth; and he entered, and all that we brought to him, into the ark, and the Lord closed it from without on the seventeenth evening.

C.38 This is a big topic that I cover extensively in the **APPENDIX** concerning the time discrepancies between the different books of: The Bible, The Septuagint, Book of Enoch, Book of Jasher & This Book of Jubilees. According to the King James Bible 'The Great Flood' happened in 1658 A.M, and not 1308 A.M, as stated in this book of Jubilees. Why is there a discrepancy of 350 years? Hopefully we can find an answer to this question. (See the Appendix for the answers).

GEN.7:7 And Noah went in, and his sons, and his wife, and his sons' wives with him, into the ark, because of the waters of the flood.

GEN.7:11 In the six hundredth year of Noah's life, in the second month, the seventeenth day of the month, the same day were all the fountains of the great deep broken up, and the windows of heaven were opened.

JASHER 6.1 At that time, after the death of Methuselah, the Lord said to Noah, 'Go with thy household into the ark; behold I will gather to thee all the animals of the earth, the beasts of the field and the fowls of the air, and they shall all come and surround the ark.'

---

24 And the Lord opened **seven floodgates of heaven**, And the mouths of the fountains of the great deep, **seven mouths in number**.

C.39 Here is some new information. It is stating here that there are '7 Flood Gates in' the heavens and that there are '7 Mouths' of the 'Great deep'. Today we say that there are 7 Oceans on the planet, and it looks like there are 7 big *plugs* at the bottom of each ocean or *mouths* that can be opened. Some Christian Scientists tell us that there used to be a canopy of water surrounding the planet before the Great Flood, which was around 20 metres wide and thick. It was apparently circa 100 miles above the earth's atmosphere, as we are told that this is the very point where gravitational forces and centrifugal forces, which are in direct opposition relative to each other, cancel each other out, and thus the water could float at that exact height. Here above it is stating that the waters surrounding the planet before the Great flood had 7 gates.

JASHER 6.11 And on that day, the Lord caused the whole earth to shake, and the sun darkened, and the foundations of the world raged, and the whole earth was moved violently, and the lightning flashed, and the thunder roared, and all the fountains in the earth were broken up, such as was not known to the inhabitants before; and God did this mighty act, in order to terrify the sons of men, that there might be no more evil upon earth

> 25 And the floodgates began to pour down water from the heaven forty days and forty nights, And the fountains of the deep also sent up waters, until the whole world was full of water.

GEN.7:17 And the flood was *forty days* upon the earth; and the waters increased, and bare up the ark, and it was lift up above the earth.

JASHER 6.14 And all the fountains of the deep were broken up, and the windows of heaven were opened, and the rain was upon the earth *forty days and forty nights*.

SEPTUAGINT LXX Genesis 7.11-12 In the six hundredth year of the life of Noah, in the second month, on the twenty seventh day of the month, on this day were all the **fountains of the abyss broken up**, and the floodgates of heaven were opened. And the rain was upon the earth forty days and forty nights.

C.40 The Bible says that the 'Fountains of the Deep' were broken up, but the Septuagint is even more specific in stating the *'fountains of the* abyss' were broken up. What exactly are these abysses? (**See the APPENDIX XXXI for more on the ABYSSES and THE ABYSS (Bottomless Pit)**)

> 26 And the waters increased upon the earth: Fifteen cubits did the waters rise above all the high mountains, And the ark was lift up above the earth, And it moved upon the face of the waters.

GEN.7:20 *Fifteen cubits* upward did the waters prevail; and the mountains were covered.

> 27 And the water prevailed on the face of the earth five months one hundred and fifty days.

GEN.7:24 And the waters prevailed upon the earth an hundred and fifty days.

GEN.7:19 And the waters prevailed exceedingly upon the earth; and all the high hills, that were under the whole heaven, were covered.

> 28 And the ark went and rested on the top of Lubar, one of the mountains of Ararat.

GEN.8:4 And the ark rested in the seventh month, on the seventeenth day of the month, upon the mountains of Ararat.

JASHER 6.35 And *the waters decreased* in those days, and the *ark rested* upon the mountains of *Ararat*.

29 And (on the new moon) in the fourth month the fountains of the great deep were closed and the flood-gates of heaven were restrained; and on the new moon of the seventh month **all the mouths of the abysses of the earth were opened,** and the water began to descend into the deep below.

GEN.8:2 The fountains also of the deep and the windows of heaven were stopped, and the rain from heaven was restrained;

GEN.8:3 And the *waters returned from off the earth continually*: and after the end of the hundred and fifty days the waters were abated.

30 And on the new moon of the tenth month the tops of the mountains were seen, and on the new moon of the first month the earth became visible.

GEN.8:5 And the waters decreased continually until the tenth month: in the tenth month, on the first day of the month, were the tops of the *mountains seen.*

31 And the waters disappeared from above the earth in the fifth week in the seventh year [1309 A.M.] thereof, and on the seventeenth day in the second month the earth was dry.

C.41 The Bible states that the date 1309 A.M given in the above verse should if fact be 1658 A.M This shows a discrepancy of 347 years.

32 And on the twenty-seventh thereof he opened the ark, and sent forth from it beasts, and cattle, and birds, and every moving thing.

GEN.8:16 *Go forth of the ark*, thou, and thy wife, and thy sons, and thy sons' wives with thee.

JASHER 6.39-40 At that time, on the twenty-seventh day of the second month, the earth was dry, but Noah and his sons, and those that were with him, did not go out from the ark until the Lord told them.

40 And the day came that the Lord told them to go out, and *they all went out from the ark.*

Chapter 6: NOAH

> 1 And on the new moon of the third month he went forth from the ark and built an altar on that mountain.
>
> 2 And he made atonement for the earth and took a kid and made atonement by its blood for all the guilt of the earth; for everything that had been on it had been destroyed, save those that were in the ark with Noah.

C.1 ATONEMENT. What does this mean? Noah made a sacrifice to atone for all the souls of those who had died in the Great Flood. This shows that God Himself still had hope for those '**lost souls**'. Those in Old Testament times and Pre-Old-Testament times made sacrifices using animals, which were a mere '**figure of the sacrifice**' that the Messiah would eventually do thousands of years later in the **'sacrifice of Himself'** for all of mankind. The Messiah - Jesus Christ, even went down to hell after He died, not that He himself was a prisoner, but to deliberately **'break Satan's hold on death'** and to release many of the souls who had been prisoners down there since the time of the Great Flood.

1PE.3:18 For Christ also hath once suffered for sins, the just for the unjust, that he might bring us to God, being put to death in the flesh, but quickened by the Spirit:

1PE.3:19 By which also he went and preached unto the spirits in prison (Hell);

1PE.3:20 Which sometime were disobedient, when once the longsuffering of God waited in the days of Noah, while the ark was a preparing, wherein few, that is, eight souls were saved by water.

(More about **ATONEMENT** in the next chapter)

> 3 And he placed the fat thereof on the altar, and he took an ox, and a goat, and a sheep and kids, and salt, and a turtle-dove, and the young of a dove, and placed a burnt sacrifice on the altar, and poured thereon an offering mingled with oil, and sprinkled wine and strewed frankincense over everything, and caused a goodly savour to arise, acceptable before the Lord.
>
> 4 And the Lord smelt the goodly savour, and He made a covenant with him that there should not be any more a flood to destroy the earth; that all the days of the earth seed-time and harvest should never cease; cold and heat, and summer and winter, and day and night should not

> change their order, nor cease for ever.

C.2 *cold and heat, and summer and winter, and day and night should 'not change their order' nor cease for ever.*

Here it is stating that the 'order of the seasons of summer and winter' will not alter drastically and the *'night shall not become the day or the day night.'* Instead of it stating *'forever',* it would have been better if it had stated 'for a long period of time. Why do I say that? Because it clearly states in the Book of Daniel, talking about the last few years of man's reign on the earth in the form of the Anti-Christ, that 'He shall think to 'change times & laws'.

DAN.7:25 And he shall speak great words against the Most High and shall wear out the saints of the Most High, and think to 'change times and laws': and they shall be *'given into his hand'* until a time and times and the dividing of time.

C.3 In the Apocryphal Book of **II EZDRAS 5.4** 'After the third period (1st coming of Christ until the 2nd Coming): *'The sun shall suddenly shine forth at night, and the moon during the day.'* This sounds like the earth is spinning off its axis. This description is also mentioned in the book of Isaiah.

ISA.24:20 The earth shall reel 'to and fro' like a drunkard and shall be removed like a cottage; and the transgression thereof shall be heavy upon it; and it shall fall, and not rise again. [See my book **'EZDRAS INSIGHTS'** for many more details on this subject.]

In conclusion: The times & seasons *'will be altered'* during the Great Tribulation & The Wrath of God.

> 5 'And you, increase ye and multiply upon the earth, and become many upon it, and be a blessing upon it.
>
> 6 The fear of you and the dread of you I will inspire in everything that is on earth and in the sea.
>
> 7And behold I have given unto you all beasts, and all winged things, and everything that moves on the earth, and the fish in the waters, and all things for food; as the green herbs, I have given you all things to eat.
>
> 8 But flesh, with the life thereof, with the blood, ye shall not eat; for the life of all flesh is in the blood, lest your blood of your lives be required.
>
> 9 At the hand of every man, at the hand of every (beast) will I require the blood of man.

10 Whoso sheds man's blood by man shall his blood be shed, for in the image of God made He man.

11 And you, increase ye, and multiply on the earth.'

12 And Noah and his sons swore that they would not eat any blood that was in any flesh, and he made a covenant before the Lord God for ever throughout all the generations of the earth in this month.

C.4 Why did God make a covenant with Noah in making Noah and his family sware that they would not drink the blood of an animal or any creature including man? Was it just possible that *'drinking blood' alters the D.N.A of people* and actually makes them into *vampires* or even eventually *cannibals* as happened to the *Giants*, the *sons* of the *Fallen Watchers* before the Great Flood? We have heard that since this time the 'dark side of the spirit world' often require 'human sacrifices' to 'curry the favour of the gods' so to speak. Maybe there is a lot of truth to that ancient concept. For this reason God made a strict law concerning the blood of both humans and animals in the hope that mankind would not slip back into the type of depravity that had happened before the Great Flood. I was just reading about how the wealthy can buy young people's blood by the litre to drink for $8000/L Why do they want to drink this blood? They believe that it will help them to stay younger! **SOURCE: TRUE SCIENCE:** http://www.outofthebottomlesspit.co.uk/412513932

13 On this account He spoke to thee that thou should make a covenant with the children of Israel in this month upon the mountain with an oath, and that thou should sprinkle blood upon them because of all the words of the covenant, which the Lord made with them for ever.

14 And this testimony is written concerning you that you should observe it continually, so that you should not eat on any day any blood of beasts or birds or cattle during all the days of the earth, and the man who eats the blood of beast or of cattle or of birds during all the days of the earth, he and his seed shall be rooted out of the land.

C.5 God commanded that anyone who drank the blood of animals or birds or in fact any creature should be rooted out of the land. When God talked like that, He meant to separate out the polluting member from the pure or righteous. God always made health rules for our safety; and by God taking a very strong stand concerning the 'blood of creatures' was not to be eaten or to be drunk, it was because He knew that it could be both dangerous to humans and also destructive.

C.6 I get into this topic of the Giants and the cannibals in the APPENDIX. Just to mention here that Steve Quayle and others, while investigating the sudden demise of the whole Anasazi Indians in the South West USA around the year 1150 AD came to some startling conclusions. These Indians were known to be cannibals, and yet it would seem that they themselves were devoured suddenly over a short period of time by giants. Where did the giants come from? Apparently, there are all kinds of curses that happen to people who either eat blood of humans or eat humans. There is lots of evidence for this gruesome topic. Modern Indian tribes also mention that dimensional portals exist and that the giants came through the portals and devoured the Anasazi Indian tribes because they were cannibals. In spite of all this we find that the ancient Indians the Anasazi worshipped the race of the ancient Giants. No wonder they got devoured. – (See the book **THE CLOUD-EATERS** by Tom Horn and Steve Quayle.

VIDEO: https://youtu.be/OpiTMtc0WdM?t=944

---

15 And do thou command the children of Israel to eat no blood, so that their names and their seed may be before the Lord our God continually.

16 And for this law there is no limit of days, for it is for ever.

17 They shall observe it throughout their generations, so that they may continue supplicating on your behalf with blood before the altar; every day and at the time of morning and evening they shall seek forgiveness on your behalf perpetually before the Lord that they may keep it and not be rooted out.

18 And He gave to Noah and his sons a sign that there should not again be a flood on the earth.

19 He set His bow in the cloud for a sign of the eternal covenant that there should not again be a flood on the earth to destroy it all the days of the earth.

GEN.9:12 And God said, 'This is the token of the covenant which I make between me and you and every living creature that is with you, for perpetual generations':

GEN.9:13 'I do set my (rain)*bow* in the cloud, and it shall be for a token of a covenant between me and the earth'.

---

20 For this reason it is ordained and written on the heavenly tablets, that they should celebrate the feast of weeks in this month once a year, to renew the covenant every year.

---

21 And this whole festival was celebrated in heaven from the day of creation till the days of Noah -twenty-six jubilees and five weeks of years [1309-1659 A.M. .= '**Anno Mundi' = years of the world**]: and Noah and his sons observed it for seven jubilees and one week of years, till the day of Noah's death, and from the day of Noah's death his sons did away with (it) until the days of Abraham, and they did eat blood.

C.7 According to the Bible Time-Charts, Abraham was around 60 years old when Noah died, and he received some of his spiritual training in the House of both Noah and Shem. Perhaps the above verse simply means that after Noah died that apart from Abraham's lineage, all the other descendants of Noah went astray and started eating the blood of animals just like before the Great Flood.

C.8 These dates of [1309-1659 A.M.] are incorrect according to the Bible. The Flood happened at 1658 A.M. and Noah died 350 years after the Great Flood in the year 2006 A.M The time of Noah's death is incorrect by 347 years according to biblical Time Charts.

C.9 In Summary: God told Noah and his sons not to eat the blood of animals. This was observed from the time of the Great Flood until 350 years after the Great Flood when Noah died. Abraham knew Noah for the first 60 years of his life and lived 100 years beyond the life of Noah according to biblical charts. (See the Appendix of this book) The practice was discontinued until Abraham restarted this tradition of not eating or drinking the blood of animals. Abraham and his son Isaac and his grandson Jacob observed this law, but the law was abandoned sometime later by the children of Israel who were captive in Egypt. Later God gave this same law '*not to drink blood*' unto Moses, to give as a commandment to all the people of Israel.

22 But Abraham observed it, and Isaac and Jacob and his children observed it up to thy days, and in thy days the children of Israel forgot it until ye celebrated it anew on this mountain.

C.10 The fact is that the sons of Noah did away with the law of 'not eating the blood of animals' after their father Noah died. Did this open a door of evil to allow the evil spirits of the Giants to have returned -because of man's disobedience of drinking blood of animals?

23 And do thou command the children of Israel to observe this festival in all their generations for a commandment unto them: one day in the year in this month they shall celebrate the festival.

24 For it is the feast of weeks and the feast of first fruits: this feast

is twofold and of a double nature: according to what is written and engraven concerning it, celebrate it. For I have written in the book of the first law, in that which I have written for thee, that thou should celebrate it in its season, one day in the year, and I explained to thee its sacrifices that the children of Israel should remember and should celebrate it throughout their generations in this month, one day in every year.

C.11 This Festival of the First Fruits is a very important Festival in Jewish tradition and signifies the very first fruits of the earth right after God had judged the earth with the Great Flood of Noah's time and as most other Festivals in Israel, is held on one of the New Moons..

'One of the principles that a first fruit offering taught was that a future harvest was promised - the first fruit were just a taste of what lay in store at the end of the full ingathering of the harvest. Therefore, when a first fruit offering was brought before the Lord, it represented a prayer to Him to watch over the future harvest that was there foreshadowed by the minute proportion that was being presented'.(**SOURCE**: http://www.arlev.co.uk/ffruits.htm)

25 And on the new moon of the first month, and on the new moon of the fourth month, and on the new moon of the seventh month, and on the new moon of the tenth month are the days of remembrance, and the days of the seasons in the four divisions of the year.

26 These are written and ordained as a testimony for ever. And Noah ordained them for himself as feasts for the generations for ever, so that they have become thereby a memorial unto him.

27 And on the new moon of the first month he was bidden to make for himself an ark, and on that (day) the earth became dry and he opened (the ark) and saw the earth.

28 And on the new moon of the fourth month the mouths of the depths of the abyss beneath were closed.

29 And on the new moon of the seventh month all the mouths of the abysses of the earth were opened, and the waters began to descend into them.

C.12 On the **7th** month **all** the **abysses** of the earth were opened, and the Flood waters descended into these 'abysses. Modern man has no idea about these abysses, and probably wouldn't believe you even if you told him about them, but apparently the *'abysses'* do in fact exist.

C.13 God really likes the number 7. Why? It is a combination number in Biblical Numerology: 4 equals Creation: 3 equals the Trinity: Seven equals the 'Godhead plus Creation'. There are 7 colours in the rainbow. In fact, there are just 7 basic colours. 7 days in a week & 7 notes in musiC. The whole Bible is made up of 7's. God's Creation happened in 7 days or one could say '6 days of Creation' and the 7th day of Rest for God. The number 7 does show up a lot in both biblical and Apocryphal books. In the Book of Revelations there are 7 tall Candles standing in front of Jesus. There is a' 7 Sealed Book of the Future given to the Lamb of God. There are 7 Tribulation Angels with 7 Trumpets. There were 7 Thunders There are 7 Angels who have 7 Vials full of the Wrath of God. The Book of Revelations is really a book of 3 x 7 chapters with the 22 chapter really a continuation of the 21st chapter for double the pleasure of God's Creation of the New Heaven and the New Earth. God tells us in Daniel 9.27 that there will be a Last 7 Year Reign of the Anti-Christ. Halfway through the 7 years and equal to 3-1/2 years the infamous Great Tribulation will begin. When the 7th Trumpet sounds it will be the Rapture and all saved peoples will go up to heaven to be with Jesus forever as His Bride.

C.14 Did you know that the Communists once tried to change the 'working week' to 5 days instead of 7 days but found out that it simply did not work. (**Source**: https://www.atlasobscura.com/articles/why-cant-we-get-rid-of-the-7day-week)

C.15 Satan and mankind have been trying to 'change the times and seasons' and everything that proves that God exists. Everything that proves that Creation was made by God and that it is NOT random coincidence, the devils and demons that run this planet try to influence man to alter and change. Here is a verse in the Bible talking about the future Anti-Christ world leader:

DAN.7:25 And he shall speak great words against the most High, and shall wear out the saints of the most High, and think to 'change times and laws': and they shall be given into his hand until a time and times and the dividing of time.

C.16 HALF 7: A time is a year and half a time is half a year, so that it is stating again a time of 3 and a half years of Tribulation for God's church which represents *all* true believers in Jesus from all faiths and denominations.

C.17 It would appear from the Bible that the days will come, when it is so spiritually dark on the planet and so Satanic with the infamous 'Mark of the Beast', that millions of both Jews and Muslims along with the Christians will all rebel against the Anti-Christ. When Jesus comes in the clouds of heaven, I believe that millions of both Jews and Muslims will call on the Name of Jesus, as it will be very clear that He has come to rescue 'all of his children'.

ROM.10:13 For whosoever shall call upon the name of the Lord shall be saved. The Name of the Lord is Jesus.

ACT.2:21 And it shall come to pass, that whosoever shall call on the name of the

74

Lord shall be saved.

JOE.2:32 And it shall come to pass, that whosoever shall call on the name of the LORD shall be delivered: for in mount Zion and in Jerusalem shall be deliverance, as the LORD hath said, and in the remnant whom the LORD shall call.

C.18 Look at the number 4 or the number of Creation: There are 4 Seasons. There are 4 winds. There are 4 main Directions: North, South, East & West. There are basically 4 Weeks in the month. There are 4 x 3 = 12 months in the year. There are 4 Beasts around the Throne of God, as mentioned in Isaiah, Ezekiel and the Book of Revelation. The four Beasts also have 4 different faces. Why? Because they represent the 4 main species of Creation. 1) Face of a lion represents the wild carnivorous Beasts 2) Face of a calf represents the docile animals 3) Face of a man represents mankind 4) The face of a flying eagle represents all the flying creatures. So, as you can see the 4 Beasts really represent a picture of how the Creation itself is made up. There are 24 Elders around the Throne of God. 24 = 4 x 6.

The number 4 is the number most used in construction of any building and most man-made objects such as a table or chair or tiles and bricks etC. Most rooms have 4 sides to them. Why? Because it is the most practical way to build something.

C.19 The largest construction that we know of made by God Himself is the heavenly city: 1500 miles long, wide and high! That is 250 times higher than Mount Everest. A real piker!

REV.21:16 And the city lieth foursquare, and the length is as large as the breadth: and he measured the city with the reed, twelve thousand furlongs. The length and the breadth and the height of it are equal. <**MORE INFO**: http://www.biblestudy.org/ bibleref/meaning-of-numbers-in-bible/4.html>

C.20 The number 12 which is made up of the number of Creation 4 x no of The Trinity 3 = 12. Think of how many important things mentioned in the Bible and the Apocryphal books where the number 12 shows up? **MORE INFO**:

12 Patriarchs: 12 Tribes of Israel: 12 Disciples of Jesus.

Revelation 21 describes The Heavenly City as Having 12 Foundations and 12 Pearly Gates: 12 Angels. The Names of the Twelve Tribes on Each of the 12 Pearly Gates. The names of the 12 Disciples of Jesus on the 12 Foundation layers of precious stones. < MORE INFO: http://www.biblestudy.org/bibleref/ meaning-of-numbers-in-bible/12.html >

The Number 10 = 6 + 4. (6 = Number of mankind) + (4 = Number of Creation) = 10

10 in biblical numerology stands for the **law/leadership**.

Examples: The Pre-Flood 10 Patriarchs: 10 Pre-Flood generations until Noah. 10 generations from Noah to Abraham. The 10 Commandments: The Ten Plagues of Egypt: Chapter 10 in Revelation shows a Book of Prophecy handed to John who received the book by one of God's very powerful angels.

In the story Jesus told of the Wise Virgins: 5 were wise and 5 foolish so there were 10 Virgins in total. An important parable about the Bride of Christ. <MORE INFO: http://www.biblestudy.org/bibleref/meaning-of-numbers-in-bible/10.html>

30 And on the new moon of the tenth month the tops of the mountains were seen, and Noah was glad. And on this account he ordained them for himself as feasts for a memorial for ever, and thus are they ordained.

31 And they placed them on the heavenly tablets, each had thirteen weeks; from one to another (passed) their memorial, from the first to the second, and from the second to the third, and from the third to the fourth.

C.21 Many times, we hear mentioned the 'heavenly tablets of stone' which are mentioned not only in this Jewish book of Jubilees, but also in the Hebrew Book of Enoch. The angels told God's prophets repeatedly, that everything that was to happen from the beginning of the Creation, until the End of Time - and the New Heaven and Earth was all written down on the Heavenly tablets.

32 And all the days of the commandment will be two and fifty weeks of days, and (these will make) the entire year complete.

Thus it is engraven and ordained on the heavenly tablets. And there is no neglecting (this commandment) for a single year or from year to year.

33 And command thou the children of Israel that they observe the years according to this reckoning- three hundred and sixty-four days, and (these) will constitute a complete year, and they will not disturb its time from its days and from its feasts; for everything will fall out in them according to their testimony, and they will not leave out any day nor disturb any feasts.

C.22 Here it is clearly stating, that there are to be 52 weeks of 7 days in the year. We are also told that there were to be 364 days in each year. We were told above that that are also 4 seasons. What the years used to be like and the length of the year, and the number of days in the year before the laws of Moses - was obviously different. Now God was establishing with His people how to measure time itself correctly and not as the heathen did.

34 But if they do neglect and do not observe them according to His commandment, then they will disturb all their seasons and the years will be dislodged from this (order), [and they will disturb the seasons and the years will be dislodged] and they will neglect their ordinances.

35 And all the children of Israel will forget and will not find the path of the years, and will forget the new moons, and seasons, and sabbaths and they will go wrong as to all the order of the years.

36 For I know and from henceforth will I declare it unto thee, and it is not of my own devising; for the book (lies) written before me, and on the heavenly tablets the division of days is ordained, lest they forget the feasts of the covenant and walk according to the feasts of the Gentiles after their error and after their ignorance.

37 For there will be those who will assuredly make observations of the moon -how (it) disturbs the seasons and comes in from year to year ten days too soon.

C.23 Here it is stating that it is important to use the Solar year of 364 days and not the Lunar year of 354 days which is 10 days shorter, otherwise Israel would start to Celebrate the different sacred Festivals on the wrong days.

38 For this reason the years will come upon them when they will disturb (the order), and make an abominable (day) the day of testimony, and an unclean day a feast day, and they will confound all the days, the holy with the unclean, and the unclean day with the holy; for they will go wrong as to the months and sabbaths and feasts and jubilees.

39 For this reason I command and testify to thee that thou mayst testify to them; for after thy death thy children will disturb (them), so that they will not make the year three hundred and sixty-four days only, and for this reason they will go wrong as to the new moons and seasons and sabbaths and festivals, and they will eat all kinds of blood with all kinds of flesh.

C.24 Here is a warning not to alter the length of a year according to the seasons. Remember that God originally created the sun, the moon, and the stars for 'signs and seasons'. In other words, God created a perfect 'clock of the universe', which also controlled the seasons on the earth and the astrological star signs. The Star signs which are directly affected by the sun, the moon, the planets and the stars were created to bring variety in his creation and perfect order. This book of Jubilees is advocating that there would be 364 days in the year as stated by the Solar Calendar. Strangely though, the 'Lunar Calendar' of 354 days is the one most used by the Jews today. The '360-day Calendar' is known as the 'Prophetic Year Calendar'. (See: APPENDIX)

GEN.1:14 And God said, 'Let there be lights in the firmament of the heaven to divide the day from the night; and let them be for signs, and for seasons, and for days, and years.'

Chapter 7: CANAAN CURSED

1 And in the seventh week in the first year [1317 A.M.] thereof, in this jubilee, Noah planted vines on the mountain on which the ark had rested, named Lubar, one of the Ararat Mountains, and they produced fruit in the fourth year, [1320 A.M. = '**Anno Mundi' = years of the world**]] and he guarded their fruit, and gathered it in this year in the seventh month.

2 And he made wine therefrom and put it into a vessel, and kept it until the fifth year, [1321 A.M.] until the first day, on the new moon of the first month.

Comment:1: These dates given in the Book of Jubilees are not the same as mentioned in the Bible. [1317 A.M] should read 1658 A.C (After Creation) & [1320 A.M] should read 1661 A.C.

3 And he celebrated with joy the day of this feast, and he made a burnt sacrifice unto the Lord, one young ox and one ram, and seven sheep, each a year old, and a kid of the goats, that he might make atonement thereby for himself and his sons.

C.2 It says here *'that he might make* atonement *thereby for himself and his sons'*. In other ancient texts such as *Genesis Apochryphon* it states rather that Noah made an *atonement for the whole world*, rather than just him and his sons. Genesis Apocryphon would have been available to the writer of the Book of Jubilees apparently. "and I atoned for the whole Earth" col. X, l.13 "and particularly atonement through the use of blood".

(Source: http://orion.mscC.huji.aC.il/orion/symposiums/2nd/papers/ Werman97.html)

C.3 Noah was making a blood sacrifice of a lamb and other animals to God after the Great Flood. It would seem more logical that Noah would be making a sacrifice which would be an **atonement** for all of mankind as everything on the earth had just been destroyed.

C.4 The above **Atonement** by Noah for the sins of Noah and his sons, as well as the iniquities of all who had drowned during the Great Flood was a shadow of things yet to come, once the Messiah had come to the earth to shed His blood for all of mankind:

HEB.9:12 Neither by the blood of goats and calves, but by his own blood he entered in once into the holy place, having obtained eternal redemption for us.

HEB.9:13 For if the blood of bulls and of goats, and the ashes of an heifer sprinkling the unclean, sanctifies to the purifying of the flesh:

HEB.9:14 How much more shall the blood of Christ, who through the eternal Spirit offered himself without spot to God, purge your conscience from dead works to serve the living God?

HEB.9:15 And for this cause he is the mediator of the new testament, that by means of death, for the redemption of the transgressions that were under the first testament, they which are called might receive the promise of eternal inheritance.

> 4 And he prepared the kid first and placed some of its blood on the flesh that was on the altar which he had made, and all the fat he laid on the altar where he made the burnt sacrifice, and the ox and the ram and the sheep, and he laid all their flesh upon the altar.

HEB.9:26 For then must he often have suffered since the foundation of the world: but now once in the end of the world hath he appeared to put away sin by the sacrifice of himself.

> 5 And he placed all their offerings mingled with oil upon it, and afterwards he sprinkled wine on the fire which he had previously made on the altar, and he placed incense on the altar and caused a sweet savour to ascend acceptable before the Lord his God.

HEB.9:24 For Christ is not entered into the holy places made with hands, which are the *figures of the true*; but into heaven itself, now to appear in the presence of God for us:

HEB.9:28 So Christ was once offered to *bear the sins of many*; and unto them that look for him shall he *appear the second time without sin unto salvation.*

> 6 And he rejoiced and drank of this wine, he and his children with joy.
>
> 7 And it was evening, and he went into his tent, and being drunken he lay down and slept, and was uncovered in his tent as he slept.
>
> 8 And Ham saw Noah his father naked and went forth and told his two brethren without.
>
> 9 And Shem took his garment and arose, he and Japheth, and they placed the garment on their shoulders and went backward and covered the shame of their father, and their faces were backward.

> 10 And Noah awoke from his sleep and knew all that his younger son had done unto him, and he cursed his son and said: 'Cursed be Canaan; an enslaved servant shall he be unto his brethren.'

C.5 Noah *'curses Canaan'* his grandson, rather than his son Ham who did the sin against him. Why? You will find out in the next few chapters.

C.6 What actually happened in this story that was *so bad* that Noah cursed the descendants of Ham. There is a controversy over what actually happened to Noah. The consensus of most is that Ham committed sodomy against his father Noah who was lying down naked and drunk. Some say there is not enough evidence to support that theory. I think that the first idea is correct partly due to the above verse: *'**knew all that his younger son had done unto him'***

Just seeing his father naked is of no great consequence and certainly not the fault of Ham that his father had been both drunk and let himself fall asleep naked. Ham had to have done something to Noah as the above verse clearly states: 'his younger son had *done unto him'*

GEN.9:24 And Noah awoke from his wine and knew what his younger son had done unto him.

GEN.9:25 And he said, 'Cursed be Canaan; a servant of servants shall he be unto his brethren'.

> 11 And he blessed Shem and said: 'Blessed be the Lord God of Shem, and Canaan shall be his servant. God shall enlarge Japheth, and God shall dwell in the dwelling of Shem, and Canaan shall be his servant.'

C.7 This is amazing, because we find later on, that Canaan's descendants the Canaanites, took over all the lands that were supposed to belong to Shem's descendants. Eventually starting with Abraham and his grandson Jacob and his great grandsons the 12 sons of Jacob, they started driving the Canaanites out of the land. This was completed later in time by Moses and Joshua as they carved out the land of Israel from what had been the lands of the Canaanites.

> 12 And Ham knew that his father had cursed his younger son, and he was displeased that he had cursed his son. and he parted from his father, he and his sons with him, Cush and Mizraim and Put and Canaan.
>
> 13 And he built for himself a city and called its name after the name of his wife Ne'elatama'uk.
>
> 14 And Japheth saw it, and became envious of his brother, and he too

built for himself a city, and he called its name after the name of his wife 'Adataneses.

15 And Shem dwelt with his father Noah, and he built a city close to his father on the mountain, and he too called its name after the name of his wife Sedeqetelebab.

16 And behold these three cities are near Mount Lubar; Sedeqetelebab fronting the mountain on its east; and Na'eltama'uk on the south; 'Adatan'eses towards the west.

17 And these are the sons of Shem: Elam, and Asshur, and Arpachshad -this (son) was born two years after the flood- and Lud, and Aram.

18 The sons of Japheth: Gomer and Magog and Madai and Javan, Tubal and Meshech and Tiras: these are the sons of Noah.

19 And in the twenty-eighth jubilee [1324-1372 A.M.]

C.8 These dates given in the Book of Jubilees are not the same as mentioned in the Bible. [1324 A.M] should read 1665 A.C (After Creation) & [1324-1372 A.M] should read 1661-1709 A.C.

20 Noah began to enjoin upon his sons' sons the ordinances and commandments, and all the judgments that he knew, and he exhorted his sons to observe righteousness, and to cover the shame of their flesh, and to bless their Creator, and honour father and mother, and love their neighbour, and guard their souls from fornication and uncleanness and all iniquity.

C.9 *'cover the shame of their flesh'*. Noah commands his son's sons to 'keep their clothes on' in publiC. It sounds like common sense to us today in modern times, but why does Noah make a point of this?

C.10 Well, apparently before the Great Flood many people, would on special occasions, have *public orgies, in open sacrifice to Idols or demons/Fallen angels.*

C.11 The laws of Moses were very needed right after Israel had come out of pagan Egypt with its idol worshipping and deep satanism. The laws of Moses made sure through their severity, that there weren't any beautiful naked women walking around in public areas, who would immediately attract many men. The strict laws of Moses concerning sex and marriage were probably to try and stop any temptations & resultant *'fornication and*

82

uncleanness and all iniquity'.

C.12 Look at the difference between male and female. God created the woman to be very attractive, beautiful and in fact irresistible to the normal man. There is nothing wrong with that. Nakedness is fine in the right relationships. However, public nakedness of the women could be a very dangerous idea, although in modern times we do have 'nudity beaches' in countries like Denmark where the woman seem to be safe? Probably because the naked or topless woman on the beach has someone watching out for them.

C.13 Remember The movie 'Splash' about the beautiful mermaid. When she showed up on shore in her naked innocence, the men went wild, in at least wanting to talk her or to be close to her. If the average guy was to try the same stunt, everyone who is normal would run away in the opposite direction, and probably phone the police. Point being that God created the woman to be irresistible when naked, not the man. A very good reason given by Moses for humans to 'keep their clothes on in public'

C.14 In fact there have been public orgies as documented as having happened before the Great flood and afterwards, in places like Sodom and Gomorrah. In those situations the men in particular did not see the very serious spiritual dangers to themselves in getting involved with extremely licentious women such as the daughters of Cain. Spiritually speaking, it would appear that the **women** were used as **bait** in a **demonic trap**. The woman would incite the men into **perverse sex** which would attract the **perverse demons called succubus's**, who would then possess the men, who would then never be the same again but **effeminate** and **perverse.** These orgies of lust were often done as **unto an idol or Fallen angel god**. Shockingly, this has happened repeatedly throughout history in closed circles, or in satanic rituals and idol worshipping to the gods and demons. [**For more INFO on succubus's and incubus's: [https://thoughtcatalog.com/christine-stockton/2018/05/ everything-you-need-to-know-about-the-incubus-demon/]**

C.15 Apparently, this was also **one of the many iniquities** of Sodom and Gomorrah, and one of the reasons why God rained down fire on Sodom and Gomorrah and the other cities of the plane around 4000 years ago in the days of Abraham.

> 21 For owing to these three things came the flood upon the earth, namely, owing to the fornication wherein the Watchers against the law of their ordinances went a whoring after the daughters of men and took themselves wives of all which they chose: and they made the beginning of uncleanness.

C.16 This verse above is simply stating 'Because of these **three things the flood** came as judgment of God upon the earth.'

The above verse states that three things that brought the Great Flood upon the earth as mentioned in the following verses. Strangely there are **4 things** mentioned rather than 3:

1) The Fallen angels went *'a whoring after the daughters of men.'*

2) The Giants were the offspring of the Fallen angels and human women, who ended up being cannibals and devouring mankind. *'Naphidim, and they were all unlike, and they devoured one another' and the Giants slew the Naphil, and the Naphil slew the Eljo, and the Eljo mankind, and one man another.*

3) *The world became full of violence as everyone sold himself to work iniquity and to shed much blood, and the earth was filled with iniquity.*

4) *After this they sinned against the beasts and birds, and all that moves and walks on the earth: and much blood was shed on the earth, and every imagination and desire of men imagined vanity and evil continually.*

---

22 And they begat sons the Naphidim, and they were all unlike, and they devoured one another: and the Giants slew the Naphil, and the Naphil slew the Eljo, and the Eljo mankind, and one man another.

C.17 In the above verse we can see 3 types of giants mentioned. Each one taller than the one coming after. *'And the Giants slew the Naphil, and the Naphil slew the Eljo, and the Eljo mankind, and one man another.'*

GIANTS: http://www.outofthebottomlesspit.co.uk/411784132 & http://www.outofthebottomlesspit.co.uk/411783108

GEN.6:4 There were giants in the earth in those days (Before the Flood); and also after that, when the sons of God came in unto the daughters of men, and they bare children to them, the same became mighty men which were of old, men of renown. (More giants after the Flood)

C.18 Before the Great Flood the giants had been much bigger and there is evidence to today of skeletons found of 75 feet, 45 feet and 30 feet from Pre-Flood times. After the Great Flood there were giants of 24 feet and some of 15 feet and some of 10 feet in the cursed land of Canaan.

https://uk.search.yahoo.com/search?fr=mcasa&type=E111GB662G0&p=giant+human+skeletons+75+feet+high

C.19 Here it is stating some very important information, in that Giants began to appear again in the land of Canaan, after the Great Flood through the descendants of Ham and in particular his son Canaan who was double cursed.

C.20 The first time Canaan was cursed by Noah, when his son Ham did an iniquity against Noah himself whilst he was drunk & celebrating the 'First fruits wine', after the Flood. The 2nd time Canaan was cursed by his brethren for taking the lands belonging to Shem's descendants, who ended up being Abraham and then Isaac and then Jacob and his sons and eventually the nation of Israel.

> 23 And everyone sold himself to work iniquity and to shed much blood, and the earth was filled with iniquity.
>
> 24 And after this they sinned against the beasts and birds, and all that moves and walks on the earth: and much blood was shed on the earth, and every imagination and desire of men imagined vanity and evil continually.

C.21 How is such a thing even possible that *'they sinned against the beasts and birds'* & *'all that moves and walks on the earth: and much blood was shed on the earth'*. Obviously, the average human is *not* capable of such feats, but perhaps angels and their progeny the giants were. This is probably why it was not God's will for the Angels to make love with the women on earth and create hybrid giants in the first place. One of the characteristics of angels is that they are *shapeshifters*. According to the Book of Enoch: When those first 200 Watcher angels fell to earth, some of their powers were passed on genetically to their sons the giants. The first 200 fallen angels according to the Book of Enoch, ended up getting locked up down in the earth, but there came countless more 'Fallen angels' who descended into total madness sometime after the death of Enoch. That is to say - from around 1000 A.C (After Creation) (or circa 5000 years ago) to around 1650 AC (4500years ago) at the time of the Great Flood. It was these latter Fallen Angels and their sons the Giants who altered the DNA of both animals and birds. How did they manage to do that you might ask? Well according to stories from mythology including the story of Pan, some of those entities altered their forms to be like different creatures for the purpose of mating with them. The result was the offspring of each creature now had Nephilim D.N.A and soon after, we had the hybrid creatures such as the Minotaur, the Centaur, Harpies, mermaids and the other Chimeras of all sorts including bird and insect hybrids. The fallen angels in their depravity destroyed all of God's original creation by creating these hybrids. Why did they create these hybrids? Well that's another story. **(SEE APPENDIX for more on this topic: ARE THE GIANTS COMING BACK?:http://www.outofthebottomlesspit. co.uk/411783108)** No wonder it states in the Bible just before God destroyed almost all of His original entire creation in the Great Flood, that it grieved God at His heart:

GEN.6:6 And it repented the LORD that he had made man on the earth, and it *grieved him at his heart.*

GEN.6:7 And the LORD said, I will *destroy man* whom I have created from the face of the earth; both man, and beast, and the creeping thing, and the fowls of the air; for it repents me that I have made them.

> 25 And the Lord destroyed everything from off the face of the earth;

because of the wickedness of their deeds, and because of the blood which they had shed in the midst of the earth He destroyed everything.

26 'And we were left, I and you, my sons, and everything that entered with us into the ark, and behold I see your works before me that ye do not walk in righteousness: for in the path of destruction ye have begun to walk, and ye are parting one from another, and are envious one of another, and (so it comes) that ye are not in harmony, my sons, each with his brother.

C.22 Notice the change in writing in this last verse until the end of this chapter or verse 39 - as it sounds as if it is Noah directly speaking in the 1st person and could possibly be an inception from the original Book of Noah?

27 For I see and behold the demons have begun (their) seductions against you and against your children and now I fear on your behalf, that after my death ye will shed the blood of men upon the earth, and that ye, too, will be destroyed from the face of the earth.

C.23 AFTER THE GREAT FLOOD OF NOAH, Noah began to admonish his sons about the danger of the 'disembodied spirits of the Giants', otherwise known as 'demons' coming to seduce and harm his descendants, especially if they gave in to 'demonic influences' of 'shedding blood', 'eating or drinking blood ' and 'idol worshipping':

28 For whoso sheds man's blood, and whoso eats the blood of any flesh, shall all be destroyed from the earth.

29 And there shall not be left any man that eats blood, or that sheds the blood of man on the earth, nor shall there be left to him any seed or descendants living under heaven; For into Sheol shall they go, And into the place of condemnation shall they descend, And into the darkness of the deep shall they all be removed by a violent death.

C.24 This is a very severe law that any man who eats blood or sheds the blood of a man on the earth shall descend into hell. There is evidence that those who have both shed the blood of man and even sometimes drink his blood as a sign of a conquering army. Those that do such things will themselves be devoured by a violent death. In the case of the Mayans and Incas who were both cannibal races they were apparently suddenly devoured by Giants who seemed to come out of the ground according to recent investigations by Steve Quayle's team. <www.stevequayle.com>

30 There shall be no blood seen upon you of all the blood there shall be all the days in which ye have killed any beasts or cattle or whatever flies upon the earth, and work ye a good work to your souls by covering that which has been shed on the face of the earth.

31And ye shall not be like him who eats with blood but guard yourselves that none may eat blood before you: cover the blood, for thus have I been commanded to testify to you and your children, together with all flesh.

32 And suffer not the soul to be eaten with the flesh, that your blood, which is your life, may not be required at the hand of any flesh that sheds (it) on the earth.

C.25 Here is a very interesting statement 'suffer not the soul to be eaten with the flesh'. Well there are some verses in the Bible about this:

LEV.17:11 For the **life of the flesh** is in the **blood:** and I have given it to you upon the altar to make an atonement for your souls: for it is the blood that makes an atonement for the soul.

Spiritually speaking we also have:

JOH.6:63 It is the **spirit that quickeneth**; the flesh profits nothing: the words that I speak unto you, they are spirit, and they are life.

C.26 I admit that the above verse in **Jubilees 7.32** is very strange, as it seems to indicate that by drinking blood one '**absorbs the spirit of the animal killed'**. A very strange idea. I think that we have to make a distinction between the spirit and the flesh:

1) Physically speaking the **blood** is the **life** of the **physical body**.

2) Spiritually speaking the physical body **cannot operate** without the **life-force** of its own **spirit**. Two distinct dimensional qualities. I think it very unlikely that by drinking the blood of another creature that one would become possessed with the spirit of that creature - although there are people on this planet unfortunately that believe in such practices and especially those into very dark arts and those who believe in vampires and werewolves which creatures are all about drinking blood.

For these reasons God Himself made it very clear that we are not to drink the blood of animals or humans.

C.27 What about blood transfusions? I have personally had some of those blood transfusions, when I was in hospital with severe anaemia Apparently, it is **not the same** to have a **blood transfusion** as it is to directly **drink blood**. Our stomachs were not designed to be able to digest blood.

33 For the earth will not be clean from the blood which has been shed upon it; for (only) through the blood of him that shed it will the earth be purified throughout all its generations.

GAL.6:7 Be not deceived; God is not mocked: for whatsoever a man soweth, that shall he also reap.

GAL.6:8 For he that soweth to his flesh shall of the flesh reap corruption; but he that soweth to the Spirit shall of the Spirit reap life everlasting.

34 And now, my children, harken: work judgment and righteousness that ye maybe planted in righteousness over the face of the whole earth, and your glory lifted up before my God, who saved me from the waters of the flood.

35 And behold, ye will go and build for yourselves cities, and plant in them all the plants that are upon the earth, and moreover all fruit-bearing trees.

36 For three years the fruit of everything that is eaten will not be gathered: and in the fourth year its fruit will be accounted holy [and they will offer the first fruits], acceptable before the Most High God, who created heaven and earth and all things.

37 Let them offer in abundance the first of the wine and oil (as) first fruits on the altar of the Lord, who receives it, and what is left let the servants of the house of the Lord eat before the altar which receives (it). And in the fifth year make ye the release so that ye release it in righteousness and uprightness, and ye shall be righteous, and all that you plant shall prosper.

38 For thus did Enoch, the father of your father command Methuselah, his son, and Methuselah his son Lamech, and Lamech commanded me all the things which his fathers commanded him.

39 And I also will give you commandment, my sons, as Enoch commanded his son in the first jubilees: whilst still living, the seventh in his generation, he commanded and testified to his son and to his son's sons until the day of his death.'

Chapter 8: WRITINGS OF THE WICKED WATCHERS

> 1 In the twenty-ninth jubilee, in the first week, [1373 A.M. = 'Anno Mundi' = years of the world] in the beginning thereof Arpachshad took to himself a wife and her name was Rasu'eja, the daughter of Susan, the daughter of Elam, and she bare him a son in the third year in this week, [1375 A.M.] and he called his name Kainam.

Comment:1: According to the K.J.V of the Bible, the date that Arphaxad had his first-born son was in the year 1700 A.M, which would make the date given in this Book of Jubilees as 325 years too soon. Why is this, one might ask?

> 2 And the son grew, and his father taught him writing, and he went to seek for himself a place where he might seize for himself a city.
>
> 3 And he found a writing which former (generations) had carved on the rock, and he read what was thereon, and he transcribed it and sinned owing to it; for it contained the teaching of the Watchers in accordance with which they used to observe the omens of the sun and moon and stars in all the signs of heaven.

C.2 1'*found a writing which former (generations) had carved on the rock, and he read what was thereon, and he transcribed it and sinned owing to it; for it contained the teaching of the Watchers*'

This is a very significant verse: Apparently according to the 'Book of the Giants', they knew that the Great Flood would come. From all the evidence, it appears that the Watchers and their sons the Giants wrote down certain instructions carved in both rocks and on monoliths and great stone structures in order that their writings would most likely survive the coming Great Flood and be able to pass on instructions to those who came after the Flood. Many now believe that most of the megaliths around the world which have writings showing advanced technology were all written on from before the Great Flood, all the way from Easter Island massive statues to the pyramids dotted all around the entire planet. (See my website:

Ancient Advanced Technology: http://www.outofthebottomlesspit.co.uk/413536147)

> 4 And he (Kainam) wrote it down and said nothing regarding it; for he was afraid to speak to Noah about it, lest he should be angry with him on account of it.

C.3 Is it just possible that because Kainam hid the writings of the Watchers from Noah, that he became cursed & evil and started to write about evil things and this is why the 70 scholars at the time of the putting together of the Bible in 1611 decided to exclude Kainam from Noah's lineage down through Abraham, because he was in fact a very evil person writing about evil things that pertained to the Wicked Watchers who had left their writings engraved in the rocks; and which we read earlier that Kainam had kept to himself and didn't tell Noah, and it stated '*he transcribed it and sinned owing to it*'.

C.4 Unlike his ancestors both Enoch and Noah, Kainam son of Arphaxad, became evil due to the wicked knowledge of the former Rephaim or Giants who died before the Flood & who were sons of the Nephilim (Fallen Angels). They were also the beginning of the disembodied spirits of the giants when they died, or better known today as demons. Traditionally their fathers the Fallen Angels tend to be known also as devils.

C.5 It is very interesting that Kainam is not mentioned in the KJV of the Bible. The lineage of descent in the K.J.V of the Bible shows Arphaxad having a son called Salah. However, Kainam is also mentioned in the Septuagint version of the Old Testament or also known as LXX, as one of the sons of Arphaxad. In the Septuagint Salah is shown as the son of Kainam! Why does the Bible miss out the lineage of Kainam when Kainam is mentioned in both the Septuagint (Assembled in 300 B.C.E) and also this Book of Jubilees (Re-assembled around 200 B.C.E) The KJV of the Bible wasn't put together until 1611? The New Testament was reliable, but the Old Testament was taken from a Jewish *Masoretic version from the early centuries A.D. That was a Jewish cult in 300 AD who *re-did the Septuagint* version of the Old Testament and obviously changed the things that they didn't like.

C.6 The fact that Kainam wrote down some of the writings of the Watchers, and then deliberately hid it from Noah shows how the writings of the Wicked Watchers did in fact get passed on after the Great Flood. This Kainam was of the Shem lineage, not to be confused with Canaan who was of the lineage of Ham.

> 5 And in the thirtieth jubilee, [1429 A.M. = '**Anno Mundi' = years of the world**] in the second week, in the first year thereof, he took to himself a wife, and her name was Melka, the daughter of Madai, the son of Japheth, and in the fourth year [1432 A.M.] he begat a son, and called his name Shelah; for he said: 'Truly I have been sent.'

C.7 According to the K.J.V. of the Bible, Selah was born in the year 1700 A.M. and 44 years after the Great Flood which according to the Bible happened in the year 1658 A.M. This shows a discrepancy of 268 years.

> 6 [And in the fourth year he was born], and Shelah grew up and took to himself a wife, and her name was Mu'ak, the daughter of Kesed, his father's brother, in the one and thirtieth jubilee, in the fifth week, in the

first year [1499 A.M.] thereof.

7 And she bare him a son in the fifth year [1503 A.M.] thereof, and he called his name Eber: and he took unto himself a wife, and her name was 'Azurad, the daughter of Nebrod, in the thirty-second jubilee, in the seventh week, in the third year thereof. [1564 A.M.]

C.8 According to the Bible, Eber was born in the year 1723 A.M. This shows a difference of 220 years

8 And in the sixth year [1567 A.M.] thereof, she bare him son, and he called his name Peleg; for in the days when he was born the children of Noah began to divide the earth amongst themselves: for this reason he called his name Peleg.

C.9 According to biblical Time Charts the date of Peleg's birth was actually 1757 A.M. This means that the Book of Jubilees has placed Peleg's birth some 190 years earlier than that stated in the Bible.

9 And they divided (it) secretly amongst themselves and told it to Noah.

10 And it came to pass in the beginning of the thirty-third jubilee [1569 A.M.] that they divided the earth into three parts, for Shem and Ham and Japheth, according to the inheritance of each, in the first year in the first week, when one of us who had been sent, was with them.

C.10 Here it is stating that an angel had been sent to instruct Noah and his sons. What were they talking about?

Well let's consider the original setting. What had just happened on a world scale?

The entire planet had been cleansed from evil and any empires of the Fallen angels and their sons the giants such as ATLANTIS had been destroyed. Both the INNER EARTH AND THE OUTER EARTH can been eradicated of mankind and all creatures with the exception of the sea creatures.

At some point an angel of the Lord appears to Noah and he receives in prophecy that the **whole earth will be divided into three parts by his sons for the duration of eternity**. It states that in verse 11 *'took the writing out of the bosom of Noah, their father'*

C.11 Let's consider this very important writing as in some ways to us in modern times it would appear not to make any sense. Noah was the father of Shem and from Shem descended the Semites and Israel. As we all know Israel is a very small country today and yet it was promised by God for the **lands of the Semites to be extensive**, so what went wrong?

C.12 God's original promise given later to Abraham was that his descendants would **drive out the Canaanites** from the lands which had been assigned to Shem and his descendants the Semites. Jacob and his sons did a pretty good job of that as did Moses and Joshua and Samson and king David. Unfortunately they were not able to fully stop the evil as only the Messiah is capable of doing that completely. It is prophesied in the **Book of Zechariah** that in the **Millennium** there will be **no more evil** and **wicked persons** corrupting Israel. The whole world will have to be cleansed again as at the time of Noah's Great Flood before the Millennium can be ushered in by God Himself and all evil eradicated at least for the 1000 years of the Golden Age. (**See Appendix** for the **POST MILLENNIUM TIMES AND THE NEW HEAVEN AND NEW EARTH**)

ZEC.14:21 Yea, every pot in Jerusalem and in Judah shall be holiness unto the LORD of hosts: and all they that sacrifice shall come and take of them, and seethe therein: and in that day there **shall be no more the Canaanite** in the house of the LORD of hosts.

C13 The prophecy can't be fully fulfilled until the time of the Messiah and all evil is eradicated and the devil and his demons locked away for good. At present there are too many evil critters plaguing our planet but in the not too distant future they will all be gone and then the complete fulfilment of prophecy will come about.

REV.20:1 And I saw an angel come down from heaven, having the key of the bottomless pit and a great chain in his hand.

REV.20:2 And he laid hold on the dragon, that old serpent, which is the Devil, and Satan, and bound him a thousand years,

C.14 In verse 16 it gives something important away and that it is: 'This portion came forth by lot for Shem and his sons, that they should possess it for ever unto his generations for **evermore.'**

This was a prophecy was talking about the far future and that one day when the Golden Age of the Millennium has come and the return of the Messiah that the lands of Shem and thus by implication Israel shall expand to incorporate a much bigger land area. The lands promised to Shem for ETERNITY included in the original prophecy given to Noah not only lands of the OUTER EARTH but also lands of the INNER EARTH that are right below Israel on the INNER SURFACE of the planet.

C.15 This is why even modern Jews who know their religious books such as the Torah and the Zohar will tell you that Abraham and Sarah were buried in a double cave that was in fact a portal from the outer earth to the inner earth and that the cave descended in the earth and came out right next to the garden of Eden.

C.16 WHAT DOES ISRAEL REPRESENT - AS THE SONS OF SHEM?

ISRAEL is a spiritual location as well as a physical one

Israel represents God's promise to the **RIGHTEOUS** and those who will keep

His commandments and clearly this number of people is going to multiply during the **MILLENIUM** or the **Golden Age of the Messiah** as millions will see Jesus in person as the Messiah and will believe and receive Him. Millions will turn to Christ and Israel will increase in size as the original promise was given to Noah about his son Shem and their descendants Israel. Of course to us Christians Israel is a spiritual place where all the saved will find a haven in Christ the Messiah. The Messiah will rule from his Millennial capital of Jerusalem in Israel. Finally the pristine conditions that used to exist before the Great Flood will be restored and mankind will again live to be 1000 years old on the earth. That will give more time to both multiply and to replenish the earth as was God's original first commandment to mankind to be fruitful and multiply.

C.17 According to the K.J.V. of the Bible the Great Flood didn't happen until 1658 A.M, so the earth being divided into three parts to Shem and Ham and Japheth must have happened around 30 years after the Flood which according to the Bible would make it around 1688. This represents a difference of 99 years.

C.18 They 'divided the earth' into 'three parts', for Shem and Ham and Japheth

> 11 And he called his sons, and they drew nigh to him, they and their children, and he divided the earth into the lots, which his three sons were to take in possession, and they reached forth their hands, and took the writing out of the bosom of Noah, their father.
>
> 12 And there came forth on the writing as Shem's lot the middle of the earth which he should take as an inheritance for himself and for his sons for the generations of eternity, from the middle of the mountain range of Rafa, from the mouth of the water from the river Tina, and his portion goes towards the west through the midst of this river, and it extends till it reaches the water of the abysses, out of which this river goes forth and pours its waters into the sea Me'at, and this river flows into the great sea.

C.19 This above verse is mentioning places that *don't seem to exist today. 'Middle of the earth' Rafa, River Tina, Sea of Me'at and the Great Sea.* I see some people trying to explain it in terms of the Middle of the earth being in North Africa, but all the names including the Garden of Eden simply don't fit that map. Are these Inner Earth locations?

Where is the *real* evidence today on maps to show the above-named places accurately? [https://www.ancient-code.com/the-forbidden-land-of-agartha-the-secrets-of-the-inner-earth/]

13 And all that is towards the north is Japheth's, and all that is towards the south belongs to Shem. And it extends till it reaches Karaso: this is in the bosom of the tongue which looks towards the south.

14 And his portion extends along the great sea, and it extends in a straight line till it reaches the west of the tongue which looks towards the south: for this sea is named the tongue of the Egyptian Sea. And it turns from here towards the south towards the mouth of the great sea on the shore of (its) waters, and it extends to the west to 'Afra, and it extends till it reaches the waters of the river Gihon, and to the south of the waters of Gihon, to the banks of this river.

15 And it extends towards the east, till it reaches the Garden of Eden, to the south thereof, and from the east of the whole land of Eden and of the whole east, it turns to the east and proceeds till it reaches the east of the mountain named Rafa, and it descends to the bank of the mouth of the river Tina.

C.20 What if modern science has it all wrong and that the earth is actually *hollow*. Jewish Sages tell us that ancient Jews also believed that the earth is in fact hollow as quoted in the Zohar. The Jewish Sages also stated that the Garden of Eden is in fact inside the earth. (See my book: '**OUT OF THE BOTTOMLESS PIT'**)

C.21 There is strong evidence that the original Garden of Eden was in fact inside the earth. A lot of people do believe that the earth is in fact hollow and there is a lot of evidence to support this idea. **(See APPENDIX)**

C.22 Of those who believe that the earth is hollow, there are two possibilities for Noah and his sons. 1) Either: They lived inside the earth until the Great Flood when they were moved in the Ark to the outer surface for the very first time. 2) Or: Adam and Eve were cast out of the Garden of Eden and they were put on the outer surface of the earth. For various reasons which I will show in the Appendix - from what I have been able to study about this interesting topic so far, number 1 is the correct answer.

C.23 If this is true then **Noah and his sons must have been aware** that the **earth is in fact** hollow. This Book of Jubilees actually gives it away, in that it is describing the lands assigned to the sons of Noah. As far as I can ascertain, some of these lands and rivers mentioned are not outer earth places *but inner earth locations.* This is a big mystery and if it is true, then **why did future generations mostly forget about this information**? The answer to that question is answered in my book '**Out of the Bottomless Pit'** in that after the Great Flood, the **demons and entities took much more control of Inner Earth** and along with Satan and his Fallen angels they have done their best to keep uninvited guests out of the Inner Earth in modern times.

C.24 Importantly, it is the **power of demons** to **cloud the truth** in the **minds of humans** who are not protected by faith in God. One of the first things that the Fallen angels and demons would have wanted hidden was the knowledge about their abode inside the Inner Earth. So, it became but a myth instead of reality, like so many other so-called myths from all of history such as the demi-gods and the Titans and the infamous chimeras and monsters that roamed the earth in Pre-Flood times and devoured mankind.

C.25 It is the power of the **negative spirit world** to conceal matters from the minds of unsuspecting humans and keep them brain-washed to the kind of lying vanities put forth by modern false science such as Evolution and Global Warming. The powers that be know that these weighty topics are lies, but they use them to control the masses and thus cause them to be dumb-ed-down and thus easier to control. There are many such lies, and half-truths foisted over mankind to control them. The Elite who run our planet do the same with fake politics. Supposedly, the people have a vote to have a say in matters in a Democracy. In reality voting is always rigged in favour of the wishes and whims of the Elite. The media is the same - mostly fake Why? Because in general, those who have ruled empires and kingdoms throughout the history of the world, have been inspired and led by **demonic forces** right out of hell itself. Man does not want to do things God's way, so he has the Devil to pay, and thus does everything by force!

C.26 Another thing that is important to mention is that the **original Watcher class of angels that fell** in pre-Flood times, were **experts at understanding the 'thoughts of mankind'** and in '**communicating**' with mankind. When the angels became evil, they then used their 'special abilities' against mankind and started to plague mankind's thoughts - and thus confusing mankind about many topics. Thus, today in modern times most people don't have a clue as to what is 'going on' on this planet, and sadly many don't seem to understand the difference between right and wrong anymore, as 'anything goes' and 'all is random' to the latest generation. It is a clear sign and it proves that time is indeed late and that we are living in the Last Days. **Every empire that turned away from God and from His Spirit crumbled to dust!**

C.27 As mentioned in the Bible the Inner earth has become the location of both Hell and the Lake of Fire and also the domain of Satan and his Fallen angels and minions. It is also mentioned in the Bible that a place called Paradise and Hell are side by side inside the earth.

LUK.16:23 And in hell he lift up his eyes, being in torments, and sees Abraham afar off, and Lazarus in his bosom. (N.B *'Abraham's Bosom'* is the name given to Paradise in old Jewish texts)

LUK.16:26 And beside all this, between us (Hell and Paradise) and you there is a great gulf fixed: so that they which would pass from hence to you cannot; neither can they pass to us, that would come from thence.

C.28 Could it be wildly possible that as Noah and his sons had originally sailed out from the inner earth to the outer earth, that when land was assigned to each of them, it also included lands on the outer surface and the inner surface? It is a great mystery, as even if true, how could the sons of Noah get back into the inner earth, when even today it is very difficult and dangerous. Perhaps, with the passage of time future generations forgot about there being a *world within our world* and the *portals* mentioned by Enoch linking both the inner and outer worlds on our planet. **(See the Appendix for 'THE DEGENERATION OF THE INNER WORLD')**

16 This portion came forth by lot for Shem and his sons, that they should possess it for ever unto his generations for evermore.

17 And Noah rejoiced that this portion came forth for Shem and for his sons, and he remembered all that he had spoken with his mouth in prophecy; for he had said: 'Blessed be the Lord God of Shem.

C.29 This verse is one of the keys to this very revealing chapter. 'spoken with his mouth in prophecy'

18 And may the Lord dwell in the dwelling of Shem.'

19 And he knew that the Garden of Eden is the holy of holies, and the dwelling of the Lord, and Mount Sinai the centre of the desert, and Mount Zion - the centre of the navel of the earth: these three were created as holy places facing each other.

C.30 This verse is amazingly revealing: 'Garden of Eden is the 'holy of holies' What is the definition of the Holy of Holies? Strictly speaking and very simplified, it is *something inside something else.* You know you have the temple and the sanctuary within it and the Holy of Holies is the Inner Sanctum Santorum within the sanctuary. In my opinion, this is in fact stating in so many words, that the *Garden of Eden is within the earth* where it is 'protected like a baby in the womb' of the earth. This above verse also gives the 'hollow earth' theory credibility in stating: '**Mount Zion - the centre of the navel of the earth.** The word 'navel' implies **something inside something else, (hollow earth)** such as a baby in the womb.

II EZDRAS: 4. 41 And he said unto me, 'In Hades the '*chambers of the souls*' are like the '*womb*'.

II EZDRAS 5.48 He said to me, 'even so have I given the 'womb of the earth' to those who from time to time are sown in it' (See my book '**Ezdras Insights**' at Amazon.co.uk or Amazon.com)

C.31 Why does God Himself call the earth '*like a 'womb'*, unless He is making a valid point. A womb is hollow in order that it can *contain something* and that is to say water and a baby, which is similar to Inner Earth. The inner earth contains an inner sun, lands and water as well as Hell and The Lake of Fire in lower dimensions.

C.32 MACHPELAH was the cave where Abraham buried Sarah and it is located in the mountains in Hebron some 20 miles south of Jerusalem. This was no ordinary cave according to the **Jewish book** of the **Zohar** but a **double cave**.

The **Zohar**, and ancient **Jewish book** of **mysticism** writes that the Cave is "the very entranceway to the Garden of Eden." The Hebrew word Machpelah means **twofold.** The Cave is considered "twofold," because it **bridges the material and spiritual worlds**, linking them by serving as an **entrance from one to the other**. The name of the city in which the Cave is situated, Hebron, also bears the etymological roots of "**connection**."

SOURCE: https://torah.org/torah-portion/legacy-5768-chayeisarah/

C.33 I am of course hypothesizing here that 'if the **earth is hollow'**, which I certainly believe it to be then:

The above verse 19 is revealing **incredible secrets** about **the earth** and about the **inner earth for those who have 'eyes to see' and 'ears to hear'.** *'Garden of Eden is the holy of holies, and the dwelling of the Lord, and Mount Sinai the centre of the desert, and Mount Zion - the centre of the navel of the earth: these three were created as holy places facing each other'.*

C.34 According to modern maps, the distance from Mount Zion in Jerusalem to Mount Sinai in Egypt is around 500 KM or 300 miles. The thickness of the crust of the earth is allegedly around 300 miles also. The distance from Jerusalem to Machpelah, which is in the mountains of Israel south of Jerusalem some 20 miles.

C.35 Fascinating mathematical calculations: If one does a little maths drawing a triangle with two sides being equidistant. One side is 300 miles, another side is 300 miles. The long side will be 444 miles.

'these three were created as holy places facing each other.'

If all locations are facing each other, then the middle point between them would have to be around 150 miles down in the earth and equidistant from both Mount Sinai and Mount Zion. All these calculations are possible by going through the famous cave systems at **MACPELAH**, where Abraham and Sarah were both buried. **A place that represents eternal life** and is supposed to be directly above the **Garden of Eden according to the Zohar,** which is situated on the **inner surface of the earth** some **300 miles** below the **caves of Machpelah**.

C.36 There must also be an exact location deep down in the earth where the distance to all three locations is equal and that is at some location around 150 miles down in the earth or halfway through the **earth's crust which I believe to be 300 miles thick** and halfway between Mount Zion and Mount Sinai and half the distance down in the earth to the Garden of Eden. That exact location is the focal point between Mt Zion, Mt Sinai and Mt Machpelah and is approximately 222 miles distant from each of those three locations.

[**Editor**: *Note that many others will state that the crust of the **hollow earth** is around 700 - 800 miles thick, however there are important reasons to believe that the earth is closer to only 300 miles thick. - See the **Appendix** to learn more].

C.37 When doing these calculations, I did not know the exact distances. I realized that the distance down in the earth from Machpelah in Hebron to the Garden of Eden and the distance from Mt Zion to Mount Sinai would have to be around the same distance. It turned out that when I found the distance of Mount Zion at Jerusalem to Mount Sinai in /Egypt that it was indeed approximately 300 miles. I think that this is more than just co-incidence, and it makes it possible mathematically for the **three locations mentioned in this chapter verse 19 'to be facing each other perfectly'**.

C.38 What would one find at the place exactly equidistance from all three locations is anyone's guess, but it will be half-way down through the crust of the earth where the middle point between all three is to be found?(**Editor:** The above calculations are all approximate in their distances and not exact.

C.39 See my book '**ENOCH INSIGHTS**': **Here is a preview:** In the amazing Book of Enoch, Enoch speaks of proceeding to 'the **middle** of the earth', where he beheld a 'blessed land', 'happy and fertile. He also sees '**many mountains of fire'**. The angel Uriel shows him 'the first and last secrets in heaven above and the depths of the earth: There are said to be cavities in the earth and 'mighty waters' under it . Enoch sees an abyss 'opened in the midst of the earth, which was full of fire' There is also a reference to seven great rivers, four of which 'take their course in the cavity of the north' (**ENOCH INSIGHTS** available at Amazon.com or Amazon.co.uk)

> 20 And he blessed the God of gods, who had put the word of the Lord into his mouth, and the Lord for evermore.

C.40 Why does this above verse state '**God of gods'**

PSA.82:6 I have said, Ye are *gods*; and all of you are children of the most High.

JOH.10:34 Jesus answered them, Is it not written in your law, I said, Ye are *gods*?

1SA.28:13 And the king said unto her, Be not afraid: for what sawest thou? And the woman said unto Saul, I saw *gods* ascending out of the earth.

1SA.28:14 And he said unto her, What form is he of? And she said, An old man cometh up; and he is covered with a mantle. And Saul perceived that it was Samuel, and he stooped with his face to the ground, and bowed himself.

C.41 We are made in the image of God and thus he calls us gods because we have the ability to **choose** to do either good or evil. The fallen angels are also known as 'gods' and their sons with human woman as demi-gods. For the time being whilst we are being 'tested' by God in the earth life - the Psalms makes it clear that:

PSA.8:4 What is *man*, that thou art mindful of him? and the son of man, that thou visit him?

PSA.8:5 For thou hast made him a *'little lower than the angels'*, and hast crowned him with glory and honour.

C.41 Once we have been resurrected and gone to be with the Lord in heaven it is stated:

1CO.6:2 Do ye not know that the *saints shall judge the world*? and if the world shall be judged by you, are ye unworthy to judge the smallest matters?

1CO.6:3 Know ye not that we shall *judge angels*? how much more things that pertain to this life?

---

21 And he knew that a blessed portion and a blessing had come to Shem and his sons unto the generations for ever -the whole land of Eden and the whole land of the Red Sea, and the whole land of the east and India, and on the Red Sea and the mountains thereof, and all the land of Bashan, and all the land of Lebanon and the islands of Kaftur, and all the mountains of Sanir and 'Amana, and the mountains of Asshur in the north, and all the land of Elam, Asshur, and Babel, and Susan and Ma'edai, and all the mountains of Ararat, and all the region beyond the sea, which is beyond the mountains of Asshur towards the north, a blessed and spacious land, and all that is in it is very good.

22 And for Ham came forth the second portion, beyond the Gihon towards the south to the right of the Garden, and it extends towards the south and it extends to all the *mountains of fire*, and it extends towards the west to the sea of 'Atel and it extends towards the west till it reaches the sea of Ma'uk -that (sea) into which everything which is not destroyed descends.

C.42 If the sons of Noah divided the earth from a position near Mount Ararat in Turkey, where the ark of Noah originally landed after the Great Flood then where did these *'mountains of fire'* come from? . (See **C.39** above)

There are only a handful of volcanos in Turkey, the Middle East on even on North Africa. What 'mountains of fire' or 'mountain ranges of fire' - unless it is talking about mountain ranges inside the earth or the Inner Earth. **Inner earth** is described as the place of a **'thousand mountains of fire'**. Just a possibility that somehow mankind still had access to Inner Earth right after the Flood

- but how? In my book II Ezdras chapter 13 there is a very strange description of the 10 missing tribes of Israel going to a faraway land by going to a 'hidden place' by going in through a passageway near the river Euphrates. What is that talking about

C.43 Here is the exact passage from my book '**Ezdras Insights**':

II Ezdras 13.17 But they formed this plan for themselves, that they would leave the multitude of the nations and go to a more distant region, where mankind had never lived; that there at least they might keep their statutes which they had not kept in their own land; and they went in by the narrow passages of the Euphrates river. **C.44** This is indeed a mind-boggling verse as it reveals some AMAZING secrets:

THE LOST 10 TRIBES OF ISRAEL. This 17th verse most definitely gives the impression that a group of people representing the 10 Tribes made some sort of pact with God, whereby they wanted to live His laws to the full, without corruption coming back in, as it had done back in their land of Israel countless times. It would seem, that these people, were given special instructions to 'go to a more distant region' where 'mankind had never lived' and that they 'went in by the narrow passages of the Euphrates river'. The fact that it states here that the 10 tribes or representatives of those 10 tribes, went to a place where mankind had never lived before! Very odd! There are many sites on the internet that claim that the 10 Tribes disappeared inside the earth and descended into the INNER EARTH. It is also stated that these ten tribes will return to Israel at the time of the MESSIAH or the 2nd coming of Christ.

(End of excerpt from EZDRAS INSIGHTS)

---

23 And it goes forth towards the north to the limits of Gadir, and it goes forth to the coast of the waters of the sea to the waters of the great sea till it draws near to the river Gihon and goes along the river Gihon till it reaches the right of the Garden of Eden.

24 And this is the land which came forth for Ham as the portion which he was to occupy for ever for himself and his sons unto their generations for ever.

25 And for Japheth came forth the third portion beyond the river Tina to the north of the outflow of its waters, and it extends north-easterly to the whole region of Gog, and to all the country east thereof.

26 And it extends northerly to the north, and it extends to the mountains of Qelt towards the north, and towards the sea of Ma'uk, and it goes forth to the east of Gadir as far as the region of the waters of the

---

sea. And it extends until it approaches the west of Fara and it returns towards 'Aferag, and it extends easterly to the waters of the sea of Me'at.

28 And it extends to the region of the river Tina in a north-easterly direction until it approaches the boundary of its waters towards the mountain Rafa, and it turns round towards the north.

29 This is the land which came forth for Japheth and his sons as the portion of his inheritance which he should possess for himself and his sons, for their generations for ever; five great islands, and a great land in the north.

30 But it is cold, and the land of Ham is hot, and the land of Shem is neither hot nor cold, but it is of blended cold and heat.

C.45 CONCLUSION about the **TIME SEQUENCE 1:** Is it just possible that the Book of Jubilees was using a different system of measuring time than the King James Bible. The 'Solar year' is known to be 364 days and the 'Lunar year' 354 days and the 'Prophetic year' is 360 days.

C.46 CONCLUSION about the **TIME SEQUENCE 2:** According to the modern Jewish calendar, the earth is around 5775 years old, whilst according to the King James Version of the Bible it is around 6000 years old. Going by the Septuagint LXX it is around 6650 years old. So, which is right you may well ask? Well, all of the calculations of the Biblical and Apocryphal Books are reasonably close to each other in Time sequence.

Thank God the earth certainly isn't millions or billions of years old as the unproven 'mantra of Evolution' would have you believe. See the **APPENDIX** to find out more about this fascinating topic of TIME.

Chapter 9: SONS OF NOAH DIVIDE THE LAND

1 And Ham divided amongst his sons, and the first portion came forth for Cush towards the east, and to the west of him for Mizraim, and to the west of him for Put, and to the west of him [and to the west thereof] on the sea for Canaan.

2 And Shem also divided amongst his sons, and the first portion came forth for Ham and his sons, to the east of the river Tigris till it approaches the east, the whole land of India, and on the Red Sea on its coast, and the waters of Dedan, and all the mountains of Mebri and Ela, and all the land of Susan and all that is on the side of Pharnak to the Red Sea and the river Tina.

3 And for Asshur came forth the second Portion, all the land of Asshur and Nineveh and Shinar and to the border of India, and it ascends and skirts the river.

4 And for Arpachshad came forth the third portion, all the land of the region of the Chaldees to the east of the Euphrates, bordering on the Red Sea, and all the waters of the desert close to the tongue of the sea which looks towards Egypt, all the land of Lebanon and Sanir and 'Amana to the border of the Euphrates.

5 And for Aram there came forth the fourth portion, all the land of Mesopotamia between the Tigris and the Euphrates to the north of the Chaldees to the border of the mountains of Asshur and the land of 'Arara.

6 And there came forth for Lud the fifth portion, the mountains of Asshur and all appertaining to them till it reaches the Great Sea, and till it reaches the east of Asshur his brother.

7 And Japheth also divided the land of his inheritance amongst his sons.

8 And the first portion came forth for Gomer to the east from the north

side to the river Tina; and in the north there came forth for Magog all the inner portions of the north until it reaches to the sea of Me'at.

Comment:1: Is the earth hollow? Why does it state the *'inner portions of the north'*? Is this talking about lands inside a Hollow Earth? Many of the names mentioned of the places given to the sons of Noah are not known today. The names were very strange to us. Why is that? It is just possible that Noah and his family were originally inside a Hollow earth at the time of the Great Flood, but then God brought Noah and his family on the Ark through one of the openings either the North or the South Poles onto the outer surface. If Noah had been aware of the change in the topography of the new lands, then it is logical that when he divided up the land to his descendants then it is conceivable that he would have divided up the lands of the Inner Earth as well as the Outer Earth. This could also explain why at least half of the names mentioned above are not know to us in modern times.

C.2 This brings up another important question: *How did the ancients get from the outer earth to the inner earth?* The **Book of Enoch** mentions portals from the inner earth to the outer earth. It is also mentioned in my books both **Enoch Insights** & **Ezdras Insights** about the **portals**: The following is from '**Ezdras Insights'**. The angel Uriel is talking with Ezra:

II EZDRAS 6.1 1 And he said unto me, "At the beginning of the '**circle** of the earth', before the **portals** of the **world** were in place .

C.3 Is it just possible that places like the '**Bermuda Triangle'** are **portals** or even '**places between dimensions'.** I think it is likely that at one time there used to exist portals from the Outer Earth to the Inner Earth but just like the Bermuda Triangle, the Portals no longer function correctly. Why is that? Now that is a very good question for which I would like to find an answer. Consider the following: Allegedly there are 12 Triangles like the Bermuda Triangle around the world. They are apparently all at 30o Latitude. Today most of them are under water. In ancient times the sea level was much lower, and it is very likely that all the Triangles used to be on the land. That is when they were acting as portals. Unfortunately, in modern times these 'Bermuda Triangles' are famous for malfunctioning. Ships, planes disappear and often are never to be seen again! Why does this happen? [To know more about this topic read my books '**Enoch Insights**' and **Out of the Bottomless Pit**]

C.4 Notice that God in speaking to Ezra two and a half thousand years ago and clearly mentions that the earth is a 'circle'. In other words it is round or spherical and certainly not 'flat'!

9 And for Madai came forth as his portion that he should possess from the west of his two brothers to the islands, and to the coasts of the islands.

10 And for Javan came forth the fourth portion every island and the

103

islands which are towards the border of Lud.

GEN.10:4 And the sons of Javan; Elishah, and Tarshish, Kittim, and Dodanim.

GEN.10:5 By these were the isles of the Gentiles divided in their lands; every one after his tongue, after their families, in their nations

11 And for Tubal there came forth the fifth portion in the midst of the tongue which approaches towards the border of the portion of Lud to the second tongue, to the region beyond the second tongue unto the third tongue.

12 And for Meshech came forth the sixth portion, all the region beyond the third tongue till it approaches the east of Gadir.

13 And for Tiras there came forth the seventh portion, four great islands in the midst of the sea, which reach to the portion of Ham [and the islands of Kamaturi came out by lot for the sons of Arpachshad as his inheritance].

14 And thus the sons of Noah divided unto their sons in the presence of Noah their father, and he bound them all by an oath, imprecating a curse on every one that sought to seize the portion which had not fallen (to him) by his lot.

C.5 Noah causes his sons to 'bind themselves to an oath and to a curse', that if any of his sons transgress the oath they will be cursed. None of his sons was allowed to seize upon the territory of his brother. Why did God through Noah make such a law with a curse behind it for severe punishment if they transgressed this oath? When we look at today in modern times, why is it that nations go to war with each other? Is it not some dispute over some piece of land as to who would be the owner thereof?

C.6 The law to keep Noah's sons in their own territories was made in the hope of avoiding wars and disputes and a descent into violence and the resultant barbarity that goes with wars such as raping and pillaging and murdering innocent peoples. All for the benefit of some rich people's land grab!

15 And they all said, 'So be it; so be it ' for themselves and their sons for ever throughout their generations till the day of judgment, on which the Lord God shall judge them with a sword and with fire for all the unclean wickedness of their errors, wherewith they have filled the earth

with transgression and uncleanness and fornication and sin.

Chapter 10: DEMONS & THE TOWER OF BABEL

> 1 And in the third week of this jubilee the unclean demons began to lead astray the children of the sons of Noah, and to make to err and destroy them.
>
> 2 And the sons of Noah came to Noah their father, and they told him concerning the demons which were leading astray and blinding and slaying his sons' sons.

Comment:1: Here, we see the beginning of the spiritual warfare beginning after the Great Flood, when *what used to be the Giants before the Great Flood*, who had all been swept away of the Flood, their *spirits became the demons*, which started to afflict and oppress mankind.

C.2 It would also appear that **all diseases and sicknesses** started after the Great Flood when the earth had become physically very different, with no layer of water around the earth to protect it from cosmic rays which cause the ageing of mankind. In studying the **Book of Enoch** and the **Book of Jasher** which are the books which mention the most about the times before the Great Flood, there is simply **no mention of sicknesses** at all.

C.3 After the Great Flood *the demons (who are the dis-embodied spirits of the Giants)*, were no longer directly oppressing mankind face-to face in the physical realm, but more indirectly through the spiritual realm, influencing mankind through their thoughts, feelings, desires and lusts and causing mankind to be tempted with perversions, corruptions and violence. The demons also cause contentions between peoples. Many people contend that all sicknesses are brought by demons. (See verses 10 -13 *of this very chapter which show the* origins of medicine *to combat sicknesses. Notice that they are all natural cures shown by God's angels to Noah.*)

C.4 Before the Flood, the fight against the bad spirits in the giants was directly physical, but after the Flood they came back yet again to oppress mankind spiritually. Before the Flood the evil of the giants and their fathers the Fallen angels was very obvious and visible. After the Flood it was *much more deceptive* and *'hidden'* across the *'veil of dimensions'*.

EPH.6:12 For we wrestle not against flesh and blood, but against principalities, against powers, against the rulers of the darkness of this world, against spiritual wickedness in high places.

2CO.10:4 (For the weapons of our warfare are not carnal, but mighty through God to the pulling down of strong holds;)

2CO.10:5 Casting down imaginations, and every high thing that exalts itself against the knowledge of God, and bringing into captivity every thought to the obedience of Christ;

C.5 Until recently it would seem that these entities mostly plagued mankind in our thoughts in trying to oppress us. However there has been evidence that the demons or the disembodied spirits of the former giants, have found a way to come more directly into our physical dimension through **portals**. Fortunately, so far this has been very limited in scope and has only been observed in areas of great conflict and confusion such as warzones.

Why has this started to happen in modern times? It has been reported by both the American and Russian special forces as happening in Afghanistan and in Morocco and Syria. **(See APPENDIX XXI for VIDEO LINKS)**

C.6 Strangely I have also heard on Steve Quayle's site that something **really odd** happened to the **Anastasi Indians** in Mexico along with the **Aztecs** and possibly even the **Mayans**. These Indian civilizations were both barbaric and **cannibalistiC.**

The Anastasi Indians also worshipped the ancient Giants from Pre-Flood times. It has been reported that their **whole community was suddenly destroyed** by red-headed Annunaki Giants which **came out of portals** and **tore the people apart limb from limb** and **devoured them** - and then disappeared again as suddenly as they came. That was about 1000 years ago.

That would prove that the disembodied spirits of the former Pre-flood giants have indeed found a way into our physical plane through some kind of portals. [**Steve Quayle is the expert on Giants and the Annunaki**: www. stevequayle.com]

C.7 WEAPONS against demons? This story just goes to prove that you should **not worship demons or devils,** as witches do. Or they may tend to turn around and rend and destroy you both physically and spiritually. Believe in God's Word and in Salvation in Jesus - who is the **Word of God** and then you can just **rebuke the demons** in **spirit** in the **name** of the Messiah **Jesus** before they cause you any harm.

JOH.1:1 In the beginning was the Word, and the Word was with God, and the Word was God.

JOH.1:2 The same was in the beginning with God.

JOH.1:3 All things were made by him; and without him was not anything made that was made.

---

3 And he prayed before the Lord his God, and said: 'God of the spirits of all flesh, who hast shown mercy unto me And hast saved me and my sons from the waters of the flood, And hast not caused me to perish as Thou didst the sons of perdition: For Thy grace has been great towards

---

me, And great has been Thy mercy to my soul;

Let Thy grace be lift up upon my sons And let not wicked spirits rule over them Lest they should destroy them from the earth.

4 But do Thou bless me and my sons, that we may increase and Multiply and replenish the earth.

5 And Thou know how Thy Watchers, the fathers of these spirits, acted in my day: and as for these spirits which are living, imprison them and hold them fast in the place of condemnation, and let them not bring destruction on the sons of thy servant, my God; for these are malignant, and created in order to destroy.

C.8 The demons are as brute beasts and totally malignant. Just like Satan who is totally insane, you cannot 'talk' to these malignant beings, no more than you would talk with a fire-breathing dragon. The only thing one can do is to 'rebuke' them in the name of Jesus and command them to leave, just as the Saviour did to the evil spirits and demons while He lived on earth and cast out demons through His Word.

2PE.2:12 But these, as natural **brute beasts**, made to be taken and destroyed, speak evil of the things that they understand not; and shall utterly perish in their own corruption

JUD.1:10 But these speak evil of those things which they know not: but what they know naturally, as **brute beasts**, in those things they corrupt themselves

C.9 This last verse reminds me of many modern scientists who are *trying to alter humans* and *'make them more advanced'*. They sound totally 'insane' like Dr Frankenstein, being not content with what God has created, they want to create *'Transhuman beings'*.

C.10 THE IMAGE OF THE BEAST from **Revelations 13**: The problem with depending too much on micro-circuits and A.I. for our future is that the *demons* can get into the micro-chips and totally fritz them up. Of course, modern technology is heading towards the 'total control' of humans and the 'human mind' through the infamous 'Mark of the Beast' and 'Image of the Beast' – brought in through the Anti-Christ which the **New World Order Globalists** will embrace – themselves being **Satanists.**

C.11 All part of Satan's crazy plan to enslave all of mankind even more effectively than he has already done. The ultimate of technology will be the soon coming of the 'Mark of the Beast' Total enslavement and *total control of all humans by A.I. and the Devil and his demons behind it all.*

DANIEL 11:32 "And the transgressors shall bring about a covenant by deceitful ways: but a people knowing their God shall prevail, and do valiantly. Daniel 11:32

REV.13:16 And he causes all, both small and great, rich and poor, free and bond, to receive a mark in their right hand, or in their foreheads:

REV.13:17 And that no man might buy or sell, save he that had the mark, or the name of the beast, or the number of his name.

REV.13:18 Here is wisdom. Let him that hath understanding count the number of the beast: for it is the number of a man; and his number is Six hundred threescore and six. (666)

---

6 And let them not rule over the spirits of the living; for Thou alone canst exercise dominion over them.

7 And let them not have power over the sons of the righteous from henceforth and for evermore.'

8 And the Lord our God bade us to bind all. And the chief of the spirits, Mastema, came and said: 'Lord, Creator, let some of them remain before me, and let them harken to my voice, and do all that I shall say unto them; for if some of them are not left to me, I shall not be able to execute the power of my will on the sons of men; for these are for corruption and leading astray before my judgment, for great is the wickedness of the sons of men.'

C.12 Mastema is the Old Hebrew name for Satan. See **Jubilees chapter 17.16** concerning Abraham sacrificing Isaac on an altar as suggested by prince Mastema

For more information about **MASTEMA**: https://www.ancient-origins.net/human-origins-religions/mastema-persecutor-god-001018

This above-mentioned site brings up some important points about Mastema

A) He seems to be working for God Himself

Satan is God's prosecuting attorney. He falsely accuses the Saints and the innocent.

REV.12:10 And I heard a loud voice saying in heaven, Now is come salvation, and strength, and the kingdom of our God, and the power of his Christ: for *the accuser of our brethren is cast down*, which *accused them before our God day and night.*

B) Satan is often used by God Himself to bring God's judgements upon mankind.

JOB.1:7 And the LORD said unto Satan, 'Whence came thou?' Then Satan answered the LORD, and said, 'From going to and fro in the earth, and from walking up and down in it'.

JOB.1:8 And the LORD said unto Satan, Hast thou considered my servant Job, that there is none like him in the earth, a perfect and an upright man, one that fears God, and eschews evil?

JOB.1:9 Then Satan answered the LORD, and said, Doth Job fear God for nought?

JOB.1:10 Hast not thou made an hedge about him, and about his house, and about all that he hath on every side? thou hast blessed the work of his hands, and his substance is increased in the land.

JOB.1:11 But put forth thine hand now, and touch all that he hath, and he will curse thee to thy face.

JOB.1:12 And the LORD said unto Satan, Behold, all that he hath is in thy power; only upon himself put not forth thine hand. So Satan went forth from the presence of the LORD.

> 9 And He said: Let the tenth part of them remain before him and let nine parts descend into the place of condemnation.'

C.13 Here, it is clear that Satan and God are counselling together, and that God takes Satan's advice sometimes. God here in the above verse commands that one tenth of the Fallen angels be given over to Satan to enable him to do his evil deeds on earth. As Satan himself said unto God *'execute the power of my will on the sons of men; for these are for corruption and leading astray before my judgment, for great is the wickedness of the sons of men.'*

JER.17:9 The heart is deceitful above all things, and desperately wicked: who can know it?

PSA.58:3 The wicked are estranged from the womb: they go astray as soon as they be born, speaking lies.

JOH.8:44 Ye are of your father the devil, and the lusts of your father ye will do. He was a murderer from the beginning, and abode not in the truth, because there is no truth in him. When he speaks a lie, he speaks of his own: for he is a liar, and the father of it.

C.14 MORE CONCERNING MASTEMA AND EVIL. CAN GOD DO EVIL, OR ONLY THE DEVIL?

According to the embedded article concerning **Mastema** here are some relevant Bible verses.

"I am he that prepared light, and formed darkness; who make peace, and create evil; I am the Lord God, that does all these things." -Isaiah 45.7

It doesn't say that God "does" evil but that he creates evil.(or allows it to ferment for a season until His judgments are due)

10 And one of us He commanded that we should teach Noah all their medicines; for He knew that they would not walk in uprightness, nor strive in righteousness.

11 And we did according to all His words: all the malignant evil ones we bound in the place of condemnation and a tenth part of them we left that they might be subject before Satan on the earth.

12 And we explained to Noah all the medicines of their diseases, together with their seductions, how he might heal them with herbs of the earth.

C.15 This is important information about how the angels taught Noah about the *different herbs* and how that they *cured different diseases*. There is apparently a herb to cure every disease known to man. The modern massive Pharmaceutical industries don't like natural cures as they tend to use chemicals instead which often have many bad side effects. God's original herbs as suggested by his angels to Noah are in general the best solution for infirmities apart from straight miracles from heaven.

13 And Noah wrote down all things in a book as we instructed him concerning every kind of medicine. Thus the evil spirits were precluded from (hurting) the sons of Noah.

C.16 A very interesting point is brought out here about both healing and getting rid of evil spirits. Why? Because it is often evil spirits causing the sicknesses in the first place. Notice how that in the New Testament, Jesus often cast out evil spirits from people and *then* they were healed.

LUK.8:2 And certain women, which had been healed of evil spirits and infirmities, Mary called Magdalene, out of whom went seven devils,

14 And he gave all that he had written to Shem, his eldest son; for he loved him exceedingly above all his sons.

C.17 Noah wrote a book or books and passed them on to Shem. Sadly, today we have next to no record of the **Books of Noah**, apart from around five chapters penned inside the **Book of Enoch**. The **Book of Herbs and Spices and Cures** would have been invaluable & exceedingly useful to have.

Is it just possible that like many other books, that the Books of Noah Have been deliberately 'hidden away'? After all, if everyone knew how to cure themselves just using herbs and spices and fruits and vegetables, then who would need the biggest industry in the whole world: **BIG PHARMA**? My hope is that a copy of the book of Noah will yet show up!

C.18 It is mentioned by modern Jews that there was the **Book of Remedies** as mentioned by the Talmud. Here is some interesting information about that ancient book which some say came from the sons of Noah or even Noah himself.

The book was apparently banned by an ancient king of Israel, called Hezekiah, who incidentally according to the Book of Isaiah in the Bible, was himself miraculously healed by God Himself. God told Hezekiah to hide the Book of Remedies away, because the people relied more on the **BOOK OF REMEDIES** and forgot about God Himself. This was in the 8th century BCE

C.19 THE DANGERS OF WORSHIPPING ICONS

Why was the **Book of Remedies** banned? It was because the book showed how to make 'magical spells' and incantations for remedies of health problems. Initially this might have been all right, but God observed that the knowledge of the incantations was misused and eventually led the hearts of the people astray from God and led to the worship of idols and inadvertently demons/fallen angels. Therefore, God told Hezekiah the king to hide the Book of Remedies away as it was being misused.

[Ref: https://www.jpost.com/Jewish-World/Judaism/World-of-the-Sages-Books-of-Remedies]

C.20 I would say that we have had the same problem in the Catholic church where people start to believe in physical objects or paintings and revere them so much that they become idols, which take away faith in God Himself. We also see this problem occurring in the New testament that when certain freedoms were presented to the early church that unfortunately the freedoms had to be taken away because they were misused, and it resulted in fornication and the worship of idols as mentioned clearly in **Revelation 2**

REV.2:20 Notwithstanding I have a few things against thee, because thou suffer that woman Jezebel, which calleth herself a prophetess, to teach and to seduce my servants to commit fornication, and to eat things sacrificed unto idols.

C.21 The ancient book of TOBIAS Chapters 6 & 8 (around the same time as King Hezekiah mentioned above in the Book of Isaiah):

This book talks about an **angel** instructing God's prophet to kill a certain large fish and to take out the **heart, liver and gall**. He later used the heart and liver by **smoking them with incense** to drive away a very bad spirit called Asmodeus, which was strangling the husbands of a beautiful young woman called Sara, as soon as they tried to make love with her. She apparently lost seven young husbands this way, because of this very bad spirit. The prophet also used the **gall** to heal his father of 'whiteness in the eyes' sickness - which used to cause **blindness.**

C.22 BLINDNESS, the **root cause** of which is mentioned in the very first verse of this **chapter 10 of JUBILEES**, which is **caused by demons.**

C.23 SORCERY

Apparently people started to learn sorcery by using that ancient Book of Remedies and making all kinds of incantations to ward off evil spirits as well as to heal people, and even to bring up the dead as clearly shown by the Witch of Endor, who at King Saul's request, summoned up the deceased prophet Samuel, who had just died in Saul's time, and Saul was in a pinch because of his enemies the Philistines.

1SA.28:7 Then said Saul unto his servants, Seek me a woman that hath a familiar spirit, that I may go to her, and enquire of her. And his servants said to him, Behold, there is a woman that hath a familiar spirit at Endor.

[See APPENDIX XXV: IDOL WORSHIPPING & SORCERY]

> 15 And Noah slept with his fathers and was buried on Mount Lubar in the land of Ararat.
>
> 16 Nine hundred and fifty years he completed in his life, nineteen jubilees and two weeks and five years. [1659 A.M. = 'Anno Mundi' = years of the world]

C.24 This date given for the death of Noah has to be wrong: [1659 A.M.] Why? The date is far too early! According to the Bible and other sources the Great Flood happened in the year 1658 A.M and Noah died 448 years after the Great Flood

According to both the Bible and other sources Noah died in the year 2006 A.M, at the ripe old age of 950 years old. This means that there is an error in the Timeline in the Book of Jubilees by a factor of 2006-1659 = 347 years. Why is this?

> 17 And in his life on earth he excelled the children of men save Enoch because of the righteousness, wherein he was perfect.
>
> 18 For Enoch's office was ordained for a testimony to the generations of the world, so that he should recount all the deeds of generation unto generation, till the day of judgment.

C.25 A very important detail here about Enoch stating that he was extra special in that God had showed him the history of the world from the very beginning to the very end of time itself.

> 19 And in the three and thirtieth jubilee, in the first year in the second week, Peleg took to himself a wife, whose name was Lomna the daughter of Sina'ar, and she bare him a son in the fourth year of this week, and he called his name Reu; for he said: 'Behold the children of men

113

> have become evil through the wicked purpose of building for themselves a city and a tower in the land of Shinar.'

C.26 How could the peoples of the earth *'become evil through the wicked purpose of building for themselves a city and a tower in the land of Shinar.'* It had to do with the intent of them wanting to build the Tower of Babel which was in defiance of God and in open rebellion against Him. It was indeed the malignant spirits of the 'disembodied spirits of the giants' under Satan's command that inspired those on earth to build the tower of Babel.

C.27 Reu was born around 1800 A.M and was the great-great grandfather of Abraham. People married much younger than before the Great Flood or circa 30 years old. Why? Because God had told Noah at the time of the Flood that He was going to cut man's life short and down to 120 years only. At the time of Reu people also still lived to be well over 200 years old but not as old as Eber at 464 years old who was the grandfather of Reu. That means that Abraham was alive at the same time as Reu and his father Peleg and his father Eber all the way back to Noah. Abraham was alive at the same time as all of them even all ten generations that came before Abraham.

> 20 For they departed from the land of Ararat eastward to Shinar; for in his days they built the city and the tower, saying, 'Go to, let us ascend thereby into heaven.' And they began to build, and in the fourth week they made brick with fire, and the bricks served them for stone, and the clay with which they cemented them together was asphalt which comes out of the sea, and out of the fountains of water in the land of Shinar.

C.28 It Is interesting that here it states that they made actual 'bricks' in the fire. It also states that they used asphalt for mortar which comes out of the sea. Today asphalt is like a tar substance that it used in making the roads. The asphalt mentioned here is more likely to be LIME or Calcium Bicarbonate. **(See APPENDIX)**

C.29 Shinar means 'The land of the Giants'.

GEN.11:1 And the whole earth was of one language, and of one speech.

GEN.11:2 And it came to pass, as they journeyed from the east, that they found a plain in the land of *Shinar;* and they dwelt there.

GEN.11:3 And they said one to another, Go to, let us make brick, and burn them thoroughly. And they had brick for stone, and slime had they for mortar.

GEN.11:4 And they said, Go to, let us *build us a city and a tower*, whose *top may reach unto heaven*; and let us make us a name, lest we be scattered abroad upon the face of the whole earth.

> 21 And they built it: forty and three years [1645-1688 A.M. = '**Anno**

> **Mundi' = years of the world**] were they building it; its breadth was 203 bricks, and the height (of a brick) was the third of one; its height amounted to 5433 cubits and 2 palms, and (the extent of one wall was) thirteen stades (and of the other thirty stades). And the Lord our God said unto us: Behold, they are one people, and (this) they begin to do, and now nothing will be withholden from them.

C.30 *'nothing will be withholden from them'*. This is a very strong statement by God Himself talking with His angels and the hosts of heaven. It sounds like mankind was somehow gaining access to supernatural powers. But how? So much so, that God here states that 'man will be able to do anything that he desires to do' if he is not immediately restrained. This sounds ominously similar to what happened in the Garden of Eden just before Adam and Eve were kicked out by God because of their rebellion against Him.

GEN.3:22 And the LORD God said, Behold, the man is become as one of us, to know good and evil: and now, lest he put forth his hand, and take also of the tree of life, and eat, and live for ever:

GEN.3:23 Therefore the LORD God sent him forth from the garden of Eden, to till the ground from whence he was taken.

GEN.3:24 So he drove out the man; and he placed at the east of the garden of Eden Cherubim, and a flaming sword which turned every way, to keep the way of the tree of life.

C.31 Were the Giants working together with Nimrod who himself was also a giant and king of the giants, trying to find the secret to eternal life but without God? Is it just possible that Nimrod and the Giants had inherited 'special powers' from their spiritual and perhaps even physical fathers the 'Fallen angels'? What if Nimrod was not only seeking to build a tall skyscraper, but that the tower had a specific purpose to climb up to heaven and to enter heaven and to replace God with man's Idols and demon gods?

JASHER 9.21 And all the princes of Nimrod and his great men took counsel together; Phut, Mitzraim, Cush and Canaan with their families, and they said to each other, Come let us build ourselves a city and in it a strong tower, and its top reaching heaven, and we will make ourselves famed, so that we may reign upon the whole world, in order that the evil of our enemies may cease from us, that we may reign mightily over them, and that we may not become scattered over the earth on account of their wars.

C.32 Notice that it was the sons of Ham who counselled together with Nimrod, the son of Cush to build the Tower of Babel in rebellion against God. Canaan had already been cursed by Noah and now they all become cursed by building the tower. The Canaanities along with other sons of Ham had obviously been cursed by God and now in their rebellion they brought back the powers of the Nephilim and also brought back the Rephaim giants. Nimrod was the

115

son of Cush, the son of Ham, who somehow 'became a giant'. In other words he had Nephilim (Satan's seed) blood in him.

LXX SEPTUAGINT GENESIS 9.8 'Nimrod began to be a giant upon the earth.' He was a giant hunter before the Lord. The beginning of his kingdom was Babylon and Orech and Archad and Charlanne in the land of Shinar. Out of that land came Assur and built Ninevah. And Misraim (son of Ham) begot the Ludiim and Nephthalim and the Enementiim and the Labiim (races of Giants)

C.33 The sons of Canaan, who himself was a son of Ham, were also of Nephilim (Fallen angel) D.N.A and there were thus giants after the Great flood as well as before the Great flood. The Tower of Babel was built by a race of giants, thus explaining how they managed to build it so high. (8000 feet high in 43 years)

C.34 A stade which is short for stadium and is defined as being 180 meters or 600 feet. One wall was of the tower of Babel is stated in the above verse as 30 stades. This would equal 30 x 600 feet = 18,000 feet. One of the other walls was 13 stades. This equals 13 x 600 = 7800 feet long. Why build a tower with one of the walls as 18,000 feet wide which is over 3 miles wide! Even the lesser wall was around 8000 feet wide. The height was around 10,000 feet high

Now let's look at the size of the bricks mentioned: One wall was 18,000 feet long and it was made up of 203 bricks in its baseline. 1800 divided by 203 gives us single bricks which were around 90 feet long and a 1/3 of 9 for the height = 30 feet. What about the width of each brick? We are not told. Looking at bricks and slabs of stone especially with the foundation stones in mind, generally the width is half the length. Often in modern times the height of bricks is only 1/5 the length. Why did those build the Tower with the measurements given above – that is to say the height of the brick was 1/3 the length? Probably as the width of the stones which is normally as I have mentioned is around half the length. It is possible that in the case of the Tower of Babel as the builders intended to build it exceptionally high that they therefore build the foundation amazingly strong with very big slabs of rock measuring at least 90 feet x 45 feet x 30 feet high. Imagine the people having to lift these stones and assemble millions of them into place to build the Tower of Babel for 43 years. It is stated that over 700,000 workers(slaves) were used to build the Tower. Today in modern times it would be totally impossible to build such a Tower even with modern technology and massive cranes. Something was very different back then! How was the Tower of Babel built? By what sort of amazingly strong people? Well the answer is that the tower was built by giants. It Is even stated that Nimrod the king and orchestrator of the Tower of Babel himself was a Nephilim or a giant son - born of the Fallen angels.

C.35 Have any stones this size ever been found at other locations on the planet? Yes! [At the southern entrance of Baalbeck is a quarry where the stones used in the temples were cut. A huge block, considered the largest hewn stone in the world, still sits where it was cut almost 2,000 years ago.

Called the "Stone of the Pregnant Woman", it is 21.5m (71 feet) x 4.8m(16 feet) x 4.2 meters (14 feet) in size and weighs an estimated 1,000 tons] I have heard of a stone that there is an even bigger slab of stone which is 3000 tons.<**SOURCE**: http://blog.world-mysteries.com/strange-artifacts/the-trylithon-at-baalbeck/

C.36 CONCLUSION: The Tower of Babel was built with stones as big as or even a bit larger than those slabs of rock at Baalbeck. How were the massive slabs of stone moved into place?

SOME OF THE MOST AMAZING CYCLOPIAN STRUCTURES IN THE WORLD:

https://youtu.be/JgomdsVZZM4?list=PL9SHD8shR4ZNmcDkjQ8D6IMN8Z3qzqGRW&t=23

C.37 Could Baalbeck have been one of the quarries from which Nimrod's Giants obtained the massive stones for building the Tower of Babel. Baalbeck is in Lebanon and the Land of the Giants (Shinar) is in Northern Iraq?

C.38 1) How could such Slabs of stone, which are over 1000 tons each, and measuring 90 feet x 30 x 45 (According to the measurements given in this Book of Jubilees) be cut & quarried in the first place?

2) Secondly, how could these gargantuan stones be transported long distance?

3) Thirdly, how could these gargantuan stones even be lifted into place one upon the other?

ANSWER: Apparently those very deeply into the occult and into satanism had the ability of being able to levitate large objects. Maybe, but that still doesn't explain how such massive stones were quarried?

There is a lot of evidence that those of the very far past and I am talking about Pre-Diluvian times used some sort of *crystal* energy similar to lasers of today which enabled them to cut the large stones quickly. Not only are there large slabs of stone as mentioned here, but also many tunnels have been found honey-combing our planet and perfectly formed as by a very strong laser. Obviously, because the giants before the Great Flood had very advanced technology with which they were able to perform feats of engineering that we can only dream of today.

4) Fourthly how could the 700,000 slaves helping to build the Tower of Babel been able to do the gargantuan task? It is possible that massive giants could have been involved but what use would the normal humans have been, in helping to move such massive stones?

It is indeed a very big mystery which no-one so far has been able to fully solve because obviously conditions on the planet were very different in many ways back then. We humans are actually much smaller than humans of the past in direct contradiction to the modern doctrine of Evolution.

C.39 There is much evidence from all over the world of Giant megaliths and pyramids and *giant steps* in Peru that are 12 feet high?! Who would use such steps?

C.40 The grave of Noah and his wife showed that they must have been around 12 feet tall. So it is feasible that there used to be giants of 24 feet and perhaps 35 and even 45 feet high right after the great Flood. Perhaps they were strong enough to move those gargantuan slabs of stone.

C.41 The real date of the Tower of Babel should read [1645 + 347 = 1992 AM = **Anno Mundi' = years of the world**] Abraham was born in 1948 and would have been circa 44 years old years old when the Tower of Babel was built according to the Jewish Book of Jasher. (See my book '**Jasher Insights'**)

C.42 Here is some staggering information about the Tower of Babel, which is described in a lot more detail in the Book of Jasher. See my book Jasher Insights for a lot more details about Nimrod and the Tower of Babel. In this last verse it is stating that the tower of Babel was '*5433 cubits and 2 palms'* A cubit is defined as being between 18-25 inches or say 1 & a half to 2 feet. So, the Tower was somewhere between *8150 to 11,000 feet high!* Quite a skyscraper! It was around 7 times higher than the Twin Towers that also met the same fate. It also mentioned that it took them 43 years to build it.

GEN.11:5 And the LORD came down to see the city and the tower, which the children of men builded.

> 22 Go to, let us go down and confound their language, that they may not understand one another's speech, and they may be dispersed into cities and nations, and one purpose will no longer abide with them till the day of judgment.'

GEN.11:6 And the LORD said, Behold, the people is one, and they have all one language; and this they begin to do: and now nothing will be restrained from them, which they have imagined to do.

GEN.11:7 Go to, let us go down, and there confound their language, that they may not understand one another's speech.

C.43 The above verse '*now nothing will be restrained from them, which they have imagined to do'* is exceptionally strong and meaningful because of what it is implying.

It is in fact stating that unless God 'restrains man and the giants who were building the tower that they might be capable of doing anything monstrous and evil as according to the Book of **Jasher** the people building the Tower were attempting to built it high enough to 'get into heaven' and place their idols there and to take over that domain. Not that demons and giants and fallen angels are any match for God and His angels - they are not but they are very deluded into thinking that they will win the battle of Good versus evil. The Devil and his crowd need to take a very good and long look at **Revelations 12.7**

REV.12:7 And there was **war in heaven**: Michael and his angels fought against the **dragon (Satan)**; and the dragon fought and his angels,

REV.12:8 And prevailed not; neither was their place found any more in heaven.

C.44 A restriction like above was also put on Adam and Eve after their disobedience in the Garden of Eden

GEN.3:22 And the LORD God said, Behold, **the man is become as one of us,** to **know good and evil:** and now, lest he put forth his hand, and take also of the **tree of life**, and eat, and **live for ever**:

GEN.3:23 Therefore the LORD God sent him forth from the garden of Eden, to till the ground from whence he was taken.

GEN.3:24 So he drove out the man; and he placed at the east of the garden of Eden Cherubims, and a flaming sword which turned every way, to keep the way of the **tree of life**.

C.45 Is it just possible that the new 'After the Flood' Giants along with fallen man at the Tower of Babel, thought that they could reach a 'portal in the sky' at a certain altitude and gotten into heaven? Perhaps they thought that somehow if they could have gotten some **fruit** from the **Tree of Life** then that they might live forever. Being as twisted in mind as they indeed were . It would not at all surprise me. In modern times Portals have indeed been discovered in the air and in the sea and down into the ground into the Inner Earth. No wonder God changed the lifespan of mankind at the time of the Great Flood to only 120 years. See what damage mankind had done before the Great Flood when he had lived up to 900 years old.

C.46 Concerning the Giants: Why was that important for them to reach into heaven? Because they themselves were not created by God - so that they were not fully human but a hybrid of humans and Fallen angels and therefore could **not live forever**. They were of Nephilim DNA or Satan's seed. Neither could they find Salvation through the Messiah - because Salvation is only for humans.

C.47 Many would state that the **Tree of Life** is supposed to be inside the **Garden of Eden** which many also believe to be **inside the earth** or inner earth. Look at the following verses from my book '**Enoch Insights'** chapter 25:

*ENOCH 25.4 And as for this fragrant tree, **no mortal is permitted to touch** it till the **great judgement**, when He shall take vengeance on all and bring everything to its consummation for ever. It shall then be given to the righteous and holy.*

*ENOCH 25.5 Its fruit shall be for food to the elect. It shall be **transplanted** to the holy place, to the temple of the Lord, the Eternal King.*

TIMEFRAME: THE HEAVEN AND NEW EARTH – AFTER THE 1000 YEAR GOLDEN AGE (MILLENNIAL) RULE OF THE MESSIAH & HIS SAINTS

REV.22:2 In the midst of the street of it, and on either side of the river, was there the **Tree of Life**, which bare twelve manner of fruits, and yielded her fruit every month: and the leaves of the tree were for the **healing of the nations**.

C.48 God certainly didn't want those at the Tower of Babel in their 'depraved state' to gain the ability to 'live forever' and be spreading their evil around just like the Fallen angels who also live forever - and so as God said above: *'let us go down, and there confound their language, that they may not understand one another's speech'*

C.49 Wow, these deluded 'fallen state' peoples had no idea that their 'one language' which they all spoke and was Hebrew - the language of Creation - could be 'confused by God Himself in just a moment of time, leaving them helpless and forced to scatter all over the world, as they could no longer understand each other's language.

> 23 And the Lord descended, and we descended with him to see the city and the tower which the children of men had built.
>
> 24 And he confounded their language, and they no longer understood one another's speech, and they ceased then to build the city and the tower.
>
> 25 For this reason the whole land of Shinar is called Babel, because the Lord did there confound all the language of the children of men, and from thence they were dispersed into their cities, each according to his language and his nation.

GEN.11:8 So the LORD scattered them abroad from thence upon the face of all the earth: and they left off to build the city.

GEN.11:9 Therefore is the name of it called Babel; because the LORD did there confound the language of all the earth: and from thence did the LORD scatter them abroad upon the face of all the earth.

> 26 And the Lord sent a mighty wind against the tower and overthrew it upon the earth, and behold it was between Asshur and Babylon in the land of Shinar, and they called its name 'Overthrow'.

C.50 What kind of a wind could blow down a mighty tower over 8000 feet high? Obviously, the wind must have been accompanied by earthquakes and the land subsiding, causing the Tower to collapse.

> 27 In the fourth week in the first year [1688 A.M. = **'Anno Mundi'** = **years of the world**] in the beginning thereof in the four and thirtieth

120

jubilee, were they dispersed from the land of Shinar.

JASHER 9.38 And as to the tower which the sons of men built, the earth opened its mouth and swallowed up one third part thereof, and a fire also descended from heaven and burned another third, and the other third is left to this day, and it is of that part which was aloft, and its circumference is three days' walk.

C.51 According to the Bible the Great Flood occurred in 1658 A.M. = '**Anno Mundi' = years of the world** and not [1328 years A.M.] as given by this Book of Jubilees.

28 And Ham and his sons went into the land which he was to occupy, which he acquired as his portion in the land of the south.

29 And Canaan saw the land of Lebanon to the river of Egypt, that it was very good, and he went not into the land of his inheritance to the west (that is to) the sea, and he dwelt in the land of Lebanon, eastward and westward from the border of Jordan and from the border of the sea.

30 And Ham, his father, and Cush and Mizraim his brothers said unto him: 'Thou hast settled in a land which is not thine, and which did not fall to us by lot: do not do so; for if thou dost do so, thou and thy sons will fall in the land and (be) accursed through sedition; for by sedition ye have settled, and by sedition will thy children fall, and thou shalt be rooted out for ever.

C.52 This is an important point in time as it shows Canaan going against what Noah had originally told his sons when he divided up the lands and Canaan forcibly took over the lands that were supposed to go to the Semites. Canaan had already been cursed directly by Noah and here we see Canaan being cursed yet again by his own father and brethren for taking over the land of Shem. Of course, this caused lots of problems that we shall now read about.

31 Dwell not in the dwelling of Shem; for to Shem and to his sons did it come by their lot.

32 Cursed art thou, and cursed shalt thou be beyond all the sons of Noah, by the curse by which we bound ourselves by an oath in the presence of the holy judge, and in the presence of Noah our father.'

33 But he did not harken unto them and dwelt in the land of Lebanon

> from Hamath to the entering of Egypt, he and his sons until this day.

C.53 This well explains why the descendants of Canaan were cursed and the Canaanites actually became the new Giants in the land. The Canaanites somehow gained Nephilim D.N.A as before the Great Flood and giants were born unto their women.

> 34 And for this reason that land is named Canaan. And Japheth and his sons went towards the sea and dwelt in the land of their portion, and Madai saw the land of the sea and it did not please him, and he begged a (portion) from Ham and Asshur and Arpachshad, his wife's brother, and he dwelt in the land of Media, near to his wife's brother until this day.
>
> 35 And he called his dwelling-place, and the dwelling-place of his sons, Media, after the name of their father Madai.

C.54 For more very interesting details about the Tower of Babel see my book **'JASHER INSIGHTS'**.

C.55 Modern structural engineers who have built the world's largest structures talk about one day making a building as high as Mt Everest or over 8000 meters (30,000 feet) : https://www.businessinsider.com.au/someday-we-could-build-a-skyscraper-taller-than-mount-everest-2012-8

C.56 COMPARISON OF THE 'TOWER OF BABEL' WITH THE 'TWIN TOWERS'

Recapping on what we talked about above: 'One wall of the tower of Babel is stated in the above verse as 30 stades. This would equal 30 x 600 feet = 18000 feet. One of the other walls was 13 stades. This equals 13 x 600 = 7800 feet long. Why build a tower with one of the walls as 18,000 feet wide which is over 3 miles wide Even the lesser wall was around 8000 feet wide. The height was around 10,000 feet high. If one was to compare the dimensions of the Twin Towers with the Tower of Babel, we come up with some remarkable facts: The Twin Towers were over 400 meters high or around 1400 feet high. The base of the Twin Towers was around 60m (200 feet) x 30 m (100 feet) The Base (Length x breadth x height) Ratio was 2:1:14. The base/height ratio of the Tower of Babel on the other hand was approx. 2:1:2 In other words, the height of the Tower of Babel that was built with such gargantuan stone blocks, of up to 90 feet long and 20 feet high and 30 feet wide, could have been at least 10 times higher as compared to the Twin Towers. If the base wall of the Twin Towers was only 200 feet and the base wall of the tower of Babel 18,000 feet. The base wall of the Tower of Babel was around 90 times wider than the base of the Twin towers widest side! the Tower of Babel was around 10,000 feet high and clearly 'uncompleted', then it could have been built to being over 90,000 feet high or maybe even much

122

higher! That is just comparing it with the Twin Towers. However, the Tower of Babel was built with stronger 'mountain materials' of solid gargantuan slabs of stone. The Twin Towers was made of re-enforced concreate with iron-girders. Only God Himself knows how high that Tower of Babel could have grown to, if He hadn't intervened to stop the Giants and their Tower of Babel.

C.57 MORE CONCLUSIONS CONCERNING THE TOWER OF BABEL

My personal opinion concerning the Tower of Babel is the following. A lot more than Nimrod and 700,000 human slaves and Giants were involved in the building of this Tower. They were up to something much more important than just building a Tower to reach the Sky. But what exactly? Let's consider the following:

1) God had wiped out the Pre-Flood Giants and humans by a Great Flood

2) The dead Giants became the 'disembodied spirits of the Giants' or better known today as demons.

3) After the Flood these demonic spirits started to plague mankind.

4) The demons wanted revenge for having been locked up in the negative spirit world inside the earth but in a lower dimension.

5) Their only way to come back to the earth was to possess both people, but better still possess Chimeras. A creature that God simply had not made. This had been common practice before the Great Flood

6) It is stated that Nimrod the king, became a Giant. How we are not told, except it could have been in his D.N.A and was initially dormant, when he was young but made itself manifest when he was an adult.

7) According to the Books of Jasher and Jubilees as well as the Bible, those in charge of building the Tower of Babel wanted to 'ascend into heaven' and replace God. They wanted to put their Idols in heaven instead. They also wanted to kill all the 'hosts of heaven'. Obviously, these 'disembodied malignant spirits of the Giants' wanted revenge for them having been forcibly locked up in hell and sought a new location and these are the heavenly realms.

8) When Nimrod, who was a descendant of Ham came onto the scene, the disembodied spirits of the Giants had their chance, as they 'possessed the descendants of Ham' and again new generations of giants were born in the land of Canaan.

9) Now that the Giants were back in the physical plane, they were now seeking for a way to get into the heavenly dimensions. They somehow thought that if they could build a Tower high enough then they would reach Heaven and kick God out. I know that sounds very stupid to us in modern times, but is it? Perhaps and almost certainly, the giants knew about the Portals as mentioned in the Book of Enoch

10) In looking at the dimensions described in this **Book of Jubilees of the Tower of Babel**, where the base was 18,000 feet across and around 8000 feet wide, and around 10,000 high. With a base that big, the Tower of Babel

could have been constructed to end up being very much higher. How high did the builders want to go, or should I say get to? That is a mystery. Perhaps there is a Portal at a certain height in the sky over the Land of Shinar which is in northern Iraq, and not far from where the original fallen angels came down onto mount Hermon before the Great Flood and made love with the human women and started having Giants for sons.

11) COMPARING LAND AREA USED TO BUILD THE TOWER OF BABEL TO MODERN CITIES AROUND THE WORLD TODAY

The New York City metro area is approximately 5395 square miles. (8683 km)

Tokyo/Yokohama is approximately 4345 square miles. (6993 km)

Chicago is approximately 3416 square miles. (5498 km)

The Tower of Babel was approximately 225 miles in circumference. (450 km)

If my math was correct, then The Tower of Babel was approximately 4028 square miles. (6482 km)

The big difference is that modern cities are spread out much more laterally than built vertically, while the tower of Babel was one massive tower that could have been as high as 11000 feet or 10 times higher than the highest buildings on earth today - that went straight up to far above the clouds.

12) Many Portals have been detected in modern times and some have been detected in the skies. A spiral portal in Norway comes to mind.

13) Fortunately, God and His angels came down and ruined the plans of the Giants, and I believe that the giants were mostly killed off and the humans dispersed all over the planet as God confused their tongues and languages.

Chapter 11: WARS BEGIN AGAIN

1 And in the thirty-fifth jubilee, in the third week, in the first year [1681 A.M. = **'Anno Mundi' = years of the world**] thereof, Reu took to himself a wife, and her name was 'Ora, the daughter of 'Ur, the son of Kesed, and she bare him a son, and he called his name Seroh, in the seventh year of this week in this jubilee. [1687 A.M.]

Comment:1: Again, these dates do not match those given in the Biblical Time charts. According to the biblical time charts Reu had his first born in the year 1819 A.M.

2 And the sons of Noah began to war on each other, to take captive and to slay each other, and to shed the blood of men on the earth, and to eat blood, and to build strong cities, and walls, and towers, and individuals (began) to exalt themselves above the nation, and to found the beginnings of kingdoms, and to go to war people against people, and nation against nation, and city against city, and all (began) to do evil, and to acquire arms, and to teach their sons war, and they began to capture cities, and to sell male and female slaves.

C.2 What was the single-most factor that caused mankind to start making wars against each other after the Great Flood? Well, according to scripture, it is always PRIDE & CONTENTION. Look at the following amazing Bible verses from the book of James, that really nail the topic in the head:

JAM.4:1 From whence come **wars** and **fighting** among you? come they not hence, even of your **lusts** that **war** in your **members**?

JAM.4:2 Ye **lust**, and have not: ye **kill**, and **desire to have**, and **cannot obtain**: ye **fight** and **war**, yet ye have not, because ye ask not.

JAM.4:3 Ye ask, and receive not, because ye ask amiss, that ye may **consume** it upon your **lusts.**

JAM.4:4 Ye **adulterers** and **adulteresses,** know ye not that the friendship of the world is enmity with God? whosoever therefore will be a **friend of the world** is the **enemy of God**.

JAM.4:5 Do ye think that the scripture saith in vain, the **spirit** that dwelleth in us **lusts to envy?**

JAM.4:6 But he giveth more grace. Wherefore he saith, God resists the **proud**, but giveth **grace** unto the **humble**.

JAM.4:7 **Submit** yourselves therefore **to God. Resist the Devil**, and he will flee from you.

C.3 Talking about the great monster on the planet and within the planet the **Great Red Dragon Satan** himself, according to **Revelation 12.7**. **Satan** is the one who stirs up contentions & wars, inciting the nations through **PRIDE**.

REV.12:7 And there was **war** in heaven: Michael and his angels fought against the **dragon**; and the **dragon fought and his angels**.

JOB.41:33 Upon earth there is not his like, who is made **without fear**.

JOB.41:34 He beholds (exalts) all **high things**: he is a **king** over **all the children of pride**.

---

3 And 'Ur, the son of Kesed, built the city of 'Ara of the Chaldees, and called its name after his own name and the name of his father.

4 And they made for themselves molten images, and they worshipped each the idol, the molten image which they had made for themselves, and they began to make graven images and unclean simulacra, and malignant spirits assisted and seduced (them) into committing transgression and uncleanness.

C.4 a) **'graven images and unclean simulacra'.** Here it is clearly talking about two different things although somewhat similar. What is the difference between graven images and Simulacra? Apparently, by using special incantations and sorcery or witchcraft *certain idols* of the gods and demi-gods would sometimes *actually appear alive* and seem to come alive to their *worshippers* and followers. This has been clearly shown in certain movies about the Demi-gods.

C.5 b) **'malignant spirits assisted and seduced (them) into committing transgression and uncleanness'.** Here we see how that the 'disembodied spirits of the Giants' clearly became the demons or 'malignant spirits' which started to plague mankind after the Great Flood, and they started to seduce mankind into 'transgression and uncleanness'.

---

5 And the prince Mastema exerted himself to do all this, and he sent forth other spirits, those which were put under his hand, to do all manner of wrong and sin, and all manner of transgression, to corrupt and destroy and to shed blood upon the earth.

C.6 People need to realise that Mastema or Satan is never the friend of mankind. He is nothing but a deceiver and his ultimate goal is to destroy all of God's creation including all the people on the planet. People who so-called befriend Satan, even unknowingly, are putting themselves in mortal danger. Satan loves to set people up for a very big fall one way or the other. Satan tempts people to commit crimes and then turns right around and accuses and condemns them for those crimes. In many cases driving people to insanity and even demon possession and even suicide. He uses and then abuses his victims. For this reason, it is very important to have a strong faith in God and His Son Jesus the Messiah.

> 6 For this reason he called the name of Seroh Serug, for everyone turned to do all manner of sin and transgression.

C.7 It wasn't even 250 years after the Great Flood that mankind again went astray as before the Great Flood, and it was in the days of both Peleg and his grandson Serug, that the Tower of Babel was built by Nimrod's people & which was a great transgression against God.

> 7 And he grew up, and dwelt in Ur of the Chaldees, near to the father of his wife's mother, and he worshipped idols, and he took to himself a wife in the thirty-sixth jubilee, in the fifth week, in the first year thereof, [1744 A.M. = **Anno Mundi' = years of the world**] and her name was Melka, the daughter of Kaber, the daughter of his father's brother.
>
> 8 And she bare him Nahor in the first year of this week, and he grew and dwelt in Ur of the Chaldees, and his father taught him the researches of the Chaldees to divine and augur, according to the signs of heaven.

C.8 'taught him the researches of the Chaldees to divine and augur, according to the signs of heaven'. Here it is clearly talking about the link between astrology, witchcraft and sorcery. Astrology in itself is not bad, and is merely the study of the stars and how they influence mankind. God having afforded 12 basic star signs to mankind in order to make diversity in the characters of the humans. However, if the knowledge of astrology causes awe to the beholders when the star-gazers and prognosticators prophecy things that cause fear then astrology is being used for the dark side, and can even use spells and incantations. Almost all of Satan's power of witchcraft is in using and instilling fear in his subjects one way or the other. The ancient kings all had their astrologers and magicians. Notice that in the Book of Daniel it states that Daniel and his three countrymen Shadrach, Meshech and Abednego were ten times wiser than the soothsayers according to King Nebuchadnezzar.

DAN.1:19 And the king communed with them; and among them all was found none like Daniel, Hananiah, Mishael, and Azariah: therefore stood they before the king.

DAN.1:20 And in all matters of wisdom and understanding, that the king enquired of them, he found them **ten times better than all the magicians and astrologers** that were in all his realm.

> 9 And in the thirty-seventh jubilee in the sixth week, in the first year

thereof, [1800 A.M.] he took to himself a wife, and her name was 'Ijaska, the daughter of Nestag of the Chaldees.

10 And she bare him Terah in the seventh year of this week. [1806 A.M.]

11 And the prince Mastema sent ravens and birds to devour the seed which was sown in the land, in order to destroy the land, and rob the children of men of their labours. Before they could plough in the seed, the ravens picked (it) from the surface of the ground.

12 And for this reason he called his name Terah because the ravens and the birds reduced them to destitution and devoured their seed.

13 And the years began to be barren, owing to the birds, and they devoured all the fruit of the trees from the trees: it was only with great effort that they could save a little of all the fruit of the earth in their days.

C.9 The fruit of wickedness and disobedience of part of Shem's descendants: Serug and his son Nahor and his son Terah resulted in the curse of the Ravens devouring the seeds in the fields and thus causing famine in the land.

14 And in this thirty-ninth jubilee, in the second week in the first year, [1870 A.M.] Terah took to himself a wife, and her name was 'Edna, the daughter of 'Abram, the daughter of his father's sister.

15 And in the seventh year of this week [1876 A.M.] she bare him a son, and he called his name Abram, by the name of the father of his mother; for he had died before his daughter had conceived a son.

16 And the child began to understand the errors of the earth that all went astray after graven images and after uncleanness, and his father taught him writing, and he was two weeks of years old, [1890 A.M.] and he separated himself from his father, that he might not worship idols with him.

C.10 Finally a son is born in the Shem lineage, who sought after God, and also emphatically decried the Idol-worshipping of both his father, grand-father and great-grand-father. Because of Abraham's obedience many were made righteous. Indeed, the promised nation of Israel came forth from Abraham because of his righteousness, after God had severely tested him on at least ten occasions.

17 And he began to pray to the Creator of all things that He might save him from the errors of the children of men, and that his portion should not fall into error after uncleanness and vileness.

18 And the seed time came for the sowing of seed upon the land, and they all went forth together to protect their seed against the ravens, and Abram went forth with those that went, and the child was a lad of fourteen years.

19 And a cloud of ravens came to devour the seed, and Abram ran to meet them before they settled on the ground and cried to them before they settled on the ground to devour the seed, and said, ' Descend not: return to the place whence ye came,' and they proceeded to turn back.

20 And he caused the clouds of ravens to turn back that day seventy times, and of all the ravens throughout all the land where Abram was there settled there not so much as one.

C.11 Because of his obedience to God at the young age of fourteen, God listened to the voice and prayers of Abraham; and obviously rebuked Mastema and his horrid ravens and sent them away. The name of Abraham or Abram as he was still called when only fourteen years of age was much set-by, by the people of the Chaldees.

21 And all who were with him throughout all the land saw him cry out, and all the ravens turn back, and his name became great in all the land of the Chaldees.

22 And there came to him this year all those that wished to sow, and he went with them until the time of sowing ceased: and they sowed their land, and that year they brought enough grain home and eat and were satisfied.

23 And in the first year of the fifth week [1891 A.M.] Abram taught those who made implements for oxen, the artificers in wood, and they made a vessel above the ground, facing the frame of the plough, in order to put the seed thereon, and the seed fell down therefrom upon the share of the plough, and was hidden in the earth, and they no longer

feared the ravens.

C.12 Abraham taught mankind how to use a *'fairly modern type of plough'* which cut the earth open and at the same time introduced the seeds into the hole in the ground and covered the hole again; thus prohibiting the birds and in particular the ravens from devouring the sown seeds which had been a plague sent by Mastema (Satan). Abraham was obviously guided by God Himself and His agents the angels of God to know how to both get rid of the attacking pest of the ravens and to also build a better plough. This amazing knowledge given to Abraham 4000 years ago of how to make a more modern plough where the seeds didn't get lost or fall by the wayside, but that all the seeds got planted underground and immediately covered up with earth! Wow! What happened to that very knowledge?

C.13 Notice how that by New Testament times 2000 years after Abraham, mankind had forgotten the use of the above-mentioned type of plough, as designed by Abraham, even though it was clearly much better than the 'old fashioned way' of just digging holes and scattering the seeds by hand. This was clearly illustrated in the New Testament by Jesus Himself the normal way in his time as to how to plant seeds in the ground. It was illustrated aptly in the parable of the sower:

MAT.13:3 And he spoke many things unto them in parables, saying, Behold, a sower went forth to sow;

MAT.13:4 And when he sowed, some seeds fell by the wayside, and the fowls came and devoured them **up.** *(Just like the ravens in Abram's time)*

MAT.13:5 Some fell upon stony places, where they had not much earth: and forthwith they sprung up, because they had no deepness of earth:

MAT.13:6 And when the sun was up, they were scorched; and because they had no root, they withered away.

MAT.13:7 And some fell among thorns; and the thorns sprung up, and choked them:

MAT.13:8 But other fell into good ground, and brought forth fruit, some an hundredfold, some sixtyfold, some thirtyfold.

MAT.13:9 Who hath ears to hear, let him hear.

C.14 Modern ploughing today is in fact similar to Abraham's idea of plough-ing, using a machine that both digs furrows & turns over the earth at the same time as planting the seeds under the ground, and thus zero loss of the seeds. Quite an amazing story about Abraham.

It would seem that when a righteous man like Abraham lived, then God poured out more blessings of godly knowledge which was very helpful at that particular time. 1) To drive away the pests of the ravens 2) Create a machine that protects the seeds from being devoured again by the ravens.

Unfortunately, it would also seem, that mankind has often lost very important knowledge due to his wickedness and arrogant blatant disobedience against God. Man has learned many things over and over again.

C.15 ANCIENT KNOWLEDGE DESTROYED Man has written things down and even put his discovered knowledge into countless books, which were then assembled in libraries until there were more than a million books. Such was the case at the Grecian Library in Alexandria in Egypt in the times before Christ. That library apparently contained much of the ancient knowledge. Then some new leader or religion arises that decided it does not like the ancient knowledge. Some leader insists that they would prefer to keep future generations in the *dark*, so they burned all the books at Alexandria. How many times has that happened throughout history?

C.16 DEAD SEA SCROLLS That was probably why we have the **Dead Sea Scrolls**. A Jewish sect around 100 A.D. decided to hide the ancient scrolls in a cave because they were afraid of the Romans destroying the books. It is wonderful that a small Arab boy found the Dead Sea Scrolls in a cave in Israel in around 1949. Just that one discovery has enlightened the world through the many books that were revealed. Finding the Dead Sea Scrolls proved that many apocryphal books were originally written in Hebrew and thus were indeed genuine according to Jewish scholars thinking.

C.17 FIFTEEN APOCRYPHAL BOOKS REMOVED FROM THE BIBLE IN 1885. In 1885 fifteen of the Apocryphal books were taken out of the King James version of the Bible under the pretext that because they were supposedly not written in Hebrew then they must be fake. Well the discovery of the Dead Sea Scrolls in 1949 *proved them wrong* as many of the apocryphal books were found in the original Hebrew including the books of **Enoch, II Ezdras, Sirach** and many others.

ECC.2:26 For God giveth to a man that is good in his sight wisdom, and knowledge, and joy: but to the sinner he giveth travail, to gather and to heap up, that he may give to him that is good before God. This also is vanity and vexation of spirit.

> 24 And after this manner they made (vessels) above the ground on all the frames of the ploughs, and they sowed and tilled all the land, according as Abram commanded them, and they no longer feared the birds.

Chapter 12: ABRAHAM

Comment:1: Abraham was a very unusual man who followed God, in spite of the fact that his ancestors being Serug his great grand-father, Nahor his grandfather, and Terah his father were all Idol worshippers. Abraham was an Idol smasher. Quite a feat considering the 10 Commandments as given by God to Moses didn't happen for another 500 years from the time of Abraham. 'The Tenth Commandment', was: 'Thus shalt *not worship any graven images*'. (See Appendix for more on IDOL WORSHIPPING)

1 And it came to pass in the sixth week, in the seventh year thereof, [1904 A.M. = **Anno Mundi' = years of the world**] that Abram said to Terah his father, saying, 'Father!' And he said, 'Behold, here am I, my son.'

2 And he said, 'What help and profit have we from those idols which thou dost worship, And before which thou dost bow thyself.

3 For there is no spirit in them, For they are dumb forms, and a misleading of the heart. Worship them not:

4 Worship the God of heaven, Who causes the rain and the dew to descend on the earth And does everything upon the earth,

And has created everything by His word, And all life is from before His face.

5 Why do ye worship things that have no spirit in them For they are the work of (men's) hands, And on your shoulders do ye bear them, And ye have no help from them, But they are a great cause of shame to those who make them, And a misleading of the heart to those who worship them: Worship them not.'

6 And his father said unto him, I also know it, my son, but what shall I do with a people who have made me to serve before them.

7 And if I tell them the truth, they will slay me; for their soul cleaves to them to worship them and honour them.

8 Keep silent, my son, lest they slay thee.'

9 These words he spoke to his two brothers, and they were angry with him and he kept silent. And in the fortieth jubilee, in the second week, in the seventh year thereof, [1925 A.M.] Abram took to himself a wife, and her name was Sarai, the daughter of his father, and she became his wife.

10 And Haran, his brother, took to himself a wife in the third year of the third week, [1928 A.M.] and she bare him a son in the seventh year of this week, [1932 A.M.] and he called his name Lot.

11 And Nahor, his brother, took to himself a wife.

12 And in the sixtieth year of the life of Abram, that is, in the fourth week, in the fourth year thereof, [1936 A.M.] Abram arose by night, and burned the house of the idols, and he burned all that was in the house and no man knew it.

13 And they arose in the night and sought to save their gods from the midst of the fire.

14 And Haran hasted to save them, but the fire flamed over him, and he was burnt in the fire, and he died in Ur of the Chaldees before Terah his father, and they buried him in Ur of the Chaldees.

15 And Terah went forth from Ur of the Chaldees, he and his sons, to go into the land of Lebanon and into the land of Canaan, and he dwelt in the land of Haran, and Abram dwelt with Terah his father in Haran two weeks of years.

16 And in the sixth week, in the fifth year thereof, [1951 A.M.] Abram sat up throughout the night on the new moon of the seventh month to observe the stars from the evening to the morning, in order to see what would be the character of the year with regard to the rains, and he was alone as he sat and observed.

17 And a word came into his heart and he said: All the signs of the stars, and the signs of the moon and of the sun are all in the hand of the Lord. Why do I search (them) out?

18 If He desires, He causes it to rain, morning and evening; And if He desires, He withholds it, And all things are in his hand.'

19 And he prayed that night and said, 'My God, God Most High, Thou alone art my God, And Thee and Thy dominion have I chosen. And Thou hast created all things, And all things that are the work of thy hands.

20 Deliver me from the hands of evil spirits who have dominion over the thoughts of men's hearts, And let them not lead me astray from Thee, my God. And stablish Thou me and my seed for ever That we go not astray from henceforth and for evermore.'

C.2 Abraham was very conscious of the fact that evil spirits can have access & even dominion over the thoughts of mankind; especially when mankind doesn't bother to pray and take notice of God and His Holy Spirit, but proudly goes ahead in his own thoughts and in his own strength.

EPH.6:12 For we wrestle not against flesh and blood, but against principalities, against powers, against the rulers of the darkness of this world, against spiritual wickedness in high places.

C.3 The rulers of the earth have become just like the bad spirits that they entertain:

PSA.73:8 They are corrupt and speak wickedly concerning oppression: they speak loftily.

PSA.73:9 They set their mouth against the heavens, and their tongue walketh through the earth.

21 And he said, 'Shall I return unto Ur of the Chaldees who seek my face that I may return to them, am I to remain here in this place The right path before Thee prosper it in the hands of Thy servant that he may fulfil (it) and that I may not walk in the deceitfulness of my heart, O my God.'

JER.17:9 The heart is deceitful above all things, and desperately wicked: who can know it?

22 And he made an end of speaking and praying and behold the word of the Lord was sent to him through me, saying: 'Get thee up from thy country, and from thy kindred and from the house of thy father unto a land which I will show thee, and I shall make thee a great and numerous

nation.

23 And I will bless thee, And I will make thy name great, And thou shalt be blessed in the earth, And in Thee shall all families of the earth be blessed, And I will bless them that bless thee, And curse them that curse thee.

24 And I will be a God to thee and thy son, and to thy son's son, and to all thy seed: fear not, from henceforth and unto all generations of the earth I am thy God.'

GEN.12:1 Now the LORD had said unto Abram, Get thee out of thy country, and from thy kindred, and from thy father's house, unto a land that I will shew thee:

GEN.12:2 And I will make of thee a great nation, and I will bless thee, and make thy name great; and thou shalt be a blessing:

GEN.12:3 And I will bless them that bless thee and curse him that curse thee: and in thee shall all families of the earth be blessed.

25 And the Lord God said: 'Open his mouth and his ears, that he may hear and speak with his mouth, with the language which has been revealed'; for it had ceased from the mouths of all the children of men from the day of the overthrow (of Babel).

C.4 *'Open his mouth and his ears, that he may hear and speak with his mouth, with the language which has been revealed.'* Here God is stating that the *'language of Hebrew which was the original language of Creation as spoken by Adam and Eve',* had been taken away from mankind at the 'time of the confusion of tongues' caused by God Himself at the Tower of Babel; and that now God was giving back the Hebrew language to Abraham.

26 And I opened his mouth, and his ears and his lips, and I began to speak with him in Hebrew in the tongue of the creation.

C.5 *'Hebrew: in the tongue of the creation'.* Now that is a very revealing bit of information, that the first language ever spoken upon earth by Adam and Eve was Hebrew and was thus the language of all mankind prior to the Great Flood.

27And he took the books of his fathers, and these were written in Hebrew, and he transcribed them, and he began from henceforth to study them, and I made known to him that which he could not (understand), and he studied them during the six rainy months.

C.6 This verse is also revealing what is in fact is quite staggering! God is saying that *Abraham's ancestors* used to *write books* in the *Hebrew language*. He also just stated that the language of Hebrew hadn't been available since the time of the Tower of Babel, which happened around 200 years after the Flood. What does that mean? The only writer who came from Pre-Flood times and was still alive at the time of the tower of Babel was Noah. Here's where it gets interesting: If Noah lost the Hebrew language at the time of the Tower of Babel, then any books written in Hebrew had to have been written down before the Tower of Babel. There are only two writers mentioned in scriptures who could have qualified for the above description given by God of: **'books of his fathers, and these were written in Hebrew':** One was Noah and the other was Noah's great-grandfather Enoch. (See my book '**Enoch Insights',** as it also has around *5-6 chapters included*, which were *written by Noah*.)

C.7 '**He began from henceforth to study them'** (The Books of Enoch & the Books of Noah), **and I (Angel) 'made known to him that which he could not (understand)'.**

What this is saying is really very important. The angel of the Lord is stating that he taught Abraham both the original language of creation, being Hebrew, and he also helped him to understand the ancient Books of both Noah and Enoch. Why did God go to all the trouble of teaching Abraham how to read the Books of Noah and Enoch, (through his angel), unless these books were very important?

C.8 Since I came to discover the Book of Enoch around 7 years ago, I immediately sensed that this **book is invaluable in 'connecting the dots'** between our **modern times** and the **most ancient past**; The Book of Enoch shows greater details than that merely afforded by the Bible itself.

C.9 This makes it essential for every Bible student to study the **Book of Enoch**. We fortunately do still have a copy of the Book of Enoch which just happens to include some of the chapters from Noah's book. However, at least so far, we do not have a complete Book of Noah available today in modern times to the best of my knowledge.

---

28 And it came to pass in the seventh year of the sixth week [1953 A.M. = **Anno Mundi' = years of the world**] that he spoke to his father and informed him, that he would leave Haran to go into the land of Canaan to see it and return to him.

29 And Terah his father said unto him; Go in peace:

May the eternal God make thy path straight. And the Lord [(be) with thee, and] protect thee from all evil, And grant unto thee grace, mercy and favour before those who see thee, And may none of the children of men have power over thee to harm thee; Go in peace.

---

30 And if thou see a land pleasant to thy eyes to dwell in, then arise and take me to thee and take

31 Lot with thee, the son of Haran thy brother as thine own son: the Lord be with thee. And Nahor thy brother leave with me till thou return in peace, and we go with thee all together.'

Chapter 13: SHECHEM

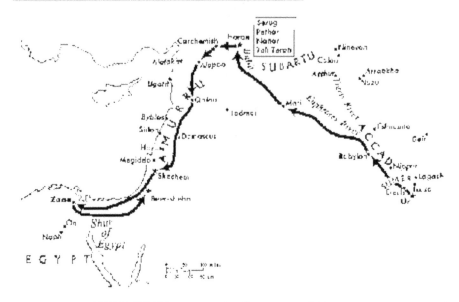

Comment:1: SHECHEM These are the first steps of Abram on the pages of Scripture as Abram enters the land of Canaan. From Ur, across the Fertile Crescent and down into Canaan, the Bible mentions Shechem as the first city to which Abram came (**GEN 12.6**)

[https://bible.org/article/geographical-historical-spiritual-significance-shechem]

GEN.12:6 And Abram passed through the land unto the place of Sichem (Shechem), unto the plain of Moreh. And the Canaanite was then in the land.

> 1 And Abram journeyed from Haran, and he took Sarai, his wife, and Lot, his brother Haran's son, to the land of Canaan, and he came into Asshur, and proceeded to Shechem, and dwelt near a lofty oak.

GEN.12:5 And Abram took Sarai his wife, and Lot his brother's son, and all their substance that they had gathered, and the souls that they had gotten in Haran; and they went forth to go into the land of Canaan; and into the land of Canaan they came.

C.2 It is important to take note that it was when Abraham came to *Shechem* and pitched his tent under a lofty oak tree, that God promised to give him all the land that was around him, and in fact promised the land to his descendants the Children of Israel.

> 2 And he saw, and, behold, the land was very pleasant from the entering of Hamath to the lofty oak.

> 3 And the Lord said to him: 'To thee and to thy seed will I give this land.' And he built an altar there, and he offered thereon a burnt sacrifice to the Lord, who had appeared to him.

GEN.12:7 And the LORD appeared unto Abram, and said, Unto thy seed will I give this land: and there builded he an altar unto the LORD, who appeared unto him.

C.3 Who was it who actually appeared unto Abraham? Was it God the Father or was it God the Son?

JOH.1:18 No man hath **seen** God (The Father) at any time, the only begotten Son, which is in the bosom of the Father, he hath **declared** him.

C.4 Notice how John who received from Jesus in heaven the Book of the Revelation - stated in his early Gospel in the New Testament that *'No man hath seen God' (The Father) at any time* …John then goes on to state that the only begotten Son of God (**JESUS**), which is in the bosom of the Father …**He** hath declared **Him (God the Father)**.

C.5 Is it not likely therefore, that it has been **Jesus**, the **Son of God -the Messiah** and **not** God the Father who appeared unto the prophets and the patriarchs and even unto Adam and Eve in the Garden of Eden… as no man hath seen God (The Father) at any time and lived.

C.6 After the Great Flood, Noah had divided the earth into three sections and given one to each of his sons. However, Canaan the grandson of Noah disobeyed, and took over part of the lands promised to Shem's descendants. In the above verse we see God Himself reiterating that this land does in fact belong to both Abraham (descendant of Shem) and his descendants. This is why in later times Israel adamantly drove out the Canaanites in the times of both Moses and Joshua around 500 years after Abraham's time.

> 5 And he removed from thence unto the mountain . . . Bethel on the west and Ai on the east and pitched his tent there.

C.7 The areas in Canaan which Abram spent most of his life were along the Route of the Patriarchs, namely in Shechem, Bethel and Ai (12:8; 13:2), Hebron (13:18; 14:13), and in the Negev (13:1; 20:1, notably Gerar).

> 6 And he saw and behold, the land was very wide and good, and everything grew thereon: vines and figs and pomegranates, oaks and **ilexes** (holly), and **terebinths** (and oil trees, and cedars and cypresses and date trees, and all trees of the field, and there was water on the mountains.

C.8 Def. of the **terebinth**--Pistacia terebinthus (Natural Order, Anacardiaceae), Arabic Butm]--is a tree allied to the P. vera, which produces the pistachio nut, and to the familiar "pepper tree" (Schinus molle) so extensively cultivated in modern Palestine. Like the latter the terebinth has red berries, like small immature grapes. The leaves are pinnate, four to six pairs, and they change color and fall in autumn, leaving the trunk bare (Isaiah 1.:30)

> 7 And he blessed the Lord who had led him out of Ur of the Chaldees and had brought him to this land.
>
> 8 And it came to pass in the first year, in the seventh week, on the *new moon of the first month, 1954 A.M. = Anno Mundi' = years of the world] that he built an altar on this mountain, and called on the name of the Lord: 'Thou, the eternal God, art my God.'

C.9 In Modern times we do know that the **moon** effects the **TIDES** twice a day. What about the '**Phases of the moon**' Do they have influence?.

Some hairdressers even in modern times state the following: *'Lunar hair care is one way that astrology fans have incorporated the **power of the stars** into their recent self-care practices. It involves syncing hair trims with the **lunar cycles**, letting cosmic timing set the pace of an otherwise mundane task.'* (https://www.mindbodygreen.com/0-21990/lunar-hair-care-cutting-your-hair-by-the-moons-phases.html)

C.10 Women's **menstrual cycle** is apparently influenced by the moon's **28 day cycle**. Babies are **conceived in the middle of the cycle**.

So the moon has a lot of influence on the **reproduction** of all of **Creation**

C.11 I may not personally agree with everything that is written in the following article, but I did find it fascinating and very inform-ative: '**Are people's feelings or spirits influenced by the phases of the moon'**?: http://thespiritscience.net/2016/06/21/the-connection-between-the-moon-cycles-and-your-mood/

C.12 The Lord himself put a lot of emphasis on ancient Israel keeping the different Festivals on the **NEW MOON** but why? Did the **phase of the moon** influence the different **festivals?**

One was called the '**Festival of the First Fruits**' and thus plants and fruits were involved.

Many gardeners state that **plants and vegetables grow better** if planted either at the **new moon** or the full moon. Is this true and if so why?: https://originalhomesteading.com/simple-guide-to-planting-by-the-moon/

C.13 See all the **Jewish Festivals** and when exactly celebrated today: http://www3.telus.net/public/kstam/en/temple/details/calendar.htm

9 And he offered on the altar a burnt sacrifice unto the Lord that He should be with him and not forsake him all the days of his life.

C.14 Here we see Abraham make an altar, and to also make a sacrifice unto God, so that God would not forsake him all the days of his life. Abraham didn't want to end up like his father, grandfather and great-grand-father as an Idol worshipper, knowing not God, and losing His blessing, as had happened repeatedly to so many both before the Great flood and afterwards.

C.15 Both Noah and Abraham established the making of sacrifices unto God as an atonement for sins. This physical sacrifice was later fully fulfilled in the greatest sacrifice of all, when God sacrificed His only Begotten Son Jesus on the cross for the sins of the whole world, and in fact for all who had or whoever will live on the earth.

C.16 Abraham's sacrifice was a physical symbol of the spiritual realities which would yet be fully accomplished in God's sacrifice of Jesus on the altar of Salvation & the Redemption for all the sins of the whole world. Wow! What an amazing sacrifice that only God Himself could have made for us all.

ROM.5:8 But God commends his love toward us, in that, while we were yet sinners, Christ died for us.

JOH.3:16 For God so loved the world, that he gave his only begotten Son, that whosoever believeth in him should not perish, but have everlasting life.

---

10 And he removed from thence and went towards the south, and he came to Hebron and Hebron was built at that time, and he dwelt there two years, and he went (thence) into the land of the south, to Bealoth, and there was a famine in the land.

11 And Abram went into Egypt in the third year of the week, and he dwelt in Egypt five years before his wife was torn away from him.

GEN.12:14 And it came to pass, that, when Abram was come into Egypt, the Egyptians beheld the woman that she was very fair.

---

12 Now Tanais in Egypt was at that time built seven years after Hebron.

13 And it came to pass when Pharaoh seized Sarai, the wife of Abram that the Lord plagued Pharaoh and his house with great plagues because of Sarai, Abram's wife.

GEN.12:17 And the LORD plagued Pharaoh and his house with great plagues because of Sarai Abram's wife.

---

14 And Abram was very glorious by reason of possessions in sheep, and cattle, and asses, and horses, and camels, and menservants, and maidservants, and in silver and gold exceedingly.

GEN.13:2 And Abram was very rich in cattle, in silver, and in gold.

15 And Lot also his brother's son, was wealthy. And Pharaoh gave back Sarai, the wife of Abram, and he sent him out of the land of Egypt, and he journeyed to the place where he had pitched his tent at the beginning, to the place of the altar, with Ai on the east, and Bethel on the west, and he blessed the Lord his God who had brought him back in peace.

16 And it came to pass in the forty-first jubilee in the third year of the first week, [1963 A.M. = **Anno Mundi' = years of the world**] that he returned to this place and offered thereon a burnt sacrifice, and called on the name of the Lord, and said: 'Thou, the Most High God, art my God for ever and ever.'

17 And in the fourth year of this week [1964 A.M.] Lot parted from him, and Lot dwelt in Sodom, and the men of Sodom were sinners exceedingly.

GEN.13:10 And Lot lifted up his eyes, and beheld all the plain of Jordan, that it was well watered every where, before the LORD destroyed Sodom and Gomorrah, even as the garden of the LORD, like the land of Egypt, as thou comest unto Zoar.

GEN.13:11 Then Lot chose him all the plain of Jordan; and Lot journeyed east: and they separated themselves the one from the other.

18 And it grieved him in his heart that his brother's son had parted from him; for he had no children.

19 In that year when Lot was taken captive, the Lord said unto Abram, after that Lot had parted from him, in the fourth year of this week: 'Lift up thine eyes from the place where thou art dwelling, northward and southward, and westward and eastward.

20 For all the land which thou see I will give to thee and to thy seed for ever, and I will make thy seed as the sand of the sea: though a man may number the dust of the earth, yet thy seed shall not be numbered.

21 Arise, walk (through the land) in the length of it and the breadth of it, and see it all; for to thy seed will I give it.'

22 And Abram went to Hebron and dwelt there.

> 23 And in this year came Chedorlaomer, king of Elam, and Amraphel, king of Shinar, and Arioch king of Sellasar, and Tergal, king of nations, and slew the king of Gomorrah, and the king of Sodom fled, and many fell through wounds in the vale of Siddim, by the Salt Sea.

C.17 Here is a very important point, as it mentions Amraphel, king of Shinar. Why is this so important? Both the Books of Jubilees and the Book of Jasher both state that Abraham was alive at the same time as Nimrod. This is very important as it means that 3 books agree on the Biblical time-line from after the Great Flood times, and that they do not agree with the Biblical time-lines as put out in the Septuagint, because the Septuagint has deliberately added 100 years to the patriarchs born after the Great Flood, then, according to the Septuagint version of the Old Testament, Abraham couldn't have been alive at the same time as Nimrod, who was born just a few generations after the Great Flood.

C.18 I have covered this topic as to how the Septuagint version of the Old Testament was deliberately altered or falsified in this particular point of the biblical timeframe in order to make it appear that the Egyptians built the Pyramids, when in fact the pyramids were built in Pre-Flood Times. (See my book '**JASHER INSIGHTS**' for more on this topiC.)

C.19 Amraphel, king of Shinar was also known as Nimrod:

JASHER 11.6 And Nimrod dwelt in Babel, and he there renewed his reign over the rest of his subjects, and he reigned securely, and the subjects and princes of Nimrod called his name *Amraphel*, saying that at the tower his princes and men fell through his means.

> 24 And they took captive Sodom and Adam and Zeboim, and they took captive Lot also, the son of Abram's brother, and all his possessions, and they went to Dan.
>
> 25 And one who had escaped came and told Abram that his brother's son had been taken captive and (Abram) armed his household servants . . . . . . for Abram, and for his seed, a tenth of the first fruits to the Lord, and the Lord ordained it as an ordinance for ever that they should give it to the priests who served before Him, that they should possess it for ever.

C.20 Now here is where it gets very interesting: In this verse 25 we see something very important although **not much** is actually revealed, except that Abraham '*armed his household servants*'. Why is this above verse both confusing and incomplete? Fortunately, we can check with our Bibles in the book of **Genesis**:

GEN.14:14 And when Abram heard that his brother was taken captive, **he armed his trained servants**, born in his own house, three hundred and eighteen, and pursued them unto Dan.

GEN.14:15 And he divided himself against them, he and his servants, by night, and smote them, and pursued them unto Hobah, which is on the left hand of Damascus.

GEN.14:16 And he brought back all the goods, and also brought again his brother Lot, and his goods, and the women also, and the people.

C.21 This next verse appears to be introducing **TITHING:** or the giving of 10% of one's income unto the Lord, through giving to the priests at the temple, which were the **LEVITE TRIBE,** once the nation of Israel had come into existence through Abraham's grandson Jacob.

---

26 And to this law there is no limit of days; for He hath ordained it for the generations for ever that they should give to the Lord the tenth of everything, of the seed and of the wine and of the oil and of the cattle and of the sheep.

27 And He gave (it) unto His priests to eat and to drink with joy before Him.

28 And the king of Sodom came to him and bowed himself before him, and said: 'Our Lord Abram, give unto us the souls which thou hast rescued, but let the booty be thine.' And Abram said unto him: 'I lift up my hands to the Most High God, that from a thread to a shoe-latchet I shall not take aught that is thine lest thou should say, I have made Abram rich; save only what the young men have eaten, and the portion of the men who went with me -Aner, Eschol, and Mamre. These shall take their portion.'

GEN.14:17 And the king of Sodom went out to meet him after his return from the slaughter of Chedorlaomer, and of the kings that were with him, at the valley of Shaveh, which is the king's dale.

C.22 This chapter leaves out a **very important story** as told in the Bible about a very mysterious person known as **MELCHIZADECH, a 'King of kings'** who came to visit Abraham with two other unearthly beings after the **'Slaughter of the Kings'. Why did Abraham tithe 10% to this seeming stranger?** It would seem that this story had been deliberately **'cut out'** of this 'Book of Jubilees'. I wonder why? Here is the missing story as told in the Bible:

GEN.14:18 And **Melchizedek** king of Salem brought forth bread and wine: and he

144

was the **priest of the most high God.**

GEN.14:19 And he blessed him, and said, Blessed be Abram of the most high God, possessor of heaven and earth:

GEN.14:20 And blessed be the most high God, which hath delivered thine enemies into thy hand. And he (Abraham) gave him tithes of all.

C.23 The New Testament explains who this Melchisedec (King of kings was):

HEB.6:20 Whither the forerunner is for us entered, even Jesus, made an high priest for ever after the order of MelchisedeC.

HEB.7:1 For this Melchisedec, king of Salem, priest of the most high God, who met Abraham returning from the slaughter of the kings, and blessed him;

HEB.7:2 To whom also Abraham gave a tenth part of all; first being by interpretation King of righteousness, and after that also King of Salem, which is, King of peace;

HEB.7:3 Without father, without mother, without descent, having neither beginning of days, nor end of life; but made **like unto the Son of God;** abideth a priest continually.

HEB.7:4 Now consider how great this man was, unto whom even the patriarch Abraham gave the tenth of the spoils.

HEB.7:5 And verily they that are of the sons of Levi, who receive the office of the priesthood, have a commandment to take tithes of the people according to the law, that is, of their brethren, though they come out of the loins of Abraham:

HEB.7:6 But he whose descent is not counted from them received tithes of Abraham, and blessed him that had the promises.

HEB.7:7 And without all contradiction the less is blessed of the better.

C.24 In my opinion, the reason why verse 25 seems both **incomplete and confusing** is because **most of the story was deliberately 'cut out'**. Why? Because the **Book of Jubilees was originally a very religious Jewish book**, and they did not like the reference to **Melchisedec** implying that He was a **King of Kings** and that it was clearly referring to the **Messiah - Jesus. THE KING OF KINGS.** So they cut out that part of the story which is **clearly shown in Genesis**.

C.25 Here are also some very powerful corresponding verses from both the Bible and the Book of Enoch:

REV.19:16 And he hath on his vesture and on his thigh a name written, **KING OF KINGS**, AND LORD OF LORDS.

BOOK OF ENOCH 84.2 Blessed be thou 'O Lord King. Great and mighty Thy greatness, Lord of the whole Creation of heaven'. **King of Kings** and God of the whole world and thy power and thy kingship and greatness abide for ever and ever, and throughout all generations. Thy dominion and all the heavens are Thy throne for ever,

C.26 Look as thee other similar verses about the **MESSIAH** written in the **Book of Daniel** in **500-600 BC**:

DAN.7:9 I beheld till the thrones were cast down, and the Ancient of days did sit, whose garment was white as snow, and the hair of his head like the pure wool: his throne was like the fiery flame, and his wheels as burning fire.

DAN.7:13 I saw in the night visions, and, behold, one like the **Son of man (Son of God)** came with the clouds of heaven, and came to the Ancient of days, and they brought him near before him.

DAN.7:14 And there was given him dominion, and glory, and a kingdom, that all people, nations, and languages, should serve him: **his dominion is an everlasting dominion, which shall not pass away, and his kingdom that which shall not be destroyed.**

Chapter 14: GOD CALLS ABRAHAM

1 After these things, in the fourth year of this week, on the new moon of the third month, the word of the Lord came to Abram in a dream, saying: 'Fear not, Abram; I am thy defender, and thy reward will be exceeding great.'

GEN.15:1 After these things the word of the LORD came unto Abram in a vision, saying, Fear not, Abram: I am thy shield, and thy exceeding great reward.

2 And he said: 'Lord, Lord, what wilt thou give me, seeing I go hence childless, and the son of Maseq, the son of my handmaid, is the Dammasek Eliezer: he will be my heir, and to me thou hast given no seed.'

3 And he said unto him: 'This (man) will not be thy heir, but one that will come out of thine own bowels; he will be thine heir.'

4 And He brought him forth abroad and said unto him: 'Look toward heaven and number the stars if thou art able to number them.'

5 And he looked toward heaven and beheld the stars.

6 And He said unto him: 'So shall thy seed be.'

7 And he believed in the Lord, and it was counted to him for righteousness.

GEN.15:6 And he believed in the LORD; and he counted it to him for righteousness.

8 And He said unto him: 'I am the Lord that brought thee out of Ur of the Chaldees, to give thee the land of the Canaanites to possess it for ever; and I will be God unto thee and to thy seed after thee.'

Comment:1: At a time just after the Great Flood, Canaan, son of Ham was cursed by Noah because of a sin that his son Ham had done against him (Noah). Later in time, all of his brothers and relatives told Canaan that he would be *double cursed* if he was to take the land of Canaan for an inheritance, as that land belonged to the descendants of Shem. However, Canaan would not listen to his brethren and took over the land of what became called the land of Canaan anyway. Now some hundreds of years later, the curse on

Canaan is to be fulfilled as both Abraham and his grandson Jacob as well as Jacob's sons, followed by Moses and the Israelites when they came out of Egypt some 500 years after Abraham, all slaughtered the Canaanites. Thus, the double curse on Canaan was indeed fulfilled.

> 9 And he said: 'Lord, Lord, whereby shall I know that I shall inherit (it)' And He said unto him: 'Take Me an heifer of three years, and a goat of three years, and a sheep of three years, and a turtle-dove, and a pigeon.'

C.2 Abraham wanted to know how he could really be sure that God would indeed fulfil His promises to him; and cause great nations to come forth from him and that he would be father of a very special nation: Israel. So, God told him to make a specific sacrifice to acknowledge that God would indeed keep His Word to Abraham.

C.3 Here we see God Himself specifying the exact sacrifice that He wanted Abraham to make. This sacrificial ceremony was later passed on to the Children of Israel.

> 10 And he took all these in the middle of the month and he dwelt at the oak of Mamre, which is near Hebron.
>
> 11 And he built there an altar and sacrificed all these; and he poured their blood upon the altar, and divided them in the midst, and laid them over against each other; but the birds divided he not.

C.4 Noah the 10th Ancestor in succession before Abraham offered a similar sacrifice unto God after God had delivered him from the great worldwide Flood some 350 years earlier.

GEN.8:20 And Noah built an altar unto the LORD; and took of *every clean beast*, and of *every clean fowl*, and *offered burnt offerings on the altar*.

C.5 Why did God specify: *'Take Me an heifer of three years, and a goat of three years, and a sheep of three years, and a turtle-dove, and a pigeon?'* Is it just possible that God told Abraham to take animals of three years old for the sacrifice, because this sacrifice was a reminder of the sacrifice which Noah had made for all of mankind right after the Great Flood? Both the sacrifices of Noah and Abraham are similar: The following verses describing Noah's sacrifice unto God right after the Great Flood:

Jubilees: 6. 1-3: And on the new moon of the third month he went forth from the ark and built an altar on that mountain. And he made atonement for the earth and took a kid and made atonement by its blood for all the guilt of the earth; for everything that had been on it had been destroyed, save those that were in the ark with Noah. And he placed the fat thereof on the altar, and he took an ox, and a goat, and a sheep and kids…

C.6 Could it just be possible that God asked Abraham to sacrifice animals which were *3 years old* to symbolize the fact that Noah came out of the Ark on the *3rd month* and made his sacrifice to God on behalf of all of those slain at the time of the Great Flood?

C.7 These *early sacrifices* by both Noah and Abraham were *precursors* that the *Messiah* would one day come and *shed His blood* and *be sacrificed* and *die for all sinners.*

HEB.10:1 For the *law* having a *shadow of good things to come,* and *not the very image* of the things, *can never with those sacrifices which they offered year by year continually make the comers thereunto perfect.*

HEB.9:28 So *Christ* was once *offered* to *bear the sins of many*; and unto them that look for him shall he appear the second time without sin unto *salvation.*

JOH.3:36 He that believeth on the Son hath everlasting life: and he that believeth not the Son shall not see life; but the wrath of God abides on him.

C.8 For more about Jesus as the sacrificial Lamb of God: (https://www.compellingtruth.org/Jesus-lamb-of-God.html)

> 12 And birds came down upon the pieces, and Abram drove them away, and did not suffer the birds to touch them.
>
> 13 And it came to pass, when the sun had set, that an ecstasy fell upon Abram, and lo ! an horror of great darkness fell upon him, and it was said unto Abram: 'Know of a surety that thy seed shall be a stranger in a land (that is) not theirs, and they shall bring them into bondage, and afflict them four hundred years.

C.9 Here we see the *beginnings* of *animal sacrifices* unto God by Abraham. *God is prophesying through his angel to Abraham that his descendants will be 400 years in bondage in Egypt* and history bears out *that is exactly what happened* during the time of his grandson Jacob and his great grandchildren who first went down into Egypt and their descendants came out of the bondage of Egypt some 400 years later. < See **APPENDIX XIV** about the explanation of these 400 years>

C.10 What does this verse mean? *'an ecstasy fell upon Abram', and lo an 'horror of great darkness' fell upon him.*

God is revealing the 'extreme Joy & Ecstasy' that exists in 'being very close to God Himself' and the opposite: The terrible 'horror of Darkness' that has descended upon the earth because of Satan and man's disobedience and 'what it feels like to be far away from God'.

> 14 And the nation also to whom they will be in bondage will I judge, and after that they shall come forth thence with much substance.

C.11 This above verse as the: 'nation also to whom they will be in bondage will I judge' is an amazing prophecy given to Abraham, by God Himself, some 400-500 years before it was marvellously fulfilled. It is indeed amazingly fulfilled in the **EXODUS** and the '**10 PLAGUES of EGYPT**' - where finally Pharaoh lets Israel as a nation depart from Egypt, whilst Egypt itself was totally destroyed by the **10 PLAGUES. (See Exodus: Chapters: 5-14)**

EXO.14:26 And the LORD said unto Moses, Stretch out thine hand over the sea, that the waters may come again upon the **Egyptians**, upon their chariots, and upon their horsemen.

EXO.14:27 And Moses stretched forth his hand over the sea, and the sea returned to his strength when the morning appeared; and the Egyptians fled against it; and the **LORD overthrew the Egyptians in the midst of the sea.**

EXO.14:28 And the waters returned, and covered the chariots, and the horsemen, and **all the host of Pharaoh that came into the sea after them; there remained not so much as one of them.**

---

15 And thou shalt go to thy fathers in peace and be buried in a good old age.

16 But in the fourth generation they shall return hither; for the iniquity of the Amorites is not yet full.'

17 And he awoke from his sleep, and he arose, and the sun had set; and there was a flame, and behold a furnace was smoking, and a flame of fire passed between the pieces.

18 And on that day the Lord made a covenant with Abram, saying: 'To thy seed will I give this land, from the river of Egypt unto the great river, the river Euphrates, the Kenites, the Kenizzites, the Kadmonites, the Perizzites, and the Rephaim (Giants), the Phakorites, and the Hivites, and the Amorites, and the Canaanites, and the Girgashites, and the Jebusites.

19 And the day passed, and Abram offered the pieces, and the birds, and their fruit offerings, and their drink offerings, and the fire devoured them.

20 And on that day we made a covenant with Abram, according as we had covenanted with Noah in this month; and Abram renewed the

---

festival and ordinance for himself for ever.

C.12 In this verse it clearly makes the connection between Abraham and Noah's covenants which God made with them. It also states that God did these covenants in the exact same months. The third month of the year. It is a covenant of peace between God and man.

21 And Abram rejoiced, and made all these things known to Sarai his wife; and he believed that he would have seed, but she did not bear.

22 And Sarai advised her husband Abram and said unto him: 'Go in unto Hagar, my Egyptian maid: it may be that I shall build up seed unto thee by her.'

23 And Abram harkened unto the voice of Sarai his wife, and said unto her, 'Do (so).' And Sarai took Hagar, her maid, the Egyptian, and gave her to Abram, her husband, to be his wife.

24 And he went in unto her, and she conceived and bare him a son, and he called his name Ishmael, in the fifth year of this week [1965 A.M.]; and this was the eighty-sixth year in the life of Abram.

Chapter 15

1 And in the fifth year of the fourth week of this jubilee, [1979 A.M. = **Anno Mundi' = years of the world**] in the third month, in the middle of the month, Abram celebrated the feast of the first fruits of the grain harvest.

2 And he offered new offerings on the altar, the first-fruits of the produce, unto the Lord, an heifer and a goat and a sheep on the altar as a burnt sacrifice unto the Lord; their fruit offerings and their drink offerings he offered upon the altar with frankincense.

3 And the Lord appeared to Abram, and said unto him:

4 'I am God Almighty; approve thyself before me and be thou perfect. And I will make My covenant between Me and thee, and I will multiply thee exceedingly.'

5 And Abram fell on his face, and God talked with him, and said:

6 'Behold my ordinance is with thee, And thou shalt be the father of many nations.

7 Neither shall thy name any more be called Abram, But thy name from henceforth, even for ever, shall be Abraham.

8 For the father of many nations have I made thee.

And I will make thee very great, And I will make thee into nations, And kings shall come forth from thee.

Comment:1: What a very great promise God made to Abraham, not only telling him that he would become the father of many nations, but also that kings would come from Abraham. This was fulfilled in King David and his son Solomon the richest and wisest king ever except for Jesus - King of Kings, who came later to also fulfil the above promise made by God directly Abraham. So, the Messiah himself, also came through the lineage of Abraham.

9 And I shall establish My covenant between Me and thee, and thy seed

after thee, throughout their generations, for an eternal covenant, so that I may be a God unto thee, and to thy seed after thee.

C.2 'establish My covenant between Me and thee'. This Eternal Covenant is a covenant of peace made between God and Abraham. God also made a similar covenant with Noah, which was for the benefit of all mankind, right after the Great Flood, when God gave the symbol of the rainbow in the clouds.

GEN.9:12 And God said, 'This is the token of the covenant which I make between me and you and every living creature that is with you, for perpetual generations':

GEN.9:13 I do set my bow in the cloud, and it shall be for a token of a covenant between me and the earth.

GEN.9:14 And it shall come to pass, when I bring a cloud over the earth, that the bow shall be seen in the cloud:

GEN.9:15 And I will remember my covenant, which is between me and you and every living creature of all flesh; and the waters shall no more become a flood to destroy all flesh.

GEN.9:16 And the bow shall be in the cloud; and I will look upon it, that I may remember the everlasting covenant between God and every living creature of all flesh that is upon the earth.

GEN.9:17 And God said unto Noah, This is the token of the covenant, which I have established between me and all flesh that is upon the earth.

C.3 We also see this symbol of God's covenant around the throne of God itself.

REV.4:3 And he that sat was to look upon like a jasper and a sardine stone: and there was a *rainbow* round about the throne, in sight like unto an emerald.

C.4 There are some beautiful verses in the Book of Isaiah about God's 'covenant of peace' with us:

ISA.54:10 For the mountains shall depart, and the hills be removed; but my kindness shall not depart from thee, neither shall the '*covenant of my peace*' be removed, saith the LORD that hath mercy on thee.

10 The land where thou hast been a sojourner, the land of Canaan, that thou mayst possess it for ever, and I will be their God.'

C.5 It is important here to see how that God has promised Abraham and his descendants the land of Canaan. This makes it easier to explain why the sons of Jacob and in fact the great grandchildren of Abraham would cause such havoc & slaughter of the Canaanites such as the city of Shechem in the land of Canaan. This is very well shown in the Book of Jasher. (See my book

> 11 And the Lord said unto Abraham: 'And as for thee, do thou keep my covenant, thou and thy seed after thee: and circumcise ye every male among you, and circumcise your foreskins, and it shall be a token of an eternal covenant between Me and you.
>
> 12 And the child on the eighth day ye shall circumcise, every male throughout your generations, him that is born in the house, or whom ye have bought with money from any stranger, whom ye have acquired who is not of thy seed.
>
> 13 He that is born in thy house shall surely be circumcised, and those whom thou hast bought with money shall be circumcised, and My covenant shall be in your flesh for an eternal ordinance.

C.6 God gives His Covenant of Circumcision. This was a physical illustration of an actual change of heart and mind and spirit. The Old Testament in Abraham and the Laws of Moses brought a figure of the true. Like childish illustrations for a hardened people such as the Children of Israel who just came out of Egypt.

C.7 The real issues are expressed by God himself and complimented much late in time in the New Testament with all the laws of Moses and Abraham fulfilled by the Messiah Jesus Christ.

JOH.1:17 For the law was given by Moses, but grace and truth came by Jesus Christ.

MAT.5:17 Think not that I am come to destroy the law, or the prophets: I am not come to destroy, but to fulfil.

MAT.5:18 For verily I say unto you, Till heaven and earth pass, one jot or one tittle shall in no wise pass from the law, till all be fulfilled.

C.8 Who is really a Jew in the eyes of God, after the Sacrifice of God's Son the Messiah who redeemed all mankind from their sins?

ROM.2:28 For he is not a Jew, which is one outwardly; neither is that circumcision, which is outward in the flesh:

ROM.2:29 But he is a Jew, which is one inwardly; and circumcision is that of the heart, in the spirit, and not in the letter; whose praise is not of men, but of God.

> 14 And the uncircumcised male who is not circumcised in the flesh of his foreskin on the eighth day, that soul shall be cut off from his people, for he has broken My covenant.'

15 And God said unto Abraham: 'As for Sarai thy wife, her name shall no more be called Sarai, but Sarah shall be her name.

16 And I will bless her, and give thee a son by her, and I will bless him, and he shall become a nation, and kings of nations shall proceed from him.'

17 And Abraham fell on his face, and rejoiced, and said in his heart: 'Shall a son be born to him that is a hundred years old, and shall Sarah, who is ninety years old, bring forth'

18 And Abraham said unto God: 'O that Ishmael might live before thee!'

19 And God said: 'Yea, and Sarah also shall bear thee a son, and thou shalt call his name Isaac, and I will establish My covenant with him, an everlasting covenant, and for his seed after him.

20 And as for Ishmael also have I heard thee, and behold I will bless him, and make him great, and multiply him exceedingly, and he shall beget twelve princes, and I will make him a great nation.

21 But My covenant will I establish with Isaac, whom Sarah shall bear to thee, in these days, in the next year.'

22 And He left off speaking with him, and God went up from Abraham.

23 And Abraham did according as God had said unto him, and he took Ishmael his son, and all that were born in his house, and whom he had bought with his money, every male in his house, and circumcised the flesh of their foreskin.

24 And on the self-same day was Abraham circumcised, and all the men of his house, and all those, whom he had bought with money from the children of the stranger, were circumcised with him.

25 This law is for all the generations for ever, and there is no circumcision of the days, and no omission of one day out of the eight days; for

it is an eternal ordinance, ordained and written on the heavenly tablets.

26 And every one that is born, the flesh of whose foreskin is not circumcised on the eighth day, belongs not to the children of the covenant which the Lord made with Abraham, but to the children of destruction; nor is there, moreover, any sign on him that he is the Lord's, but (he is destined) to be destroyed and slain from the earth, and to be rooted out of the earth, for he has broken the covenant of the Lord our God.

27 For all the angels of the presence and all the angels of sanctification have been so created from the day of their creation, and before the angels of the presence and the angels of sanctification He hath sanctified Israel, that they should be with Him and with His holy angels.

28 And do thou command the children of Israel and let them observe the sign of this covenant for their generations as an eternal ordinance, and they will not be rooted out of the land.

29 For the command is ordained for a covenant, that they should observe it for ever among all the children of Israel.

30 For Ishmael and his sons and his brothers and Esau, the Lord did not cause to approach Him, and he chose them not because they are the children of Abraham, because He knew them, but He chose Israel to be His people.

31 And He sanctified it and gathered it from amongst all the children of men; for there are many nations and many peoples, and all are His, and over all hath He placed spirits in authority to lead them astray from Him.

32 But over Israel He did not appoint any angel or spirit, for He alone is their ruler, and He will preserve them and require them at the hand of His angels and His spirits, and at the hand of all His powers in order that He may preserve them and bless them, and that they may be His and He may be theirs from henceforth for ever.

33 And now I announce unto thee that the children of Israel will not

keep true to this ordinance, and they will not circumcise their sons according to all this law; for in the flesh of their circumcision they will omit this circumcision of their sons, and all of them, sons of Beliar, will leave their sons uncircumcised as they were born.

34 And there will be great wrath from the Lord against the children of Israel. because they have forsaken His covenant and turned aside from His word, and provoked and blasphemed, inasmuch as they do not observe the ordinance of this law; for they have treated their members like the Gentiles, so that they may be removed and rooted out of the land. And there will no more be pardon or forgiveness unto them [so that there should be forgiveness and pardon] for all the sin of this eternal error. (Meaning of the word **oblation**: offering unto God by the people, normally through the priest: http://bibletruthandprophecy. com/wp-content/uploads/2018/10/Chapter-15-The-holy-oblation. pdf)

Chapter 16

> 1 And on the new moon of the fourth month we appeared unto Abraham, at the oak of Mamre, and we talked with him, and we announced to him that a son would be given to him by Sarah his wife.

Comment:1: Notice that it starts off with *"us"*. Who is we? This whole narrative of Jubilees appears to be God's angels talking to Moses and revealing to him all kinds of happenings since the beginning of Creation until his time, and sometimes even revealing the future to him. This happening of the angels of God revealing the History of the world from the Beginning to the End has happened many times through all of the prophets. Some more than others.

C.2 ENOCH & EZRA

Unto Enoch was revealed the whole panorama of 7000 years of World History, mostly by the angels of God. To Ezra was also revealed many things from the Creation and leading up to the Wrath of God and the end of the world. God gave the books back to Ezra in visions because Israel was in captivity and the biblical History records had been destroyed by the Babylonians. [See my books **'ENOCH INSIGHTS'** & **EZDRAS INSIGHTS**]

> 2 And Sarah laughed, for she heard that we had spoken these words with Abraham, and we admonished her, and she became afraid, and denied that she had laughed on account of the words.
>
> 3 And we told her the name of her son, as his name is ordained and written in the heavenly tablets (i.e.) IsaaC.
>
> 4 And, (that) when we returned to her at a set time, she would have conceived a son.
>
> 5 And in this month the Lord executed his judgments on Sodom, and Gomorrah, and Zeboim, and all the region of the Jordan, and He burned them with fire and brimstone, and destroyed them until this day, even as [lo] I have declared unto thee all their works, that they are wicked and sinners exceedingly, and that they defile themselves and commit fornication in their flesh, and work uncleanness on the earth.
>
> 6 And, in like manner, God will execute judgment on the places where they have done according to the uncleanness of the Sodomites, like unto the judgment of Sodom.

7 But Lot we saved; for God remembered Abraham, and sent him out from the midst of the overthrow.

8 And he and his daughters committed sin upon the earth, such as had not been on the earth since the days of Adam till his time; for the man lay with his daughters.

9 And, behold, it was commanded and engraven concerning all his seed, on the heavenly tablets, to remove them and root them out, and to execute judgment upon them like the judgment of Sodom, and to leave no seed of the man on earth on the day of condemnation.

10 And in this month Abraham moved from Hebron, and departed and dwelt between Kadesh and Shur in the mountains of Gerar.

11 And in the middle of the fifth month he moved from thence, and dwelt at the Well of the Oath.

12 And in the middle of the sixth month the Lord visited Sarah and did unto her as He had spoken and she conceived.

13 And she bare a son in the third month, and in the middle of the month, at the time of which the Lord had spoken to Abraham, on the festival of the first fruits of the harvest, Isaac was born.

14 And Abraham circumcised his son on the eighth day: he was the first that was circumcised according to the covenant which is ordained for ever.

15 And in the sixth year of the fourth week we came to Abraham, to the Well of the Oath, and we appeared unto him [as we had told Sarah that we should return to her, and she would have conceived a son.

16 And we returned in the seventh month, and found Sarah with child before us] and we blessed him, and we announced to him all the things which had been decreed concerning him, that he should not die till he should beget six sons more, and should see (them) before he died; but (that) in Isaac should his name and seed be called:

17 And (that) all the seed of his sons should be Gentiles, and be reckoned with the Gentiles; but from the sons of Isaac one should become a holy seed, and should not be reckoned among the Gentiles.

18 For he should become the portion of the Most High, and all his seed had fallen into the possession of God, that it should be unto the Lord a people for (His) possession above all nations and that it should become a kingdom and priests and a holy nation.

19 And we went our way, and we announced to Sarah all that we had told him, and they both rejoiced with exceeding great joy.

20 And he built there an altar to the Lord who had delivered him, and who was making him rejoice in the land of his sojourning, and he celebrated a festival of joy in this month seven days, near the altar which he had built at the Well of the Oath.

21 And he built booths for himself and for his servants on this festival, and he was the first to celebrate the feast of tabernacles on the earth.

22 And during these seven days he brought each day to the altar a burnt offering to the Lord, two oxen, two rams, seven sheep, one he-goat, for a sin offering, that he might atone thereby for himself and for his seed.

23 And, as a thank-offering, seven rams, seven kids, seven sheep, and seven he-goats, and their fruit offerings and their drink offerings; and he burnt all the fat thereof on the altar, a chosen offering unto the Lord for a sweet smelling savour.

24 And morning and evening he burnt fragrant substances, frankincense and galbanum, and stackte, and nard, and myrrh, and spice, and costume; all these seven he offered, crushed, mixed together in equal parts (and) pure.

25 And he celebrated this feast during seven days, rejoicing with all his heart and with all his soul, he and all those who were in his house, and there was no stranger with him, nor any that was uncircumcised.

> 26 And he blessed his Creator who had created him in his generation, for He had created him according to His good pleasure; for He knew and perceived that from him would arise the plant of righteousness for the eternal generations, and from him a holy seed, so that it should become like Him who had made all things.

C.3 'perceived that *from him (Abraham)* would arise the *'plant of righteousness'* for the *eternal generations,* and from him a *'holy seed'* Here it is stating that *from Abraham* would come both the *Messiah* and the promised seed of *Israel* (Zion)

ISA.61:3 To appoint unto them that mourn in Zion, to give unto them beauty for ashes, the oil of joy for mourning, the garment of praise for the spirit of heaviness; that they might be called *trees of righteousness*, the *planting of the LORD*, that *he might be glorified.*

C.4 Jesus the Messiah said of Himself:

JOH.15:4 'Abide in me, and I in you. As the *branch* cannot bear fruit of itself, except it abide in the *vine*; no more can ye, except ye abide in me'.

JOH.15:5 'I am the *vine*, ye are the *branches:* He that abides in me, and I in him, the same bringeth forth much fruit: for *without me* ye can do *nothing.'*

HOS.10:12 Sow to yourselves *in righteousness*, reap in mercy; break up your fallow ground: for it is time to seek the LORD, till *He* come and rain *righteousness upon you.*

PHI.1:11 Being filled with *the fruits of righteousness*, which are *by Jesus Christ*, unto the *glory and praise of God.*

> 27 And he blessed and rejoiced, and he called the name of this festival the festival of the Lord, a joy acceptable to the Most High God.
>
> 28 And we blessed him for ever, and all his seed after him throughout all the generations of the earth, because he celebrated this festival in its season, according to the testimony of the heavenly tablets.
>
> 29 For this reason it is ordained on the heavenly tablets concerning Israel, that they shall celebrate the feast of tabernacles seven days with joy, in the seventh month, acceptable before the Lord -a statute for ever throughout their generations every year.
>
> 30 And to this there is no limit of days; for it is ordained for ever regarding Israel that they should celebrate it and dwell in booths, and set

wreaths upon their heads, and take leafy boughs, and willows from the brook.

31 And Abraham took branches of palm trees, and the fruit of goodly trees, and every day going round the altar with the branches seven times [a day] in the morning, he praised and gave thanks to his God for all things in joy.

Chapter 17

1 And in the first year of the fifth week Isaac was weaned in this jubilee, [1982 A.M. = '**Anno Mundi**' = **years of the world**] and Abraham made a great banquet in the third month, on the day his son Isaac was weaned.

2 And Ishmael, the son of Hagar, the Egyptian, was before the face of Abraham, his father, in his place, and Abraham rejoiced and blessed God because he had seen his sons and had not died childless.

3 And he remembered the words which He had spoken to him on the day on which Lot had parted from him, and he rejoiced because the Lord had given him seed upon the earth to inherit the earth, and he blessed with all his mouth the Creator of all things.

4 And Sarah saw Ishmael playing and dancing, and Abraham rejoicing with great joy, and she became jealous of Ishmael and said to Abraham, 'Cast out this bondwoman and her son; for the son of this bondwoman will not be heir with my son, IsaaC.'

5 And the thing was grievous in Abraham's sight, because of his maid-servant and because of his son, that he should drive them from him.

6 And God said to Abraham 'Let it not be grievous in thy sight, because of the child and because of the bondwoman; in all that Sarah hath said unto thee, harken to her words and do (them); for in Isaac shall thy name and seed be called.

7 But as for the son of this bondwoman I will make him a great nation, because he is of thy seed.'

8 And Abraham rose up early in the morning, and took bread and a bottle of water, and placed them on the shoulders of Hagar and the child and sent her away.

9 And she departed and wandered in the wilderness of Beersheba, and the water in the bottle was spent, and the child thirsted, and was not

able to go on, and fell down.

10 And his mother took him and cast him under an olive tree, and went and sat her down over against him, at the distance of a bow-shot; for she said, 'Let me not see the death of my child,' and as she sat she wept.

11 And an angel of God, one of the holy ones, said unto her, 'Why weep thou, Hagar. Arise take the child and hold him in thine hand; for God hath heard thy voice, and hath seen the child.'

12 And she opened her eyes, and she saw a well of water, and she went and filled her bottle with water, and she gave her child to drink, and she arose and went towards the wilderness of Paran.

13 And the child grew and became an archer, and God was with him, and his mother took him a wife from among the daughters of Egypt.

14 And she bare him a son, and he called his name Nebaioth; for she said, 'The Lord was nigh to me when I called upon him.'

15 And it came to pass in the seventh week, in the first year thereof, [2003 A.M.] in the first month in this jubilee, on the twelfth of this month, there were voices in heaven regarding Abraham, that he was faithful in all that He told him, and that he loved the Lord, and that in every affliction he was faithful.

16 And the prince Mastema came and said before God, 'Behold, Abraham loves Isaac his son, and he delights in him above all things else; bid him offer him as a burnt-offering on the altar, and Thou wilt see if he will do this command, and Thou wilt know if he is faithful in everything wherein Thou dost try him.

Comment:1: A Very strange scene: Satan in the form of Mastema comes before God and practically tells God what to do. Satan is very cheeky, as well as hateful as a trickster. There is no other being in the spirit world as far as I know who can behave like Satan. He is indeed the 'Accuser of the Saints', and like some prosecuting lawyer who is able to come into the 'Courts of Heaven' and to accuse the saints before God day and night.

JOB.1:6 Now there was a day when the sons of God came to present themselves before the LORD, and Satan came also among them.

JOB.1:7 And the LORD said unto Satan, Whence came thou? Then Satan answered the LORD, and said, From going to and fro in the earth, and from walking up and down in it.

JOB.1:8 And the LORD said unto Satan, Hast thou considered my servant Job, that there is none like him in the earth, a perfect and an upright man, one that fears God, and eschews evil?

JOB.1:9 Then Satan answered the LORD, and said, Doth Job fear God for nought?

JOB.1:10 Hast not thou made an hedge about him, and about his house, and about all that he hath on every side? thou hast blessed the work of his hands, and his substance is increased in the land.

JOB.1:11 But put forth thine hand now, and touch all that he hath, and he will curse thee to thy face.

JOB.1:12 And the LORD said unto Satan, Behold, all that he hath is in thy power; only upon himself put not forth thine hand. So Satan went forth from the presence of the LORD.

C.2 The good news is that one day Satan or *Mastema* will finally be cast out of the Heavenly courts, and will no longer be able to *accuse the righteous* before God day and night:

REV.12:7 And there was war in heaven: Michael and his angels fought against the Dragon (Satan); and the Dragon fought and his angels,

REV.12:8 And prevailed not; neither was their place found any more in heaven.

REV.12:9 And the great dragon was cast out, that old serpent, called the Devil, and Satan, which deceives the whole world: he was cast out into the earth, and his angels were cast out with him.

REV.12:10 And I heard a loud voice saying in heaven, Now is come salvation, and strength, and the kingdom of our God, and the power of his Christ: for the accuser of our brethren is cast down, which accused them before our God day and night.

REV.12:11 And they overcame him by the blood of the Lamb, and by the word of their testimony; and they loved not their lives unto the death.

REV.12:12 Therefore rejoice, ye heavens, and ye that dwell in them. Woe to the inhabitants of the earth and of the sea! for the devil is come down unto you, having great wrath, because he knows that he hath but a short time.

> 17 And the Lord knew that Abraham was faithful in all his afflictions; for He had tried him through his country and with famine, and had tried him with the wealth of kings, and had tried him again through his wife, when she was torn (from him), and with circumcision; and had

tried him through Ishmael and Hagar, his maid-servant, when he sent them away.

18 And in everything wherein He had tried him, he was found faithful, and his soul was not impatient, and he was not slow to act; for he was faithful and a lover of the Lord.

C.3 This last verse shows how we are supposed to live our lives: Allow God to 'try us' and make us into what he wants to make us into through 'trials of affliction, pain and sorrow & disappointment'. One who loves God in spite of it all, with all of ones might. One who both listens to God regularly and obeys specifically what He tells one to do.

Chapter 18

Comment:1: There is another example in the Bible where God listens to His Heavenly Court advisors on both sides of the spectrum: spirits of the good and of the evil:

1KI.22:19 And he said, "Hear thou therefore the word of the LORD: I saw the LORD sitting on his throne, and all the host of heaven standing by him on his right hand and on his left".

1KI.22:20 And the LORD said, 'Who shall persuade Ahab, that he may go up and fall at Ramoth Gilead? And one said on this manner, and another said on that manner'.

1KI.22:21 And there came forth a spirit, and stood before the LORD, and said, 'I will persuade him'.

1KI.22:22 And the LORD said unto him, Wherewith? And he said, 'I will go forth, and I will be a *lying spirit* in the *mouth of all his prophets*'. And he said, 'Thou shalt persuade him, and prevail also: go forth, and do so'.

C.2 Here, it would appear that God *did* take *Satan's advice* concerning Abraham sacrificing his only son Isaac as a burnt offering.

---

1 And God said to him, 'Abraham, Abraham'; and he said, Behold, (here) am I.'

2 And he said, 'Take thy beloved son whom thou love (even) Isaac, and go unto the high country, and offer him on one of the mountains which I will point out unto thee.'

3 And he rose early in the morning and saddled his ass, and took his two young men with him, and Isaac his son, and clave the wood of the burnt offering, and he went to the place on the third day, and he saw the place afar off.

4 And he came to a well of water, and he said to his young men, 'Abide ye here with the ass, and I and the lad shall go (yonder), and when we have worshipped we shall come again to you.'

5 And he took the wood of the burnt-offering and laid it on Isaac his son, and he took in his hand the fire and the knife, and they went both of them together to that place.

---

6 And Isaac said to his father, 'Father;' and he said, 'Here am I, my son.' And he said unto him, 'Behold the fire, and the knife, and the wood; but where is the sheep for the burnt-offering, father'

7 And he said, 'God will provide for himself a sheep for a burnt-offering, my son.' And he drew near to the place of the mount of God.

8 And he built an altar, and he placed the wood on the altar, and bound Isaac his son, and placed him on the wood which was upon the altar and stretched forth his hand to take the knife to slay Isaac his son.

9 And I stood before him, and before the prince Mastema, and the Lord said, 'Bid him not to lay his hand on the lad, nor to do anything to him, for I have shown that he fears the Lord.'

10 And I called to him from heaven, and said unto him: 'Abraham, Abraham;' and he was terrified and said: 'Behold, (here) am I.' And I said unto him: 'Lay not thy hand upon the lad, neither do thou anything to him; for now I have shown that thou fearest the Lord, and hast not withheld thy son, thy first-born son, from me.'

11And the prince Mastema was put to shame; and Abraham lifted up his eyes and looked, and, behold a ram caught . . . by his horns, and Abraham went and took the ram and offered it for a burnt offering in the stead of his son.

C.3 Good to see Mastema (Satan) put to shame and proven to be wrong. Satan always seems to think that he can trick mankind into doing the wrong thing one way or the other. I think he assumes falsely that everyone is as proud as he is himself. A good movie about Satan himself is: *The Devil's Advocate*. It really shows how Satan operates in the land of the living.

12 And Abraham called that place 'The Lord hath seen', so that it is said the Lord hath seen: that is Mount Sion.

C.4 Another name for Mt Zion is 'The Lord hath seen'

13 And the Lord called Abraham by his name a second time from heaven, as he caused us to appear to speak to him in the name of the Lord.

14 And he said: 'By Myself have I sworn, saith the Lord, Because thou hast done this thing, 'And hast not withheld thy son, thy beloved son, from Me, That in blessing I will bless thee, and in multiplying I will multiply thy seed As the stars of heaven, And as the sand which is on the seashore.

15 And thy seed shall inherit the cities of its enemies, and in thy seed shall all nations of the earth be blessed: Because thou hast obeyed My voice, And I have shown to all that thou art faithful unto Me in all that I have said unto thee: Go in peace.'

16 And Abraham went to his young men, and they arose and went together to Beersheba, and Abraham [2010 A.M. = **Anno Mundi'** **= years of the world**] dwelt by the Well of the Oath. And he celebrated this festival every year, seven days with joy, and he called it the festival of the Lord according to the seven days during which he went and returned in peace.

C.6 'Well of Oath'. A place close to where God had promised to Abraham that he would 'multiply his seed' as the stars of heaven. So, this location became a place for yearly festivals to Abraham and his family.

17 And accordingly has it been ordained and written on the heavenly tablets regarding Israel and its seed that they should observe this festival seven days with the joy of festival.

169

Chapter 19

> 1 And in the first year of the first week in the forty-second jubilee, Abraham returned and dwelt opposite Hebron, that is Kirjath Arba, two weeks of years.

> 2 And in the first year of the third week of this jubilee the days of the life of Sarah were accomplished, and she died in Hebron.

Comment:1: *'days of the life of Sarah were accomplished'*

This sounds like the length of Sarah's life was 'predestined'. At least that's what it sounds like from the text. Now, why do you suppose that in Sarah's particular case, her life was predestined by God Himself?

I think that the answer to that question is quite clear: God had promised to make Abraham the Father of many nations, and Abraham had had only one son through Sarah and one son through Hagar. Hagar died first and then Sarah. Sarah died at 127 years old whilst Abraham lived until he was 175. In modern terms it was as if Sarah had died in modern terms at 60 and Abraham 80 years old respectively. Abraham remarried at the age of 137 or around 65 in modern times and still managed to have yet 6 sons. Quite a miracle of God in itself. So, *God's promises to Abraham were fulfilled*, by him have *seed through both Sarah, Hagar and Keturah.* Thus, arose the Hebrews, the Arabs and the Ishmaelites. So, God had a great purpose in both Sarah and also Hagar dying younger than Abraham.

> 3 And Abraham went to mourn over her and bury her, and we tried him to see if his spirit were patient and he was not indignant in the words of his mouth; and he was found patient in this and was not disturbed.

C.2 *'He was not indignant in the words of his mouth; and he was found patient in this and was not disturbed'.*

What this verse shows is how God 'tries and tests people's spirits' to see how they will behave, and if they will show restraint under duress. Whether they will Thank God and be full of praise for what God allows to be dished out to them or whether they get bitter and curse God.

Look at the following example in the Bible about righteous Job who lived around the same time as Abraham or perhaps slightly earlier: Satan was allowed by God to practically totally destroy Job including kill all of his many sons and daughters:

JOB.2:9 Then said his wife unto him, Dost thou still retain thine integrity? Curse God, and die.

JOB.2:10 But he said unto her, Thou speak as one of the foolish women speak.

What? shall we receive good at the hand of God, and shall we not receive evil? In all this did not Job sin with his lips.

> 4 For in patience of spirit he conversed with the children of Heth, to the intent that they should give him a place in which to bury his dead.
>
> 5 And the Lord gave him grace before all who saw him, and he besought in gentleness the sons of Heth, and they gave him the land of the double cave over against Mamre, that is Hebron, for four hundred pieces of silver.

C.3 Abraham was both a kind and generous man and because of that God blessed him with abundance

> 6 And they besought him saying, 'We shall give it to thee for nothing', but he would not take it from their hands for nothing, for he gave the price of the place, the money in full, and he bowed down before them twice, and after this he buried his dead in the double cave.

C.4 1000 years later king David did something similar:

2 SA.24:24 And King David said, 'But I will surely buy it of thee at a price: neither will I offer burnt offerings unto the LORD my God of that which doth cost me nothing'. So David bought the threshing floor and the oxen for fifty shekels of silver.

> 7 And all the days of the life of Sarah were one hundred and twen-ty-seven years, that is, two jubilees and four weeks and one year: these are the days of the years of the life of Sarah.
>
> 8 This is the tenth trial wherewith Abraham was tried, and he was found faithful, patient in spirit.

C.5 God is mentioning how that Abraham was tried with **10 severe tests** and that he was found **faithful** and **patient.**

LUK.21:19 In your **patience** possess ye your souls.

JAM.1:4 But let **patience** have her perfect work, that ye may be perfect and entire, wanting nothing.

1PE.1:7 That the trial of your faith, being much more precious than of gold that perishes, though it be tried with fire, might be found unto praise and honour and glory at the appearing of Jesus Christ:

> 9 And he said not a single word regarding the rumour in the land how

that God had said that He would give it to him and to his seed after him, and he begged a place there to bury his dead; for he was found faithful and was recorded on the heavenly tablets as the friend of God.

C.6 Considering how that Abraham's great-grandsons, the sons of Jacob were one day to slaughter the Canaanites and the emerging nation of Israel would continue to do so after them, perhaps it was in fact very wise of Abraham not to say a word of God's promise to him, that one day his seed would inherit all the lands of the Canaanites.

10 And in the fourth year thereof he took a wife for his son Isaac and her name was Rebecca [2020 A.M.] [the daughter of Bethuel, the son of Nahor, the brother of Abraham] the sister of Laban and daughter of Bethuel; and Bethuel was the son of Melca, who was the wife of Nahor, the brother of Abraham.

11 And Abraham took to himself a third wife, and her name was Keturah, from among the daughters of his household servants, for Hagar had died before Sarah.

12 And she bare him six sons, Zimram, and Jokshan, and Medan, and Midian, and Ishbak, and Shuah, in the two weeks of years.

13 And in the sixth week, in the second year thereof, Rebecca bare to Isaac two sons, Jacob and Esau, and [2046 A.M. = **Anno Mundi' = years of the world**] Jacob was a smooth and upright man, and Esau was fierce, a man of the field, and hairy, and Jacob dwelt in tents.

C.7 These dates mentioned in the above verses, according to the Bible are correct. It is strange how the dates leading up to the Great Flood seem to be different than the Bible and off by up to 350 years, but after the Great Flood & by the time of Abraham and his sons the dates seem to parallel the Bible.

14 And the youths grew, and Jacob learned to write; but Esau did not learn, for he was a man of the field and a hunter, and he learnt war, and all his deeds were fierce.

15 And Abraham loved Jacob, but Isaac loved Esau.

16 And Abraham saw the deeds of Esau, and he knew that in Jacob should his name and seed be called; and he called Rebecca and gave

commandment regarding Jacob, for he knew that she (too) loved Jacob much more than Esau. And he said unto her:

My daughter watch over my son Jacob for he shall be in my stead on the earth, And for a blessing in the midst of the children of men,

17 And for the glory of the whole seed of Shem.

C.8 Here is a unique account that you won't find even in the Bible or the Book of Jasher or even the Septuagint – This discourse between Abraham and Rebecca explains why later Rebecca persuaded Jacob to steal Esau's birth rite.

C.9 Verses **16-29** which are Abraham's 'heart wish' to Rebecca his daughter in law for his future heir in Jacob and not his older brother Esau, who was not a godly man and had Canaanite wives whom Rebecca found licentious and excessively lustful as well as idol worshippers and did not like having them around, as they behaved in a very ungodly manner as stated in this very book.

C.10 Abraham could not mention this to his son Isaac at the time as Isaac preferred his older son Esau to inherit his family lineage.

18 For I know that the Lord will choose him to be a people for possession unto Himself, above all peoples that are upon the face of the earth.

19 And behold, Isaac my son loves Esau more than Jacob, but I see that thou truly love Jacob.

20 Add still further to thy kindness to him and let thine eyes be upon him in love; For he shall be a blessing unto us on the earth from henceforth unto all generations of the earth.

21 Let thy hands be strong and let thy heart rejoice in thy son Jacob; For I have loved him far beyond all my sons.

He shall be blessed for ever, and his seed shall fill the whole earth.

22 If a man can number the sand of the earth, His seed also shall be numbered.

C.11 What a tremendous prophecy and vision God had given Abraham because of his continued faithfulness - that his seed would become as numerous as the sand on the seashore. Did this prophecy get fulfilled? It did so

173

miraculously!

HEB.11:12 Therefore sprang there even of one, and him as good as dead, so many as the stars of the sky in multitude, and as the sand which is by the sea shore innumerable.

---

23 And all the blessings wherewith the Lord hath blessed me and my seed shall belong to Jacob and his seed always.

24 And in his seed shall my name be blessed, and the name of my fathers, Shem, and Noah, and Enoch, and Mahalalel, and Enos, and Seth, and Adam.

25 And these shall serve to lay the foundations of the heaven, and to strengthen the earth, and to renew all the luminaries which are in the firmament.

C.12 Verses **24- 25** are a very powerful verses and give a lot of information.

It is stating that in the seed of Jacob shall the 'name of Abraham' be blessed – in Israel and Jacob will continue the original intent of God Himself which started with Adam and all the great men of God such as Abraham, Noah and Enoch.

C.13 Remember that the original language of Creation was Hebrew. ThIs language was lost at the time of the 'Tower of Babel' and re-taught to Abraham by the angels of God according to this very Book of Jubilees. Jacob's descendants would therefore have the blessing of the language of 'Creation'.

C.14 Imagine if Isaac had gotten his wish - and that Esau had inherited his name: Then Israel the 'promised seed' would have never come into existence.

It would seem that God took a direct hand in both Jacob stealing Esau's birth rite in an unguarded moment in the case of Esau himself - and later Rebecca persuading Jacob to disguise himself as Esau in order to the get his 'blind' father Isaac's blessing before he died.

C.15 What is the following talking about: '*25 And these shall serve to lay the **foundations** of the **heaven**, and to strengthen the earth, and to renew all the luminaries which are in the firmament.*'

1) What are the 'foundations of heaven'? They are the foundations of the eternal life. See **Revelation 21**.

REV.21:1 And I saw a **new heaven** and a **new earth:** for the first heaven and the first earth were passed away;

REV.21:14 And the wall of the city had **twelve foundations**, and in them the names of the twelve apostles of the Lamb.

174

2) To 'strengthen the earth' God chose Jacob and his descendants to be a 'faithful witness' of the **truth** of **God's Word** to the whole world unto eternity and thus 'strengthen the earth'. See **Revelation 21**

REV.21:12 And had a wall great and high, and had **twelve gates**, and at the gates twelve angels, and names written thereon, which are the names of the **twelve tribes** of the **children of Israel:**

3) 'Renew *the* luminaries *which are in the firmament'* – this is talked about in the **Book of the Luminaries** which is a section in the 1st **Book of Enoch** - see my book 'Enoch Insights' Basically, stars are representing angels, and some of the angels have fallen which are also called '**wondering stars'**.

JUD.1:13 Raging waves of the sea, foaming out their own shame; **wandering stars**, to whom is reserved **the blackness of darkness** for ever.

JUD.1:14 And **Enoch** also, the seventh from Adam, prophesied of these, saying, Behold, the Lord cometh with ten thousands of his saints,

JUD.1:15 To **execute judgment** upon all, and to convince all that are ungodly among them of all their ungodly deeds which they have ungodly committed, and of all their hard speeches which ungodly sinners have spoken against him.

C.16 More on 'Renew the Luminaries' is talking about a time when all evil has been destroyed and there are no more evil angels or evil people. This happens just before the Heavenly City comes down to the surface of the earth at the Great White Throne Judgment of God at the very end of the Golden age of the Millennium and both Satan and the fallen angels are cast into the Lake of Fire along with the incalcitrant wicked people.

REV.20:11 And I saw a great white throne, and him that sat on it, from whose face the earth and the heaven fled away; and there was found no place for them.

JUD.1:6 And the angels which kept not their first estate, but left their own habitation, he hath reserved in everlasting chains under darkness unto the judgment of the great day.

C.17 In other words Abraham was telling Rebecca that in **Jacob** was the **promised seed** and that he would **affect the entire earth** from Jacob's time until the **New Heaven and New earth**.

Israel would become a blessing to all mankind and would continue to be a blessing until eternity **if they obeyed God** as his '**chosen people**'.

---

26 And he called Jacob before the eyes of Rebecca his mother, and kissed him, and blessed him, and said: 'Jacob, my beloved son, whom my soul loveth, may God bless thee from above the firmament, and may He give thee all the blessings wherewith He blessed Adam, and Enoch, and Noah, and Shem;

> 27 And all the things of which He told me, and all the things which He promised to give me, may he cause to cleave to thee and to thy seed for ever, according to the days of heaven above the earth.
>
> 28 And the Spirits of Mastema shall not rule over thee or over thy seed to turn thee from the Lord, who is thy God from henceforth for ever.

C.18 Mastema is Satan. Why does it state the '*spirits*' of *Mastema*. Surely Satan only has one spirit? In the Book of Enoch it also uses the word Satan in the plural: Satans. It is probably referring to the 'hosts of Satan' or the 'Fallen angels' who have been with him since before the creation of the physical universe. As Enoch talked about them 'They do as if THEY were the Lord'. (See my book 'Enoch Insights' for more on this topic)

DAN.8:10 And it waxed great, even to the 'host of heaven'; and it cast down some of the host and of the stars to the ground and stamped upon them.

REV.12:4 And his tail drew the third part of the stars of heaven and did cast them to the earth: and the dragon stood before the woman which was ready to be delivered, for to devour her child as soon as it was born.

> 29 And may the Lord God be a father to thee and thou the first-born son, and to the people always. Go in peace, my son.'
>
> 30 And they both went forth together from Abraham.
>
> 31 And Rebecca loved Jacob, with all her heart and with all her soul, very much more than Esau; but Isaac loved Esau much more than Jacob.

C.19 ABRAHAM'S BLESSING ON JACOB: The above story of Abraham giving his blessing to Jacob and encouraging Rebecca the mother of Jacob, (the younger twin to his brother Esau), to choose Jacob over Esau, is a very important piece of information. As far as I am aware of, this Book of Jubilees is the only book to mention this fact.

C.20 Isaac the father of Esau and Jacob, wanted to give his blessing to Esau, but God had other plans, because Esau had proven himself not to be worthy of inheriting the kingdom of Abraham and his descendants Israel.

C.21 Why is this particular point so important? Well, according to the account of Jacob and Esau given in the Bible, it gives the impression that Rebecca and Jacob were deceiving Isaac when he was old and blind. Rebecca told Jacob to disguise himself as his brother Esau, in order to steal the birth rite.

C.22 Rebecca was in fact obeying Abraham's wishes, because his own son Isaac was not realizing God's will in this matter. How could Isaac bless his son Esau who was a reprobate son doing all kinds of evil?

176

C.23 Why did God allow Isaac to go blind when he was old? Well, if we analyse the situation: we see that Jacob and Rebecca could never have tricked Isaac if he hadn't been blind at that exact time - by Jacob trying to disguise himself as Esau, as Isaac would have clearly noticed the deception.

Because Isaac was insisting that Esau his first born would indeed inherit his family title as was the normal tradition for the first born to inherit the family line, therefore God had to intervene so that Jacob would become the forefather of Israel - with the full blessing of his grandfather Abraham and Rebecca his mother.

C.24 Interestingly enough, later in this Book of Jubilees, Isaac changes his mind and realizes that it should be Jacob who inherits the promises as he finally realized how evil his first born son Esau is. It is also stated in this book of Jubilees, that later on in this book when Jacob brought two of his 11 sons to visit Isaac when Isaac was already blind, that the Lord opened his eyes again so that he could actually see the sons of Jacob Judah and Levi - which clearly showed that God could take away blindness when necessary.

C.25 Also remember that it was prophesied at the birth of Esau and Jacob that the older would serve the younger. Thus was it fulfilled, and Jacob eventually became Israel.

GEN.25:22 And the children struggled together within her; and she said, If it be so, why am I thus? And she went to enquire of the LORD.

GEN.25:23 And the LORD said unto her, Two nations are in thy womb, and two manner of people shall be separated from thy bowels; and the one people shall be stronger than the other people; and the elder shall serve the younger.

Chapter 20

> 1 And in the forty-second jubilee, in the first year of the seventh week, Abraham called Ishmael, [2052 (2045) A.M. = **Anno Mundi' = years of the world**] and his twelve sons, and Isaac and his two sons, and the six sons of Keturah, and their sons.

Comment:1: Here it is wonderful to see that at one time in the past families used to work together, and families used to have many children. Even up to just over 100 years ago quite a few people had large families. Some, in order to keep their family line going, and perhaps others even to keep their businesses going. Today there is such *disobedience* to even *God's 1st Commandment*: 'Be fruitful and multiply'.

C.2 TODAY IN MODERN TIMES IN THE WEST, THE BIRTH RATE HAS DECLINED TO 1.3 IN THE UK and we need 2.1/couple just to maintain the population. What does this mean? It means that the reason these Western governments insist on inviting so many foreigners into the country is not because they care about the immigrants or the 'so-called refugees' but it is simply so that they have enough workers to do the jobs, otherwise the businesses would fail.

C.3 SOVEREIGNTY OF NATIONS The tragedy is that the indigenous sovereignty of the different races of Europe is fast disappearing, because most people no longer either get married or have children. I would however like to see more young people getting married and having at least 2-3 kids here in the UK. People today don't even see that it is disobedience to God himself to 'forbid to marry' & 'withhold from having children' for 'convenience sake', in our so-called modern and progressive society. Where are we progressing to? In fact, we are going backwards in every sense of the word! It was just reported in 2020 that during the 'LOCKDOWN' for the Covid-19 in the UK, there were 3,000,000 children who were from single-child homes in England alone. Imagine so many children today without brothers and sisters!

> 2 And he commanded them that they should observe the way of the Lord; that they should work righteousness, and love each his neighbour, and act on this manner amongst all men; that they should each so walk with regard to them as to do judgment and righteousness on the earth.

Today unfortunately the world has become just like the following description in the Book of Romans 1:

ROM.1:20 For the invisible things of him from the creation of the world are clearly seen, being understood by the things that are made, even his eternal power and Godhead; so that they are without excuse:

ROM.1:21 Because that, when they knew God, they glorified him not as God, neither were thankful; but became vain in their imaginations, and their foolish heart was darkened.

ROM.1:22 Professing themselves to be wise, they became fools,

3 That they should circumcise their sons, according to the covenant which He had made with them, and not deviate to the right hand or the left of all the paths which the Lord had commanded us; and that we should keep ourselves from all fornication and uncleanness, [and renounce from amongst us all fornication and uncleanness].

4 And if any woman or maid commit fornication amongst you, burn her with fire and let them not commit fornication with her after their eyes and their heart; and let them not take to themselves wives from the daughters of Canaan; for the seed of Canaan will be rooted out of the land.

C.4 '**woman or maid commit fornication amongst you, burn her with fire**' I know that to many 'advanced thinking' people of today, that this above verse seems very cruel. On the surface I would also tend to agree, but let's now examine the depth of what this verse is really talking about? Why did God allow the laws of Abraham and some 500 years later, the Laws of Moses to be so severe? Let's consider a few points. According to this book of Jubilees as well as the Bible and also the Book of Jasher, Abraham was alive at the same time as both Noah and Shem. According to the Book of Jasher Abraham was taught at the feet of Noah and Shem. He studied the Books of both Enoch and Noah. I suspect that *Abraham was thinking about the dangers that used to exist before the Great Flood*, and he didn't want these dangers to return. Women acting promiscuously could attract the same evil spirits that destroyed the earth before the great Flood. Women enticing Fallen angels to make love with them and thus causing the same problems again as before the Great Flood.

C.5 Solomon 1000 years later warned about these spirits of seduction. In the book of Enoch he called them Sirens. The problem was that the 'fornication' was one of the traits of witchcraft and the deliberate summoning of evil spirits or entities. For this reason, God made very severe laws so that no one would dare to disobey and open the door to these dark entities and bring chaos yet again. At least that was the idea.

5 And he told them of the judgment of the giants, and the judgment of the Sodomites, how they had been judged on account of their wickedness, and had died on account of their fornication, and uncleanness, and mutual corruption through fornication.

6 'And guard yourselves from all fornication and uncleanness, And from all pollution of sin,

Lest ye make our name a curse, And your whole life a hissing,

And all your sons to be destroyed by the sword, And ye become accursed like Sodom, And all your remnant as the sons of Gomorrah.

7 I implore you, my sons, love the God of heaven And cleave ye to all His commandments. And walk not after their idols, and after their uncleanness, And make not for yourselves molten or graven gods;

C.6 Here we can clearly see that Abraham has made the point, that all his life he has been an Idol Smasher as he had seen how much evil these Idols had caused in their time. Ceremonies with Idols often had to do with *fornication both physical and spiritual* which would indeed summon the evil spirits. The Idols might just be dead wood, but when a lot of attention is given to them, and especially if the Idol represents a Fallen angel or a demon god, then it would cause the demons to show up and cause chaos and confusion. Abraham having been an Idol smasher all his life wanted that his descendants would get off to a good start by *not allowing such iniquity in their camp.* Thus, the *severe laws* concerning *fornication and idol worshipping.*

C.7 Here is how God dealt with both Idol worshipping and fornication in the time of Moses:

NUM.25:1 And Israel abode in Shittim, and the people began to *commit whoredom* with the *daughters of Moab.*

NUM.25:2 And they called the people unto the *sacrifices of their gods*: and the people did eat and *bowed down to their gods.*

NUM.25:3 And Israel joined himself unto Baalpeor: and the anger of the LORD was kindled against Israel.

NUM.25:4 And the LORD said unto Moses, *Take all the heads of the people*, and hang them up before the LORD against the sun, that the fierce anger of the LORD may be turned away from Israel.

NUM.25:5 And Moses said unto the judges of Israel, *Slay ye everyone* his men that were *joined unto Baalpeor.*

C.8 Another point is that in the far past in order for the men of Israel to be with the women of another nation it involved *worshipping their Idols* or gods of that nation or presumably the men wouldn't be given the women. This turned out to be Solomon's downfall and how he lost the Kingdom:

1KI.11:1 But king Solomon loved many strange women, together with the daughter of Pharaoh, women of the Moabites, Ammonites, Edomites, Zidonians, and Hittites:

1KI.11:2 Of the nations concerning which the LORD said unto the children of Israel, Ye shall not go into them, neither shall they come in unto you: for surely they will *turn away your heart* after their **gods:** Solomon clave unto these in love.

1KI.11:4 For it came to pass, when Solomon was old, that his wives turned away his heart after other gods: and his heart was not perfect with the LORD his God, as was the heart of David his father.

1KI.11:5 For Solomon went after Ashtoreth the goddess of the Zidonians, and after Milcom the abomination of the Ammonites.

1KI.11:11 Wherefore the LORD said unto Solomon, Forasmuch as this is done of thee, and thou hast not kept my covenant and my statutes, which I have commanded thee, I will surely rend the kingdom from thee, and will give it to thy servant.

---

8 For they are vanity, And there is no spirit in them;

For they are work of (men's) hands, And all who trust in them, trust in nothing.

REV.2:20 Notwithstanding I have a few things against thee, because thou suffer that woman *Jezebel*, which *calleth herself a prophetess*, to teach and to *seduce my servants* to *commit fornication*, and to *eat things sacrificed* unto *idols*.

---

9 Serve them not, nor worship them, But serve ye the most high God, and worship Him continually: And hope for His countenance always, And work uprightness and righteousness before Him,

That He may have pleasure in you and grant you His mercy, And send rain upon you morning and evening,

And bless all your works which ye have wrought upon the earth, And bless thy bread and thy water,

And bless the fruit of thy womb and the fruit of thy land, And the herds of thy cattle, and the flocks of thy sheep.

10 And ye will be for a blessing on the earth, And all nations of the earth will desire you,

And bless your sons in my name, That they may be blessed as I am.

11 And he gave to Ishmael and to his sons, and to the sons of Keturah, gifts, and sent them away from Isaac his son, and he gave everything to Isaac his son.

---

12 And Ishmael and his sons, and the sons of Keturah and their sons, went together and dwelt from Paran to the entering in of Babylon in all the land which is towards the East facing the desert.

13 And these mingled with each other, and their name was called Arabs, and Ishmaelites.

Chapter 21

1 And in the sixth year of the seventh week of this jubilee Abraham called Isaac his son, and [2057 (2050) A.M. = **Anno Mundi' = years of the world**] commanded him: saying, 'I am become old, and know not the day of my death, and am full of my days.

2 And behold, I am one hundred and seventy-five years old, and throughout all the days of my life I have remembered the Lord and sought with all my heart to do His will, and to walk uprightly in all His ways.

Comment:1: I think it likely that *biblical numerology* often has *great significance* in showing the *order of Creation* and thus there has to be a *divine Designer.*

Abraham died at **175** years old **175 = 25 x 7 or 52 x 7** Do these number mean something?: We know that the **number 7** *is God's number.* What about double 5 or **5 x 5**? How does it apply to Abraham?

The Meaning of Numbers: The Number 5

The number **5** symbolizes **God's grace**, **goodness** and **favour toward humans** and is mentioned **318** times in Scripture.

Five is the **number** of **grace**, and **multiplied by itself**, which is **5 x 5 = 25,** is **'grace upon grace' (John 1:16)**. The **Ten Commandments** contains **two sets of 5** commandments. The **first five** commandments are related to our treatment and **relationship with God**, and the **last five** concern **our relationship with others humans**.

C.2 For a lot more interesting details about the number five:

Source: https://www.biblestudy.org/bibleref/meaning-of-numbers-in-bible/5.html

C.3 I find this **biblical numerology** assessment of the number **7 x 5 x 5** as applied to Abraham to be quite remarkable - having both **God's number 7** and the **double 5** meaning '**Grace** upon **Grace**'

C.4 If one was to describe **Abraham's life in a sentence**, it would be: 'A man who '**loved God with all his heart**' and a man who was '**known to kind and generous to those whom he met**'.

C.5 Abraham was an excellent example of living the two most important commandments: How many people who have ever lived have held that high a standard?

MAT.22:37-8 Jesus said unto him, Thou shalt love the Lord thy God with all thy heart, and with all thy soul, and with all thy mind .. and thy neighbour as thyself.

3 My soul has hated idols, given my heart and spirit that I might observe to do the will of Him who created me.

4 For He is the living God, and He is holy and faithful, and He is righteous beyond all, and there is with Him no accepting of (men's) persons and no accepting of gifts; for God is righteous, and executeth judgment on all those who transgress His commandments and despise His covenant.

5 And do thou, my son, observe His commandments and His ordinances and His judgments, and walk not after the abominations and after the graven images and after the molten images.

6 And eat no blood at all of animals or cattle, or of any bird which flies in the heaven.

7 And if thou dost slay a victim as an acceptable peace offering, slay ye it, and pour out its blood upon the altar, and all the fat of the offering offer on the altar with fine flour and the meat offering mingled with oil, with its drink offering offer them all together on the altar of burnt offering; it is a sweet savour before the Lord.

8 And thou wilt offer the fat of the sacrifice of thank offerings on the fire which is upon the altar, and the fat which is on the belly, and all the fat on the inwards and the two kidneys, and all the fat that is upon them, and upon the loins and liver thou shalt remove, together with the kidneys.

9 And offer all these for a sweet savour acceptable before the Lord, with its meat-offering and with its drink-offering, for a sweet savour, the bread of the offering unto the Lord.

10 And eat its meat on that day and on the second day, and let not the sun on the second day go down upon it till it is eaten, and let nothing be left over for the third day; for it is not acceptable [for it is not approved] and let it no longer be eaten, and all who eat thereof will bring sin upon themselves; for thus I have found it written in the books of my forefa-

thers, and in the words of Enoch, and in the words of Noah.

C.6 Here we can clearly see that Abraham is referring to the Books of both Noah and the Book of Enoch and most importantly pointing to these books as an *authority of God's Word*. The big question is what happened to the books of Noah? We have the book of Enoch and in it are perhaps five chapters from the Book of Noah but where is the original complete book or the books of Noah. These would be amazing to find.

C.7 From reading this book of Jubilees alone we can see that the angels passed on to Noah the *knowledge of all the herbs and spices* and which ailments they could cure. We are also told that *different herbs can drive away certain bad spirits* which are actually responsible for the sicknesses or diseases in the first place. So, the *book of healing by Noah would be an invaluable book* to have. I suspect that in modern times that there are certain pharmaceutical companies who would not like an alternative to their modern chemical solutions for healings which often only treat the symptoms of diseases but never get to the root of the diseases. Probably done deliberately as permanently curing someone does not make money but dependence of the pharmaceutical companies does! The pharmaceutical companies would probably finance the 'getting rid of ancient herbal knowledge'. Why? Because that would truly help people to heal themselves and thus not need modern Western medicines. The oriental medical cures are much closer to nature in their use of herbs and spices and much more effecting in curing people.

11 And on all thy oblations thou shalt strew salt and let not the salt of the covenant be lacking in all thy oblations before the Lord.

12 And as regards the wood of the sacrifices, beware lest thou bring (other) wood for the altar in addition to these: cypress, bay, almond, fir, pine, cedar, savin, fig, olive, myrrh, laurel, aspalathus.

13 And of these kinds of wood lay upon the altar under the sacrifice, such as have been tested as to their appearance, and do not lay (thereon) any split or dark wood, (but) hard and clean, without fault, a sound and new growth; and do not lay (thereon) old wood, [for its fragrance is gone] for there is no longer fragrance in it as before.

14 Besides these kinds of wood there is none other that thou shalt place (on the altar), for the fragrance is dispersed, and the smell of its fragrance goes not up to heaven.

15 Observe this commandment and do it, my son, that thou mayst be

upright in all thy deeds.

16 And at all times be clean in thy body and wash thyself with water before thou approach to offer on the altar, and wash thy hands and thy feet before thou draw near to the altar; and when thou art done sacrificing, wash again thy hands and thy feet.

17 And let no blood appear upon you nor upon your clothes; be on thy guard, my son, against blood, be on thy guard exceedingly; cover it with dust.

18 And do not eat any blood for it is the soul; eat no blood whatever.

C.8 As has been correctly stated in the New Testament 'The Life of the body is in the blood. If the flow of blood stops when the heart stops then we die. Here Abraham is telling his son that life itself is sacred and that he should not touch the blood of any creature as it was the life-flow of that creature.

19 And take no gifts for the blood of man, lest it be shed with impunity, without judgment; for it is the blood that is shed that causes the earth to sin, and the earth cannot be cleansed from the blood of man save by the blood of him who shed it.

C.9 Here Abraham is telling us some very important points. If a man kills another man, then the earth itself could not be cleansed from this evil except by the blood of him who committed the crime.

C.10 Like other prophets of God, Abraham is inferring that the earth itself has a conscious or is somewhat alive and knows everything that goes on in it. This is also brought out in the apocryphal book of II Ezdras.

II Ezdras: 5.30 (God speaking through his angel Uriel): He said unto me, 'Even so have I given the womb of the earth to those who from time to time are sown in it.'

II Ezdras 5.31 'Is our Mother (Earth) of whom thou has told me still young…?

C.11 This is where the Mosaic laws some 400 years later stated 'Eye for an eye and 'Tooth for a tooth' came from. These laws were finally done away with the shedding of the blood of the Messiah – Jesus who took upon Himself all the sins of the whole world upon Himself and thus the world was cleansed from all sins. For this reason, when we confess Christ and receive Him into our hearts, He cleanses us from all of our sins by His own sacrifice in His own blood shed upon the cross.

1JN.1:9 If we confess our sins, he is faithful and just to forgive us our sins, and to cleanse us from all unrighteousness

C.12 Before the Messiah came along it was as if the earth itself wanted retribution for all the crimes committed in itself

NUM.32:23 But if ye will not do so, behold, ye have sinned against the LORD: and be sure your sin will find you out.

A very interesting choice of words in the above verse *'your sin will find you out'*. This verse also makes out as if your sin has the power to bring retribution? Is sin somehow at least in extreme cases linked to 'demons that torment people' for their crimes?

GAL.6:7 Be not deceived; God is not mocked: for whatsoever a man soweth, that shall he also reap.

GAL.6:8 For he that soweth to his flesh shall of the flesh reap corruption; but he that soweth to the Spirit shall of the Spirit reap life everlasting.

C.13 Let's examine this very interesting topiC. The first person whose blood was shed on the earth was Abel the son of Adam and Eve...

GEN.4:10 And he said, What hast thou done? the voice of thy brother's blood crieth unto me from the ground.

GEN.4:11 And now art thou cursed from the earth, which hath opened her mouth to receive thy brother's blood from thy hand;

Look what happens to Cain's bloodline according to the book of Enoch

ENOCH 22.5 'This is the spirit that went forth from Abel whom Cain slew and makes his suit against him until his seed is destroyed from the earth annihilated from amongst the seed of men.

According to the **Book of Jasher** Cain was killed by one of his own descendants called Lamech. Apparently Lamech was the last person in the bloodline of Cain. We can clearly see that in the case of Cain, God did wipe out his descendants and also Cain himself was killed as retribution for his iniquities.

C.14 There is a consequence for our sins and iniquities and that is why we all need the Saviour Jesus Christ. Without Christ's sacrificing His blood for us, we are truly totally lost in darkness and our own sins will indeed be 'seeking us out'!

C.15 HAUNTED? I have heard countless stories of people stating that they have been haunted for one reason or another because of evil deeds that they had done. It has happened to countless soldiers coming back from wars. It happens to murderers. It has happened to women who have had abortions. It can happen for many reasons.

C.16 The truth is exactly what Abraham has stated above to his son Isaac 'He that sheds the blood of mankind - of mankind shall his blood be required' or better said Mother Earth or the Spirit World will take retribution on a person who is not protected by the blood of Jesus Christ. If you believe in Jesus, then you have nothing to fear as in regard to your sins. Jesus Christ forgives them all and washes them away with His blood.

C.17 Look at the following verses which were directly prophesising about the Messiah 800-1000 years before Jesus was even born.

ISA.53:5 But he was wounded for our transgressions, he was bruised for our iniquities: the chastisement of our peace was upon him; and with his stripes we are healed.

PSA.22:16 For dogs have compassed me: the assembly of the wicked have unclosed me: they pierced my hands and my feet.

PSA.22:17 I may tell all my bones: they look and stare upon me.

PSA.22:18 They part my garments among them, and cast lots upon my vesture.

---

20 And take no present or gift for the blood of man: blood for blood, that thou mayest be accepted before the Lord, the Most High God; for He is the defence of the good: and that thou mayest be preserved from all evil, and that He may save thee from every kind of death.

21 I see, my son, That all the works of the children of men are sin and wickedness, And all their deeds are uncleanness and an abomination and a pollution, And there is no righteousness with them.

22 Beware, lest thou shouldest walk in their ways And tread in their paths, And sin a sin unto death before the Most High God.

Else He will hide His face from thee and give thee back into the hands of thy transgression, and root thee out of the land, and thy seed likewise from under heaven, and thy name and thy seed shall perish from the whole earth.

23 Turn away from all their deeds and all their uncleanness, and observe the ordinance of the Most High God, and do His will and be upright in all things.

24 And He will bless thee in all thy deeds, and will raise up from thee a plant of righteousness through all the earth, throughout all generations of the earth, and my name and thy name shall not be forgotten under heaven for ever.

25 Go, my son in peace. May the Most High God, my God and thy

---

> God, strengthen thee to do His will, And may He bless all thy seed and the residue of thy seed for the generations for ever, with all righteous blessings, That thou mayest be a blessing on all the earth.'
>
> 26 And he went out from him rejoicing.

C.18 Here are some very good verses from the New Testament about the above-mentioned topic of blood sacrifices.

HEB.9:11 But Christ being come an high priest of good things to come, by a greater and more perfect tabernacle, not made with hands, that is to say, not of this building;

HEB.9:12 Neither by the blood of goats and calves, but by his own blood he entered in once into the holy place, having obtained eternal redemption for us.

HEB.9:13 For if the blood of bulls and of goats, and the ashes of an heifer sprinkling the unclean, pp to the purifying of the flesh:

HEB.9:14 How much more shall the blood of Christ, who through the eternal Spirit offered himself without spot to God, purge your conscience from dead works to serve the living God?

HEB.9:15 And for this cause he is the mediator of the new testament, that by means of death, for the redemption of the transgressions that were under the first testament, they which are called might receive the promise of eternal inheritance.

Chapter 22

1 And it came to pass in the first week in the forty-fourth jubilee, in the second year, that is, the year in which Abraham died, that Isaac and Ishmael came from the Well of the Oath to celebrate the feast of weeks -that is, the feast of the first fruits of the harvest-to Abraham, their father, and Abraham rejoiced because his two sons had come.

2 For Isaac had many possessions in Beersheba, and Isaac was wont to go and see his possessions and to return to his father.

3 And in those days Ishmael came to see his father, and they both came together, and Isaac offered a sacrifice for a burnt offering, and presented it on the altar of his father which he had made in Hebron.

4 And he offered a thank offering and made a feast of joy before Ishmael, his brother: and Rebecca made new cakes from the new grain, and gave them to Jacob, her son, to take them to Abraham, his father, from the first fruits of the land, that he might eat and bless the Creator of all things before he died.

5 And Isaac, too, sent by the hand of Jacob to Abraham a best thank offering, that he might eat and drink.

6 And he ate and drank, and blessed the Most High God, Who hath created heaven and earth, Who hath made all the fat things of the earth, And given them to the children of men That they might eat and drink and bless their Creator.

7 'And now I give thanks unto Thee, my God, because thou hast caused me to see this day: behold, I am one hundred three score and fifteen years, an old man and full of days, and all my days have been unto me peace.

Comment:1: '*one hundred three score and fifteen years*.' A Score is 20, so three score is 60. Add 100 +15 and you get a total of 175 years old.

8 The sword of the adversary has not overcome me in all that Thou hast given me and my children all the days of my life until this day.

9 My God, may Thy mercy and Thy peace be upon Thy servant, and upon the seed of his sons, that they may be to Thee a chosen nation and an inheritance from amongst all the nations of the earth from henceforth unto all the days of the generations of the earth, unto all the ages.'

10 And he called Jacob and said: 'My son Jacob, may the God of all bless thee and strengthen thee to do righteousness, and His will before Him, and may He choose thee and thy seed that ye may become a people for His inheritance according to His will always.

11 And do thou, my son, Jacob, draw near and kiss me.' And he drew near and kissed him, and he said:

'Blessed be my son Jacob And all the sons of God Most High, unto all the ages:

May God give unto thee a seed of righteousness; And some of thy sons may He sanctify in the midst of the whole earth;

May nations serve thee, And all the nations bow themselves before thy seed.

12 Be strong in the presence of men, And exercise authority over all the seed of Seth.

Then thy ways and the ways of thy sons will be justified, So that they shall become a holy nation.

C.2 Where is the sense of discipline today? What happened to morals and scruples? Why are so many people without a backbone in not knowing what they believe in? Why are most who say that they believe in God severely compromised and hardly know right from wrong?

Abraham certainly knew the difference and God Himself encouraged him to stand up for his convictions in spite of great adversity. God instructed him to be an example to others.

C.3 According to the Bible there is coming the Golden Age of the Messiah where Jesus rules in person on the earth with his angelized saints.

What kind of rule is that going to be? Well it certainly wont be a wishy washy 'anything goes' sort of rule of Liberalism!

'He shall rule them with a rod of iron' according to Psalm 2 - as it will be needed to subdue any incorrigibles. The 'selfishness' and 'do your own thing' and 'anything goes' morality of today as well as the 'defiance of Satan and his satanists' God will have long since disappeared into the smokes of hell

191

with all the Mark of the Beast people.

13 May the Most High God give thee all the blessings Wherewith He has blessed me And wherewith He blessed Noah and Adam; May they rest on the sacred head of thy seed from generation to generation for ever.

14 And may He cleanse thee from all unrighteousness and impurity, That thou mayest be forgiven all the transgressions; which thou hast committed ignorantly.

And may He strengthen thee, And bless thee. And mayest thou inherit the whole earth,

15 And may He renew His covenant with thee. That thou mayest be to Him a nation for His inheritance for all the ages, And that He may be to thee and to thy seed a God in truth and righteousness throughout all the days of the earth.

16 And do thou, my son Jacob, remember my words, And observe the commandments of Abraham, thy father:

Separate thyself from the nations, And eat not with them:

And do not according to their works, And become not their associate;

For their works are unclean, And all their ways are a Pollution and an abomination and uncleanness.

2CO.6:17 Wherefore come out from among them, and be ye separate, saith the Lord, and touch not the unclean thing; and I will receive you.

C.4 *'All their ways are a Pollution and an abomination and uncleanness.'*
Now, that is a very strong statement! Why does Abraham say that to his grandson Jacob just before he died? There are clearly some things which are indeed a Pollution or an Abomination or an Uncleanness unto the Lord. Later Moses would *list all of these things* in the Book of Leviticus and other Books of the Law. Let's face it today in modern times the reason why our planet is totally polluted and has become an abomination where so many peoples are 'unclean' is because of the way people choose to live with 1) Non-Kosher food. Or food that is not good for the human body and therefore unclean. The saying 'You are what you eat is true'. God clearly lists in the books of the Laws of Moses which foods are Kosher and which are unclean. Abomination is when people deliberately do the opposite of what God teaches His people. For example: The Greek ruler Antiochus Epiphanes* who deliberately placed

192

the head of a pig on the Jewish altar in Jerusalem (*SOURCE: https://www.gotquestions.org/Antiochus-Epiphanes.html) The Bible predicts that in the very Last days of man upon the earth there shall arise the most evil man of all time: The Anti-Christ. He also will place an ABOMINATION in the soon to be built 3rd Temple in Jerusalem.

C.5 MORE on ABOMINATIONS: MAT.24:15 When ye therefore shall see the *abomination of desolation*, spoken of by Daniel the prophet, stand in the holy place, (whoso reads, let him understand:)

DAN.9:27 And he shall confirm the covenant with many for one week: and in the midst of the week he shall cause the sacrifice and the oblation to cease, and for the overspreading of *abominations* he shall make it desolate, even until the consummation, and that determined shall be poured upon the desolate.

REV.13:14 And deceives them that dwell on the earth by the means of those miracles which he had power to do in the sight of the beast; saying to them that dwell on the earth, that they should make an image to the beast, which had the wound by a sword, and did live.

REV.13:15 And he had power to give life unto the image of the beast, that the image of the beast should both speak, and cause that as many as would not worship the image of the beast should be killed.

REV.13:16 And he causes all, both small and great, rich and poor, free and bond, to receive a mark in their right hand, or in their foreheads:

REV.13:17 And that no man might buy or sell, save he that had the mark, or the name of the beast, or the number of his name.

REV.13:18 Here is wisdom. Let him that hath understanding count the number of the beast: for it is the number of a man; and his number is Six hundred threescore and six.

> 17 They offer their sacrifices to the dead And they worship evil spirits,
>
> And they eat over the graves, And all their works are vanity and noth-ingness.

C.6 This is talking about a type of ancestral worship of the Dead, which is nothing more than Idol worshipping rather than worshipping God. This practice is apparently still common today in Africa, Japan & Korea

(**Source:** https://repository.up.aC.za/bitstream/handle/2263/25045/Complete.pdf?sequence=10)

> 18 They have no heart to understand And their eyes do not see what their works are,
>
> And how they err in saying to a piece of wood: 'Thou art my God,' And to a stone: 'Thou art my Lord and thou art my deliverer.' [And they

have no heart.]

C.7 This verse is quite revealing: *'they err in saying to a piece of wood: 'Thou art my God,' And to a stone: 'Thou art my Lord and thou art my deliverer.'* Today this is exactly what is preached in the false doctrine of Evolution. That mankind came from a stone or a rock in the pre-historic primordial soup some billions of years ago. The following verses describe the False Doctrine of Evolution 1850 to 2350 years before Charles Darwin fabricated the Doctrine of Evolution:

JER.2:27 Saying to a *stock (tree),* Thou art my father; and to a *stone, Thou hast brought me forth*: for they have *turned their back unto me,* and not their face: but in the time of their trouble they will say, Arise, and save us

ROM.1:22 Professing themselves to be wise, they *became fools,*

ROM.1:23 And *changed the glory* of the *uncorruptible God* into an *image* made like to *corruptible man,* and to *birds,* and *four-footed beasts, and creeping things.*

19 And as for thee, my son Jacob, May the Most High God help thee And the God of heaven bless thee And remove thee from their uncleanness and from all their error.

20 Be thou ware, my son Jacob, of taking a wife from any seed of the daughters of Canaan; For all his seed is to be rooted out of the earth.

21 For, owing to the transgression of Ham, Canaan erred, And all his seed shall be destroyed from off the earth and all the residue thereof, And none springing from him shall be saved on the day of judgment.

C.8 This verse does not say that all the descendants of Ham or the Black races shall be destroyed, but *only the seed of Canaan.* Why? Canaan was double cursed, and because of his actions, the Giants of the Nephilim (Fallen Angels) came back again after the Great Flood. For that reason, they were to be rooted out to stop more giants from emerging on the surface of the earth due to the extreme wickedness such as was seen in Sodom and Gomorrah, as they were indeed Canaanites. God didn't want the same situation as before the Great Flood happening yet again so soon after the Great Flood.

22 And as for all the worshippers of idols and the profane (b) There shall be no hope for them in the land of the living; (c) And there shall be no remembrance of them on the earth; (c) For they shall descend into Sheol, (d) And into the place of condemnation shall they go,

As the children of Sodom were taken away from the earth So will all

194

those who worship idols be taken away.

C.9 This verse also reveals a lot of information, showing that those who *worship Idols* often become *demon possessed*. This is also stated in the book of Revelation very clearly.

REV.9:20 And the rest of the men which were not killed by these plagues yet repented not of the works of their hands, that they should not *worship devils*, and idols of gold, and silver, and brass, and stone, and of wood: which neither can see, nor hear, nor walk:

REV.9:21 Neither repented they of their *murders*, nor of their *sorceries*, nor of their *fornication*, nor of their thefts.

'As the children of Sodom were taken away from the earth So will all those who worship idols be taken away.'

C.10 As in God's violent destruction of Sodom and Gomorrah by sending fire and brimstone down from heaven. It turns out that the greatest iniquities of those Canaanite cities was their *extreme cruelty* to *strangers*. Cruelty without a cause, just for the sake of being cruel in other words Satanic & demoniC.

---

23 Fear not, my son Jacob, And be not dismayed, O son of Abraham:

May the Most High God preserve thee from destruction, And from all the paths of error may he deliver thee.

24 This house have I built for myself that I might put my name upon it in the earth: [it is given to thee and to thy seed for ever], and it will be named the house of Abraham; it is given to thee and to thy seed for ever; for thou wilt build my house and establish my name before God for ever: thy seed and thy name will stand throughout all generations of the earth.'

25 And he ceased commanding him and blessing him.

26 And the two lay together on one bed, and Jacob slept in the bosom of Abraham, his father's father and he kissed him seven times, and his affection and his heart rejoiced over him.

C.11 'Bosom of Abraham'. From this verse comes the example that has been used as an expression of Paradise inside the earth ever since. In the New Testament Jesus mentions Lazarus as being 'In the Bosom of Abraham':

LUK.16:22 And it came to pass, that the beggar died, and was carried by the angels into *'Abraham's bosom'*: the rich man also died and was buried;

LUK.16:23 And in hell he lifted up his eyes, being in torments, and saw Abraham afar off, and Lazarus in his bosom.

LUK.16:24 And he cried and said, Father Abraham, have mercy on me, and send Lazarus, that he may dip the tip of his finger in water, and cool my tongue; for I am tormented in this flame.

LUK.16:25 But Abraham said, Son, remember that thou in thy lifetime received thy good things, and likewise Lazarus evil things: but now he is comforted, and thou art tormented.

LUK.16:26 And beside all this, between us and you there is a great gulf fixed: so that they which would pass from hence to you cannot; neither can they pass to us, that would come from thence.

C.12 It is held by Jewish writings, that Hell and Paradise (Abraham's Bosom) are side by side, inside the earth; which Jesus's Parable of the Rich and the Beggar seem to also confirm.

---

27 And he blessed him with all his heart and said: 'The Most High God, the God of all, and Creator of all, who brought me forth from Ur of the Chaldees that he might give me this land to inherit it for ever, and that I might establish a holy seed-blessed be the Most High for ever.'

28 And he blessed Jacob and said: 'My son, over whom with all my heart and my affection I rejoice, may Thy grace and Thy mercy be lift up upon him and upon his seed always.

29 And do not forsake him, nor set him at nought from henceforth unto the days of eternity, and may Thine eyes be opened upon him and upon his seed, that Thou mayst preserve him, and bless him, and mayest sanctify him as a nation for Thine inheritance;

30 And bless him with all Thy blessings from henceforth unto all the days of eternity and renew Thy covenant and Thy grace with him and with his seed according to all Thy good pleasure unto all the generations of the earth.'

C.13 God made a Covenant with Jacob that he should follow in Abraham's footsteps and teach righteousness unto his descendants and that God would make a great nation of Jacob. God's promises were marvellously fulfilled in Jacobs 12 sons.

REV.7:4 And I heard the number of them which were sealed: and there were sealed an hundred and forty and four thousand of all the tribes of the children of Israel.

C.14 The Book of Revelations in Chapter 21 goes on to name all those *sealed by God* of the Tribes of Israel (12 sons of Jacob):

REV.7:5 Of the tribe of Juda were sealed twelve thousand. Of the tribe of Reuben were sealed twelve thousand. Of the tribe of Gad were sealed twelve thousand.

REV.7:6 Of the tribe of Asher were sealed twelve thousand. Of the tribe of Nephthalim were sealed twelve thousand. Of the tribe of Manasses were sealed twelve thousand.

REV.7:7 Of the tribe of Simeon were sealed twelve thousand. Of the tribe of Levi were sealed twelve thousand. Of the tribe of Issachar were sealed twelve thousand.

REV.7:8 Of the tribe of Zabulon were sealed twelve thousand. Of the tribe of Joseph were sealed twelve thousand. Of the tribe of Benjamin were sealed twelve thousand.

C.15 Jacob's sons are so well known, that God even honoured them by calling the gates of His heavenly city by the names of Jacobs sons.

REV.21:12 And had a wall great and high, and had twelve gates, and at the gates twelve angels, and names written thereon, which are the names of the *twelve tribes of the children of Israel*:

C.16 Look how long God worked in Abraham's life. He made a promise to him that his seed would be as the stars of the sky in multitude, but he was nearly a hundred years old before his wife Sarah first got pregnant and had IsaaC. But Abraham endured, even undergoing the test on Mount Moriah when the Lord tested him to see if he'd give up Isaac, and he became the father of faith, and example of faithfulness and endurance. The Lord said that 'after he had patiently endured, he received the promise.' And what a wonderful promise and victory it was!

HEB.11:8 By faith Abraham, when he was called to go out into a place which he should after receive for an inheritance, obeyed; and he went out, not knowing whither he went.

HEB.11:9 By faith he sojourned in the land of promise, as in a strange country, dwelling in tabernacles with Isaac and Jacob, the heirs with him of the same promise:

HEB.11:10 For he looked for a city which hath foundations, whose builder and maker is God.

HEB.11:11 Through faith also Sara herself received strength to conceive seed, and was delivered of a child when she was past age, because she judged him faithful who had promised.

HEB.11:12 Therefore sprang there even of one, and him as good as dead, so many as the stars of the sky in multitude, and as the sand which is by the sea shore innumerable.

HEB.11:13 These all died in faith, not having received the promises, but having seen them afar off, and were persuaded of them, and embraced them, and confessed that they were strangers and pilgrims on the earth.

Chapter 23

1 And he placed two fingers of Jacob on his eyes, and he blessed the God of gods, and he covered his face and stretched out his feet and slept the sleep of eternity, and was gathered to his fathers.

2 And notwithstanding all this Jacob was lying in his bosom, and knew not that Abraham, his father's father, was dead.

3 And Jacob awoke from his sleep, and behold Abraham was cold as ice, and he said 'Father, father'; but there was none that spoke, and he knew that he was dead.

4 And he arose from his bosom and ran and told Rebecca, his mother; and Rebecca went to Isaac in the night, and told him; and they went together, and Jacob with them, and a lamp was in his hand, and when they had gone in they found Abraham lying dead.

5 And Isaac fell on the face of his father and wept and kissed him.

6 And the voices were heard in the house of Abraham, and Ishmael his son arose, and went to Abraham his father, and wept over Abraham his father, he and all the house of Abraham, and they wept with a great weeping.

7 And his sons Isaac and Ishmael buried him in the double cave, near Sarah his wife, and they wept for him forty days, all the men of his house, and Isaac and Ishmael, and all their sons, and all the sons of Keturah in their places; and the days of weeping for Abraham were ended.

8 And he lived three jubilees and four weeks of years, one hundred and seventy-five years, and completed the days of his life, being old and full of days.

9 For the days of the forefathers, of their life, were nineteen jubilees; and after the Flood they began to grow less than nineteen jubilees, and to decrease in jubilees, and to grow old quickly, and to be full of their

> days by reason of manifold tribulation and the wickedness of their ways, with the exception of Abraham.

Comment:1: One Jubilee is 50 years. Here it is stating that Adam and Eve, and those before the Great Flood lived to be 'nineteen jubilees' or almost 950 years old. It is also stating that because of '*manifold tribulation and the wickedness*' mankind started to '*grow old quickly*' after the Great Flood. This is very evident and can be seen in the **BIBLE LONGEVITY CHART** in the **APPENDIX**

> 10 For Abraham was perfect in all his deeds with the Lord, and well-pleasing in righteousness all the days of his life; and behold, he did not complete four jubilees in his life, when he had grown old by reason of the wickedness and was full of his days.
>
> 11 And all the generations which shall arise from this time until the day of the great judgment shall grow old quickly, before they complete two jubilees, and their knowledge shall forsake them by reason of their old age and all their knowledge shall vanish away.

C.2 This is very revealing information: '*shall grow old quickly, before they complete two jubilees*'. Here, it is saying the days would come after Abraham's time when people would live to be less than a 100-years old. '*and their knowledge shall forsake them by reason of their old age*'. Mankind would be cursed to lose his knowledge in his old age. This is not as it used to be as it used to be the case that those that are the oldest were often the wisest and most knowledgeable. People today do lose their knowledge when they get old by modern disease such as Parkinson's, Altzeimer's and Dementia.

'*until the day of the great judgment (they) shall grow old quickly.*' This is also interesting, as normally we talk about the '*great judgement*' as the Great White Throne Judgement at the end of the Millennium.

REV.20:11 And I saw a great white throne, and him that sat on it, from whose face the earth and the heaven fled away; and there was found no place for them.

REV.20:12 And I saw the dead, small and great, stand before God; and the books were opened: and another book was opened, which is the book of life: and the dead were judged out of those things which were written in the books, according to their works.

REV.20:13 And the sea gave up the dead which were in it; and death and hell delivered up the dead which were in them: and they were judged every man according to their works.

REV.20:14 And death and hell were cast into the lake of fire. This is the second death.

REV.20:15 And whosoever was not found written in the book of life was cast into the lake of fire.

Here however it states that people will grow old until the great judgement. One thing we know is that after Christ returns there will be a period of 1000 Millennium when people get as old as in Pre-Flood times, that is up to 1000 years old. So the above verse in mentioning the great judgement could be talking about the 'Wrath of God' right before the Millennium.

REV.16:1 And I heard a great voice out of the temple saying to the seven angels, Go your ways, and pour out the vials of the wrath of God upon the earth.

> 12 And in those days, if a man live a jubilee and a-half of years, they shall say regarding him: 'He has lived long, and the greater part of his days are pain and sorrow and tribulation, and there is no peace:

C.3 Here it is stating that man's lifespan will be reduced even more 'man live a jubilee and a-half of years' =75 years.

> 13 For calamity follows on calamity, and wound on wound, and tribulation on tribulation, and evil tidings on evil tidings, and illness on illness, and all evil judgments such as these, one with another, illness and overthrow, and snow and frost and ice, and fever, and chills, and torpor, and famine, and death, and sword, and captivity, and all kinds of calamities and pains.'
>
> 14 And all these shall come on an evil generation, which transgresses on the earth: their works are uncleanness and fornication, and pollution and abominations.
>
> 15 Then they shall say: 'The days of the forefathers were many (even), unto a thousand years, and were good; but behold, the days of our life, if a man has lived many, are three score years and ten, and, if he is strong, four score years, and those evil, and there is no peace in the days of this evil generation.'

C.4 Here it states that man's life will end up being only 70 and full of trials, sorrows and pains because of wickedness. This is exactly what King David stated 1000 years after Abraham.

PSA.90:10 The days of our years are threescore years and ten; and if by reason of strength they be fourscore years yet is their strength labour and sorrow; for it is soon cut off, and we fly away.

16 And in that generation the sons shall convict their fathers and their elders of sin and unrighteousness, and of the words of their mouth and the great wickedness which they perpetrate, and concerning their forsaking the covenant which the Lord made between them and Him, that they should observe and do all His commandments and His ordinances and all His laws, without departing either to the right hand or the left.

17 For all have done evil, and every mouth speaks iniquity and all their works are an uncleanness and an abomination, and all their ways are pollution, uncleanness and destruction.

C.5 What does it mean by *'uncleanness' and an 'abomination'* These are obviously used in a very strong way. Often these words are linked with witch-craft and human sacrifices in the very worst-case scenarios and *uncleanness* sometimes indicates people that are *demon possessed.* This is mentioned in the prophets as becoming extreme in the last days of man's rule on earth. The Book of Revelations talks about an *unclean Whore*:

REV.17:4 And the woman was arrayed in purple and scarlet colour, and decked with gold and precious stones and pearls, having a golden cup in her hand full of abominations and *filthiness* of her fornication:

REV.17:5 And upon her forehead was a name written, MYSTERY, BABYLON THE GREAT, THE MOTHER OF HARLOTS AND *ABOMINATIONS* OF THE EARTH.

In the Book of Daniel it talks about the *Abomination of Desolation* which is also mentioned in the Book of Revelation 13. The days will come when a Satanic world leader will arise whom we call the Anti-Christ. He will demand the worship of himself as god. Now that is what I would call an *abomination*.

DAN.9:27 And he shall confirm the covenant with many for one week: and in the midst of the week he shall cause the sacrifice and the oblation to cease, and for the overspreading of *abominations* he shall make it desolate, even until the consummation, and that determined shall be poured upon the desolate.

18 Behold the earth shall be destroyed on account of all their works, and there shall be no seed of the vine, and no oil; for their works are altogether faithless, and they shall all perish together, beasts and cattle and birds, and all the fish of the sea, on account of the children of men.

C.6 This chapter is clearly talking about the conditions on the earth at the End of Days.

II EZDRAS 16.4 Behold, calamities are sent forth, and shall not return until they come over the earth. The fire is kindled and shall not be put out until it consumes the foundations of the earth. Just as an arrow shot by a mighty archer does not return, so the calamities that are sent upon the earth shall not return. Alas for me! Alas for me! Who will deliver me in those days?

> 19 And they shall strive one with another, the young with the old, and the old with the young, the poor with the rich, the lowly with the great, and the beggar with the prince, on account of the law and the covenant; for they have forgotten commandment, and covenant, and feasts, and months, and Sabbaths, and jubilees, and all judgments.
>
> 20 And they shall stand swords and war to turn them back into the way; but they shall not return until much blood has been shed on the earth, one by another.

II EZDRAS 16.5 The beginning of sorrows, when there shall be much lamentation; the beginning of famine, when many shall perish; the beginning of wars, when the powers shall be terrified; the beginning of calamities, when all shall tremble. What shall ye do in these circumstances, when the calamities come?

> 21 And those who have escaped shall not return from their wickedness to the way of righteousness, but they shall all exalt themselves to deceit and wealth, that they may each take all that is his neighbour's, and they shall name the great name, but not in truth and not in righteousness, and they shall defile the holy of holies with their uncleanness and the corruption of their pollution.

II EZDRAS 16.6 Behold, famine and plague, tribulation and anguish are sent as scourges for the correction of men. Yet for all this, they will not turn from their iniquities, nor be always mindful of the scourges. Behold, provision will be so cheap upon earth that men will imagine that peace is assured for them, and then the calamities shall spring up on the earth the sword, famine, and great confusion.

> 22 And a great punishment shall befall the deeds of this generation from the Lord, and He will give them over to the sword and to judgment and to captivity, and to be plundered and devoured.

C.7 This is clearly talking about 'Days of Jacob's Trouble' in the Last Days:

JER.30:3 For, lo, the days come, saith the LORD, that I will bring again the captivity of my people Israel and Judah, saith the LORD: and I will cause them to return to the land that I gave to their fathers, and they shall possess it.

203

JER.30:7 Alas! for that day is great, so that none is like it: it is even the time of Jacob's trouble, but he shall be saved out it.

> 23 And He will wake up against them the sinners of the Gentiles, who have neither mercy nor compassion, and who shall respect the person of none, neither old nor young, nor any one, for they are more wicked and strong to do evil than all the children of men. And they shall use violence against Israel and transgression against Jacob, And much blood shall be shed upon the earth, And there shall be none to gather and none to bury.

II EZDRAS 16.7 For many of those who live on the earth shall perish by famine; and those who survive the famine shall die by the sword. And the dead shall be cast out like dung, and there shall be no one to console them; for the earth shall be left desolate, and its cities shall be demolished.

C.8 According to Ezekiel Chapters 38-39: *Two thirds* of the population of Israel will be destroyed in the 'Time of the End', by an Invasion led Russia, Iran, Turkey and Germany on behalf of the World leader the Anti-Christ.

EZE.38:8 After many days thou shalt be visited: in the latter years thou shalt come into the land that is brought back from the sword, and *is gathered out of many people*, against the mountains of Israel, which have been always waste: but it is *brought forth out of the nations*, and they shall dwell safely all of them.

EZE.38:9 Thou shalt ascend and come like a storm, thou shalt be like a cloud to cover the land, thou, and all thy bands, and many people with thee.

EZE.38:16 And thou shalt come up against my people of Israel, as a cloud to cover the land; it shall be in the latter days, and I will bring thee against my land, that the heathen may know me, when I shall be sanctified in thee, O Gog, before their eyes.

> 24 In those days they shall cry aloud, And call and pray that they may be saved from the hand of the sinners, the Gentiles; But none shall be saved.

ENOCH 1.1 The words of the blessing of Enoch, wherewith he blessed the elect and righteous, who will be living in the 'day of tribulation', when all the wicked and godless are to be removed.

> 25 And the heads of the children shall be white with grey hair, And a child of three weeks shall appear old like a man of one hundred years, And their stature shall be destroyed by tribulation and oppression.

C.9 Here is an interesting comparison with:

II EZDRAS Chapter 3.4 'Menstruous women shall bring forth monsters; and salty waters shall be found in the sweet, and all friends shall conquer one another'. (*See my book '**EZDRAS INSIGHTS**' for a lot more information)

> 26 And in those days the children shall begin to study the laws, And to seek the commandments, And to return to the path of righteousness.

C.10 A time will come when many shall turn to righteousness and will again seek after the Laws of God and in New Testament terms will turn to God's Word for inspiration and instruction. This could be referring to all of those who go through the Great Tribulation and hold on to their faith in God. Many will turn to God and His Word in the coming days of Tribulation that will overtake the whole world under the Satanic world-wide government of the Anti-Christ.

REV.7:9 After this I beheld, and, lo, a great multitude, which no man could number, of all nations, and kindreds, and people, and tongues, stood before the throne, and before the Lamb, clothed with white robes, and palms in their hands;

REV.7:10 And cried with a loud voice, saying, Salvation to our God which sits upon the throne, and unto the Lamb.

REV.7:14 And he said to me, 'These are they which came out of **great tribulation**, and have washed their robes, and made them white in the blood of the Lamb'.

REV.7:15 Therefore are they before the throne of God and serve him day and night in his temple: and he that sits on the throne shall dwell among them.

> 27 And the days shall begin to grow many and increase amongst those children of men till their days draw nigh to one thousand years. And to a greater number of years than (before) was the number of the days.

C.11 Here we can see that God will again change the conditions on the earth at the time of the Golden age to come. Conditions will go back to the pristine conditions that existed upon the earth before the Great Flood. People will start to live to be almost 1000 years old again. A man dying at 100 years old will be considered but a child.

ISA.65:20 There shall be no more thence an infant of days, nor an old man that hath not filled his days: for the child shall die an hundred years old; but the sinner being an hundred years old shall be accursed.

> 28 And there shall be no old man nor one who is satisfied with his days, for all shall be (as) children and youths.
>
> 29 And all their days they shall complete and live in peace and in joy, and there shall be no Satan nor any evil destroyer. For all their days shall be days of blessing and healing.

C.12 Wonderful news! No more Satan, well at least for 1000 years! Peace at last with no more war or violence tolerated. The golden Age of the Messiah and his saints who shall rule the whole earth during the soon coming Millennium.

REV.20:2 And he laid hold on the dragon, that old serpent, which is the Devil, and Satan, and bound him a thousand years,

REV.20:3 And cast him into the bottomless pit, and shut him up, and set a seal upon him, that he should deceive the nations no more, till the thousand years should be fulfilled: and after that he must be *loosed a little season.*

C.13 At the end of the Golden Age and the Final Battle of God and Magog, Satan is tossed into the Lake of Fire and all his followers burned up by 'fire from the sky' by the hand of God himself.

REV.20:7 And when the thousand years are expired, Satan shall be loosed out of his prison,

REV.20:8 And shall go out to deceive the nations which are in the four quarters of the earth, Gog, and Magog, to gather them together to battle: the number of whom is as the sand of the sea.

REV.20:9 And they went up on the breadth of the earth, and compassed the camp of the saints about, and the beloved city: and fire came down from God out of heaven and devoured them.

REV.20:10 And the devil that deceived them was cast into the lake of fire and brimstone, where the beast and the false prophet are, and shall be tormented day and night for ever and ever.

---

30 And at that time the Lord will heal His servants, And they shall rise up and see great peace, And drive out their adversaries.

And the righteous shall see and be thankful, And rejoice with joy for ever and ever, And shall see all their judgments and all their curses on their enemies.

31 And their bones shall rest in the earth, And their spirits shall have much joy, And they shall know that it is the Lord who executes judgment, And shows mercy to hundreds and thousands and to all that love Him

---

C.14 Here we see the beginning of the Eternal Age of the New Heaven and New Earth and no more Satan or evil ever again.

REV.21:3 And I heard a great voice out of heaven saying, Behold, the tabernacle of God is with men, and he will dwell with them, and they shall be his people, and God himself shall be with them, and be their God.

REV.21:4 And God shall wipe away all tears from their eyes; and there shall be no more death, neither sorrow, nor crying, neither shall there be any more pain: for the former things are passed away.

> 32 And do thou, Moses, write down these words; for thus are they written, and they record (them) on the heavenly tablets for a testimony for the generations for ever.

C.15 Consider God's great men who have walked the face of the earth, and the great and mighty things that they have done. You look at their greatness and the way they were so mightily used of God, that they were God's mouthpieces, they were his Word, they wrought miracles, they brought forth great wonders, they delivered great messages, and they accomplished God's will greatly. Why could they do these things? Because they were faithful in that which was least. Because God tested them, and tried them and proved them, and they came through as faithful men, as obedient men, as yielded men. The things that you read about them were the outcroppings, the peaks, the highlights. They had these things because day by day, hour by hour, minute by minute, they obeyed God, they followed God, they served God. They learned in the little things so that they would be faithful in the big things.

Chapter 24

1 And it came to pass after the death of Abraham, that the Lord blessed Isaac his son, and he arose from Hebron and went and dwelt at the Well of the Vision in the first year of the third week [2073 A.M. = **'Anno Mundi' = years of the world**] of this jubilee, seven years.

Comment:1: Isaac is famous for being the son of Abraham and the father of Jacob who became Israel and who fathered the 12 Patriarchs. Abraham was very famous because of his faith and integrity, generosity as well as being an Idol Smasher and valiant in battle as if God Himself fought for him. What about Isaac his son? He inherited everything from his father Abraham but what is he remembered for?

Was Isaac a pacifist or actually a wise diplomat?

It would seem from the Bible that Isaac was a pacifist who allowed the Philistines to fill in the wells that he dug. Not much else is mentioned about him in the Bible apart from him going blind when he got old and being 'deceived' by Jacob stealing his father's blessing from Esau.

C.2 The Book of Jubilees shows more about Isaac than even the Bible does

However, in this Book of Jubilees it makes it clear that Isaac was much more than a pacifist. What is notable is that every time he came to dig new **wells** is that the Lord God came and spake to him – In effect bringing him 'Living Waters', as He had with Abraham his father.

I think in actuality **Isaac was a wise diplomat in dealing with the Philistines** who are infamous in biblical history for filling in three of the wells that Isaac dug. I think that the Philistines filled in the wells that Isaac dug in order to persuade him to move further away from the Philistines land, whose king had told Isaac that he needed to move from their lands as he was far richer than they were. (Verse 17 of this chapter)

C.3 Isaac and his wife Rebecca got some amazing prophecies which came true according to this amazing Book of Jubilees.

Isaac ended up cursing the Philistines and prophesied that they would cease to exist in the future because of their extreme wickedness, and Rebecca prophesied that her son Jacob would begat 12 Patriarchs -which he did.

C.4 I also believe that the fathers of the patriarchs in travelling through Canaan or what was to become future Israel, were making 'Israel to bud' physically by digging wells.

We know that Israel is described in the Bible in the time of Moses as being a land being very fruitful or a 'land flowing with milk and honey'.

DEU.31:20 For when I shall have brought them into the land which I sware unto their fathers, that flows with milk and honey.

C.5 Fruitful Israel: I believe that Israel had many underground rivers, in a land that often initially could look barren. But was it? Apparently, all it took was for someone to diligently build wells – some of which could have turned into fountains, because of the underground rivers.

C.6 Israel an Oasis. Water is the most important thing to sustain life. Once a well had been dug and upon occasion a fountain of water had been struck, then an oasis would follow and then the trees and herbs would grow in what beforehand had been almost barren land.

With enough oasis's well placed throughout the land both the vegetation would increase as well as both the people and animals would come and towns would begin to form.

C.7 In order to understand this fully we have to realize that back then there were relatively few people in the land of Canaan. The mode of transport was relatively slow - either walking or using camels, donkeys. Only the wealthy had horses - like princes. How far could a person or a family or even a whole tribe of 400 people like Isaac's travel in one day? I would say best to be able to travel from on oasis to another within a day. So a tribe the size of Abraham's or his son Isaac were in a perfect situation to have some of their workers dig wells wherever they travelled. A small family would not be able to do that however.

C.8 As you can see, 'digging wells' was actually a very important job as in regards to making Israel easy to cross by 'making it fertile' and a blessing so that it was possible for a lone traveller much later in time such as the Messiah Jesus Christ and his 12 disciples to travel to the Well at Sichem (Shechem) which had been dug by Jacob, Isaac's son 2000 years earlier and it was actually still there!

JOH.4:5 Then cometh he to a city of Samaria, which is called Sychar, near to the parcel of ground that Jacob gave to his son Joseph.

JOH.4:6 Now Jacob's well was there. Jesus therefore, being wearied with his journey, sat thus on the well: and it was about the sixth hour.

C.9 I believe it very possible that Isaac was doing a very important job in digging wells to irrigate the land of Israel ahead of the birth of the nation. We also know that spiritually he fed his tribe the 'Living waters' of scriptures as handed down from his father Abraham who had been directly mentored by both Noah and his son Shem.

---

2 And in the first year of the fourth week a famine began in the land, [2080 A.M.] besides the first famine, which had been in the days of Abraham.

3 And Jacob sod lentil pottage, and Esau came from the field hungry. And he said to Jacob his brother: 'Give me of this red pottage.'

---

4 And Jacob said to him: 'Sell to me thy [primogeniture, this] birthright and I will give thee bread, and also some of this lentil pottage.'

5 And Esau said in his heart: 'I shall die; of what profit to me is this birth right 'And he said to Jacob: 'I give it to thee.'

6 And Jacob said: 'Swear to me, this day,' and he swore unto him.

7 And Jacob gave his brother Esau bread and pottage, and he eat till he was satisfied, and Esau despised his birth right; for this reason was Esau's name called Edom, on account of the red pottage which Jacob gave him for his birth right.

C.10 This story is almost identical with the version give of this story in the Bible in Genesis. However, when we read the Book of Jasher we find the reason why Esau was so off-hand about his birth right on that occasion. Esau had apparently just slain Nimrod and two of his men and just barely escaped with his life to his family being totally exhausted and very hungry. It was at that exact moment that Jacob basically said to Esau, 'No food unless to give me your birth right. Esau was too exhausted at that moment to be bothered with his birth right, and so flippantly give it away to Jacob in order to get the much need nourishment after a big fight with three men including king Nimrod. The fuller story in the Book of Jasher gives a background to Esau's behaviour that makes a lot of sense. (See **Chapter 27** from my book '**Jasher Insights'**)

JASHER 27.12 And he said unto his brother Jacob, Behold I shall die this day, and wherefore then do I want the birth right? And Jacob acted wisely with Esau in this matter, and Esau sold his birth right to Jacob, for it was so brought about by the Lord.

8 And Jacob became the elder, and Esau was brought down from his dignity.

9 And the famine was over the land, and Isaac departed to go down into Egypt in the second year of this week and went to the king of the Philistines to Gerar, unto Abimelech.

10 And the Lord appeared unto him and said unto him: 'Go not down into Egypt; dwell in the land that I shall tell thee of, and sojourn in this land, and I will be with thee and bless thee.

C.11 Prophecy given to Isaac, with a warning not to go down to Egypt and that God Himself was directing his every move and would bless him

PSA.37:23 The steps of a good man are ordered by the LORD: and he delights in his way.

PSA.37:22 For such as be blessed of him shall inherit the earth; and they that be cursed of him shall be cut off.

---

11 For to thee and to thy seed will I give all this land, and I will establish My oath which I swore unto Abraham thy father, and I will multiply thy seed as the stars of heaven, and will give unto thy seed all this land.

12 And in thy seed shall all the nations of the earth be blessed, because thy father obeyed My voice, and kept My charge and My commandments, and My laws, and My ordinances, and My covenant; and now obey My voice and dwell in this land.' And he dwelt in Gelar three weeks of years.

13 And Abimelech charged concerning him, [2080-2101 A.M. = **Anno Mundi' = years of the world**] and concerning all that was his, saying: 'Any man that shall touch him or aught that is his shall surely die.'

14 And Isaac waxed strong among the Philistines, and he got many possessions, oxen and sheep and camels and asses and a great household.

15 And he sowed in the land of the Philistines and brought in a hundredfold, and Isaac became exceedingly great, and the Philistines envied him.

16 Now all the wells which the servants of Abraham had dug during the life of Abraham, the Philistines had stopped them after the death of Abraham and filled them with earth.

17 And Abimelech said unto Isaac: 'Go from us, for thou art much mightier than we', and Isaac departed thence in the first year of the seventh week, and sojourned in the valleys of Gerar.

18 And they digged again the wells of water which the servants of Abraham, his father, had digged, and which the Philistines had closed after the death of Abraham his father, and he called their names as Abraham

---

his father had named them.

19 And the servants of Isaac dug a well in the valley, and found living water, and the shepherds of Gerar strove with the shepherds of Isaac, saying: 'The water is ours'; and Isaac called the name of the well 'Perversity', because they had been perverse with us.

20 And they dug a second well, and they strove for that also, and he called its name 'Enmity'.

21 And he arose from thence and they digged another well, and for that they strove not, and he called the name of it 'Room', and Isaac said: 'Now the Lord hath made room for us, and we have increased in the land.'

22 And he went up from thence to the Well of the Oath in the first year of the first week in the [2108 A.M.] forty-fourth jubilee. And the Lord appeared to him that night, on the new moon of the first month, and said unto him: 'I am the God of Abraham thy father; fear not, for I am with thee, and shall bless thee and shall surely multiply thy seed as the sand of the earth, for the sake of Abraham my servant.'

23 And he built an altar there, which Abraham his father had first built, and he called upon the name of the Lord, and he offered sacrifice to the God of Abraham his father.

24 And they digged a well and they found living water.

C.12 I have often wondered about **this verse** as it is odd that it says 'living water' is it just possible that **Isaac,** being a king and prophet of sorts, was comparing **physical waters** with **spiritual waters or was he even prophesying about the coming Messiah?**

Look at the following from **John chapter 4:**

JOHN.4:5 Then cometh he to a city of Samaria, which is called Sychar, near to the parcel of ground that Jacob gave to his son Joseph.

JOHN.4:6 Now Jacob's well was there. Jesus therefore, being wearied with his journey, sat thus on the well: and it was about the sixth hour.

JOHN.4:7 There cometh a woman of Samaria to draw water: Jesus saith unto her, Give me to drink.

JOHN.4:8 (For his disciples were gone away unto the city to buy meat.)

JOHN.4:9 Then saith the woman of Samaria unto him, How is it that thou, being a Jew, askest drink of me, which am a woman of Samaria? for the Jews have no dealings with the Samaritans.

JOHN.4:10 Jesus answered and said unto her, If thou knew the gift of God, and who it is that saith to thee, Give me to drink; thou would have asked of him, and he would have given thee living water.

JOH.4:11 The woman saith unto him, Sir, thou hast nothing to draw with, and the well is deep: from whence then hast thou that living water?

JOHN.4:12 Art thou greater than our father Jacob, which gave us the well, and drank thereof himself, and his children, and his cattle?

JOHN.4:13 Jesus answered and said unto her, Whosoever drinketh of this water shall thirst again:

JOHN.4:14 But whosoever drinketh of the water that I shall give him shall never thirst; but the water that I shall give him shall be in him a well of water springing up into everlasting life.

JOH.4:15 The woman saith unto him, Sir, give me this water, that I thirst not, neither come hither to draw.

C.13 Here is another beautiful bible verse about spiritual *'Living Waters'*

JOHN.7:38 He that believeth on me, as the scripture hath said, out of his belly shall flow *rivers of living water*.

JOHN.7:39 (But this spake he of the Spirit, which they that believe on him should receive: for the Holy Ghost was not yet given; because that Jesus was not yet glorified.)

> 25 And the servants of Isaac digged another well and did not find water, and they went and told Isaac that they had not found water, and Isaac said: 'I have sworn this day to the Philistines and this thing has been announced to us.'
>
> 26 And he called the name of that place the Well of the Oath; for there he had sworn to Abimelech and Ahuzzath his friend and Phicol the prefect or his host.
>
> 27 And Isaac knew that day that under constraint he had sworn to them to make peace with them.

28 And Isaac on that day cursed the Philistines and said: 'Cursed be the Philistines unto the day of wrath and indignation from the midst of all nations; may God make them a derision and a curse and an object of wrath and indignation in the hands of the sinners the Gentiles and in the hands of the Kittim.

C.14 Why did Isaac curse the Philistines? It would seem that he realised that their race had a mischievous spirit. After all who would go around filling in wells that someone else had just dug up?

29 And whoever escapes the sword of the enemy and the Kittim, may the righteous nation root out in judgment from under heaven; for they shall be the enemies and foes of my children throughout their generations upon the earth.

30 And no remnant shall be left to them, Nor one that shall be saved on the day of the wrath of judgment; For destruction and rooting out and expulsion from the earth is the whole seed of the Philistines (reserved), And there shall no longer be left for these Caphtorim a name or a seed on the earth.

31 For though he ascend unto heaven, Thence shall he be brought down,

And though he make himself strong on earth, Thence shall he be dragged forth,

And though he hide himself amongst the nations, Even from thence shall he be rooted out; and though he descend into Sheol, There also shall his condemnation be great, And there also he shall have no peace.

32 And if he go into captivity, By the hands of those that seek his life shall they slay him on the way, And neither name nor seed shall be left to him on all the earth; For into eternal malediction shall he depart.'

33 And thus is it written and engraved concerning him on the heavenly tablets, to do unto him on the day of judgment, so that he may be rooted out of the earth.

ANALYSIS OF THIS CHAPTER:
C.15 From this chapter **24 verses 28-32** we see Isaac cursing the Philistines,

whom he also mentions as them being Caphtorim - meaning related to the Giants.

Here it would seem that Isaac cursed the Philistines because they kept filling in the wells that he had just dug up.

This curse was fulfilled in both Samson some 700 years after Isaac's time:

JDG.16:30 And Samson said, 'Let me die with the Philistines. And he bowed himself with all his might; and the house fell upon the lords, and upon all the people that were therein. So the dead which he slew at his death were more than they which he slew in his life.

C.16 And also Isaac's curse against the Philistines was also fulfilled by a youthful David (who later became king David), in slaying Goliath the giant champion of the Philistines, and in king Saul in around 1000 BC. (See: **I Samuel 17**)

C.17) Verse 31 is the key verse about this topic as it is clearly talking about Satan and his future destruction for leading the nations astray through his own 'Satanic seed' races like the Philistines, who had Nephilim (Fallen angel) DNA.

C.18 Verse 31 sounds like **Ezekiel 28** in describing Satan:

EZE.28:13 Thou hast been in Eden the garden of God; every precious stone was thy covering, the sardius, topaz, and the diamond, the beryl, the onyx, and the jasper, the sapphire, the emerald, and the carbuncle, and gold: the workmanship of thy tabrets and of thy pipes was prepared in thee in the day that thou wast created.

EZE.28:14 Thou art the anointed cherub that covereth; and I have set thee so: thou wast upon the holy mountain of God; thou hast walked up and down in the midst of the stones of fire.

EZE.28:15 Thou wast perfect in thy ways from the day that thou wast created, till iniquity was found in thee.

C.19 Isaiah 14.9-21 Here are some of those verses about Satan himself::

14:9 Hell from beneath is moved for thee to meet thee at thy coming: it stirreth up the dead for thee, even all the chief ones of the earth; it hath raised up from their thrones all the kings of the nations.

ISA.14:12 How art thou fallen from heaven, O Lucifer, son of the morning! how art thou cut down to the ground, which didst weaken the nations!

ISA.14:13 For thou hast said in thine heart, I will ascend into heaven, I will exalt my throne above the stars of God: I will sit also upon the mount of the congregation, in the sides of the north:

ISA.14:14 I will ascend above the heights of the clouds; I will be like the most High.

ISA.14:16 They that see thee shall narrowly look upon thee, and consider thee, saying, Is this the man that made the earth to tremble, that did shake kingdoms;

ISA.14:21 Prepare slaughter for his children for the iniquity of their fathers; that they do not rise, nor possess the land, nor fill the face of the world with cities.

C.20 More Verses about Satan: Revelations 20.1-3

REV.20:1 And I saw an angel come down from heaven, having the key of the bottomless pit and a great chain in his hand.

REV.20:2 And he laid hold on the dragon, that old serpent, which is the Devil, and Satan, and bound him a thousand years,

REV.20:3 And cast him into the bottomless pit, and shut him up, and set a seal upon him, that he should deceive the nations no more, till the thousand years should be fulfilled: and after that he must be loosed a little season.

C.21 The Book of Enoch also mentioned that there would be no peace for the Fallen angels but as verse 32 of this chapter of Jubilees states: *'they will have an eternal malediction'*

C.22 So Isaac is in effect not just cursing the Philistines for being mischievous or deceitful – but he is describing the judgement of Satan and all the demons for creating such wicked nations as the Philistines who did things that had no sanity to them.

C.23 There was a similar description given about Sodom and Gomorrah in the book of Jasher where the Sodomities killed the visitors to their city for no sane reason – again mischievous as demons. See my book '**Jasher Insights'**

Chapter 25

1 And in the second year of this week in this jubilee, Rebecca called Jacob her son, and spoke unto [2109 A.M. = **Anno Mundi' = years of the world**] him, saying: 'My son, do not take thee a wife of the daughters of Canaan, as Esau, thy brother, who took him two wives of the daughters of Canaan, and they have embittered my soul with all their unclean deeds: for all their deeds are fornication and lust, and there is no righteousness with them, for (their deeds) are evil.

Comment:1: Rebecca tells her son Jacob not to take a wife of the Canaanites as their women did 'unclean deeds' of fornication and lust. They are totally evil Rebecca tells her son. They were constantly sacrificing unto Idols and demons in some sort of sexual orgy. Like the wives of Solomon who led him astray when he got old.

1KI.11:4 For it came to pass, when Solomon was old, that his wives turned away his heart after other gods: and his heart was not perfect with the LORD his God, as was the heart of David his father.

1KI.11:5 For Solomon went after Ashtoreth the goddess of the Zidonians, and after Milcom the abomination of the Ammonites.

1KI.11:6 And Solomon did evil in the sight of the LORD, and went not fully after the LORD, as did David his father.

1KI.11:7 Then did Solomon build an high place for Chemosh, the abomination of Moab, in the hill that is before Jerusalem, and for Molech, the abomination of the children of Ammon.

1KI.11:8 And likewise did he for all his strange wives, which burnt incense and sacrificed unto their gods.

2 And I, my son, love thee exceedingly, and my heart and my affection bless thee every hour of the day and watch of the night.

3 And now, my son, hearken to my voice, and do the will of thy mother, and do not take thee a wife of the daughters of this land, but only of the house of my father, and of my father's kindred.

4 Thou shalt take thee a wife of the house of my father, and the Most High God will bless thee, and thy children shall be a righteous generation and a holy seed.'

5 And then spoke Jacob to Rebecca, his mother, and said unto her: 'Behold, mother, I am nine weeks of years old, and I neither know nor have I touched any woman, nor have I betrothed myself to any, nor even think of taking me a wife of the daughters of Canaan.

C.2 Jacob is stating that he was 9 weeks old at that time. Meaning: 9 x 7 years old. That means he was 63 years old and he hadn't yet married a wife.

6 For I remember, mother, the words of Abraham, our father, for he commanded me not to take a wife of the daughters of Canaan, but to take me a wife from the seed of my father's house and from my kindred.

7 I have heard before that daughters have been born to Laban, thy brother, and I have set my heart on them to take a wife from amongst them.

8 And for this reason I have guarded myself in my spirit against sinning or being corrupted in all my ways throughout all the days of my life; for with regard to lust and fornication, Abraham, my father, gave me many commands. And, despite all that he has commanded me, these two and twenty years my brother has striven with me, and spoken frequently to me and said: 'My brother, take to wife a sister of my two wives'; but I refuse to do as he has done.

9 I swear before thee, mother, that all the days of my life I will not take me a wife from the daughters of the seed of Canaan, and I will not act wickedly as my brother has done.

C.3 It would appear than any time when Abraham's descendants took a wife of the daughters of the Canaanites, that it only caused lot of subsequent trouble.

10 Fear not, mother; be assured that I shall do thy will and walk in uprightness, and not corrupt my ways for ever.'

11 And thereupon she lifted up her face to heaven and extended the fingers of her hands and opened her mouth and blessed the Most High God, who had created the heaven and the earth, and she gave Him thanks and praise.

12 And she said: 'Blessed be the Lord God, and may His holy name be

blessed for ever and ever, who has given me Jacob as a pure son and a holy seed; for he is Thine, and Thine shall his seed be continually and throughout all the generations for evermore.

13 Bless him, O Lord, and place in my mouth the blessing of righteousness, that I may bless him.'

14 And at that hour, when the spirit of righteousness descended into her mouth, she placed both her hands on the head of Jacob, and said:

15 Blessed art thou, Lord of righteousness and God of the ages And may He bless thee beyond all the generations of men.

May He give thee, my Son, the path of righteousness, And reveal righteousness to thy seed.

16 And may He make thy sons many during thy life, And may they arise according to the number of the months of the year. And may their sons become many and great beyond the stars of heaven, And their numbers be more than the sand of the sea.

17 And may He give them this goodly land -as He said He would give it to Abraham and to his seed after him always- And may they hold it as a possession for ever.

18 And may I see (born) unto thee, my son, blessed children during my life, And a blessed and holy seed may all thy seed be.

19 And as thou hast refreshed thy mother's spirit during her life, The womb of her that bare thee blesses thee thus,

[My affection] and my breasts bless thee And my mouth and my tongue praise thee greatly.

20 Increase and spread over the earth, And may thy seed be perfect in the joy of heaven and earth for ever;

And may thy seed rejoice, And on the great day of peace may it have peace.

21 And may thy name and thy seed endure to all the ages, And may the Most High God be their God,

And may the God of righteousness dwell with them, And by them may His sanctuary be built unto all the ages.

22 Blessed be he that blesses thee, And all flesh that curses thee falsely, may it be cursed.'

23 And she kissed him and said to him; 'May the Lord of the world love thee As the heart of thy mother and her affection rejoice in thee and bless thee.' And she ceased from blessing.

C.4 Rebecca really prayed for her son Jacob to be blessed by the Lord and that he would give him many children. Well God certainly answered Rebecca's heart-felt prayers as Jacob ended up with 4 wives and 12 sons and one daughter. Of course, this was all part of God's plan for Israel to multiply, prosper and became a great nation. This was indeed God's commandment to Adam and Eve at the very beginning of Creation and again after the Great Flood when growth of the human population had been restarted with Noah and his three sons.

GEN.1:28 And God blessed them, and God said unto them, 'Be fruitful, and multiply, and replenish the earth, and subdue it: and have dominion over the fish of the sea, and over the fowl of the air, and over every living thing that moves upon the earth'.

GEN.9:1 And God blessed Noah and his sons, and said unto them, 'Be fruitful, and multiply, and replenish the earth'.

C.5 VEGAN OR VEGETARIAN? Notice how that before the Great Flood people ate vegetables, fruits and herbs. After the Great Flood God commanded mankind to also eat meat because the planet was different, and meat was given to preserve mankind from the ravages of a planet that now would progressively age quickly instead of very slowly as before the Great Flood.

C.6 AMINO ACIDS: Apparently, certain amino acids and vitamins are only afforded by eating meat which became necessary after the Great Flood. Before the Great Flood, humans didn't need to eat meat, but after the Great Flood the protective canopy of water around the earth was gone and humans became much more susceptible to dangerous radiation. Thus, the need for meat to help sustain the deteriorating and diminishing body of mankind.

C.7 LARGER FAMILIES: In starting a nation in the past, the rulers have always encouraged its peoples to have large families, and after a war or serious crisis sometimes have encouraged its peoples to have larger families by rewarding them; but now in modern times people are discouraged from having large families, as they are told that the population of the planet is too great, when this is actually a totally erroneous lie.

C.8 CONTROL: We are told that humans are part of the Global Warming problem, which is another insidious lie. There is plenty of room for more people on the planet if the rich and powerful were not so totally selfish and destructive with their deliberate wars to destroy mankind in modern times with their Eugenics policies.

C.9 POPULATION: As we speak it is getting critical. The facts are that the ratio of children born in the West is below 2.0 /couple especially among the white races. The ratio is as low as 1.2 in some Western countries. What does this mean? It is necessary to have a minimum of 2.1/couple in order to sustain any given race.

C.10 BORDERS? Because of the diminishing Western population, the governments of the West can only manage their companies by constantly importing loads of foreigners one way or the other. This is the real reason why the rich all encourage open 'border policies', in order to keep their factories running. The rich don't really care about the refugees and the poor of the world, they seek more ways to exploit them and use them as slaves.

C.11 GENOCIDE: The West is committing genocide by refusing to have children anymore. Even worse, the latest stats show that 20% of males in Denmark can't even have children. So much for disobeying God's commands to 'Be fruitful and multiply'.

C.12 ABORTION: Now many opt to abort or better said murder millions of babies instead. Is it any wonder that our planet is going down, and will soon face the Wrath of God? Just before the Golden Age to come, and all of God's children have been taken up to heaven in the Rapture, most of the rest of the planet will be wiped out and destroyed, and God will have to start again with a few faithful few to whom he will say: 'Be fruitful and multiply'.

Chapter 26

1 And in the seventh year of this week Isaac called Esau, his elder Son, and said unto him: ' I am [2114 A.M. = '**Anno Mundi' = years of the world**] old, my son, and behold my eyes are dim in seeing, and I know not the day of my death.

Comment:1: See this whole story in **Genesis 27.**

2 And now take thy hunting weapons thy quiver and thy bow, and go out to the field, and hunt and catch me (venison), my son, and make me savoury meat, such as my soul loveth, and bring it to me that I may eat, and that my soul may bless thee before I die.'

3 But Rebecca heard Isaac speaking to Esau.

4 And Esau went forth early to the field to hunt and catch and bring home to his father.

5 And Rebecca called Jacob, her son, and said unto him: 'Behold, I heard Isaac, thy father, speak unto Esau, thy brother, saying: "Hunt for me, and make me savoury meat, and bring (it) to me that I may eat and bless thee before the Lord before I die."

C.2 Initially it doesn't sound right that Rebecca is teaching Jacob to be deceitful and to steal his brother Esau's blessing. In the Bible it doesn't give the important extra details afforded by the Apocryphal books such as Jubilees and Jasher. By reading these books we find out that it was Abraham that told Rebecca that God's blessing was to be though Jacob and not Esau. The problem was that Isaac wanted Esau to be his heir, whilst Rebecca wanted Jacob to be the heir. Maybe, this is why God allowed Isaac to become blind physically, because he also wasn't seeing things spiritually the way that God saw them at least concerning his heir. Why couldn't Isaac see that his son Esau was an evil and violent person? So, God Himself took a hand in the situation, to ensure that Jacob would be the heir and that Israel would come from Jacob, Isaac and Abraham. Israel certainly could not have come through Esau who was an evil & violent man.

6 And now, my son, obey my voice in that which I command thee: Go to thy flock and fetch me two good kids of the goats, and I will make them savoury meat for thy father, such as he loves, and thou shalt bring (it) to thy father that he may eat and bless thee before the Lord before

he die, and that thou mayst be blessed.'

7 And Jacob said to Rebecca his mother: 'Mother, I shall not withhold anything which my father would eat, and which would please him: only I fear, my mother, that he will recognise my voice and wish to touch me.

8 And thou know that I am smooth, and Esau, my brother, is hairy, and I shall appear before his eyes as an evildoer and shall do a deed which he had not commanded me, and he will be wroth with me, and I shall bring upon myself a curse, and not a blessing.'

9 And Rebecca, his mother, said unto him: 'Upon me be thy curse, my son, only obey my voice.'

C.3 So Jacob becomes Jacob the Deceiver as also his name means. However, both Rebecca and Jacob deceiving poor old Isaac would end up causing them lots of pain and sorrow before *finally things got put right*. God is always working in the background with us humans, even if we are more like marionets that are sometimes rather like spastics fumbling around, in our wrong decisions and choosing to go the wrong way. God always works out His better purpose in the end despite our dumb mistakes, deceits and sins. From what seems like a defeat to us, come some of God's greatest victories.

ROM.8:28 And we know that all things work together for good to them that love God, to them who are the called according to his purpose.

10 And Jacob obeyed the voice of Rebecca, his mother, and went and fetched two good and fat kids of the goats, and brought them to his mother, and his mother made them savoury meat such as he loved.

11 And Rebecca took the goodly raiment of Esau, her elder son, which was with her in the house, and she clothed Jacob, her younger son, (with them), and she put the skins of the kids upon his hands and on the exposed parts of his neck.

12 And she gave the meat and the bread which she had prepared into the hand of her son Jacob.

13 And Jacob went in to his father and said: 'I am thy son: I have done according as thou bade me: arise and sit and eat of that which I have caught, father, that thy soul may bless me.'

14 And Isaac said to his son: 'How hast thou found so quickly, my son.

15 'And Jacob said: 'Because (the Lord thy God caused me to find.'

16 And Isaac said unto him: Come near, that I may feel thee, my son, if thou art my son Esau or not.'

17 And Jacob went near to Isaac, his father, and he felt him and said:

18 'The voice is Jacob's voice, but the hands are the hands of Esau,' and he discerned him not, because it was a dispensation from heaven to remove his power of perception and Isaac discerned not, for his hands were hairy as his brother Esau's, so that he blessed him.

19 And he said: 'Art thou my son Esau ' and he said: 'I am thy son': and he said, 'Bring near to me that I may eat of that which thou hast caught, my son, that my soul may bless thee.'

20 And he brought near to him, and he did eat, and he brought him wine and he drank.

21 And Isaac, his father, said unto him: 'Come near and kiss me, my son.

22 And he came near and kissed him. And he smelled the smell of his raiment, and he blessed him and said: 'Behold, the smell of my son is as the smell of a (full) field which the Lord hath blessed.

23 And may the Lord give thee of the dew of heaven And of the dew of the earth, and plenty of corn and oil:

Let nations serve thee, And peoples bow down to thee.

24 Be lord over thy brethren, And let thy mother's sons bow down to thee;

And may all the blessings wherewith the Lord hath blessed me and blessed Abraham, my father; Be imparted to thee and to thy seed for ever:

Cursed be he that curses thee and blessed be he that blesses thee.'

25 And it came to pass as soon as Isaac had made an end of blessing his son Jacob, and Jacob had gone forth from Isaac his father he hid himself and Esau, his brother, came in from his hunting.

26 And he also made savoury meat, and brought (it) to his father, and said unto his father: 'Let my father arise and eat of my venison that thy soul may bless me.'

27 And Isaac, his father, said unto him: 'Who art thou 'And he said unto him: 'I am thy first born, thy son Esau: I have done as thou hast commanded me.'

28 And Isaac was very greatly astonished and said: 'Who is he that hath hunted and caught and brought (it) to me, and I have eaten of all before thou came and have blessed him: (and) he shall be blessed, and all his seed for ever.'

29 And it came to pass when Esau heard the words of his father Isaac that he cried with an exceeding great and bitter cry, and said unto his father:

30 'Bless me, (even) me also, father.' And he said unto him: 'Thy brother came with guile, and hath taken away thy blessing.'

31 And he said: 'Now I know why his name is named Jacob: behold, he hath supplanted me these two times: he took away my birth-right, and now he hath taken away my blessing.'

C.4 Jacob the Deceiver walked off with both Esau's birth-right and his blessing. No wonder that Esau got hopping mad at Jacob and sought to kill him for being 'Jacob the Gypper'. Jacob eventually learned not to be deceptive, but only by God allowing him to have to work under the oversight of his corrupt uncle Laban, who in 21 years had gypped Jacob out of his wages 14 times and even his wife was supplanted by her older sister Leah in the night of Jacob and Rachel's wedding, Jacob being unaware!. But that's another story.

32 And he said: 'Hast thou not reserved a blessing for me, father' and Isaac answered and said unto Esau: 'Behold, I have made him thy lord, And all his brethren have I given to him for servants, And with plenty of corn and wine and oil have I strengthened him: And what now shall

I do for thee, my son' And Esau said to Isaac, his father: 'Hast thou but one blessing, O father Bless me, (even) me also, father: '

33 And Esau lifted up his voice and wept. And Isaac answered and said unto him: 'Behold, far from the dew of the earth shall be thy dwelling, And far from the dew of heaven from above.

34 And by thy sword wilt thou live, And thou wilt serve thy brother.

And it shall come to pass when thou become great, And dost shake his yoke from off thy neck, Thou shalt sin a complete sin unto death, And thy seed shall be rooted out from under heaven.'

C.5 This is strong language, in stating that eventually Esau's descendants will be totally rooted out. Does this mean that a race will be annihilated in the times of the End because of the crimes of that nation? Is it possible that Esau was like unto Cain of the Pre-Flood times? < **See APPENDIX**>

35 And Esau kept threatening Jacob because of the blessing where-with his father blessed him, and he: said in his heart: 'May the days of mourning for my father now come, so that I may slay my brother Jacob.'

Chapter 27

1 And the words of Esau, her elder son, were told to Rebecca in a dream, and Rebecca sent and called Jacob her younger son, and said unto him: 'Behold Esau thy brother will take vengeance on thee, so as to kill thee.

Comment:1: See **Genesis 27-28** for this continuing story with a similar description.

2 Now, therefore, my son, obey my voice, and arise and flee thou to Laban, my brother, to Haran, and tarry with him a few days until thy brother's anger turns away, and he remove his anger from thee, and forget all that thou hast done; then I will send and fetch thee from thence.'

3 And Jacob said: 'I am not afraid; if he wishes to kill me, I will kill him.'

4 But she said unto him: 'Let me not be bereft of both my sons on one day.'

5 And Jacob said to Rebecca his mother: 'Behold, thou know that my father has become old, and does not see because his eyes are dull, and if I leave him it will be evil in his eyes, because I leave him and go away from you, and my father will be angry, and will curse me.

6 I will not go; when he sends me, then only will I go.'

7 And Rebecca said to Jacob: 'I will go in and speak to him, and he will send thee away.'

8 And Rebecca went in and said to Isaac: 'I loathe my life because of the two daughters of Heth, whom Esau has taken him as wives; and if Jacob take a wife from among the daughters of the land such as these, for what purpose do I further live, for the daughters of Canaan are evil.'

9 And Isaac called Jacob and blessed him and admonished him and said unto him: 'Do not take thee a wife of any of the daughters of Canaan; arise and go to Mesopotamia, to the house of Bethuel, thy

mother's father, and take thee a wife from thence of the daughters of Laban, thy mother's brother.

10 And God Almighty bless thee and increase and multiply thee that thou mayest become a company of nations, and give thee the blessings of my father Abraham, to thee and to thy seed after thee, that thou mayest inherit the land of thy sojournings and all the land which God gave to Abraham: go, my son, in peace.'

11 And Isaac sent Jacob away, and he went to Mesopotamia, to Laban the son of Bethuel the Syrian, the brother of Rebecca, Jacob's mother.

12 And it came to pass after Jacob had arisen to go to Mesopotamia that the spirit of Rebecca was grieved after her son, and she wept.

13 And Isaac said to Rebecca: 'My sister, weep not on account of Jacob, my son; for he goes in peace, and in peace will he return.

14 The Most High God will preserve him from all evil, and will be with him; for He will not forsake him all his days;

15 For I know that his ways will be prospered in all things wherever he goes, until he return in peace to us, and we see him in peace.

C.2 Here Isaac is prophesising that Jacob will safely return because he is a godly man and that God Himself will protect him, which He mostly certainly did.

16 Fear not on his account, my sister, for he is on the upright path and he is a perfect man: and he is faithful and will not perish. Weep not.'

17 And Isaac comforted Rebecca on account of her son Jacob and blessed him.

18 And Jacob went from the Well of the Oath to go to Haran on the first year of the second week in the forty-fourth jubilee, and he came to Luz on the mountains, that is, Bethel, on the new moon of the first month of this week, [2115 A.M. = **'Anno Mundi' = years of the world**] and he came to the place at even and turned from the way to the west of the road that night: and he slept there; for the sun had set.

GEN.28:10 And Jacob went out from Beersheba, and went toward Haran.

> 19 And he took one of the stones of that place and laid under the tree, and he was journeying alone, and he slept.

GEN.28:11 And he lighted upon a certain place, and tarried there all night, because the sun was set; and he took of the stones of that place, and put them for his pillows, and lay down in that place to sleep.

> 20 And he dreamt that night, and behold a ladder set up on the earth, and the top of it reached to heaven, and behold, the angels of the Lord ascended and descended on it: and behold, the Lord stood upon it.

GEN.28:12 And he dreamed, and behold a ladder set up on the earth, and the top of it reached to heaven: and behold the angels of God ascending and descending on it.

C.3 Here is where God makes His first important contact with the Patriarch Jacob

> 21 And he spoke to Jacob and said: 'I am the Lord God of Abraham, thy father, and the God of Isaac; the land whereon thou art sleeping, to thee will I give it, and to thy seed after thee.

GEN.28:13 And, behold, the LORD stood above it, and said, I am the LORD God of Abraham thy father, and the God of Isaac: the land whereon thou liest, to thee will I give it, and to thy seed;

> 22 And thy seed shall be as the dust of the earth, and thou shalt increase to the west and to the east, to the north and the south, and in thee and in thy seed shall all the families of the nations be blessed.

GEN.28:14 And thy seed shall be as the dust of the earth, and thou shalt spread abroad to the west, and to the east, and to the north, and to the south: and in thee and in thy seed shall all the families of the earth be blessed.

> 23 And behold, I will be with thee, and will keep thee whithersoever thou goes, and I will bring thee again into this land in peace; for I will not leave thee until I do everything that I told thee of.'

GEN.28:15 And, behold, I am with thee, and will keep thee in all places whither thou goest, and will bring thee again into this land; for I will not leave thee, until I have done that which I have spoken to thee of.

> 24 And Jacob awoke from his sleep, and said, 'Truly this place is the

house of the Lord, and I knew it not.'

GEN.28:16 And Jacob awaked out of his sleep, and he said, Surely the LORD is in this place; and I knew it not.

25 And he was afraid and said: 'Dreadful is this place which is none other than the house of God, and this is the gate of heaven.'

GEN.28:17 And he was afraid, and said, How dreadful is this place! this is none other but the house of God, and this is the gate of heaven.

26 And Jacob arose early in the morning and took the stone which he had put under his head and set it up as a pillar for a sign, and he poured oil upon the top of it. And he called the name of that place Bethel; but the name of the place was Luz at the first.

GEN.28:18 And Jacob rose up early in the morning, and took the stone that he had put for his pillows, and set it up for a pillar, and poured oil upon the top of it.

GEN.28:19 And he called the name of that place Bethel: but the name of that city was called Luz at the first.

27 And Jacob vowed a vow unto the Lord, saying: 'If the Lord will be with me, and will keep me in this way that I go, and give me bread to eat and raiment to put on, so that I come again to my father's house in peace, then shall the Lord be my God, and this stone which I have set up as a pillar for a sign in this place, shall be the Lord's house, and of all that thou give me, I shall give the tenth to thee, my God.'

GEN.28:20 And Jacob vowed a vow, saying, If God will be with me, and will keep me in this way that I go, and will give me bread to eat, and raiment to put on,

GEN.28:21 So that I come again to my father's house in peace; then shall the LORD be my God:

GEN.28:22 And this stone, which I have set for a pillar, shall be God's house: and of all that thou shalt give me I will surely give the tenth unto thee.

C.4 Jacob sees what we would call today a 'portal' up to heaven. He names the place Bethel and makes a vow to God that if He will keep Jacob safely until he returns to his father's house then he will tithe to God, which is giving 10% of his income to God.

Chapter 28

Comment:1: See **Genesis 29** for a more complete version of how Jacob came to live with his uncle Laban and how he worked for 7 years for his wife Leah, 7 years for Rachel, and 7 years for the herds and flocks under a very deceitful uncle. Jacob has 'gypped' his brother out his birth right, but he soon learned how to stay close to God when he had to work under a much more deceitful person than himself.

1 And he went on his journey, and came to the land of the east, to Laban, the brother of Rebecca, and he was with him, and served him for Rachel his daughter one week.

2 And in the first year of the third week [2122 A.M. = **'Anno Mundi' = years of the world**] he said unto him: 'Give me my wife, for whom I have served thee seven years '; and Laban said unto Jacob: 'I will give thee thy wife.'

3 And Laban made a feast, and took Leah his elder daughter, and gave (her) to Jacob as a wife, and gave her Zilpah his handmaid for an hand maid; and Jacob did not know, for he thought that she was Rachel.

4 And he went in unto her, and behold, she was Leah; and Jacob was angry with Laban, and said unto him: 'Why hast thou dealt thus with me Did not I serve thee for Rachel and not for Leah Why hast thou wronged me Take thy daughter, and I will go; for thou hast done evil to me.'

C.2 Jacob got a lot more than he bargained for. He perhaps thought that he would just marry Rachel but ended up having 4 wives and 13 children because of it. God obviously allowed it in order to create the 12 Tribes of Israel.

5 For Jacob loved Rachel more than Leah; for Leah's eyes were weak, but her form was very handsome; but Rachel had beautiful eyes and a beautiful and very handsome form.

6 And Laban said to Jacob: 'It is not so done in our country, to give the younger before the elder.'

7 And it is not right to do this; for thus it is ordained and written in the

heavenly tablets, that no one should give his younger daughter before the elder; but the elder, one gives first and after her the younger -and the man who does so, they set down guilt against him in heaven, and none is righteous that does this thing, for this deed is evil before the Lord.

8 And command thou the children of Israel that they do not this thing; let them neither take nor give the younger before they have given the elder, for it is very wicked. And Laban said to Jacob: 'Let the seven days of the feast of this one pass by, and I shall give thee Rachel, that thou mayst serve me another seven years, that thou mayst pasture my sheep as thou didst in the former week.'

9 And on the day when the seven days of the feast of Leah had passed, Laban gave Rachel to Jacob, that he might serve him another seven years, and he gave to Rachel Bilhah, the sister of Zilpah, as a handmaid.

10 And he served yet other seven years for Rachel, for Leah had been given to him for nothing.

11 And the Lord opened the womb of Leah, and she conceived and bare Jacob a son, and he called his name Reuben, on the fourteenth day of the ninth month, in the first year of the third week. [2122 A.M.]

12 But the womb of Rachel was closed, for the Lord saw that Leah was hated and Rachel loved.

13 And again Jacob went in unto Leah, and she conceived, and bare Jacob a second son, and he called his name Simeon, on the twenty-first of the tenth month, and in the third year of this week. [2124 A.M.]

14 And again Jacob went in unto Leah, and she conceived, and bare him a third son, and he called his name Levi, in the new moon of the first month in the sixth year of this week. [2127 A.M.]

15 And again Jacob went in unto her, and she conceived, and bare him a fourth son, and he called his name Judah, on the fifteenth of the third month, in the first year of the fourth week. [2129 A.M.]

16 And on account of all this Rachel envied Leah, for she did not bear, and she said to Jacob: 'Give me children'; and Jacob said: 'Have I withheld from thee the fruits of thy womb Have I forsaken thee'

17 And when Rachel saw that Leah had borne four sons to Jacob, Reuben and Simeon and Levi and Judah, she said unto him: 'Go in unto Bilhah my handmaid, and she will conceive, and bear a son unto me.' (And she gave (him) Bilhah her handmaid to wife).

18 And he went in unto her, and she conceived, and bare him a son, and he called his name Dan, on the ninth of the sixth month, in the sixth year of the third week. [2127 A.M.]

19 And Jacob went in again unto Bilhah a second time, and she conceived, and bare Jacob another son, and Rachel called his name Napthali, on the fifth of the seventh month, in the second year of the fourth week. [2130 A.M. = **'Anno Mundi' = years of the world**]

20 And when Leah saw that she had become sterile and did not bear, she envied Rachel, and she also gave her handmaid Zilpah to Jacob to wife, and she conceived, and bare a son, and Leah called his name Gad, on the twelfth of the eighth month, in the third year of the fourth week. [2131 A.M.]

21 And he went in again unto her, and she conceived, and bare him a second son, and Leah called his name Asher, on the second of the eleventh month, in the fifth year of the fourth week. [2133 A.M.]

22 And Jacob went in unto Leah, and she conceived, and bare a son, and she called his name Issachar, on the fourth of the fifth month, in the fourth year of the fourth week [2132 A.M.] and she gave him to a nurse.

23 And Jacob went in again unto her, and she conceived, and bare two (children), a son and a daughter, and she called the name of the son Zabulon, and the name of the daughter Dinah, in the seventh of the seventh month, in the sixth year of the fourth week. [2134 A.M.]

24 And the Lord was gracious to Rachel, and opened her womb, and she conceived, and bare a son, and she called his name Joseph, on the new moon of the fourth month, in the sixth year in this fourth week. [2134 A.M.]

25 And in the days when Joseph was born, Jacob said to Laban: 'Give me my wives and sons, and let me go to my father Isaac, and let me make me an house; for I have completed the years in which I have served thee for thy two daughters, and I will go to the house of my father.'

26 And Laban said to Jacob: 'Tarry with me for thy wages, and pasture my flock for me again, and take thy wages.'

27 And they agreed with one another that he should give him as his wages those of the lambs and kids which were born black and spotted and white, (these) were to be his wages.

28 And all the sheep brought forth spotted and speckled and black, variously marked, and they brought forth again lambs like themselves, and all that were spotted were Jacob's and those which were not were Laban's.

29 And Jacob's possessions multiplied exceedingly, and he possessed oxen and sheep and 30 asses and camels, and menservants and maid-servants.

30 And Laban and his sons envied Jacob, and Laban took back his sheep from him, and he observed him with evil intent.

C.3 See **Genesis Chapters 30 -31** for the full story of how Jacob managed to make the cattle bear offspring which were spotted and speckled and brown using the sticks from trees

GEN.30:37 And Jacob took him rods of green poplar, and of the hazel and chestnut tree; and pilled white strakes in them, and made the white appear which was in the rods.

GEN.30:38 And he set the rods which he had pilled before the flocks in the gutters in the watering troughs when the flocks came to drink, that they should conceive when they came to drink.

GEN.30:39 And the flocks conceived before the rods, and brought forth cattle ringstraked, speckled, and spotted.

C.4 BIBLICAL QUESTIONS & ANSWERS

Was the method of God - or was it of Evil Craftiness?

Genesis 31.10-12 would seem to indicate that it was in fact *by divine instruction.*

GEN.31:10 And it came to pass at the time that the cattle conceived, that I lifted up mine eyes, and saw in a dream, and, behold, the rams which **leaped upon the cattle (mating)** were ringstraked, speckled, and grisled.

GEN.31:11 And the angel of God spake unto me in a dream, saying, Jacob: And I said, Here am I.

GEN.31:12 And he said, Lift up now thine eyes, and see, all the rams which leap upon the cattle are ringstraked, speckled, and grisled: for I have seen all that Laban doeth unto thee.

How did Jacob in Genesis chapter 30-31 enable many ringed and spotted animals to be born to his advantage?

This **Book of Jubilees** mentions the '**speckled and spotted'** animals but does **not mention** the **methodology** of Genesis 30.

C.4 Some wise person has stated that '**Suspicion** is more often **wrong** than right'. It seems to be human nature that when we **don't fully understand something** that we often **assume the worst**. It is therefore in my opinion **very necessary** to **study fully** the **events in the Bible** that would otherwise possibly **cause someone to doubt** or **think evil** of that **particular event**.

The following **LINK** explains what Jacob did to **cause his cattle** to be **spotted** and **ringstraked** according to **modern husbandry**:

https://answersingenesis.org/genetics/animal-genetics/
jacobs-odd-breeding-program-genesis-30/

Chapter 29

1 And it came to pass when Rachel had borne Joseph, that Laban went to shear his sheep; for they were distant from him a three days' journey.

2 And Jacob saw that Laban was going to shear his sheep, and Jacob called Leah and Rachel, and spoke kindly unto them that they should come with him to the land of Canaan.

3 For he told them how he had seen everything in a dream, even all that He had spoken unto him that he should return to his father's house, and they said: 'To every place whither thou goes we will go with thee.'

4 And Jacob blessed the God of Isaac his father, and the God of Abraham his father's father, and he arose and mounted his wives and his children, and took all his possessions and crossed the river, and came to the land of Gilead, and Jacob hid his intention from Laban and told him not.

5 And in the seventh year of the fourth week Jacob turned (his face) toward Gilead in the first month, on the twenty-first thereof. [2135 A.M. = '**Anno Mundi' = years of the world**] And Laban pursued after him and overtook Jacob in the mountain of Gilead in the third month, on the thirteenth thereof.

6 And the Lord did not suffer him to injure Jacob; for he appeared to him in a dream by night. And Laban spoke to Jacob.

7 And on the fifteenth of those days Jacob made a feast for Laban, and for all who came with him, and Jacob swore to Laban that day, and Laban also to Jacob, that neither should cross the mountain of Gilead to the other with evil purpose.

8 And he made there a heap for a witness; wherefore the name of that place is called: 'The Heap of Witness,' after this heap.

9 But before they used to call the land of Gilead the land of the Rephaim; for it was the land of the Rephaim, and the Rephaim were born (there),

> giants whose height was ten, nine, eight down to seven cubits.

Comment:1: Rephaim is another name for giants. A cubit is between 18 inches to 25 inches. So here it was talking about giants from 22-25 feet high, 19-20 feet high, 16-18 feet high down to 12-14 feet high. These giants were much higher than Goliath whom a young king David slew. Goliath was around 10 feet tall. King David slew Goliath around 800 years after Jacob's time. Had the giants all be been slain by king David's time. We know that Joshua's men when they spied out the land of Canaan which was to become Israel said there were giants in the land so tall that they made Joshua's men feel like grasshoppers.

NUM.13:32 And they brought up an evil report of the land which they had searched unto the children of Israel, saying, The land, through which we have gone to search it, is a land that eats up the inhabitants thereof; and all the people that we saw in it are men of a great stature.

NUM.13:33 And there we saw the *giants, the sons of Anak*, which come of the giants: and we were in our own sight as *grasshoppers*, and so we were in their sight.

> 10 And their habitation was from the land of the children of Ammon to Mount Hermon, and the seats of their kingdom were Karnaim and Ashtaroth, and Edrei, and Misur, and Beon.
>
> 11 And the Lord destroyed them because of the evil of their deeds; for they were very malignant, and the Amorites dwelt in their stead, wicked and sinful, and there is no people to-day which has wrought to the full all their sins, and they have no longer length of life on the earth.

C.2 According to the Apocryphal Book of Enoch, God commanded his angels to provoke the giants to fight the one against the other until they were all consumed:

ENOCH 10.9 'And destroy all the spirits of the reprobate and the children (giants) of the Watchers (Fallen Angels), because they have wronged mankind. Destroy all wrong from the face of the earth, and let every evil work come to an end, and let the Plant of Righteousness appear'.

C.3 That might explain how that between Abraham's time and King David 1000 years later *most of the giants* had been killed and there were only a few small ones left in king David's time of almost 10 feet tall, such as Goliath and his brothers.

> 12 And Jacob sent away Laban, and he departed into Mesopotamia, the land of the East, and Jacob returned to the land of Gilead.

13 And he passed over the Jabbok in the ninth month, on the eleventh thereof. And on that day Esau, his brother, came to him, and he was reconciled to him, and departed from him unto the land of Seir, but Jacob dwelt in tents.

14 And in the first year of the fifth week in this jubilee [2136 A.M.] he crossed the Jordan, and dwelt beyond the Jordan, and he pastured his sheep from the sea of the heap unto Bethshan, and unto Dothan and unto the forest of Akrabbim.

15 And he sent to his father Isaac of all his substance, clothing, and food, and meat, and drink, and milk, and butter, and cheese, and some dates of the valley.

16 And to his mother Rebecca also four times a year, between the times of the months, between ploughing and reaping, and between autumn and the rain (season) and between winter and spring, to the tower of Abraham.

17 For Isaac had returned from the Well of the Oath and gone up to the tower of his father Abraham, and he dwelt there apart from his son Esau.

18 For in the days when Jacob went to Mesopotamia, Esau took to himself a wife Mahalath, the daughter of Ishmael, and he gathered together all the flocks of his father and his wives, and went Up and dwelt on Mount Seir, and left Isaac his father at the Well of the Oath alone.

19 And Isaac went up from the Well of the Oath and dwelt in the tower of Abraham his father on the mountains of Hebron,

20 And thither Jacob sent all that he did send to his father and his mother from time to time, all they needed, and they blessed Jacob with all their heart and with all their soul.

Chapter 30 DINAH & SHECHEM

Comment:1: **SHECHEM** Located in the Hill Country of Ephraim, the city of Shechem played a vital role in the history of Israel. This location, in the middle of the nation, provided the most important crossroads in central Israel. The city lay along the northern end of "The Way of the Patriarchs." This road, also called the "Ridge Route" (because it followed a key mountain ridge stretching 50 miles south), travelled from Shechem through Shiloh, Bethel/Ai, Ramah, Gibeah, Jerusalem, Bethlehem, and Hebron. This route appears continuously in the Biblical text. [https://bible.org/article/geographical-historical-spiritual-significance-shechem]

1 And in the first year of the sixth week [2143 A.M. = '**Anno Mundi' = years of the world**] he went up to Salem, to the east of Shechem, in peace, in the fourth month.

2 And there they carried off Dinah, the daughter of Jacob, into the house of Shechem, the son of Hamor, the Hivite, the prince of the land, and he lay with her and defiled her, and she was a little girl, a child of twelve years.

Comment:1: This story is also mentioned in detail in the **Book of Jasher**. See my book '**Jasher Insights' Book I**. Here, it tells us how old Dinah was, being only a child of twelve years old. No wonder her brothers were so angry when they found out what Shechem had done to her. This prince Shechem would be labelled as a paedophile today.

3 And he besought his father and her brothers that she might be given to him to wife. And Jacob and his sons were wroth because of the men of Shechem; for they had defiled Dinah, their sister, and they spoke to them with evil intent and dealt deceitfully with them and beguiled them.

4 And Simeon and Levi came unexpectedly to Shechem and executed judgment on all the men of Shechem, and slew all the men whom they found in it, and left not a single one remaining in it: they slew all in torments because they had dishonoured their sister Dinah.

C.2 '*Slew all in torments*' What exactly is that talking about? According to both the K.J.V of the Bible and the Book of Jasher, Jacob's sons tricked Shechem and his father Hamah into believing that if they and the people in their city would get circumcised then Shechem would be allowed to marry their sister Dinah. To which happily they agreed, but it was a ruse. The sons of Jacob knew that after three days those who had been newly circumcised would be in a lot of pain and therefore unfit for fighting in battle. Therefore, Simeon and Levi attacked the them on the 3rd day and slaughtered all the males in the town and took some of the young women and men as slaves.

GEN.34:25 And it came to pass on the third day, when they were sore, that two of the sons of Jacob, Simeon and Levi, Dinah's brethren, took each man his sword, and came upon the city boldly, and slew all the males.

GEN.34:26 And they slew Hamor and Shechem his son with the edge of the sword, and took Dinah out of Shechem's house, and went out.

C.3 In Old times these sons of Jacob believed in retribution against the paedophile Shechem. Why does our modern society let most of the paedophiles get away with their atrocities? Because they are mostly people in high places and seemingly above the law. I wouldn't want to be those criminals when **Hell finally opens up her mouth to receive them**. They will get what they dished out and much more-you can be certain of that, as God is just and righteous in all of His judgements.

PSA.9:15 The heathen are sunk down in the pit that they made: in the net which they hid is their own foot taken.

PSA.9:16 The LORD is known by the judgment which he executeth: the wicked is snared in the work of his own hands. Higgaion. Selah.

PSA.9:17 The wicked shall be turned into hell, and all the nations that forget God.

> 5 And thus let it not again be done from henceforth that a daughter of Israel be defiled; for judgment is ordained in heaven against them that they should destroy with the sword all the men of the Shechemites because they had wrought shame in Israel.

C4 Here we clearly see how that the rape of women is not to be allowed and yet some cultures today promote raping women. God is very much against any kind of rape and especially anything involving minors or children. There are a lot of sick people on this planet today, who should get slaughtered like the town of Shechem, because they abuse the innocent and those too young to even defend themselves. Often their lives are ruined after being abused as children.

C.5 Many people ask why does God seemingly just sit back and do nothing about the evil on our planet? Now that is a good question. From experience, I would say that it *only appears that way*. When I prayed about this point, God told me that He does protect many people and children from terrible things happening to them, especially when others pray for them and their protection.

C.6 The problem in modern times is that Western society in general, is getting away from its Christian/Judeo moral values and not enough people are praying for protection from evil. As a direct, result more and more horrors are happening on this planet. Many atrocities are committed by the ruling classes especially. Why? Because they are often guided by demons and devils and certainly not by the spirit of God. What they don't seem to realise is that God will not be mocked:

GAL.6:7 Be not deceived, God is not mocked.

GAL.6:8 For what things a man shall sow, those also shall he reap. For he that soweth in his flesh, of the flesh also shall reap corruption. But he that soweth in the spirit, of the spirit shall reap life everlasting.

C.7 I wouldn't want to be in the shoes of those who go around murdering other human beings and raping women and abusing children. Hellish murderers, rapists and pedophiles is what they are! Those people who do those things are cowards and bullies and have been led astray by evil entities or demons and devils who seek to harm and destroy all of God's creation.

C.8 The day of retribution will indeed come down on the heads of the vile wicked people who commit such crimes as mentioned in the story of Shechem, where a 12-year old girl was raped and forcibly taken away from her parents and brethren. In Old Testament times God often enacted vengeance through His people Israel at the times when Israel was obedient.

C.9 In modern times it is now supposed to be different if society abides by decent values. Fortunately, we do have the police and the Law, so we can report crimes to them.

C.10 Since the times of Jesus, the Messiah, he commanded us not to take matters into our own hands. Not to kill others who are evil, but to love one's enemies and to pray that God Himself will take retribution for the sins and iniquities of mankind and that we as Christians will not act as vigilantes seeking for revenge against criminal activities.

MAT.5:38 You have heard that it hath been said, An eye for an eye, and a tooth for a tooth.

MAT.5:39 But I say to you not to resist evil: but if one strike thee on thy right cheek, turn to him also the other:

MAT.5:43 You have heard that it hath been said, Thou shalt love thy neighbor, and hate thy enemy.

MAT.5:44 But I say to you, Love your enemies: do good to them that hate you: and pray for them that persecute and calumniate you:

MAT.5:45 That you may be the children of your Father who is in heaven.

C.11 This does not mean that Christians are supposed to be on the defensive like so many of the so-called Christian churches today.

All true believers are supposed to be '**Warriors of the Spirit**', not letting down their guard to **Evil,** but fighting against it according to **Ephesians 6.12-18**

241

which shows us where the **real** warfare is:

EPH.6:12 For we wrestle not against flesh and blood, but against principalities, against powers, against the rulers of the darkness of this world, against spiritual wickedness in high places.

EPH.6:13 Wherefore take unto you the whole armour of God, that ye may be able to withstand in the evil day, and having done all, to stand.

EPH.6:14 Stand therefore, having your loins girt about with truth, and having on the breastplate of righteousness;

EPH.6:15 And your feet shod with the preparation of the gospel of peace;

EPH.6:16 Above all, taking the shield of faith, wherewith ye shall be able to quench all the fiery darts of the wicked.

EPH.6:17 And take the helmet of salvation, and the sword of the Spirit, which is the word of God:

EPH.6:18 Praying always with all prayer and supplication in the Spirit, and watching thereunto with all perseverance and supplication for all saints;

C.12 In Jacob and his sons time however there were **no police and no 'law and order'**. It was pretty much 'kill or be killed' as Jacob and his sons were surrounded by enemies on every side, and they had no choice but to fight or they would have been slaughtered time and time again.

JAM.1:20 For the wrath of man worketh not the righteousness of God.

C.13 Things changed when the Messiah came to earth. Jesus in effect said let God be the judge and let Him bring retribution for iniquity. We do have laws in modern Western society against all the crimes that I have mentioned.

C.14 Why is **LAW and ORDER** still a very big problem? There are laws for the poor which the elite break at will and think nothing of, because some of the rulers are 'hardly human' and often have little or 'no conscience' about committing what we would think of as 'outrageous crimes. God however sees all, and their day will come when into the furnace they will go. Good riddance to bad rubbish I say! God calls them the '**Merchants**' who have **no conscience and exploit and plunder all the nations**.

REV.18:23 For thy merchants were the great men of the earth; for by thy sorceries were all nations deceived.

REV.18:24 And in her was found the blood of prophets, and of saints, and of all that were slain upon the earth.

C.15 Religious people of any Faith who go around slaughtering others, as the Muslim extremists do in Nigeria and in the Middle-East are certainly not going to a cushy harem-heaven, but will be thrust down into the heart of a fiery hell, where everything they did to others will be done to them.

242

C.16 Disclaimer by author: I accept that the vast majority of Muslims are not machete-wielding bomb makers waiting to explode. That image is mere propaganda. It is not just fanatical ISIS (IS) in the Middle East who are killing innocent people. Many Western nations kill innocent peoples in their hellish wars that slay MILLIONS of the innocent. All the slaughter of the nations in the past 100 years or so has been for what? It has been only for exploitation, power, domination and control as well as eugenics.

C.17 Look how countries justify going to war, where millions are slaughtered. If any normal person kills another person, then it is defined as murder, but going to war and killing others is justified and made to look even heroic? The fact is that it is mostly innocent women and children who are the real victims of wars.

> 6 And the Lord delivered them into the hands of the sons of Jacob that they might exterminate them with the sword and execute judgment upon them, and that it might not thus again be done in Israel that a virgin of Israel should be defiled.

C.18 How was it even possible that only two men managed to take out a whole town single-handedly? The sons of Jacob were empowered by God and were thus much more agile than normal people and much stronger. It is stated that then the sons of Jacob went to battle that they slew their enemies like someone with a machete knife slicing through many gourds in a mere few seconds. Their enemies didn't have a chance. Today we would call them **X-Men or supermen**. I am not exaggerating. If God is on your side, then anything is possible.

LUK.1:37 Because nothing is impossible with God.

> 7 And if there is any man who wishes in Israel to give his daughter or his sister to any man who is of the seed of the Gentiles he shall surely die, and they shall stone him with stones; for he hath wrought shame in Israel; and they shall burn the woman with fire, because she has dishonoured the name of the house of her father, and she shall be rooted out of Israel.

C.19 The reason the laws were made so severe in the times of Moses was as a severe deterrent. Why is there so much crime today in modern Western society? The West has given up its Christian values and society is fast turning into anarchy where 'anything goes' and there are 'no rules' because according to the liberalists and evolutionists there is seemingly no God, and we all just evolved from monkeys. The stance of ATHEISM is: You are basically just a beast so why not just behave like one? That is the devilish doctrine of Evolution that is being taught in schools and universities today when in fact there is absolutely no proof of evolution whatsoever. It is merely another LIE of Satan. There is a Creator and he is indeed wonderful to know.

> 8 And let not an adulteress and no uncleanness be found in Israel throughout all the days of the generations of the earth; for Israel is holy unto the Lord, and every man who has defiled (it) shall surely die: they shall stone him with stones.

C.20 If a woman committed adultery, she was to be stoned according to the Old Mosaic law, but what did Jesus say in His time: **Jesus was a lot more merciful** than the cruel Laws of Moses:

JOHN.8:3 And the scribes and Pharisees brought unto him a woman taken in adultery; and when they had set her in the midst,

JOHN.8:4 They say unto him, Master, this woman was taken in adultery, in the very act.

JOHN.8:5 Now Moses in the law commanded us, that such should be stoned: but what sayest thou?

JOHN.8:6 This they said, tempting him, that they might have to accuse him. But Jesus stooped down, and with his finger wrote on the ground, as though he heard them not.

JOHN.8:7 So when they continued asking him, he lifted up himself, and said unto them, He that is without sin among you, let him first cast a stone at her.

JOHN.8:8 And again he stooped down and wrote on the ground.

JOHN.8:9 And they which heard it, being convicted by their own conscience, went out one by one, beginning at the eldest, even unto the last: and Jesus was left alone, and the woman standing in the midst.

JOHN.8:10 When Jesus had lifted up himself, and saw none but the woman, he said unto her, Woman, where are those thine accusers? hath no man condemned thee?

JOHN.8:11 She said, No man, Lord. And Jesus said unto her, Neither do I condemn thee: go, and sin no more.

> 9 For thus has it been ordained and written in the heavenly tablets regarding all the seed of Israel: he who defiles (it) shall surely die, and he shall be stoned with stones.
>
> 10 And to this law there is no limit of days, and no remission, nor any atonement: but the man who has defiled his daughter shall be rooted out in the midst of all Israel, because he has given of his seed to Moloch, and wrought impiously so as to defile it.

11And do thou, Moses, command the children of Israel and exhort them not to give their daughters to the Gentiles, and not to take for their sons any of the daughters of the Gentiles, for this is abominable before the Lord.

12 For this reason I have written for thee in the words of the Law all the deeds of the Shechemites, which they wrought against Dinah, and how the sons of Jacob spoke, saying: 'We will not give our daughter to a man who is uncircumcised; for that were a reproach unto us.'

13 And it is a reproach to Israel, to those who live, and to those that take the daughters of the Gentiles; for this is unclean and abominable to Israel.

14 And Israel will not be free from this uncleanness if it has a wife of the daughters of the Gentiles or has given any of its daughters to a man who is of any of the Gentiles.

MAT.19:7 They say unto him, Why did Moses then command to give a writing of divorcement, and to put her away?

MAT.19:8 He saith unto them, Moses because of the **hardness of your hearts** suffered you to **put away your wives: but from the beginning it was not so.**

MAT.19:9 And I say unto you, Whosoever shall put away his wife, except it be for fornication, and shall marry another, committeth adultery: and whoso marrieth her which is put away doth commit adultery.

MAT.5:7 Blessed are the merciful: for they shall obtain mercy.

15 For there will be plague upon plague, and curse upon curse, and every judgment and plague and curse will come : if he do this thing, or hide his eyes from those who commit uncleanness, or those who defile the sanctuary of the Lord, or those who profane His holy name, (then) will the whole nation together be judged for all the uncleanness and profanation of this man.

16 And there will be no respect of persons [and no consideration of persons] and no receiving at his hands of fruits and offerings and burnt-offerings and fat, nor the fragrance of sweet savour, so as to accept it: and so fare every man or woman in Israel who defiles the sanctuary.

245

17 For this reason I have commanded thee, saying: 'Testify this testimony to Israel: see how the Shechemites fared and their sons: how they were delivered into the hands of two sons of Jacob, and they slew them under tortures, and it was (reckoned) unto them for righteousness, and it is written down to them for righteousness.

18 And the seed of Levi was chosen for the priesthood, and to be Levites, that they might minister before the Lord, as we, continually, and that Levi and his sons may be blessed for ever; for he was zealous to execute righteousness and judgment and vengeance on all those who arose against Israel.

19 And so they inscribe as a testimony in his favour on the heavenly tablets blessing and righteousness before the God of all:

20 And we remember the righteousness which the man fulfilled during his life, at all periods of the year; until a thousand generations they will record it, and it will come to him and to his descendants after him, and he has been recorded on the heavenly tablets as a friend and a righteous man.

21 All this account I have written for thee and have commanded thee to say to the children of Israel, that they should not commit sin nor transgress the ordinances nor break the covenant which has been ordained for them, (but) that they should fulfil it and be recorded as friends.

22 But if they transgress and work uncleanness in every way, they will be recorded on the heavenly tablets as adversaries, and they will be destroyed out of the book of life, and they will be recorded in the book of those who will be destroyed and with those who will be rooted out of the earth.

23 And on the day when the sons of Jacob slew Shechem a writing was recorded in their favour in heaven that they had executed righteousness and uprightness and vengeance on the sinners, and it was written for a blessing.

C.21 Even though Simeon and Levi had slaughtered a whole town of people containing 720 men they were not arrested for 'War Crimes' as would happen

246

today for sure. Why? Because they were used by God Himself to enact His judgements upon the wicked which was alright for that time. A time in which there were no police and no Law and Order. For that reason, Simon and Levi were the 'law' in the hands of an angry God, who enacted swift vengeance and retribution upon His very wicked enemies.

---

24 And they brought Dinah, their sister, out of the house of Shechem, and they took captive everything that was in Shechem, their sheep and their oxen and their asses, and all their wealth, and all their flocks, and brought them all to Jacob their father.

25 And he reproached them because they had put the city to the sword for he feared those who dwelt in the land, the Canaanites and the Perizzites.

26 And the dread of the Lord was upon all the cities which are around about Shechem, and they did not rise to pursue after the sons of Jacob; for terror had fallen upon them.

C.22 CONCLUSION: The Laws of Moses were seemingly very harsh in their time. They certainly sound harsh to us today in modern times, but were they? The **LAWS of MOSES** served a very good purpose in their time as a **deterrent** against **crime**, but with the coming of the **MESSIAH** came **FORGIVENESS** and **MERCY.**

JOH.1:17 For the law was given by Moses, but grace and truth came by Jesus Christ.

Chapter 31

1 And on the new moon of the month Jacob spoke to all the people of his house. saying: 'Purify yourselves and change your garments, and let us arise and go up to Bethel, where I vowed a vow to Him on the day when I fled from the face of Esau my brother, because he has been with me and brought me into this land in peace, and put ye away the strange gods that arc among you.'

2 And they gave up the strange gods and that which was in their ears and which was on their necks and the idols which Rachel stole from Laban her father she gave wholly to Jacob.

3 And he burnt and brake them to pieces and destroyed them and hid them under an oak which is in the land of Shechem.

C.1 Jacob is still living in the land of Shechem and he gets rid of all the idols that Rachel had brought with her from her father's house. She originally brought these idols belonging to her father Laban as she didn't want him using them to divine where Jacob and she had gone when they had just fled from Laban's house. Not that her actions helped anything as Laban simply used other idols to discern where Jacob and Rachel had fled to and he did manage to overtake them and say good-bye before letting them go. Rachel taking the idols was not a good idea and it probably cost her an early death as she died young in the childbirth of her son Benjamin at around 46 years old.

4 And he went up on the new moon of the seventh month to Bethel.

5 And he built an altar at the place where he had slept, and he set up a pillar there, and he sent word to his father Isaac to come to him to his sacrifice, and to his mother Rebecca. And Isaac said: 'Let my son Jacob come, and let me see him before I die.'

6 And Jacob went to his father Isaac and to his mother Rebecca, to the house of his father Abraham, and he took two of his sons with him, Levi and Judah, and he came to his father Isaac and to his mother Rebecca.

7 And Rebecca came forth from the tower to the front of it to kiss Jacob and embrace him; for her spirit had revived when she heard: 'Behold

Jacob thy son has come'; and she kissed him.

8 And she saw his two sons, and she recognised them, and said unto him: 'Are these thy sons, my son' and she embraced them and kissed them, and blessed them, saying: 'In you shall the seed of Abraham become illustrious, and ye shall prove a blessing on the earth.'

9 And Jacob went in to Isaac his father, to the chamber where he lay, and his two sons were with him, and he took the hand of his father, and stooping down he kissed him, and Isaac clung to the neck of Jacob his son and wept upon his neck.

10 And the darkness left the eyes of Isaac, and he saw the two sons of Jacob, Levi, and Judah, and he said: '

C.2 Here is an example of a miracle, that a blind man's sight is restored long enough for him to see the sons of Jacob. Presumably after this event Isaac became blind again but the story doesn't directly tell us so perhaps God in His great mercy took away his blindness permanently? Why did God open the eyes of blind Isaac at this time?

11 Are these thy sons, my son for they are like thee.' And he said unto him that they were truly his sons: 'And thou hast truly seen that they are truly my sons'.

12 And they came near to him, and he turned and kissed them and embraced them both together.

13 And the spirit of prophecy came down into his mouth, and he took Levi by his right hand and Judah by his left.

14 And he turned to Levi first, and began to bless him first, and said unto him: May the God of all, the very Lord of all the ages, bless thee and thy children throughout all the ages.

15 And may the Lord give to thee and to thy seed greatness and great glory, and cause thee and thy seed, from among all flesh, to approach Him to serve in His sanctuary as the angels of the presence and as the holy ones. (Even) as they, shall the seed of thy sons be for glory and greatness and holiness, and may He make them great unto all the ages.

16 And they shall be judges and princes, and chiefs of all the seed of the sons of Jacob;

They shall speak the word of the Lord in righteousness and they shall judge all His judgments in righteousness.

And they shall declare My ways to Jacob And My paths to Israel.

The blessing of the Lord shall be given in their mouths to bless all the seed of the beloved.

17 Thy mother has called thy name Levi, And justly has she called thy name;

Thou shalt be joined to the Lord And be the companion of all the sons of Jacob; Let His table be thine, And do thou and thy sons eat thereof;

And may thy table be full unto all generations, And thy food fail not unto all the ages.

18 And let all who hate thee fall down before thee, And let all thy adversaries be rooted out and perish; And blessed be he that blesses thee And cursed be every nation that curses thee.'

C.3 We see here a very important prophecy and blessing being given to Levi and exalting him as the father of the tribe of Levi which was the tribe of the priesthood that would represent God Himself from now on. Amazing insight that God gave to Isaac about the future of his grandson Levi.

19 And to Judah he said: 'May the Lord give thee strength and power

To tread down all that hate thee; A prince shalt thou be, thou and one of thy sons, over the sons of Jacob;

20 May thy name and the name of thy sons go forth and traverse every land and region. Then shall the Gentiles fear before thy face,

And all the nations shall quake [And all the peoples shall quake].

In thee shall be the help of Jacob, And in thee be found the salvation of Israel.

21 And when thou sits on the throne of honour of thy righteousness

> There shall be great peace for all the seed of the sons of the beloved;
>
> Blessed be he that blesses thee, And all that hate thee and afflict thee and curse thee Shall be rooted out and destroyed from the earth and be accursed.'

C.4 Again, a miraculous scene as Isaac is blessing Judah and stating that his tribe of Judah is to be the ruling tribe of the kings that are to come forth from Israel. The tribe of Judah had the symbol of the **LION**. It was later prophesied that the Messiah would come from the tribe of Judah - or the tribe of the kings.

> 22 And turning he kissed him again and embraced him and rejoiced greatly; for he had seen the sons of Jacob his son in very truth.

C.5 Of all of Jacobs sons that he could have taken to see his father Isaac he chose to take Levi and Judah. Why? Did he perceive what would happen when he went to visit his aged father IsaaC. Or did God specifically tell him to take these particular sons to their grandfather to get a special blessing before he died? We are not told in this story, but it would seem that Jacob had been instructed by God to take those particular sons to see his father IsaaC. This story shows clearly how the Patriarchs could hear clearly from God and that they had great discernment and wisdom given to them by God because of their obedience to Him. God really tried the Patriarchs and they came closer to God by reason of their many calamities, dangers, afflictions, sorrows and heartbreaks.

> 23 And he went forth from between his feet and fell down and bowed down to him, and he blessed them and rested there with Isaac his father that night, and they eat and drank with joy.
>
> 24 And he made the two sons of Jacob sleep, the one on his right hand and the other on his left, and it was counted to him for righteousness.
>
> 25 And Jacob told his father everything during the night, how the Lord had shown him great mercy, and how he had prospered (him in) all his ways, and protected him from all evil.
>
> 26 And Isaac blessed the God of his father Abraham, who had not withdrawn his mercy and his righteousness from the sons of his servant IsaaC.
>
> 27 And in the morning Jacob told his father Isaac the vow which he had

vowed to the Lord, and the vision which he had seen, and that he had built an altar, and that everything was ready for the sacrifice to be made before the Lord as he had vowed, and that he had come to set him on an ass.

28 And Isaac said unto Jacob his son: 'I am not able to go with thee; for I am old and not able to bear the way: go, my son, in peace; for I am one hundred and sixty-five years this day; I am no longer able to journey; set thy mother (on an ass) and let her go with thee.

29 And I know, my son, that thou hast come on my account, and may this day be blessed on which thou hast seen me alive, and I also have seen thee, my son.

30 Mayest thou prosper and fulfil the vow which thou hast vowed; and put not off thy vow; for thou shalt be called to account as touching the vow; now therefore make haste to perform it, and may He be pleased who has made all things, to whom thou hast vowed the vow.'

C.6 What was this vow that Jacob had promised to give to God? It was the vow of tithing 10% of his income to God. Until God had decided which tribe would be the tribe of the priesthood, he hadn't been able to tithe to anyone representing God apart from himself. Now with Levi being anointed to become the tribe of the Priesthood of Israel now Jacob and his family could start tithing and thus increasing the house of the priesthood.

C.7 Concerning Judah: Judah was blessed to be the tribe representing the Kings of Israel. Unfortunately, after Solomon his kingdom was divided into two kingdoms because of Solomon's idolatry with his wives. Judah and Benjamin stayed together, and the other 10 tribes became the northern tribe of Israel. In around 950 BCE.

C.8 What did happen to those 10 northern tribes of Israel? It is indeed a great mystery, as they seemingly just disappeared from the face of the earth back in around 722 BCE, when taken captive by the Assyrian empire.

C.9 According to the apocryphal book of **II Ezdras** they were captured by the Assyrian empire and went into slavery, but that some of them managed to escape to a **'far away land'** where no peoples had lived before?

II EZDRAS 13.40 'These are the ten tribes which were led away from their own land into captivity I the days of king Hosea, whom Shalmaneser the king of the Assyrians led captive; he took them across the river, and they were taken to another land.

II EZDRAS 13.41 But they formed a plan for themselves, that they would leave the multitude of the nations and to a more distant region, where mankind had never lived.

C.10 Is the earth hollow and the 10 tribes took refuge inside the earth? Read the complete story in my book **EZDRAS INSIGHTS.**

II EZDRAS 13.42 That there at least they might keep their statutes which they were not able to keep in their own land.

II EZDRAS 13.43 And they went in the narrow passages of the Euphrates river. (Read more of this fascinating story about the 10 Northern Tribes some of whose representatives went to a very far away land? Where was that far away land, where you will see that they promised to come back in the last times. Well you can read all about that in my book **EZDRAS INSIGHTS)**

---

31 And he said to Rebecca: 'Go with Jacob thy son'; and Rebecca went with Jacob her son, and Deborah with her, and they came to Bethel.

32 And Jacob remembered the prayer with which his father had blessed him and his two sons, Levi and Judah, and he rejoiced and blessed the God of his fathers, Abraham and IsaaC.

33 And he said: 'Now I know that I have an eternal hope, and my sons also, before the God of all'; and thus is it ordained concerning the two; and they record it as an eternal testimony unto them on the heavenly tablets how Isaac blessed them.

C.11 Notice how that everything of importance was written down on the heavenly tablets. The same was the case in the **Book of Enoch**. See my book 'ENOCH INSIGHTS'.

Chapter 32

1 And he abode that night at Bethel, and Levi dreamed that they had ordained and made him the priest of the Most High God, him and his sons for ever; and he awoke from his sleep and blessed the Lord.

2 And Jacob rose early in the morning, on the fourteenth of this month, and he gave a tithe of all that came with him, both of men and cattle, both of gold and every vessel and garment, yea, he gave tithes of all.

3 And in those days Rachel became pregnant with her son Benjamin. And Jacob counted his sons from him upwards and Levi fell to the portion of the Lord, and his father clothed him in the garments of the priesthood and filled his hands.

4 And on the fifteenth of this month, he brought to the altar fourteen oxen from amongst the cattle, and twenty-eight rams, and forty-nine sheep, and seven lambs, and twenty-one kids of the goats as a burnt-offering on the altar of sacrifice, well pleasing for a sweet savour before God.

5 This was his offering, in consequence of the vow which he had vowed that he would give a tenth, with their fruit-offerings and their drink-offerings.

6 And when the fire had consumed it, he burnt incense on the fire over the fire, and for a thank-offering two oxen and four rams and four sheep, four he-goats, and two sheep of a year old, and two kids of the goats; and thus he did daily for seven days.

7 And he and all his sons and his men were eating (this) with joy there during seven days and blessing and thanking the Lord, who had delivered him out of all his tribulation and had given him his vow.

8 And he tithed all the clean animals, and made a burnt sacrifice, but the unclean animals he gave (not) to Levi his son, and he gave him all the souls of the men

9 And Levi discharged the priestly office at Bethel before Jacob his father in preference to his ten brothers, and he was a priest there, and Jacob gave his vow: thus he tithed again the tithe to the Lord and sanctified it, and it became holy unto Him.

10 And for this reason it is ordained on the heavenly tablets as a law for the tithing again the tithe to eat before the Lord from year to year, in the place where it is chosen that His name should dwell, and to this law there is no limit of days for ever.

11 This ordinance is written that it may be fulfilled from year to year in eating the second tithe before the Lord in the place where it has been chosen, and nothing shall remain over from it from this year to the year following.

12 For in its year shall the seed be eaten till the days of the gathering of the seed of the year, and the wine till the days of the wine and the oil till the days of its season.

13 And all that is left thereof and becomes old, let it be regarded as polluted: let it be burnt with fire, for it is unclean.

14 And thus let them eat it together in the sanctuary and let them not suffer it to become old.

15 And all the tithes of the oxen and sheep shall be holy unto the Lord, and shall belong to his priests, which they will eat before Him from year to year; for thus is it ordained and engraven regarding the tithe on the heavenly tablets.

16 And on the following night, on the twenty-second day of this month, Jacob resolved to build that place, and to surround the court with a wall, and to sanctify it and make it holy for ever, for himself and his children after him.

17 And the Lord appeared to him by night and blessed him and said unto him: 'Thy name shall not be called Jacob, but Israel shall they name thy name.'

Comment:1: An important moment where God comes to talk with Jacob in person and tells him that his name is no longer Jacob (means deceiver) but Israel (Prince of God and of man) We today in modern times would think why would anyone call their son 'Deceiver'? Well perhaps God told them to call Jacob that name as it certainly turned out to be true when he cheated his brother out of his birthright and then his blessing. Eventually though he became Israel when God had given to him a new name. This reminds me of being born again in Christ Jesus. It was probably Jesus who came to visit Jacob at the time of giving to the Patriarch Jacob a new name.

2CO.5:17 Therefore if any man be in Christ, he is a new creature: old things are passed away; behold, all things are become new.

> 18 And He said unto him again: 'I am the Lord who created the heaven and the earth, and I will increase thee and multiply thee exceedingly, and kings shall come forth from thee, and they shall judge everywhere wherever the foot of the sons of men has trodden.

JOH.1:1 In the beginning was the Word, and the Word was with God, and the Word was God.

JOH.1:2 The same was in the beginning with God.

JOH.1:3 All things were made by him; and without him was not anything made that was made.

> 19 And I will give to thy seed all the earth which is under heaven, and they shall judge all the nations according to their desires, and after that they shall get possession of the whole earth and inherit it for ever.'
>
> 20 And He finished speaking with him, and He went up from him. and Jacob looked till He had ascended into heaven.
>
> 21 And he saw in a vision of the night, and behold an angel descended from heaven with seven tablets in his hands, and he gave them to Jacob, and he read them and knew all that was written therein which would befall him and his sons throughout all the ages.
>
> 22 And he showed him all that was written on the tablets and said unto him: 'Do not build this place, and do not make it an eternal sanctuary, and do not dwell here; for this is not the place. Go to the house of Abraham thy father and dwell with Isaac thy father until the day of the death of thy father.

23 For in Egypt thou shalt die in peace, and in this land thou shalt be buried with honour in the sepulchre of thy fathers, with Abraham and IsaaC.

24 Fear not, for as thou hast seen and read it, thus shall it all be; and do thou write down everything as thou hast seen and read.'

25 And Jacob said: 'Lord, how can I remember all that I have read and seen 'And he said unto him: 'I will bring all things to thy remembrance.'

26 And he went up from him, and he awoke from his sleep, and he remembered everything which he had read and seen, and he wrote down all the words which he had read and seen.

27 And he celebrated there yet another day, and he sacrificed thereon according to all that he sacrificed on the former days, and called its name 'Addition,' for this day was added and the former days he called 'The Feast '.

28 And thus it was manifested that it should be, and it is written on the heavenly tablets: wherefore it was revealed to him that he should celebrate it and add it to the seven days of the feast.

29 And its name was called 'Addition,' because that it was recorded amongst the days of the feast days, according to the number of the days of the year.

30 And in the night, on the twenty-third of this month, Deborah Rebecca's nurse died, and they buried her beneath the city under the oak of the river, and he called the name of this place, 'The river of Deborah,' and the oak, 'The oak of the mourning of Deborah.'

31 And Rebecca went and returned to her house to his father Isaac, and Jacob sent by her hand rams and sheep and he-goats that she should prepare a meal for his father such as he desired.

32 And he went after his mother till he came to the land of Kabratan, and he dwelt there.

33 And Rachel bare a son in the night and called his name 'Son of my sorrow '; for she suffered in giving him birth: but his father called his name Benjamin, on the eleventh of the eighth month in the first of the sixth week of this jubilee. [2143 A.M.]

34 And Rachel died there, and she was buried in the land of Ephrath, the same is Bethlehem, and Jacob built a pillar on the grave of Rachel, on the road above her grave.

Chapter 33

1 And Jacob went and dwelt to the south of Magdaladra'ef. And he went to his father Isaac, he and Leah his wife, on the new moon of the tenth month.

2 And Reuben saw Bilhah, Rachel's maid, the concubine of his father, bathing in water in a secret place, and he loved her.

C.1 'When the cat's away the mice will play', is the old proverb. Perhaps it was a mistake for Jacob to leave his concubine Bilhad behind, whilst he and his wife Leah went off to visit his father Isaac, as it obviously opened the door to temptation in the case of Reuben. He apparently went to see Isaac because Isaac was passing through pain of sorrows in the death of his wife's handmaiden Deborah and also Jacob himself was in sorrow because of his wife Rachel having just died in childbirth.

3 And he hid himself at night, and he entered the house of Bilhah [at night], and he found her sleeping alone on a bed in her house.

C.2 Reuben thought that his father had too many wives and that he could spare one for the night. At least that must have been the temptation that he gave into. Notice how both sorrow and the raping of women occurred several times in the story of the life of Jacob. Apparently, men didn't treat women very well in the olden days. They seemed to have been treated as some sort of second-class citizens. Why was it only the Patriarchs that got together and talked with other 'wise men'? Why didn't they include their women? In the New Testament, refreshingly it was very different. Women could be leaders and shepherds and often were. The macho culture of old religions has not done the world any good in modern times.

C.3 According to the New Testament men and women are equal when it comes to spiritual things. Paul who had been a Pharisee made it very clear in the New Testament, although even he himself got stuck up about some things concerning women. He preferred to be a dedicated monk which certainly is not the choice of most of us men. Women are very important and should be treated with great respect. It saddens me to see so many people not marrying in modern times and not having children. The man and his wife were supposed to stick together through thick and thin.

4 And he lay with her, and she awoke and saw, and behold Reuben was lying with her in the bed, and she uncovered the border of her covering and seized him, and cried out, and discovered that it was Reuben.

5 And she was ashamed because of him, and released her hand from

him, and he fled.

6 And she lamented because of this thing exceedingly and did not tell it to anyone.

7 And when Jacob returned and sought her, she said unto him: 'I am not clean for thee, for I have been defiled as regards thee; for Reuben has defiled me, and has lain with me in the night, and I was asleep, and did not discover until he uncovered my skirt and slept with me.'

C.4 Poor girl, not only is she defiled by a relative but now her own husband will never touch her again when it wasn't even her fault? No mercy shown to her, even though she was completely innocent.

8 And Jacob was exceedingly wroth with Reuben because he had lain with Bilhah, because he had uncovered his father's skirt; and Jacob did not approach her again because Reuben had defiled her.

C.5 It was good that Bilhad was honest with Jacob especially when Reuben had forced himself upon her. Why was Reuben not punished for such a crime as rape, when his brothers Simeon and Levi slaughtered a whole town because of Shechem raping their only sister Dinah? What is the difference? It was still the crime of rape and Reuben got away with it, scot free, whilst Shechem and his whole town were slaughtered. Where is the justice and retribution against Reuben? It can't be right to have a double standard as in this case.

C.6 Well, the answer to that question is that 'Before the times of Moses', there were no official laws written out and carved in stone by the Almighty hand of God Himself.

9 And as for any man who uncovers his father's skirt his deed is wicked exceedingly, for he is abominable before the Lord.

C.7 Remember here, that it is the angel of the Lord who is talking to Moses as to what is right and what is wrong, and Moses is thus establishing the Laws for Israel. The angel even mentions that Reuben was not judged because the Law of 'not going into thy father's wife' had not yet been established

10 For this reason it is written and ordained on the heavenly tablets that a man should not lie with his father's wife, and should not uncover his father's skirt, for this is unclean: they shall surely die together, the man who lies with his father's wife and the woman also, for they have wrought uncleanness on the earth.

C.8 With the **TEN COMMANDMENTS** it was very clear that a man was not allowed to commit adultery, or he would be stoned to death along with the woman. Since Reuben lived before the time of Moses by around 400 years the law had not yet been established and fully substantiated – therefore Reuben could not be judged by the Law as it not yet been established. It does say above however that Jacob was exceeding wroth against Reuben and obviously Reuben would have been in Jacob's hot dis-pleasure for some time. So, I guess, in a sense Reuben was punished but not with the severity of the harsh Mosaic Laws. In another sense both Jacob and Bildah were also punished as well -as Jacob now saw his concubine as unclean and would no longer go into her. Where is the mercy and forgiveness in this situation, especially if Bildah was totally innocent?

---

11 And there shall be nothing unclean before our God in the nation which He has chosen for Himself as a possession.

12 And again, it is written a second time: 'Cursed be he who lieth with the wife of his father, for he hath uncovered his father's shame'; and all the holy ones of the Lord said 'So be it; so be it.'

13 And do thou, Moses, command the children of Israel that they observe this word; for it (entails) a punishment of death; and it is unclean and there is no atonement for ever to atone for the man who has committed this, but he is to be put to death and slain, and stoned with stones, and rooted out from the midst of the people of our God.

14 For to no man who does so in Israel is it permitted to remain alive a single day on the earth, for he is abominable and unclean.

15 And let them not say: to Reuben was granted life and forgiveness after he had lain with his father's concubine, and to her also though she had a husband, and her husband Jacob, his father, was still alive.

16 For until that time there had not been revealed the ordinance and judgment and law in its completeness for all, but in thy days (it has been revealed) as a law of seasons and of days, and an everlasting law for the everlasting generations.

---

17 And for this law there is no consummation of days, and no atonement for it, but they must both be rooted out in the midst of the nation: on the day whereon they committed it they shall slay them.
C.9 During these Old Testament times it is stating here that there was **no**

atonement for sin. It was only after the **Messiah** and come that we have atonement for sin. This is way the Messiah came to set us free from the Mosaic Laws that kept the people in bondage and in fear of retribution. Unfortunately, later in time and at the time of Jesus, the religious establishment had a stranglehold on the people of Israel through the Law. If they didn't like someone, they would find religious laws against that person even if they were completely innocent. The Pharisees ended up killing their own Messiah Jesus, using the Law. They stoned an innocent man Stephen, known as the first Christian martyr using the so-called Mosaic law against him because they didn't like his history of Israel lesson that he gave to them when forced to attend a 'kangaroo trial'. Then they stoned him to death using the old law.

18 And do thou, Moses, write (it) down for Israel that they may observe it, and do according to these words, and not commit a sin unto death; for the Lord our God is judge, who respects not persons and accepts not gifts.

19 And tell them these words of the covenant, that they may hear and observe, and be on their guard with respect to them, and not be destroyed and rooted out of the land; for an uncleanness, and an abomination, and a contamination, and a pollution are all they who commit it on the earth before our God.

20 And there is no greater sin than the fornication which they commit on earth; for Israel is a holy nation unto the Lord its God, and a nation of inheritance, and a priestly and royal nation and for (His own) possession; and there shall no such uncleanness appear in the midst of the holy nation.

C.10 'There is no greater sin than fornication which they commit on earth'. It sounds to me that God had to be very severe with Israel when Israel had first come out of Egypt because they had seen many evil happenings in Egypt and god had to establish some sort of code of ethics. Sometime in order to get people to change from their evil habits it necessary to be strict and stern until people change from their evil ways of both idol worship and fornication. These two were often linked together in ritual sexual sacrifice, which is the much more severe form of fornication known as witchcraft. Fornicating with demons and Fallen angels. This, God wanted to totally root out in the new nation of Israel and thus the original severity of the Laws of Moses.

21 And in the third year of this sixth week [2145 A.M. = **Anno Mundi' = years of the world**] Jacob and all his sons went and dwelt in the house of Abraham, near Isaac his father and Rebecca his mother.

22 And these were the names of the sons of Jacob: the first-born Reuben, Simeon, Levi, Judah, Issachar, Zebulon, the sons of Leah; and the sons of Rachel, Joseph and Benjamin; and the sons of Bilhah, Dan and Naphtali; and the sons of Zilpah, Gad and Asher; and Dinah, the daughter of Leah, the only daughter of Jacob. And they came and bowed themselves to Isaac and Rebecca, and when they saw them, they blessed Jacob and all his sons, and Isaac rejoiced exceedingly, for he saw the sons of Jacob, his younger son and he blessed them.

C.11 It was necessary to have harsh laws for a season until Israel could learn through a harsh deterrent. Unfortunately, the laws were eventually misused against the poor of the land by the rich and powerful and thus the laws became of no effect, as the powers that ruled became more and more corrupt. This is why God had to send His only Begotten Son to set an example of how we are supposed to live. Not using the harshness of the Old Mosaic laws but to show forgiveness and mercy and not harsh judgement anymore. The bible clearly states

MAT.26:52 For all they that take the sword shall perish with the sword.

C.12 Because the Pharisees used the 'letter of the Law' against Jesus the Messiah and had an innocent man crucified. Israel was later kicked out of its own country by the Romans some 40 years later in 70 AD. This was surely retribution by God Himself.

ROM.11:22 Behold therefore the goodness and severity of God: on them which fell, severity; but toward thee, goodness, if thou continue in his goodness: otherwise thou also shalt be cut off.

JOH.1:17 For the law was given by Moses, but grace and truth came by Jesus Christ

MAT.19:8 He saith unto them, Moses because of the hardness of your hearts suffered you to put away your wives: but from the beginning it was not so.

C.13 Strangely, if we look at all the scriptures from the beginning of time until the end of time when God finally ushers in the New Heaven and the New Earth, we find that at different seasons there does exist the harshness of the Laws of Moses and at other times the New testaments ways of Jesus of turning the other cheek and mercy and kindness and forgiveness. When does God use one set of laws and when does He use the other?

C.14 According to Revelations 20 the Messiah will be ruling and reigning over the peoples of the earth together with his angels an angelized saints with a 'Rod of Iron'. Now a 'Rod of iron' certainly doesn't sound like a 'turning the other cheek' does it? There are plenty of examples of this of the 'severity of God'. Whether God uses the severity of His laws of the Mercy of Christ very much depends on the situation and the peoples involved.

C.15 God is not a namby-pamby God for the goody-goody church go'ers who never really does anything to deal with people's sins. That is a very false conception given out by many Christian churches who have fallen asleep in their vocation. God can be very severe if He has to be. He will certainly be very severe with the final Judgement of the Fallen angels and Satan at the final Great white Throne Judgement according to Revelations chapter 20.

REV.20:11 And I saw a great white throne, and him that sat on it, from whose face the earth and the heaven fled away; and there was found no place for them.

REV.20:12 And I saw the dead, small and great, stand before God; and the books were opened: and another book was opened, which is the book of life: and the dead were judged out of those things which were written in the books, according to their works.

REV.20:10 And the devil that deceived them was cast into the lake of fire and brimstone, where the beast and the false prophet are, and shall be tormented day and night for ever and ever.

REV.20:15 And whosoever was not found written in the book of life was cast into the lake of fire.

C.16 God was not just severe in the Old Testament times but even in the New Testament. In the new Testament it shows the severity of God in Acts 5.1

ACT.5:1 But a certain man named Ananias, with Sapphira his wife, sold a possession,

ACT.5:2 And kept back part of the price, his wife also being privy to it, and brought a certain part, and laid it at the apostles' feet.

ACT.5:3 But Peter said, Ananias, why hath Satan filled thine heart to lie to the Holy Ghost, and to keep back part of the price of the land?

ACT.5:4 Whiles it remained, was it not thine own? and after it was sold, was it not in thine own power? why hast thou conceived this thing in thine heart? thou hast not lied unto men, but unto God.

ACT.5:5 And Ananias hearing these words fell down and gave up the ghost: and great fear came on all them that heard these things.

ACT.5:10 Then fell she down straightway at his feet and yielded up the ghost: and the young men came in, and found her dead, and, carrying her forth, buried her by her husband.

ACT.5:11 And great fear came upon all the church, and upon as many as heard these things.

C.17 Look at the following verse from the apocryphal Book of **II EZDRAS** written in 500 BCE by Ezra the prophet in Israel:

II EZDRAS 7.33 And the Most High shall be revealed upon the seat of Judgement, and compassion shall pass away and compassion shall pass away and patience shall be withdrawn.

II EZDRAS 7.34 But only judgement shall remain, truth shall stand, and faithfulness shall grow strong.

C.18 (See my book '**EZDRAS INSIGHTS'** for amazing information about the future Judgements of God:

See also the **APPENDIX** for more on this **TOPIC** of the **LAW**)

Chapter 34 SHECHEM

HISTORY OF SHECHEM:

Comment:1: Shechem was a very important city in Israel, near the Mediterranean Coast. It was situated between two mountains and had its origins in the times before Abraham. It is located near the modern village of Balatah, north of the highway in the beautiful valley between **Mount Ebal** and **Mount Gerizim**. This was the first place which Abraham visited in Canaan (**Gen 12:6,7**), travelling from Haran in the North. Jacob and his family came to Shechem and erected an altar and dug a well (**Gen33:18-20**). Joseph's brothers pastured their flocks there, and Joseph was buried there. (**Joshua 24:32**) Joshua gathered the tribes of Israel there.

C.2 Rehoboam, the son of Solomon was crowned there. After Solomon's death, Israel became divided into two kingdoms. The Northern Kingdom consisting of 10 tribes was called **Israel**. The other two tribes to the south were called **Judah** which included the tribe of Benjamin. The united monarchy was divided there in Shechem in the year circa 975 BCE, and Jeroboam established his residence in Shechem as the capital for the 10 Northern Tribes of Israel, whilst Jerusalem to the south was the Capital of the Southern kingdom. (See how the kingdom came to be divided in **I Kings 12**)

C.3 In the New Testament Shechem was also famous for Jesus' visit there to the well where he talked with the Samaritan woman.

JOH.4:5 Then cometh he to a city of Samaria, which is called Sychar, near to the parcel of ground that Jacob gave to his son Joseph.

C.4 To know more about the history of **SHECHEM** visit the following website: [https://bible.org/article/geographical-historical-spiritual-significance-shechem]

C.5 What is interesting to note is that the Northern tribes went into captivity to the Assyrian empire to the north of Israel in around 722 BCE. These tribes seemed to disappear from history with the exception that some of the former captives in Assyria came to live in Samaria. These people were not wholly of Jewish blood but had mixed blood. Those in Jerusalem at the time of Jesus in 30 A.D. considered the Samaritans to be an 'unclean' race as they were not a pure-blood Jewish race but a mongrel race and therefore they treated them as inferiors.

C.6 What did happen to the Northern Tribes of Israel that were taken into captivity in 722 BCE? (See my book **EZDRAS INSIGHTS** for the whole story, which is a fascinating one.)

---

1 And in the sixth year of this week of this forty-fourth jubilee [2148 A.M. = **Anno Mundi' = years of the world**] Jacob sent his sons to pasture their sheep, and his servants with them to the pastures of Shechem.

---

2 And the seven kings of the Amorites assembled themselves together against them, to slay them, hiding themselves under the trees, and to take their cattle as a prey.

3 And Jacob and Levi and Judah and Joseph were in the house with Isaac their father; for his spirit was sorrowful, and they could not leave him: and Benjamin was the youngest, and for this reason remained with his father.

4 And there came the king[s] of Taphu and the king[s] of 'Aresa, and the king[s] of Seragan, and the king[s] of Selo, and the king[s] of Ga'as, and the king of Bethoron, and the king of Ma'anisakir, and all those who dwell in these mountains (and) who dwell in the woods in the land of Canaan.

5 And they announced this to Jacob saying: 'Behold, the kings of the Amorites have surrounded thy sons, and plundered their herds.'

6 And he arose from his house, he and his three sons and all the servants of his father, and his own servants, and he went against them with six thousand men, who carried swords.

7 And he slew them in the pastures of Shechem, and pursued those who fled, and he slew them with the edge of the sword, and he slew 'Aresa and Taphu and Saregan and Selo and 'Amani-sakir and Ga[ga]'as, and he recovered his herds.

8 And he prevailed over them, and imposed tribute on them that they should pay him tribute, five fruit products of their land, and he built Robel and Tamnatares.

9 And he returned in peace, and made peace with them, and they became his servants, until the day that he and his sons went down into Egypt.

10 And in the seventh year of this week [2149 A.M. = **Anno Mundi' = years of the world**] he sent Joseph to learn about the welfare of his brothers from his house to the land of Shechem, and he found them

in the land of Dothan.

11a And they dealt treacherously with him, and formed a plot against him to slay him.

GEN.37:18 And when they saw him afar off, even before he came near unto them, they conspired against him to slay him.

GEN.37:24 And they took him, and cast him into a pit: and the pit was empty, there was no water in it.

C.7 Jacob had sent his 17-year-old son, Joseph, from Hebron to check on his brothers as they kept the flocks in Shechem (**Gen 37:12-14**). After Joseph arrived, having undoubtedly travelled up the Ridge Route, he discovered his brothers had moved on to the lush area of Dothan; so, he went to find them (Gen 37: 15-17). His brothers, filled with hatred, sold Joseph to some Ishmaelite traders who, coming through the Dothan pass, were headed for Egypt along the *Via Maris*. God used this sad turn of events to eventually take the entire family of Israel to Egypt, protecting and multiplying them. Joseph's last memories of Israel, before his brothers sold him, was of Shechem and Dothan.

11b But changing their minds, they sold him to Ishmaelite merchants, and they brought him down into Egypt, and they sold him to Potiphar, the eunuch of Pharaoh, the chief of the cooks, priest of the city of 'Elew.

C.8 It says that Potiphar was a eunuch but that must be incorrect, because both the Bible and the book of Jasher states that Potiphar had a wife who tried to seduce Joseph.

12 And the sons of Jacob slaughtered a kid, and dipped the coat of Joseph in the blood, and sent (it) to Jacob their father on the tenth of the seventh month.

13 And he mourned all that night, for they had brought it to him in the evening, and he became feverish with mourning for his death, and he said: 'An evil beast hath devoured Joseph'; and all the members of his house [mourned with him that day, and they] were grieving and mourning with him all that day.

14 And his sons and his daughter rose up to comfort him, but he refused to be comforted for his son.

15 And on that day Bilhah heard that Joseph had perished, and she died mourning him, and she was living in Qafratef, and Dinah also, his daughter, died after Joseph had perished.

16 And there came these three mournings upon Israel in one month.

17And they buried Bilhah over against the tomb of Rachel, and Dinah also, his daughter, they buried there. And he mourned for Joseph one year, and did not cease, for he said, 'Let me go down to the grave mourning for my son'.

C.9 What a terrible month for Jacob that he seemingly lost two of his children and one of his wives in the same month. Why Dinah died being so young we just don't know? It could have been a result of the extreme shock from how she had been treated by Shechem, combined with what looked like the death of her brother Joseph and the added sorrow of the death of Bilhah who had been a handmaid of Rachel, who had also already died and now she also died. Perhaps the shock of all these events happening at the same time was too much of an extra shock to Dinah and therefore she died. In reading this story in the Bible and also in the book of Jasher, one wonders, if perhaps *Jacob got too upset* about the '*seeming death of Joseph,* not realizing that his continued extreme continued sorrow for a long time for his son Joseph & him '*refusing to be comforted' & did not cease, for he said, 'Let me go down to the grave mourning for my son'.* was a stubbornness against God's Spirit & was badly affecting his young daughter Dinah? So much so, that apparently, she died of sorrow according to this Book of Jubilees!

C.10 According to the '**Book of Jasher**' Dinah did not die at that time. See my book '**Jasher Insights'**.

18 For this reason it is ordained for the children of Israel that they should afflict themselves on the tenth of the seventh month on the day that the news which made him weep for Joseph came to Jacob his father- that they should make atonement for themselves thereon with a young goat on the tenth of the seventh month, once a year, for their sins; for they had grieved the affection of their father regarding Joseph his son.

19 And this day has been ordained that they should grieve thereon for their sins, and for all their transgressions and for all their errors, so that they might cleanse themselves on that day once a year.

20 And after Joseph perished, the sons of Jacob took unto themselves wives.

C.11 Wait a minute. How can this verse state *'And after Joseph perished'*? Joseph hadn't really perished, he was still alive down in Egypt, but his father Jacob thought that Joseph had been killed by a wild animal because that is the lie his sons told him about their younger brother Joseph.

---

21 The name of Reuben's wife is 'Ada; and the name of Simeon's wife is 'Adlba'a, a Canaanite; and the name of Levi's wife is Melka, of the daughters of Aram, of the seed of the sons of Terah; and the name of Judah's wife, Betasu'el, a Canaanite; and the name of Issachar's wife, Hezaqa: and the name of Zabulon's wife, Ni'iman; and the name of Dan's wife, 'Egla; and the name of Naphtali's wife, Rasu'u, of Mesopotamia; and the name of Gad's wife, Maka; and the name of Asher's wife, 'Ijona; and the name of Joseph's wife, Asenath, the Egyptian; and the name of Benjamin's wife, 'Ijasaka.

22 And Simeon repented, and took a second wife from Mesopotamia as his brothers.

Chapter 35

1 And in the first year of the first week of the forty-fifth jubilee [2157 A.M. = **Anno Mundi' = years of the world**] Rebecca called Jacob, her son, and commanded him regarding his father and regarding his brother, that he should honour them all the days of his life.

2 And Jacob said: 'I will do everything as thou hast commanded me; for this thing will be honour and greatness to me, and righteousness before the Lord, that I should honour them.

3 And thou too, mother, know from the time I was born until this day, all my deeds and all that is in my heart, that I always think good concerning all.

4 And how should I not do this thing which thou hast commanded me, that I should honour my father and my brother!

5 Tell me, mother, what perversity hast thou seen in me and I shall turn away from it, and mercy will be upon me.'

6 And she said unto him: 'My son, I have not seen in thee all my days any perverse but (only) upright deeds.

7 And yet I will tell thee the truth, my son: I shall die this year, and I shall not survive this year in my life; for I have seen in a dream the day of my death, that I should not live beyond a hundred and fifty-five years: and behold I have completed all the days of my life which I am to live.'

Comment:1: This is the only account that I know of where it mentions the exact age of Rebecca when she died that of 155 years old. This sounds about right as her husband Isaac is stated to have lived to be 180 in the Bible. We also find out that Abraham lived to be 175 but his wife Sarah only lived to be 127, so obviously Sarah died younger than what was normal at the time.

8 And Jacob laughed at the words of his mother, because his mother had said unto him that she should die; and she was sitting opposite to him in possession of her strength, and she was not infirm in her strength; for she went in and out and saw, and her teeth were strong,

and no ailment had touched her all the days of her life.

C.2 It also states here that Rebecca had never been sick and yet she perceived that she would in fact die that very same year when she was 155 years old. This is interesting, as it is the exact opposite of what medical science teaches.

C.3 Modern science states that if a person is very strong and very fit and robust that he will live to be very old - but with Rebecca this was clearly not the case.

C.4 I think modern science being ungodly likes to push the notion of 'Self-Accomplishment' 'Self- Improvement' and so-called 'man's invincibility' is leading people into the Transhumanism movement – to improve God's original creation and make men into super-men The idea that man can live forever without God or salvation through Christ.

C.5 This above verse shows that Rebecca was spiritually very perceptive. It is very unusual for God to reveal to a human being exactly when they shall die. At least not years in advance of them dying.

C.6 I did however see a video this very week, where a doctor in the USA had been observing 1400 patients over a 10-year period, many of whom died. What he observed was that 80% of those that were to die within 2 weeks, had very vivid dreams that reassured them 'not to be afraid of death'. The doctor could not explain why this happened. It sounds to me, as if God does encourage certain people just before they die, probably by having His angels minister to the dying patients in one way or the other. Well with Rebecca, God Himself was letting Rebecca know in advance that it was soon her time to go home to Heaven.

9 And Jacob said unto her: 'Blessed am I, mother, if my days approach the days of thy life, and my strength remain with me thus as thy strength: and thou wilt not die, for thou art jesting idly with me regarding thy death.'

10 And she went in to Isaac and said unto him: 'One petition I make unto thee: make Esau swear that he will not injure Jacob, nor pursue him with enmity; for thou know Esau's thoughts that they are perverse from his youth, and there is no goodness in him; for he desires after thy death to kill him.

11 And thou know all that he has done since the day Jacob his brother went to Haran until this day: how he has forsaken us with his whole heart, and has done evil to us; thy flocks he has taken to himself, and carried off all thy possessions from before thy face.

12 And when we implored and besought him for what was our own, he did as a man who was taking pity on us.

13 And he is bitter against thee because thou didst bless Jacob thy perfect and upright son; for there is no evil but only goodness in him, and since he came from Haran unto this day he has not robbed us of aught, for he brings us everything in its season always, and rejoices with all his heart when we take at his hands and he blesses us, and has not parted from us since he came from Haran until this day, and he remains with us continually at home honouring us.'

14 And Isaac said unto her: 'I, too, know and see the deeds of Jacob who is with us, how that with all his heart he honours us; but I loved Esau formerly more than Jacob, because he was the firstborn; but now I love Jacob more than Esau, for he has done manifold evil deeds, and there is no righteousness in him, for all his ways are unrighteousness and violence, [and there is no righteousness around him.]

15 And now my heart is troubled because of all his deeds, and neither he nor his seed is to be saved, for they are those who will be destroyed from the earth and who will be rooted out from under heaven, for he has forsaken the God of Abraham and gone after his wives and after their uncleanness and after their error, he and his children.

16 And thou dost bid me make him swear that he will not slay Jacob his brother; even if he swear he will not abide by his oath, and he will not do good but evil only.

17 But if he desires to slay Jacob, his brother, into Jacob's hands will he be given, and he will not escape from his hands, [for he will descend into his hands.]

18 And fear thou not on account of Jacob; for the guardian of Jacob is great and powerful and honoured, and praised more than the guardian of Esau.'

19 And Rebecca sent and called Esau and he came to her, and she said unto him: 'I have a petition, my son, to make unto thee, and do thou

promise to do it, my son.'

20 And he said: 'I will do everything that thou says unto me, and I will not refuse thy petition.'

21 And she said unto him: 'I ask you that the day I die, thou wilt take me in and bury me near Sarah, thy father's mother, and that thou and Jacob will love each other and that neither will desire evil against the other, but mutual love only, and (so) ye will prosper, my sons, and be honoured in the midst of the land, and no enemy will rejoice over you, and ye will be a blessing and a mercy in the eyes of all those that love you.'

22 And he said: 'I will do all that thou hast told me, and I shall bury thee on the day thou die near Sarah, my father's mother, as thou hast desired that her bones may be near thy bones.

23 And Jacob, my brother, also, I shall love above all flesh; for I have not a brother in all the earth but him only: and this is no great merit for me if I love him; for he is my brother, and we were sown together in thy body, and together came we forth from thy womb, and if I do not love my brother, whom shall I love

24 And I, myself, beg thee to exhort Jacob concerning me and concerning my sons, for I know that he will assuredly be king over me and my sons, for on the day my father blessed him he made him the higher and me the lower.

25 And I swear unto thee that I shall love him, and not desire evil against him all the days of my life but good only.'

26 And he swore unto her regarding all this matter.

27 And she called Jacob before the eyes of Esau and gave him commandment according to the words which she had spoken to Esau.

28 And he said: 'I shall do thy pleasure; believe me that no evil will proceed from me or from my sons against Esau, and I shall be first in

naught save in love only.'

29 And they eat and drank, she and her sons that night, and she died, three jubilees and one week and one year old, on that night, and her two sons, Esau and Jacob, buried her in the double cave near Sarah, their father's mother.

Chapter 36

1 And in the sixth year of this week [2162 A.M. = **Anno Mundi' = years of the world**] Isaac called his two sons Esau and Jacob, and they came to him, and he said unto them: 'My sons, I am going the way of my fathers, to the eternal house where my fathers are.

GEN.35:27 And Jacob came unto Isaac his father unto Mamre, unto the city of Arbah, which is Hebron, where Abraham and Isaac sojourned.

2 Wherefore bury me near Abraham my father, in the double cave in the field of Ephron the Hittite, where Abraham purchased a sepulchre to bury in; in the sepulchre which I digged for myself, there bury me.

Comment:1: 'Double Cave'. There is a lot of talk about this very special burial place of Machpelah. Many say that this cave had a cave within a cave and that it descended into the heart of the earth. By the tradition of the Jewish **Zohar** a mystic book - on the other end of the tunnel was the Inner Earth and the Garden of Eden located.

C.2 As I mentioned in my book 'Enoch Insights', Enoch talked a lot about Portals. Portals in the sky and Portals leading down in the earth. After studying this topic at length, it is indeed true that there exist all kinds of Portals to other places and dimensions. Apparently, they are hidden most of the time but that under special circumstances these Portals or doorways to other places and dimensions open. (See: **The Cloud Eaters by Tom Horn & Steve Quayle**)

C.3 **Was the burial ground or 'Double Cave' where Abraham was buried the entrance to a Portal leading down into the Inner Earth?** According to different peoples on the planet the knowledge of the Portals used to be 'common knowledge' at one time but in more modern times we have forgotten about the existence of these Portals, which are being seen with increasing frequency in the past 10 years.

C.4 Apparently, there exist Portals between the earth and other planets, and even far away galaxies and their planets and There are also spiritual Portals to lower and higher dimensions. If it is true, then who built the physical Portals and why?

C.5 Why have most of us known nothing about Portals until very recently. Has someone been deliberately hiding this information from the general public?

3 And this I command you, my sons, that ye practise righteousness and uprightness on the earth, so that the Lord may bring upon you all that the Lord said that he would do to Abraham and to his seed.

4 And love one another, my sons, your brothers as a man who loves his own soul and let each seek in what he may benefit his brother, and act together on the earth; and let them love each other as their own souls.

5 And concerning the question of idols, I command and admonish you to reject them and hate them, and love them not, for they are full of deception for those that worship them and for those that bow down to them.

6 Remember ye, my sons, the Lord God of Abraham your father, and how I too worshipped Him and served Him in righteousness and in joy, that He might multiply you and increase your seed as the stars of heaven in multitude, and establish you on the earth as the plant of righteousness which will not be rooted out unto all the generations for ever.

7 And now I shall make you swear a great oath -for there is no oath which is greater than it by the name glorious and honoured and great and splendid and wonderful and mighty, which created the heavens and the earth and all things together- that ye will fear Him and worship Him.

8 And that each will love his brother with affection and righteousness, and that neither will desire evil against his brother from henceforth for ever all the days of your life so that ye may prosper in all your deeds and not be destroyed.

9 And if either of you devises evil against his brother, know that from henceforth everyone that devises evil against his brother shall fall into his hand, and shall be rooted out of the land of the living, and his seed shall be destroyed from under heaven.

10 But on the day of turbulence and execration and indignation and anger, with flaming devouring fire as He burnt Sodom, so likewise will He burn his land and his city and all that is his, and he shall be blotted out of the book of the discipline of the children of men, and not be recorded in the book of life, but in that which is appointed to destruc-tion, and he shall depart into eternal execration; so that their condem-

> nation may be always renewed in hate and in execration and in wrath and in torment and in indignation and in plagues and in disease for ever.

C.6 This verse sounds like something out of the Book of Enoch mentioning *'eternal execration'*. The description in the Book of Enoch is talking about the judgment of the Fallen angels and those who follow their heinous ways. Execration simply means 'cursed'.

ENOCH 5.5 'Therefore shall ye execrate your days, and the years of your life shall perish, and the years of your destruction shall be multiplied in *eternal execration* and ye shall find no mercy.

> 11 I say and testify to you, my sons, according to the judgment which shall come upon the man who wishes to injure his brother.

C.7 According to Jesus in the New Testament

MAT.5:22 But I say unto you, That whosoever is angry with his brother without a cause shall be in danger of the judgment: and whosoever shall say to his brother, Raca, shall be in danger of the council: but whosoever shall say, Thou fool, shall be in danger of hell fire.

MAT.12:36 But I say unto you, That every idle word that men shall speak, they shall give account thereof in the day of judgment.

MAT.12:37 For by thy words thou shalt be justified, and by thy words thou shalt be condemned.

C.8 Hellfire will indeed be intense for those who have committed many heinous crimes and who do not believe in the Messiah Jesus Christ. Without the Blood of Jesus, there is no redemption for our sins. Every one of us will have to give account of not only our evil deeds, but even every word that we spoke, which was 'out of place' or a lie or without love and consideration for others.

> 12 And he divided all his possessions between the two on that day and he gave the larger portion to him that was the first-born, and the tower and all that was about it, and all that Abraham possessed at the Well of the Oath.
>
> 13And he said: 'This larger portion I will give to the firstborn.'
>
> 14 And Esau said, 'I have sold to Jacob and given my birth right to Jacob; to him let it be given, and I have not a single word to say regarding it, for it is his.'

15 And Isaac said, May a blessing rest upon you, my sons, and upon your seed this day, for ye have given me rest, and my heart is not pained concerning the birth right, lest thou shouldest work wickedness on account of it.

16 May the Most High God bless the man that worketh righteousness, him and his seed for ever.'

17 And he ended commanding them and blessing them, and they eat and drank together before him, and he rejoiced because there was one mind between them, and they went forth from him and rested that day and slept.

18 And Isaac slept on his bed that day rejoicing; and he slept the eternal sleep and died one hundred and eighty years old. He completed twenty-five weeks and five years; and his two sons Esau and Jacob buried him.

GEN.35:28 And the days of Isaac were an hundred and fourscore years.

GEN.35:29 And Isaac gave up the ghost, and died, and was gathered unto his people, being old and full of days: and his sons Esau and Jacob buried him.

C.9 Isaac live to be 180 years old. Wow! No one on the planet lives to be that old anymore. I think the oldest I've ever heard about was around 110 years old. Some of the peoples who live in the mountains of Tibet, where the air is much fresher, and their diet is free of chemicals live to be exceptionally old.

19 And Esau went to the land of Edom, to the mountains of Seir, and dwelt there.

GEN.36:8 Thus dwelt Esau in mount Seir: Esau is Edom.

GEN.36:9 And these are the generations of Esau the father of the Edomites in mount Seir:

20 And Jacob dwelt in the mountains of Hebron, in the tower of the land of the sojournings of his father Abraham, and he worshipped the Lord with all his heart and according to the visible1 commands according as He had divided the days of his generations.

21 And Leah his wife died in the fourth year of the second week of the

forty-fifth jubilee, [2167 A.M.] and he buried her in the double cave near Rebecca his mother to the left of the grave of Sarah, his father's mother.

22 And all her sons and his sons came to mourn over Leah his wife with him and to comfort him regarding her, for he was lamenting her for he loved her exceedingly after Rachel her sister died; for she was perfect and upright in all her ways and honoured Jacob, and all the days that she lived with him he did not hear from her mouth a harsh word, for she was gentle and peaceable and upright and honourable.

23 And he remembered all her deeds which she had done during her life and he lamented her exceedingly; for he loved her with all his heart and with all his soul.

C.10 Why did both Rachel and her sister Leah die young? Well, only God Himself knows the answer to that question. It was also the case that Jacob's third wife or Rachel's handmaiden had also died after hearing the so-called news of Joseph's fabricated 'death'. So, Jacob ended up with only one wife and that was the handmaiden of Leah.

Chapter 37

1 And on the day that Isaac the father of Jacob and Esau died, [2162 A.M. = '**Anno Mundi**' = **years of the world**] the sons of Esau heard that Isaac had given the portion of the elder to his younger son Jacob and they were very angry.

Comment:1: There is a discrepancy of 66 years here between the K J Bible and this Book of Jubilees. The Bible states on the Time chart in front of me that Isaac died in the [year 2228 A.M] Why this discrepancy of 66 years? Now that is a good question.

2 And they strove with their father, saying 'Why has thy father given Jacob the portion of the elder and passed over thee, although thou art the elder and Jacob the younger'

3 And he said unto them 'Because I sold my birthright to Jacob for a small mess of lentils, and on the day my father sent me to hunt and catch and bring him something that he should eat and bless me, he came with guile and brought my father food and drink, and my father blessed him and put me under his hand.

4 And now our father has caused us to swear, me and him, that we shall not mutually devise evil, either against his brother, and that we shall continue in love and in peace each with his brother and not make our ways corrupt.'

5 And they said unto him, 'We shall not hearken unto thee to make peace with him; for our strength is greater than his strength, and we are more powerful than he; we shall go against him and slay him and destroy him and his sons.

6 And if thou wilt not go with us, we shall do hurt to thee also; and now hearken unto us: Let us send to Aram and Philistia and Moab and Ammon, and let us choose for ourselves chosen men who are ardent for battle, and let us go against him and do battle with him, and let us exterminate him from the earth before he grows strong.'

7 And their father said unto them, 'Do not go and do not make war

with him lest ye fall before him.'

8 And they said unto him, 'This too, is exactly thy mode of action from thy youth until this day, and thou art putting thy neck under his yoke. We shall not hearken to these words.'

9 And they sent to Aram, and to 'Aduram to the friend of their father, and they hired along with them one thousand fighting men, chosen men of war.

10 And there came to them from Moab and from the children of Ammon, those who were hired, one thousand chosen men, and from Philistia, one thousand chosen men of war, and from Edom and from the Horites one thousand chosen fighting men, and from the Kittim mighty men of war.

11 And they said unto their father: Go forth with them and lead them, else we shall slay thee.'

12 And he was filled with wrath and indignation on seeing that his sons were forcing him to go before (them) to lead them against Jacob his brother.

13 But afterward he remembered all the evil which lay hidden in his heart against Jacob his brother; and he remembered not the oath which he had sworn to his father and to his mother that he would devise no evil all his days against Jacob his brother.

C.2 It is so important in life not to hold grudges against other people, no matter what they have done to us. Of course, Esau lived in a time when it was an 'eye for and eye' and a 'tooth for a tooth'. He lived even long before that, as the Laws of Moses had not yet been written and wouldn't be written for centuries. In the New Testament it is written:

MAT.5:43 Ye have heard that it hath been said, Thou shalt love thy neighbour, and hate thine enemy.

MAT.5:44 But I say unto you, 'Love your enemies, bless them that curse you, do good to them that hate you, and pray for them which despitefully use you, and persecute you'.

14 And notwithstanding all this, Jacob knew not that they were coming

against him to battle, and he was mourning for Leah, his wife, until they approached very near to the tower with four thousand warriors and chosen men of war.

C.3 A troublesome time for Jacob, as he has just lost Leah his 2nd wife and is now left by himself and his sons. He has his fierce twin brother Esau coming to fight against him with thousands of warriors. He was in a pretty tough pickle, that's for sure.

15 And the men of Hebron sent to him saying, 'Behold thy brother has come against thee, to fight thee, with four thousand girt with the sword, and they carry shields and weapons'; for they loved Jacob more than Esau.

16 So they told him; for Jacob was a more liberal and merciful man than Esau. But Jacob would not believe until they came very near to the tower.

17 And he closed the gates of the tower; and he stood on the battlements and spoke to his brother Esau and said, 'Noble is the comfort wherewith thou hast come to comfort me for my wife who has died.

18 Is this the oath that thou didst swear to thy father and again to thy mother before they died Thou hast broken the oath, and on the moment that thou didst swear to thy father was thou condemned.'

19 And then Esau answered and said unto him, 'Neither the children of men nor the beasts of the earth have any oath of righteousness which in swearing they have sworn (an oath valid) for ever; but every day they devise evil one against another, and how each may slay his adversary and foe. And thou dost hate me and my children for ever.

20 And there is no observing the tie of brotherhood with thee. Hear these words which I declare unto thee,

If the boar can change its skin and make its bristles as soft as wool, Or if it can cause horns to sprout forth on its head like the horns of a stag or of a sheep, Then will I observe the tie of brotherhood with thee And if the breasts separated themselves from their mother, for thou hast not been a brother to me.

21 And if the wolves make peace with the lambs so as not to devour or do them violence, And if their hearts are towards them for good, Then there shall be peace in my heart towards thee

22 And if the lion becomes the friend of the ox and makes peace with him And if he is bound under one yoke with him and ploughs with him, Then will I make peace with thee.

23 And when the raven becomes white as the raza, Then know that I have loved thee And shall make peace with thee Thou shalt be rooted out, And thy sons shall be rooted out, And there shall be no peace for thee'

24 And when Jacob saw that he was (so) evilly disposed towards him with his heart, and with all his soul as to slay him, and that he had come springing like the wild boar which comes upon the spear that pierces and kills it, and recoils not from it; then he spoke to his own and to his servants that they should attack him and all his companions.

Chapter 38 ESAU IS SLAIN BY HIS TWIN BROTHER JACOB

1 And after that Judah spoke to Jacob, his father, and said unto him: 'Bend thy bow, father, and send forth thy arrows and cast down the adversary and slay the enemy; and mayst thou have the power, for we shall not slay thy brother, for he is such as thou, and he is like thee let us give him (this) honour.'

Comment:1: This clearly shows the foolishness of being over-confident. Esau and his men and even the thousands of extra hired soldiers were no match for the sons of Jacob. Simeon and Levi had slaughtered the entire Canaanite town of Shechem. Esau and his sons just failed to get the plot of the story! God has given his blessing to Jacob and not to Esau because Esau was an ungodly and wild violent man. Jacob didn't want to have to fight against his brother, but at the same time he was more than capable of doing so and was himself an expert archer. Jacob's sons slew their enemies as one who slashes through gourds.

2 Then Jacob bent his bow and sent forth the arrow and struck Esau, his brother (on his right breast) and slew him.

3 And again he sent forth an arrow and struck 'Adoran the Aramaean, on the left breast, and drove him backward and slew him

4 And then went forth the sons of Jacob, they and their servants, dividing themselves into companies on the four sides of the tower.

C.2 There are similar descriptions of Jacob and his sons fighting against their enemies in the book of Jasher. See my book 'Jasher Insights'. The Book of Jasher gives a lot more details about the fighting abilities of Jacob and his sons wiping out the Canaanite cities, just as God had promised to Abraham that the Canaanites would be driven out of the lands which should have belonged to the Semites, but had originally been usurped by Canaan against the direst command of Noah his grandfather.

5 And Judah went forth in front, and Naphtali and Gad with him and fifty servants with him on the south side of the tower, and they slew all they found before them, and not one individual of them escaped.

6 And Levi and Dan and Asher went forth on the east side of the tower,

and fifty (men) with them, and they slew the fighting men of Moab and Ammon.

7 And Reuben and Issachar and Zebulon went forth on the north side of the tower, and fifty men with them, and they slew the fighting men of the Philistines.

8 And Simeon and Benjamin and Enoch, Reuben's son, went forth on the west side of the tower, and fifty (men) with them, and they slew of Edom and of the Horites four hundred men, stout warriors; and six hundred fled, and four of the sons of Esau fled with them, and left their father lying slain, as he had fallen on the hill which is in 'Aduram.

9 And the sons of Jacob pursued after them to the mountains of Seir.

10 And Jacob buried his brother on the hill which is in 'Aduram, and he returned to his house.

11 And the sons of Jacob pressed hard upon the sons of Esau in the mountains of Seir and bowed their necks so that they became servants of the sons of Jacob.

12 And they sent to their father (to inquire) whether they should make peace with them or slay them.

13 And Jacob sent word to his sons that they should make peace, and they made peace with them, and placed the yoke of servitude upon them, so that they paid tribute to Jacob and to his sons always.

14 And they continued to pay tribute to Jacob until the day that he went down into Egypt.

15 And the sons of Edom have not got quit of the yoke of servitude which the twelve sons of Jacob had imposed on them until this day.

16 And these are the kings that reigned in Edom before there reigned any king over the children of Israel [until this day] in the land of Edom.

17 And Balaq, the son of Beor, reigned in Edom, and the name of his city was Danaba.

18 And Balaq died, and Jobab, the son of Zara of 18 Boser, reigned in his stead.

19 And Jobab died, and 'Asam, of the land of Teman, reigned in his stead.

20 And 'Asam died, and 'Adath, the son of Barad, who slew Midian in the field of Moab, reigned in his stead, and the name of his city was Avith.

21 And 'Adath died, and Salman, from 'Amaseqa, reigned in his stead.

22 And Salman died, and Saul of Ra'aboth (by the) river, reigned in his stead. And Saul died, and Ba'elunan, the son of Achbor, reigned in his stead.

23 And Ba'elunan, the son of Achbor died, and 'Adath reigned in his stead, and the name of his wife was Maitabith, the daughter of Matarat, the daughter of Metabedza'ab.

24 These are the kings who reigned in the land of Edom.

Chapter 39 JOSEPH SOLD TO POTIPHAR IN EGYPT

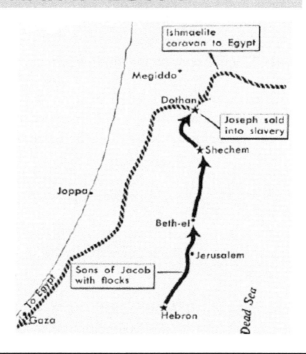

1 And Jacob dwelt in the land of his fathers sojournings in the land of Canaan. These are the generations of Jacob

2 And Joseph was seventeen years old when they took him down into the land of Egypt, and Potiphar, a eunuch of Pharaoh, the chief cook bought him.

3 And he set Joseph over all his house and the blessing of the Lord came upon the house of the Egyptian on account of Joseph, and the Lord prospered him in all that he did.

4 And the Egyptian committed everything into the hands of Joseph; for he saw that the Lord was with him, and that the Lord prospered him in all that he did.

5 And Joseph's appearance was comely [and very beautiful was his

appearance], and his master's wife lifted up her eyes and saw Joseph, and she loved him and besought him to lie with her.

C.1 How could a eunuch of Pharaoh called Potiphar have a wife? Maybe that is why his wife was after Joseph as her husband was not capable of being with her as he was a eunuch. Perhaps getting married was some sort of status symbol back there in the courts of Pharaoh. Obviously, Potiphar's wife couldn't keep her hands of Joseph or at least from strongly desiring him and trying to entice him. It is interesting to note that later in time, when the Laws of Moses came into effect in Israel, that men who were sexually defective by being a eunuch or having their privy parts cut off (from war etc) were not allowed to continue to be in the congregation of the Israelites. No more frustration for the women.

6 But he did not surrender his soul, and he remembered the Lord and the words which Jacob, his father, used to read from amongst the words of Abraham, that no man should commit fornication with a woman who has a husband; that for him the punishment of death has been ordained in the heavens before the Most High God, and the sin will be recorded against him in the eternal books continually before the Lord.

GEN.39:8 But he refused, and said unto his master's wife, Behold, my master wotteth not what is with me in the house, and he hath committed all that he hath to my hand;

GEN.39:9 There is none greater in this house than I; neither hath he kept back anything from me but thee, because thou art his wife: how then can I do this great wickedness, and sin against God?

C.2 Although this beautiful woman tried repeated to entice Joseph he did not give in to her sexy wiles. Why? Because this would have been against the laws laid down by Abraham his great-grandfather. The punishment of which could have been death back home. Also, even if Joseph had given in to her temptations, she would have used him for a while and then discarded him and he would been executed as soon as Potiphar had found out.

7 And Joseph remembered these words and refused to lie with her.

8 And she besought him for a year, but he refused and would not listen.

GEN.39:7 And it came to pass after these things, that his master's wife cast her eyes upon Joseph; and she said, Lie with me.

GEN.39:10 And it came to pass, as she spake to Joseph day by day, that he hearkened not unto her, to lie by her, or to be with her.

9 But she embraced him and held him fast in the house in order to force him to lie with her and closed the doors of the house and held him fast; but he left his garment in her hands and broke through the door and fled without from her presence.

GEN.39:11 And it came to pass about this time, that Joseph went into the house to do his business; and there was none of the men of the house there within.

GEN.39:12 And she caught him by his garment, saying, Lie with me: and he left his garment in her hand, and fled, and got him out.

GEN.39:13 And it came to pass, when she saw that he had left his garment in her hand, and was fled forth,

10 And the woman saw that he would not lie with her, and she calumniated him in the presence of his lord, saying 'Thy Hebrew servant, whom thou love, sought to force me so that he might lie with me; and it came to pass when I lifted up my voice that he fled and left his garment in my hands when I held him, and he brake through the door.'

GEN.39:14 That she called unto the men of her house, and spake unto them, saying, See, he hath brought in an Hebrew unto us to mock us; he came in unto me to lie with me, and I cried with a loud voice:

GEN.39:15 And it came to pass, when he heard that I lifted up my voice and cried, that he left his garment with me, and fled, and got him out.

GEN.39:16 And she laid up his garment by her, until his lord came home.

GEN.39:18 And it came to pass, as I lifted up my voice and cried, that he left his garment with me, and fled out.

GEN.39:19 And it came to pass, when his master heard the words of his wife, which she spake unto him, saying, After this manner did thy servant to me; that his wrath was kindled.

11 And the Egyptian saw the garment of Joseph and the broken door, and heard the words of his wife, and cast Joseph into prison into the place where the prisoners were kept whom the king imprisoned.

GEN.39:20 And Joseph's master took him, and put him into the prison, a place where the king's prisoners were bound: and he was there in the prison.

12 And he was there in the prison; and the Lord gave Joseph favour in the sight of the chief of the prison guards and compassion before him,

> for he saw that the Lord was with him, and that the Lord made all that he did to prosper.
>
> 13 And he committed all things into his hands, and the chief of the prison guards knew of nothing that was with him, for Joseph did everything, and the Lord perfected it.

GEN.39:21 But the LORD was with Joseph, and shewed him mercy, and gave him favour in the sight of the keeper of the prison.

GEN.39:22 And the keeper of the prison committed to Joseph's hand all the prisoners that were in the prison; and whatsoever they did there, he was the doer of it.

GEN.39:23 The keeper of the prison looked not to anything that was under his hand; because the LORD was with him, and that which he did, the LORD made it to prosper.

> 14 And he remained there two years. And in those days Pharaoh, king of Egypt was wroth against his two eunuchs, against the chief butler, and against the chief baker, and he put them in ward in the house of the chief cook, in the prison where Joseph was kept.
>
> 15 And the chief of the prison guards appointed Joseph to serve them; and he served before them.
>
> 16 And they both dreamed a dream, the chief butler and the chief baker, and they told it to Joseph.
>
> 17 And as he interpreted to them, so it befell them, and Pharaoh restored the chief butler to his office and the(chief) baker he slew, as Joseph had interpreted to them.

GEN.40:1 And it came to pass after these things, that the butler of the king of Egypt and his baker had offended their lord the king of Egypt.

GEN.40:2 And Pharaoh was wroth against two of his officers, against the chief of the butlers, and against the chief of the bakers.

GEN.40:3 And he put them in ward in the house of the captain of the guard, into the prison, the place where Joseph was bound.

GEN.40:4 And the captain of the guard charged Joseph with them, and he served them: and they continued a season in ward.

GEN.40:5 And they dreamed a dream both of them, each man his dream in one night, each man according to the interpretation of his dream, the butler and the baker of the king of Egypt, which were bound in the prison.

GEN.40:6 And Joseph came in unto them in the morning, and looked upon them, and, behold, they were sad.

GEN.40:7 And he asked Pharaoh's officers that were with him in the ward of his lord's house, saying, Wherefore look ye so sadly today?

GEN.40:8 And they said unto him, We have dreamed a dream, and there is no interpreter of it. And Joseph said unto them, Do not interpretations belong to God? tell me them, I pray you.

GEN.40:9 And the chief butler told his dream to Joseph, and said to him, In my dream, behold, a vine was before me;

GEN.40:10 And in the vine were three branches: and it was as though it budded, and her blossoms shot forth; and the clusters thereof brought forth ripe grapes:

GEN.40:11 And Pharaoh's cup was in my hand: and I took the grapes, and pressed them into Pharaoh's cup, and I gave the cup into Pharaoh's hand.

GEN.40:12 And Joseph said unto him, This is the interpretation of it: The three branches are three days:

GEN.40:13 Yet within three days shall Pharaoh lift up thine head and restore thee unto thy place: and thou shalt deliver Pharaoh's cup into his hand, after the former manner when thou wast his butler.

GEN.40:14 But think on me when it shall be well with thee, and shew kindness, I pray thee, unto me, and make mention of me unto Pharaoh, and bring me out of this house:

GEN.40:15 For indeed I was stolen away out of the land of the Hebrews: and here also have I done nothing that they should put me into the dungeon.

GEN.40:16 When the chief baker saw that the interpretation was good, he said unto Joseph, I also was in my dream, and, behold, I had three white baskets on my head:

GEN.40:17 And in the uppermost basket there was of all manner of bakemeats for Pharaoh; and the birds did eat them out of the basket upon my head.

GEN.40:18 And Joseph answered and said, This is the interpretation thereof: The three baskets are three days:

GEN.40:19 Yet within three days shall Pharaoh lift up thy head from off thee and shall hang thee on a tree; and the birds shall eat thy flesh from off thee.

GEN.40:20 And it came to pass the third day, which was Pharaoh's birthday, that he made a feast unto all his servants: and he lifted up the head of the chief butler and of the chief baker among his servants.

GEN.40:21 And he restored the chief butler unto his butlership again; and he gave the cup into Pharaoh's hand:

GEN.40:22 But he hanged the chief baker: as Joseph had interpreted to them.

GEN.40:23 Yet did not the chief butler remember Joseph, but forgat him.

18 But the chief butler forgot Joseph in the prison, although he had informed him what would befall him, and did not remember to inform Pharaoh how Joseph had told him, for he forgot.

Chapter 40

1 And in those days, Pharaoh dreamed two dreams in one night concerning a famine which was to be in all the land, and he awoke from his sleep and called all the interpreters of dreams that were in Egypt, and magicians, and told them his two dreams, and they were not able to declare (them).

GEN.41:1 And it came to pass at the end of two full years, that Pharaoh dreamed: and, behold, he stood by the river.

GEN.41:2 And, behold, there came up out of the river seven well favoured kine and fatfleshed; and they fed in a meadow.

GEN.41:3 And, behold, seven other kine came up after them out of the river, ill-favoured and leanfleshed; and stood by the other kine upon the brink of the river.

GEN.41:4 And the ill-favoured and leanfleshed kine did eat up the seven well favoured and fat kine. So Pharaoh awoke.

GEN.41:5 And he slept and dreamed the second time: and, behold, seven ears of corn came up upon one stalk, rank and good.

GEN.41:6 And, behold, seven thin ears and blasted with the east wind sprung up after them.

GEN.41:7 And the seven thin ears devoured the seven rank and full ears. And Pharaoh awoke, and, behold, it was a dream.

GEN.41:8 And it came to pass in the morning that his spirit was troubled; and he sent and called for all the magicians of Egypt, and all the wise men thereof: and Pharaoh told them his dream; but there was none that could interpret them unto Pharaoh

2 And then the chief butler remembered Joseph and spoke of him to the king, and he brought him forth from the prison, and he told his two dreams before him.

GEN.41:15 And Pharaoh said unto Joseph, I have dreamed a dream, and there is none that can interpret it: and I have heard say of thee, that thou canst understand a dream to interpret it.

GEN.41:16 And Joseph answered Pharaoh, saying, It is not in me: God shall give Pharaoh an answer of peace.

GEN.41:17 And Pharaoh said unto Joseph, In my dream, behold, I stood upon the bank of the river:

GEN.41:18 And, behold, there came up out of the river seven kine, fatfleshed and well favoured; and they fed in a meadow:

GEN.41:19 And, behold, seven other kine came up after them, poor and very ill favoured and leanfleshed, such as I never saw in all the land of Egypt for badness:

GEN.41:20 And the lean and the ill-favoured kine did eat up the first seven fat kine:

GEN.41:21 And when they had eaten them up, it could not be known that they had eaten them; but they were still ill favoured, as at the beginning. So I awoke.

GEN.41:22 And I saw in my dream, and, behold, seven ears came up in one stalk, full and good:

GEN.41:23 And, behold, seven ears, withered, thin, and blasted with the east wind, sprung up after them:

GEN.41:24 And the thin ears devoured the seven good ears: and I told this unto the magicians; but there was none that could declare it to me.

---

3 And he said before Pharaoh that his two dreams were one, and he said unto him: 'Seven years shall come (in which there shall be) plenty over all the land of Egypt, and after that seven years of famine, such a famine as has not been in all the land.

GEN.41:25 And Joseph said unto Pharaoh, The dream of Pharaoh is one: God hath shewed Pharaoh what he is about to do.

GEN.41:26 The seven good kine are seven years; and the seven good ears are seven years: the dream is one.

GEN.41:27 And the seven thin and ill-favoured kine that came up after them are seven years; and the seven empty ears blasted with the east wind shall be seven years of famine.

GEN.41:28 This is the thing which I have spoken unto Pharaoh: What God is about to do he sheweth unto Pharaoh.

GEN.41:29 Behold, there come seven years of great plenty throughout all the land of Egypt:

GEN.41:30 And there shall arise after them seven years of famine; and all the plenty shall be forgotten in the land of Egypt; and the famine shall consume the land;

GEN.41:31 And the plenty shall not be known in the land by reason of that famine following; for it shall be very grievous.

GEN.41:32 And for that the dream was doubled unto Pharaoh twice; it is because the thing is established by God, and God will shortly bring it to pass.

> 4 And now let Pharaoh appoint overseers in all the land of Egypt and let them store up food in every city throughout the days of the years of plenty, and there will be food for the seven years of famine, and the land will not perish through the famine, for it will be very severe.'

GEN.41:33 Now therefore let Pharaoh look out a man discreet and wise, and set him over the land of Egypt.

GEN.41:34 Let Pharaoh do this, and let him appoint officers over the land, and take up the fifth part of the land of Egypt in the seven plenteous years.

GEN.41:35 And let them gather all the food of those good years that come, and lay up corn under the hand of Pharaoh, and let them keep food in the cities.

GEN.41:36 And that food shall be for store to the land against the seven years of famine, which shall be in the land of Egypt; that the land perish not through the famine.

> 5 And the Lord gave Joseph favour and mercy in the eyes of Pharaoh, and Pharaoh said unto his servants. We shall not find such a wise and discreet man as this man, for the spirit of the Lord is with him.'

GEN.41:37 And the thing was good in the eyes of Pharaoh, and in the eyes of all his servants.

GEN.41:38 And Pharaoh said unto his servants, Can we find such a one as this is, a man in whom the Spirit of God is?

GEN.41:39 And Pharaoh said unto Joseph, Forasmuch as God hath shewed thee all this, there is none so discreet and wise as thou art:

> 6 And he appointed him the second in all his kingdom and gave him authority over all Egypt and caused him to ride in the second chariot of Pharaoh.
>
> 7And he clothed him with byssus garments, and he put a gold chain upon his neck, and (a herald) proclaimed before him ' 'El 'El was 'Abirer,' and placed a ring on his hand and made him ruler over all his house, and magnified him, and said unto him.

GEN.41:40 Thou shalt be over my house, and according unto thy word shall all my people be ruled: only in the throne will I be greater than thou.

> 8 'Only on the throne shall I be greater than thou.'

GEN.41:41 And Pharaoh said unto Joseph, See, I have set thee over all the land of Egypt.

GEN.41:42 And Pharaoh took off his ring from his hand, and put it upon Joseph's hand, and arrayed him in vestures of fine linen, and put a gold chain about his neck;

> 9 And Joseph ruled over all the land of Egypt, and all the princes of Pharaoh, and all his servants, and all who did the king's business loved him, for he walked in uprightness, for he was without pride and arrogance, and he had no respect of persons, and did not accept gifts, but he judged in uprightness all the people of the land.

GEN.41:43 And he made him to ride in the second chariot which he had; and they cried before him, Bow the knee: and he made him ruler over all the land of Egypt.

GEN.41:44 And Pharaoh said unto Joseph, I am Pharaoh, and without thee shall no man lift up his hand or foot in all the land of Egypt.

> 10 And the land of Egypt was at peace before Pharaoh because of Joseph, for the Lord was with him, and gave him favour and mercy for all his generations before all those who knew him and those who heard concerning him, and Pharaoh's kingdom was well ordered, and there was no Satan and no evil person (therein).
>
> 11 And the king called Joseph's name Sephantiphans, and gave Joseph to wife the daughter of Potiphar, the daughter of the priest of Heliopolis, the chief cook.

GEN.41:45 And Pharaoh called Joseph's name Zaphnathpaaneah; and he gave him to wife Asenath the daughter of Potipherah priest of On. And Joseph went out over all the land of Egypt.

Comment:1: Why the names are different remains a mystery. Did Pharaoh call Joseph Zaphnathpaaneah or Sephantiphans? Both these names are recognized as belonging to Joseph.

> 12 And on the day that Joseph stood before Pharaoh he was thirty years old [when he stood before Pharaoh]. And in that year Isaac died.

GEN.41:46 And Joseph was thirty years old when he stood before Pharaoh king of Egypt. And Joseph went out from the presence of Pharaoh and went throughout all the land of Egypt.

> 13 And it came to pass as Joseph had said in the interpretation of his

two dreams, according as he had said it, there were seven years of plenty over all the land of Egypt, and the land of Egypt abundantly produced, one measure (producing) eighteen hundred measures.

GEN.41:47 And in the seven plenteous years the earth brought forth by handfuls.

14 And Joseph gathered food into every city until they were full of corn until they could no longer count and measure it for its multitude.

GEN.41:48 And he gathered up all the food of the seven years, which were in the land of Egypt, and laid up the food in the cities: the food of the field, which was round about every city, laid he up in the same.

GEN.41:49 And Joseph gathered corn as the sand of the sea, very much, until he left numbering; for it was without number.

Chapter 41

1 And in the forty-fifth jubilee, in the second week, (and) in the second year, [2165 A.M. = **Anno Mundi' = years of the world**] Judah took for his first-born Er, a wife from the daughters of Aram, named Tamar.

GEN.38:6 And Judah took a wife for Er his firstborn, whose name was Tamar.

2 But he hated her, and did not lie with her, because her mother was of the daughters of Canaan, and he wished to take him a wife of the kinsfolk of his mother, but Judah, his father, would not permit him.

3 And this Er, the first-born of Judah, was wicked, and the Lord slew him.

GEN.38:7 And Er, Judah's firstborn, was wicked in the sight of the LORD; and the LORD slew him.

4 And Judah said unto Onan, his brother 'Go in unto thy brother's wife and perform the duty of a husband's brother unto her and raise up seed unto thy brother.'

5 And Onan knew that the seed would not be his, (but) his brother's only, and he went into the house of his brother's wife, and spilt the seed on the ground, and he was wicked in the eyes of the Lord, and He slew him.

6 And Judah said unto Tamar, his daughter-in-law: 'Remain in thy father's house as a widow till Shelah my son be grown up, and I shall give thee to him to wife.'

GEN.38:11 Then said Judah to Tamar his daughter in law, Remain a widow at thy father's house, till Shelah my son be grown: for he said, Lest peradventure he die also, as his brethren did. And Tamar went and dwelt in her father's house.

7 And he grew up; but Bedsu'el, the wife of Judah, did not permit her son Shelah to marry. And Bedsu'el, the wife of Judah, died [2168 A.M.] in the fifth year of this week.

GEN.38:12 And in process of time the daughter of Shuah Judah's wife died; and Judah was comforted, and went up unto his sheepshearers to Timnath, he and his friend Hirah the Adullamite.

> 8 And in the sixth year Judah went up to shear his sheep at Timnah. [2169 A.M.]
>
> 9 And they told Tamar: 'Behold thy father-in-law goes up to Timnah to shear his sheep.'

GEN.38:13 And it was told Tamar, saying, Behold thy father in law goeth up to Timnath to shear his sheep.

> 10 And she put off her widow's clothes, and put on a veil, and adorned herself, and sat in the gate adjoining the way to Timnah.

GEN.38:14 And she put her widow's garments off from her, and covered her with a vail, and wrapped herself, and sat in an open place, which is by the way to Timnath; for she saw that Shelah was grown, and she was not given unto him to wife.

> 11 And as Judah was going along, he found her, and thought her to be an harlot, and he said unto her: 'Let me come in unto thee'; and she said unto him Come in,' and he went in.

GEN.38:15 When Judah saw her, he thought her to be an harlot; because she had covered her face

GEN.38:16 And he turned unto her by the way, and said, Go to, I pray thee, let me come in unto thee; (for he knew not that she was his daughter in law.)

> 12 And she said unto him: 'Give me my hire'; and he said unto her: 'I have nothing in my hand save my ring that is on my finger, and my necklace, and my staff which is in my hand.'

GEN.38:16 And she said, What wilt thou give me, that thou mayest come in unto me?

> 13 And she said unto him 'Give them to me until thou dost send me my hire', and he said unto her: 'I will send unto thee a kid of the goats'; and he gave them to her, and she conceived by him.

GEN.38:17 And he said, I will send thee a kid from the flock. And she said, Wilt thou give me a pledge, till thou send it?

> 14 And Judah went unto his sheep, and she went to her father's house.

15 And Judah sent a kid of the goats by the hand of his shepherd, an Adullamite, and he found her not; and he asked the people of the place, saying: 'Where is the harlot who was here'

16 And they said unto him; 'There is no harlot here with us.'

17 And he returned and informed him and said unto him that he had not found her: 'I asked the people of the place, and they said unto me: "There is no harlot here." '

18 And he said: 'Let her keep (them) lest we become a cause of derision.'

19 And when she had completed three months, it was manifest that she was with child, and they told Judah, saying: 'Behold Tamar, thy daughter-in-law, is with child by whoredom.'

20 And Judah went to the house of her father and said unto her father and her brothers: 'Bring her forth, and let them burn her, for she hath wrought uncleanness in Israel.'

21 And it came to pass when they brought her forth to burn her that she sent to her father-in-law the ring and the necklace, and the staff, saying: 'Discern whose are these, for by him am I with child.'

22 And Judah acknowledged, and said: 'Tamar is more righteous than I am.

23 And therefore let them burn her not' And for that reason she was not given to Shelah, and he did not again approach her and after that she bare two sons, Perez [2170 A.M.] and Zerah, in the seventh year of this second week.

GEN.38:27 And it came to pass in the time of her travail, that, behold, twins were in her womb.

GEN.38:28 And it came to pass, when she travailed, that the one put out his hand: and the midwife took and bound upon his hand a scarlet thread, saying, This came out first.

GEN.38:29 And it came to pass, as he drew back his hand, that, behold, his brother came out: and she said, How hast thou broken forth? this breach be upon thee: therefore his name was called Pharez.

GEN.38:30 And afterward came out his brother, that had the scarlet thread upon his hand: and his name was called Zarah.

24 And thereupon the seven years of fruitfulness were accomplished, of which Joseph spoke to Pharaoh.

25 And Judah acknowledged that the deed which he had done was evil, for he had lain with his daughter-in-law, and he esteemed it hateful in his eyes, and he acknowledged that he had transgressed and gone astray, for he had uncovered the skirt of his son, and he began to lament and to supplicate before the Lord because of his transgression.

Comment:1: Why was it necessary for Judah to acknowledge that he had done wrong when it was Tamar that deceived him into lying with her? She conceived and Judah ended up marrying her. There was no sin in that. In those days it was required for a man to 'raise up seed to his brother' both of Judah's sons had died and obviously Tamar decided to choose Judah for her husband. What other choice did she have? Judah did end up marrying her.

26 And we told him in a dream that it had forgiven him because he supplicated earnestly, and lamented, and did not again commit it.

27 And he received forgiveness because he turned from his sin and from his ignorance, for he transgressed greatly before our God; and every one that acts thus, everyone who lives with his mother-in-law, let them burn him with fire that he may burn therein, for there is uncleanness and pollution upon them, with fire let them burn them.

C.2 According to the Book of Jasher, Judah ended up marrying Tamah, as his first two sons had died including Tamar's husband. These last two verses seem 'inflexibly religious' and not necessarily how God would think of the situation. God is not inflexible and unreasonable!

C.3 Judah was s no longer married, as his wife had just died and Tamar was not married anymore, so there was no reason why they could not marry.

C.4 The Problem is that Mastema or Satan loves to use the 'letter of the law' to imprison or even kill his victims. Religions often become inflexible and hard-hearted and led by the 'letter of the law' just like Satan himself.

C.5 Jesus frequently demonstrated as the Messiah that God would rather that we show mercy and forgiveness to others rather than to be guided by the

302

extremely harsh laws of Moses.

MAT.9:13 But go ye and learn what that meaneth, I will have mercy, and not sacrifice: for I am not come to call the righteous, but sinners to repentance.

C.6 Mosaic Laws: I do understand that the harshness of the law was meant as a deterrent in the time when Israel had just come out of Egypt where they had seen much wickedness and abominations of idol worship. The severity of the law was to try and deter Israel from going astray after the gods of the nation all around them. Certain crimes needed severe punishment lest Israel would do as their neighbouring nations around them.

C.7 However certain sins were classified as sins or even iniquities by religionists, which God had **never stated** and was just a religious tradition. Jesus said 'Ye by your traditions have made the Word of God of non-effect'.

C.8 Look how the Catholic church used the '**letter of the law**' during the **Inquisition** as an excuse for burning millions of people at the stake for nefarious reasons. Religions have generally lost their original meaning and have just become 'controlling mechanisms' for making money just like so many so-called charities.

C.9 Most modern religions **do not follow God** and **His commandments**. If they did, they wouldn't condone wars that slaughter innocent nations of poor peoples all over the earth.

Major protestant churches supported Adolf Hitler during W.W II.

MAR.7:13 Making the word of God of none effect through your tradition, which ye have delivered: and many such like things do ye.

---

28 And do thou command the children of Israel that there be no uncleanness amongst them, for everyone who lives with his daughter-in-law or with his mother-in-law hath wrought uncleanness; with fire let them burn the man who has lain with her, and likewise the woman, and He will turn away wrath and punishment from Israel.

29 And unto Judah we said that his two sons had not lain with her, and for this reason his seed was stablished for a second generation and would not be rooted out.

30 For in singleness of eye he had gone and sought for punishment, namely, according to the judgment of Abraham, which he had commanded his sons, Judah had sought to burn her with fire.

Chapter 42

1 And in the first year of the third week of the forty-fifth jubilee the famine began to come into the [2171 A.M. = **Anno Mundi' = years of the world**] land, and the rain refused to be given to the earth, for none whatever fell.

2 And the earth grew barren, but in the land of Egypt there was food, for Joseph had gathered the seed of the land in the seven years of plenty and had preserved it.

3 And the Egyptians came to Joseph that he might give them food, and he opened the storehouses where was the grain of the first year, and he sold it to the people of the land for gold.

4 And Jacob heard that there was food in Egypt, and he sent his ten sons that they should procure food for him in Egypt; but Benjamin he did not send and arrived among those that went (there).

5 And Joseph recognised them, but they did not recognise him, and he spoke unto them and questioned them, and he said unto them; 'Are ye not spies and have ye not come to explore the approaches of the land 'And he put them in ward.

GEN.42:1 Now when Jacob saw that there was corn in Egypt, Jacob said unto his sons, Why do ye look one upon another?

GEN.42:2 And he said, Behold, I have heard that there is corn in Egypt: get you down thither, and buy for us from thence; that we may live, and not die.

GEN.42:3 And Joseph's ten brethren went down to buy corn in Egypt.

GEN.42:4 But Benjamin, Joseph's brother, Jacob sent not with his brethren; for he said, Lest peradventure mischief befall him.

GEN.42:5 And the sons of Israel came to buy corn among those that came: for the famine was in the land of Canaan.

GEN.42:6 And Joseph was the governor over the land, and he it was that sold to all the people of the land: and Joseph's brethren came and bowed down themselves before him with their faces to the earth.

GEN.42:7 And Joseph saw his brethren, and he knew them, but made himself strange unto them, and spake roughly unto them; and he said unto them, Whence come ye? And they said, From the land of Canaan to buy food.

GEN.42:8 And Joseph knew his brethren, but they knew not him.

GEN.42:9 And Joseph remembered the dreams which he dreamed of them, and said unto them, Ye are spies; to see the nakedness of the land ye are come.

GEN.42:10 And they said unto him, Nay, my lord, but to buy food are thy servants come.

GEN.42:11 We are all one man's sons; we are true men, thy servants are no spies.

GEN.42:12 And he said unto them, Nay, but to see the nakedness of the land ye are come.

GEN.42:13 And they said, Thy servants are twelve brethren, the sons of one man in the land of Canaan; and, behold, the youngest is this day with our father, and one is not.

GEN.42:14 And Joseph said unto them, That is it that I spake unto you, saying, Ye are spies:

GEN.42:15 Hereby ye shall be proved: By the life of Pharaoh ye shall not go forth hence, except your youngest brother come hither.

GEN.42:16 Send one of you, and let him fetch your brother, and ye shall be kept in prison, that your words may be proved, whether there be any truth in you: or else by the life of Pharaoh surely ye are spies.

GEN.42:17 And he put them all together into ward three days.

---

6 And after that he set them free again, and detained Simeon alone and sent off his nine brothers.

7 And he filled their sacks with corn, and he put their gold in their sacks, and they did not know.

GEN.42:25 Then Joseph commanded to fill their sacks with corn, and to restore every man's money into his sack, and to give them provision for the way: and thus did he unto them.

GEN.42:26 And they laded their asses with the corn, and departed thence.

GEN.42:27 And as one of them opened his sack to give his ass provender in the inn, he espied his money; for, behold, it was in his sack's mouth.

GEN.42:28 And he said unto his brethren, My money is restored; and, lo, it is even in my sack: and their heart failed them, and they were afraid, saying one to another,

> 8 And he commanded them to bring their younger brother, for they had told him their father was living and their younger brother.

GEN.42:19 If ye be true men, let one of your brethren be bound in the house of your prison: go ye, carry corn for the famine of your houses:

GEN.42:20 But bring your youngest brother unto me; so shall your words be verified, and ye shall not die. And they did so.

> 9 And they went up from the land of Egypt and they came to the land of Canaan; and they told their father all that had befallen them, and how the lord of the country had spoken roughly to them and had seized Simeon till they should bring Benjamin.

GEN.42:29 And they came unto Jacob their father unto the land of Canaan, and told him all that befell unto them; saying,

GEN.42:30 The man, who is the lord of the land, spake roughly to us, and took us for spies of the country.

> 10 And Jacob said: 'Me have ye bereaved of my children! Joseph is not and Simeon also is not, and ye will take Benjamin away.
>
> 11 On me has your wickedness come.

Comment:1: Why did Jacob say: 'On me has your wickedness come'. It sounds as if Jacob knew that something was very wrong and that his sons were responsible for a wicked 'cover-up' but that he couldn't prove it. The sons of Jacob had bound themselves in a curse that if one of them told their father Jacob the truth concerning Joseph their brother then the rest of the brothers would kill that person. Therefore, none of them ever did tell Jacob the truth about his younger son Joseph having been sold into captivity in Egypt. He only found out many years later when his own sons told him that Joseph was the Pharaoh or Pharaoh's right-hand man.

> 12 'And he said: 'My son will not go down with you lest perchance he falls sick; for their mother gave birth to two sons, and one has perished, and this one also ye will take from me.

GEN.42:36 And Jacob their father said unto them, Me have ye bereaved of my children: Joseph is not, and Simeon is not, and ye will take Benjamin away: all these things are against me.

13 If perchance he took a fever on the road, ye would bring down my old age with sorrow unto death.'

GEN.42:38 And he said, My son shall not go down with you; for his brother is dead, and he is left alone: if mischief befall him by the way in the which ye go, then shall ye bring down my gray hairs with sorrow to the grave.

14 For he saw that their money had been returned to every man in his sack, and for this reason he feared to send him.

15 And the famine increased and became sore in the land of Canaan, and in all lands save in the land of Egypt, for many of the children of the Egyptians had stored up their seed for food from the time when they saw Joseph gathering seed together and putting it in storehouses and preserving it for the years of famine.

16 And the people of Egypt fed themselves thereon during the first year of their famine.

17 But when Israel saw that the famine was very sore in the land, and that there was no deliverance, he said unto his sons: 'Go again, and procure food for us that we die not.'

18 And they said: 'We shall not go; unless our youngest brother goes with us, we shall not go.'

19 And Israel saw that if he did not send him with them, they should all perish by reason of the famine.

20 And Reuben said: 'Give him into my hand, and if I do not bring him back to thee, slay my two sons instead of his soul.'

21 And he said unto him: 'He shall not go with thee.'

22 And Judah came near and said: 'Send him with me, and if I do not bring him back to thee, let me bear the blame before thee all the days of my life.'

23 And he sent him with them in the second year of this week on the

[2172 A.m.] first day of the month, and they came to the land of Egypt with all those who went, and (they had) presents in their hands, stacte and almonds and terebinth nuts and pure honey.

GEN.43:11 And their father Israel said unto them, If it must be so now, do this; take of the best fruits in the land in your vessels, and carry down the man a present, a little balm, and a little honey, spices, and myrrh, nuts, and almonds:

GEN.43:12 And take double money in your hand; and the money that was brought again in the mouth of your sacks, carry it again in your hand; peradventure it was an oversight:

GEN.43:13 Take also your brother, and arise, go again unto the man:

GEN.43:15 And the men took that present, and they took double money in their hand and Benjamin; and rose up, and went down to Egypt, and stood before Joseph.

24 And they went and stood before Joseph, and he saw Benjamin his brother, and he knew him, and said unto them: Is this your youngest brother'.

GEN.43:16 And when Joseph saw Benjamin with them, he said to the ruler of his house, Bring these men home, and slay, and make ready; for these men shall dine with me at noon.

25 And they said unto him: 'It is he.' And he said The Lord be gracious to thee, my son!'

GEN.43:17 And the man did as Joseph bade; and the man brought the men into Joseph's house.

GEN.43:18 And the men were afraid, because they were brought into Joseph's house; and they said, Because of the money that was returned in our sacks at the first time are we brought in; that he may seek occasion against us, and fall upon us, and take us for bondmen, and our asses.

GEN.43:19 And they came near to the steward of Joseph's house, and they communed with him at the door of the house,

GEN.43:20 And said, O sir, we came indeed down at the first time to buy food:

GEN.43:21 And it came to pass, when we came to the inn, that we opened our sacks, and, behold, every man's money was in the mouth of his sack, our money in full weight: and we have brought it again in our hand.

GEN.43:22 And other money have we brought down in our hands to buy food: we cannot tell who put our money in our sacks.

GEN.43:23 And he said, Peace be to you, fear not: your God, and the God of your father, hath given you treasure in your sacks: I had your money. And he brought Simeon out unto them.

---

26 And he sent him into his house and he brought forth Simeon unto them and he made a feast for them, and they presented to him the gift which they had brought in their hands.

27 And they eat before him and he gave them all a portion, but the portion of Benjamin was seven times larger than that of any of theirs.

28 And they eat and drank and arose and remained with their asses.

29 And Joseph devised a plan whereby he might learn their thoughts as to whether thoughts of peace prevailed amongst them, and he said to the steward who was over his house: 'Fill all their sacks with food, and return their money unto them into their vessels, and my cup, the silver cup out of which I drink, put it in the sack of the youngest, and send them away.'

GEN.44:1 And he commanded the steward of his house, saying, Fill the men's sacks with food, as much as they can carry, and put every man's money in his sack's mouth.

C.2 The story of Joseph and his brethren in Egypt is almost the same as in the Bible and other books. This story of Joseph is covered in detail in my book '**Jasher Insights**'. These following chapters are well worth reading however, as they do contain extra details which are not found in the Bible or in other books.

Chapter 43

1 And he did as Joseph had told him and filled all their sacks for them with food and put their money in their sacks and put the cup in Benjamin's sack.

GEN.44:2 And put my cup, the silver cup, in the sack's mouth of the youngest, and his corn money. And he did according to the word that Joseph had spoken.

GEN.44:3 As soon as the morning was light, the men were sent away, they and their asses.

2 And early in the morning they departed, and it came to pass that, when they had gone from thence, Joseph said unto the steward of his house: 'Pursue them, run and seize them, saying, "For good ye have requited me with evil; you have stolen from me the silver cup out of which my lord drinks."

GEN.44:4 And when they were gone out of the city, and not yet far off, Joseph said unto his steward, Up, follow after the men; and when thou dost overtake them, say unto them, Wherefore have ye rewarded evil for good?

GEN.44:5 Is not this it in which my lord drinketh, and whereby indeed he divineth? ye have done evil in so doing.

3 And bring back to me their youngest brother, and fetch (him) quickly before I go forth to my seat of judgment.'

4 And he ran after them and said unto them according to these words.

GEN.44:6 And he overtook them, and he spake unto them these same words.

5 And they said unto him: 'God forbid that thy servants should do this thing and steal from the house of thy lord any utensil, and the money also which we found in our sacks the first time, we thy servants brought back from the land of Canaan.

6 How then should we steal any utensil Behold here are we and our sacks search, and wherever thou find the cup in the sack of any man amongst us, let him be slain, and we and our asses will serve thy lord.'

7 And he said unto them: 'Not so, the man with whom I find, him only

shall I take as a servant, and ye shall return in peace unto your house.'

8 And as he was searching in their vessels, beginning with the eldest and ending with the youngest, it was found in Benjamin's sack.

9 And they rent their garments, and laded their asses, and returned to the city and came to the house of Joseph, and they all bowed themselves on their faces to the ground before him.

10 And Joseph said unto them: 'Ye have done evil.' And they said: 'What shall we say and how shall we defend ourselves Our lord hath discovered the transgression of his servants; behold we are the servants of our lord, and our asses also.

11 'And Joseph said unto them: 'I too fear the Lord; as for you, go ye to your homes and let your brother be my servant, for ye have done evil.

12 Know ye not that a man delights in his cup as I with this cup And yet ye have stolen it from me.'

13 And Judah said: 'O my lord, let thy servant, I pray thee, speak a word in my lord's ear two brothers did thy servant's mother bear to our father: one went away and was lost, and hath not been found, and he alone is left of his mother, and thy servant our father loves him, and his life also is bound up with the life of this (lad).

14 And it will come to pass, when we go to thy servant our father, and the lad is not with us, that he will die, and we shall bring down our father with sorrow unto death.

15 Now rather let me, thy servant, abide instead of the boy as a bondsman unto my lord, and let the lad go with his brethren, for I became surety for him at the hand of thy servant our father, and if I do not bring him back, thy servant will hear the blame to our father for ever.'

16 And Joseph saw that they were all accordant in goodness one with another, and he could not refrain himself, and he told them that he was Joseph.

17 And he conversed with them in the Hebrew tongue and fell on their neck and wept.

18 But they knew him not and they began to weep.

19 And he said unto them: 'Weep not over me but hasten and bring my father to me; and ye see that it is my mouth that speaks, and the eyes of my brother Benjamin see.

20 For behold this is the second year of the famine, and there are still five years without harvest or fruit of trees or ploughing.

21 Come down quickly ye and your households, so that ye perish not through the famine, and do not be grieved for your possessions, for the Lord sent me before you to set things in order that many people might live.

22 And tell my father that I am still alive, and ye, behold, ye see that the Lord has made me as a father to Pharaoh, and ruler over his house and over all the land of Egypt.

23 And tell my father of all my glory, and all the riches and glory that the Lord hath given me.'

24 And by the command of the mouth of Pharaoh he gave them chariots and provisions for the way, and he gave them all many-coloured raiment and silver.

25 And to their father he sent raiment and silver and ten asses which carried corn, and he sent them away.

26 And they went up and told their father that Joseph was alive and was measuring out corn to all the nations of the earth, and that he was ruler over all the land of Egypt.

27 And their father did not believe it, for he was beside himself in his mind; but when he saw the wagons which Joseph had sent, the life of his spirit revived, and he said: 'It is enough for me if Joseph lives; I will

go down and see him before I die.'

Comment:1: GREAT EXAMPLE OF GODLINESS: The story of Joseph is a wonderful example of true forgiveness and mercy. Joseph was many things, including a great leader and overseer on behalf of Pharaoh for Egypt. He was loved by the Egyptians, because he was not corrupt, but was wise & fair in all his dealings.

C.2 FAITHFULNESS & SUMMARY OF JOSEPH'S LIFE

Look at Joseph and all that the Lord put him through - being sold into slavery, spending some years in jail in Egypt after he was falsely accused by Potiphar's wife, and all that he went through there, including being separated from his family for 20 years. That was no picniC. But he stayed true to the Lord, true to his convictions, and when he had to appear before Pharaoh to pass his final test and interpret his dream, he did, and wound up running the kingdom for Pharaoh. Look at the reward he received for his faithfulness!

C.3 RULER & JUDGE Joseph was also very wise in his dealings with his brethren when they first came down to Egypt, as he wanted to see if time itself had changed them from being cruel, dishonest and deceptive men as they had been to their poor father Jacob - stating that Joseph had been killed by a wild animal when it wasn't true. The truth was that they cast a 17- year boy into a well, almost had him killed, and then sold him into slavery.

C.4 TESTINGS: As a result, of their hateful treatment of their younger brother Joseph, once down in Egypt serving as a slave, he then was falsely accused, thrown into jail for some years. Because of his faith and trust in God, he was delivered by God Himself - to literally become the overseer of all of Egypt. God gave Joseph great Grace to patiently endure his circumstances. Joseph learned through the 'hard knocks' of experience how to be wise in all of his doings.

C.5 HUMILIATION Having started out as a 'spoiled brat' who was always goading his brothers on and provoking them to anger with his tales of his own grandeur, after the humiliation of his great pride, he learnt through much suffering, deprivation, false accusations, imprisonment to totally lean on God as His Deliverer. He also didn't give into temptation in the form of a beautiful woman (the wife of Potiphar) realizing that he would only have been a pawn for a season and then cast aside as a discarded slave.

C.6 HONOUR & VALOUR God tested Joseph in every way, and yet he came through victorious where most people would have compromised and given up. That's why God could then trust Joseph to be the deliverer of the Tribes of Israel and to be responsible to both nourish and protect Israel throughout his lifetime.

C.7 VENGEANCE When Joseph saw his brethren again, he could have acted like his vengeful uncle Esau who was not able to forgive his brother Jacob after more than 20 years. He held a bitter grievance against his brother even though his brother was sorry and apologized. He was still determined to try to kill his brother. This is also how vengeance is portrayed in most movies these days; that it is OK to seek for vengeance, but certainly not to forgive, which is just like in the Old Testament Laws of Moses 'An Eye for an Eye and a Tooth for a Tooth'. That is the way of Satan: **REVENGE**. There is a deep saying that says, *'He that cannot forgive breaks the very bridge over which he himself will need someday to cross over.'*

The ways of God are Mercy and Forgiveness when the offenders are sorry for their sins and iniquities.

C.8 FORGIVENESS Unfortunately, this present world being largely under the control of Satan, has no mercy on the innocent and certainly not on those who have 'committed evil crimes. The attitude of this world is if someone has committed a serious crime such as Joseph's brothers committed, then he should be locked up for good. But would that teach them anything?

The whole plan of Creation itself is one of Forgiveness and Redemption. Here are the words of the Messiah Jesus:

MAT.5:38 Ye have heard that it hath been said, An eye for an eye, and a tooth for a tooth:

MAT.5:39 But I say unto you, 'That ye resist not evil: but whosoever shall smite thee on thy right cheek, turn to him the other also'.

MAT.6:14 For if ye forgive men their trespasses, your heavenly Father will also forgive you:

MAT.6:15 But if ye forgive not men their trespasses, neither will your Father forgive your trespasses.

Chapter 44

1 And Israel took his journey from Haran from his house on the new moon of the third month, and he went on the way of the Well of the Oath, and he offered a sacrifice to the God of his father Isaac on the seventh of this month.

2 And Jacob remembered the dream that he had seen at Bethel, and he feared to go down into Egypt.

3 And while he was thinking of sending word to Joseph to come to him, and that he would not go down, he remained there seven days, if perchance he could see a vision as to whether he should remain or go down.

4 And he celebrated the harvest festival of the first fruits with old grain, for in all the land of Canaan there was not a handful of seed [in the land], for the famine was over all the beasts and cattle and birds, and also over man.

5 And on the sixteenth the Lord appeared unto him, and said unto him, 'Jacob, Jacob'; and he said, 'Here am I.'

6 And He said unto him: 'I am the God of thy fathers, the God of Abraham and Isaac; fear not to go down into Egypt, for I will there make of thee a great nation I will go down with thee, and I will bring thee up (again), and in this land shalt thou be buried, and Joseph shall put his hands upon thy eyes.

7 Fear not; go down into Egypt.'

Comment:1: It is wonderful to see how that God talked directly to Jacob to reassure him to go down to Egypt. It is also possible for anyone to have this kind of relationship with God through Jesus as the Mediator. One can talk to Jesus and he will answer our questions, and He will also warn us of things to watch out for. He often protects us by His Holy Spirit from unforeseen dangers that we are unaware of.

PSA.91:1 He that dwelleth in the secret place of the most High shall abide under the shadow of the Almighty.

PSA.91:2 I will say of the LORD, He is my refuge and my fortress: my God; in him will I trust.

JOH.15:7 If ye abide in me, and my words abide in you, ye shall ask what ye will, and it shall be done unto you.

8 And his sons rose up, and his sons' sons, and they placed their father and their possessions upon wagons.

9 And Israel rose up from the Well of the Oath on the sixteenth of this third month, and he went to the land of Egypt.

10 And Israel sent Judah before him to his son Joseph to examine the Land of Goshen, for Joseph had told his brothers that they should come and dwell there that they might be near him.

11 And this was the goodliest (land) in the land of Egypt, and near to him, for all (of them) and for the cattle.

12 And these are the names of the sons of Jacob who went into Egypt with Jacob their father Reuben, the First-born of Israel; and these are the names of his sons Enoch, and Pallu, and Hezron and Carmi-five; Simeon and his sons; and these are the names of his sons: Jemuel, and Jamin, and Ohad, and Jachin, and Zohar, and Shaul, the son of the Zephathite woman-seven.

13 Levi and his sons; and these are the names of his sons: Gershon, and Kohath, and Merari-four.

14 Judah and his sons; and these are the names of his sons: Shela, and Perez, and Zerah-four.

15 Issachar and his sons; and these are the names of his sons: Tola, and Phua, and Jasub, and Shimron-five. Zebulon and his sons; and these are the names of his sons: Sered, and Elon, and Jahleel-four.

16 And these are the sons of Jacob and their sons whom Leah bore to Jacob in Mesopotamia, six, and their one sister, Dinah and all the souls of the sons of Leah, and their sons, who went with Jacob their father into Egypt, were twenty-nine, and Jacob their father being with them,

they were thirty.

17 And the sons of Zilpah, Leah's handmaid, the wife of Jacob, who bore unto Jacob Gad and Ashur.

18 And there are the names of their sons who went with him into Egypt.

19 The sons of Gad: Ziphion, and Haggi, and Shuni, and Ezbon, (and Eri, and Areli, and Arodi-eight.

20 And the sons of Asher: Imnah, and Ishvah, (and Ishvi), and Beriah, and Serah, their one sister-six.

21 All the souls were fourteen, and all those of Leah were forty-four.

22 And the sons of Rachel, the wife of Jacob: Joseph and Benjamin.

23 And there were born to Joseph in Egypt before his father came into Egypt, those whom Asenath, daughter of Potiphar priest of Heliopolis bare unto him, Manasseh, and Ephraim-three.

24 And the sons of Benjamin: Bela and Becher and Ashbel, Gera, and Naaman, and Ehi, and Rosh, and Muppim, and Huppim, and Ard-eleven.

25 And all the souls of Rachel were fourteen.

26 And the sons of Bilhah, the handmaid of Rachel, the wife of Jacob, whom she bare to Jacob, were Dan and Naphtali.

27 And these are the names of their sons who went with them into Egypt. And the sons of Dan were Hushim, and Samon, and Asudi and 'Ijaka, and Salomon-six.

28 And they died the year in which they entered into Egypt, and there was left to Dan Hushim alone.

29 And these are the names of the sons of Naphtali Jahziel, and Guni

and Jezer, and Shallum, and 'Iv. And 'Iv, who was born after the years of famine, died in Egypt.

30 And all the souls of Rachel were twenty-six.

31 And all the souls of Jacob which went into Egypt were seventy souls.

32 These are his children and his children's children, in all seventy, but five died in Egypt before Joseph, and had no children.

33 And in the land of Canaan two sons of Judah died, Er and Onan, and they had no children, and the children of Israel buried those who perished, and they were reckoned among the seventy Gentile nations.

Chapter 45

1 And Israel went into the country of Egypt, into the land of Goshen, on the new moon of the fourth [2172 A.M= **'Anno Mundi' = years of the world**] month, in the second year of the third week of the forty-fifth jubilee.

2 And Joseph went to meet his father Jacob, to the land of Goshen, and he fell on his father's neck and wept.

GEN.46:29 And Joseph made ready his chariot, and went up to meet Israel his father, to Goshen, and presented himself unto him; and he fell on his neck, and wept on his neck a good while.

3 And Israel said unto Joseph: 'Now let me die since I have seen thee, and now may the Lord God of Israel be blessed the God of Abraham and the God of Isaac who hath not withheld His mercy and His grace from His servant Jacob.

GEN.46:30 And Israel said unto Joseph, Now let me die, since I have seen thy face, because thou art yet alive.

4 It is enough for me that I have seen thy face whilst I am yet alive; yea, true is the vision which I saw at Bethel. Blessed be the Lord my God for ever and ever and blessed be His name.'

5 And Joseph and his brothers eat bread before their father and drank wine, and Jacob rejoiced with exceeding great joy because he saw Joseph eating with his brothers and drinking before him, and he blessed the Creator of all things who had preserved him and had preserved for him his twelve sons.

GEN.46:31 And Joseph said unto his brethren, and unto his father's house, I will go up, and shew Pharaoh, and say unto him, My brethren, and my father's house, which were in the land of Canaan, are come unto me;

GEN.46:32 And the men are shepherds, for their trade hath been to feed cattle; and they have brought their flocks, and their herds, and all that they have.

GEN.46:33 And it shall come to pass, when Pharaoh shall call you, and shall say, What is your occupation?

GEN.46:34 That ye shall say, Thy servants' trade hath been about cattle from our youth even until now, both we, and also our fathers: that ye may dwell in the land of Goshen; for every shepherd is an abomination unto the Egyptians.

6 And Joseph had given to his father and to his brothers as a gift the right of dwelling in the land of Goshen and in Rameses and all the region round about, which he ruled over before Pharaoh. And Israel and his sons dwelt in the land of Goshen, the best part of the land of Egypt and Israel was one hundred and thirty years old when he came into Egypt.

7 And Joseph nourished his father and his brethren and also their possessions with bread as much as sufficed them for the seven years of the famine.

GEN.47:12 And Joseph nourished his father, and his brethren, and all his father's household, with bread, according to their families.

GEN.47:13 And there was no bread in all the land; for the famine was very sore, so that the land of Egypt and all the land of Canaan fainted by reason of the famine.

GEN.47:14 And Joseph gathered up all the money that was found in the land of Egypt, and in the land of Canaan, for the corn which they bought: and Joseph brought the money into Pharaoh's house.

GEN.47:15 And when money failed in the land of Egypt, and in the land of Canaan, all the Egyptians came unto Joseph, and said, Give us bread: for why should we die in thy presence? for the money faileth.

GEN.47:16 And Joseph said, Give your cattle; and I will give you for your cattle, if money fail.

GEN.47:17 And they brought their cattle unto Joseph: and Joseph gave them bread in exchange for horses, and for the flocks, and for the cattle of the herds, and for the asses: and he fed them with bread for all their cattle for that year.

GEN.47:18 When that year was ended, they came unto him the second year, and said unto him, We will not hide it from my lord, how that our money is spent; my lord also hath our herds of cattle; there is not ought left in the sight of my lord, but our bodies, and our lands:

GEN.47:19 Wherefore shall we die before thine eyes, both we and our land? buy us and our land for bread, and we and our land will be servants unto Pharaoh: and give us seed, that we may live, and not die, that the land be not desolate.

GEN.47:20 And Joseph bought all the land of Egypt for Pharaoh; for the Egyptians sold every man his field, because the famine prevailed over them: so the land became Pharaoh's.

GEN.47:21 And as for the people, he removed them to cities from one end of the borders of Egypt even to the other end thereof.

GEN.47:22 Only the land of the priests bought he not; for the priests had a portion assigned them of Pharaoh, and did eat their portion which Pharaoh gave them: wherefore they sold not their lands.

GEN.47:23 Then Joseph said unto the people, Behold, I have bought you this day and your land for Pharaoh: lo, here is seed for you, and ye shall sow the land.

GEN.47:24 And it shall come to pass in the increase, that ye shall give the fifth part unto Pharaoh, and four parts shall be your own, for seed of the field, and for your food, and for them of your households, and for food for your little ones.

GEN.47:25 And they said, Thou hast saved our lives: let us find grace in the sight of my lord, and we will be Pharaoh's servants.

---

8 And the land of Egypt suffered by reason of the famine, and Joseph acquired all the land of Egypt for Pharaoh in return for food, and he got possession of the people and their cattle and everything for Pharaoh.

9 And the years of the famine were accomplished, and Joseph gave to the people in the land seed and food that they might sow (the land) in the eighth year, for the river had overflowed all the land of Egypt.

10 For in the seven years of the famine it had (not) overflowed and had irrigated only a few places on the banks of the river, but now it overflowed, and the Egyptians sowed the land, and it bore much corn that year.

11 And this was the first year of [2178 A.M. = **'Anno Mundi' = years of the world**]

the fourth week of the forty-fifth jubilee.

12 And Joseph took of the corn of the harvest the fifth part for the king and left four parts for them for food and for seed, and Joseph made it an ordinance for the land of Egypt until this day.

13 And Israel lived in the land of Egypt seventeen years, and all the

---

days which he lived were three jubilees, one hundred and forty-seven years, and he died in the fourth [2188 A.M.] year of the fifth week of the forty-fifth jubilee.

GEN.47:28 And Jacob lived in the land of Egypt seventeen years: so the whole age of Jacob was an hundred forty and seven years.

14 And Israel blessed his sons before he died and told them everything that would befall them in the land of Egypt; and he made known to them what would come upon them in the last days and blessed them and gave to Joseph two portions in the land.

GEN.47:29 And the time drew nigh that Israel must die: and he called his son Joseph, and said unto him, If now I have found grace in thy sight, put, I pray thee, thy hand under my thigh, and deal kindly and truly with me; bury me not, I pray thee, in Egypt:

15 And he slept with his fathers, and he was buried in the double cave in the land of Canaan, near Abraham his father in the grave which he dug for himself in the double cave in the land of Hebron.

GEN.47:30 But I will lie with my fathers, and thou shalt carry me out of Egypt, and bury me in their burying place. And he said, I will do as thou hast said.

GEN.47:31 And he said, Swear unto me. And he sware unto him. And Israel bowed himself upon the bed's head.

16 And he gave all his books and the books of his fathers to Levi his son that he might preserve them and renew them for his children until this day.

Chapter 46

> 1 And it came to pass that after Jacob died the children of Israel multiplied in the land of Egypt, and they became a great nation, and they were of one accord in heart, so that brother loved brother and every man helped his brother, and they increased abundantly and multiplied exceedingly, ten [2242 A.M. = **'Anno Mundi' = years of the world**] weeks of years, all the days of the life of Joseph.

GEN.50:15 And when Joseph's brethren saw that their father was dead, they said, Joseph will peradventure hate us, and will certainly requite us all the evil which we did unto him.

GEN.50:16 And they sent a messenger unto Joseph, saying, Thy father did command before he died, saying,

GEN.50:17 So shall ye say unto Joseph, Forgive, I pray thee now, the trespass of thy brethren, and their sin; for they did unto thee evil: and now, we pray thee, forgive the trespass of the servants of the God of thy father. And Joseph wept when they spake unto him.

GEN.50:18 And his brethren also went and fell down before his face; and they said, Behold, we be thy servants.

GEN.50:19 And Joseph said unto them, Fear not: for am I in the place of God?

GEN.50:20 But as for you, ye thought evil against me; but God meant it unto good, to bring to pass, as it is this day, to save much people alive.

GEN.50:21 Now therefore fear ye not: I will nourish you, and your little ones. And he comforted them, and spake kindly unto them.

GEN.50:22 And Joseph dwelt in Egypt, he, and his father's house: and Joseph lived an hundred and ten years.

GEN.50:23 And Joseph saw Ephraim's children of the third generation: the children also of Machir the son of Manasseh were brought up upon Joseph's knees.

> 2 And there was no Satan nor any evil all the days of the life of Joseph which he lived after his father Jacob, for all the Egyptians honoured the children of Israel all the days of the life of Joseph.
>
> 3 And Joseph died being a hundred and ten years old; seventeen years he lived in the land of Canaan, and ten years he was a servant, and three years in prison, and eighty years he was under the king, ruling all

323

the land of Egypt.

GEN.50:24 And Joseph said unto his brethren, I die: and God will surely visit you, and bring you out of this land unto the land which he sware to Abraham, to Isaac, and to Jacob.

GEN.50:25 And Joseph took an oath of the children of Israel, saying, God will surely visit you, and ye shall carry up my bones from hence.

GEN.50:26 So Joseph died, being an hundred and ten years old: and they embalmed him, and he was put in a coffin in Egypt.

Comment:1: Above, it states that Joseph was only 3 years in the prison. What is the length of time given in the Bible?

In **Genesis 41:46** We learn that Joseph was 30 when he was made over-seer to the king of Egypt. Since he was 17 when he was sold into Egypt, that means he spent 13 years total in Potiphar's house and prison. We know Joseph was in prison at least 2 years because Genesis 40 tells us about the servants of the king whose dreams Joseph interpreted. The first verse of chapter 41 tells us that 2 years passed after that event before the king had the dreams that Joseph was called to interpret.

So, Joseph lived in Potiphar's house 11 years or less and was in prison 2 or more years. Joseph was 17 when he was sold into Egypt

He was 30 when he was made overseer

He was 39 when his brothers first came to Egypt (second year of the famine, or nine years after being made overseer)

He was probably 41 or so when the brothers came a second time and Jacob comes to Egypt

He was 110 when he died

SOURCE: https://amazingbibletimeline.com/blog/ q27_joseph_how_long_in_prison/

4 And he died and all his brethren and all that generation.

5 And he commanded the children of Israel before he died that they should carry his bones with them when they went forth from the land of Egypt.

6 And he made them swear regarding his bones, for he knew that the Egyptians would not again bring forth and bury him in the land of Canaan, for Makamaron, king of Canaan, while dwelling in the land of Assyria, fought in the valley with the king of Egypt and slew him there, and pursued after the Egyptians to the gates of 'Ermon.

C.2 Joseph believed that God would one day return the nation to Canaan, and so he gave the command for his bones to be carried back with them and buried there (**Gen 50:25**).

> 7 But he was not able to enter, for another, a new king, had become king of Egypt, and he was stronger than he, and he returned to the land of Canaan, and the gates of Egypt were closed, and none went out and none came into Egypt.
>
> 8 And Joseph died in the forty-sixth jubilee, in the sixth week, in the second year, and they buried him in the land of Egypt, and [2242 A.M.] all his brethren died after him.

EXO.1:6 And Joseph died, and all his brethren, and all that generation.

> 9 And the king of Egypt went forth to war with the king of Canaan [2263 A.M.] in the forty-seventh jubilee, in the second week in the second year, and the children of Israel brought forth all the bones of the children of Jacob save the bones of Joseph, and they buried them in the field in the double cave in the mountain.
>
> 10 And the most (of them) returned to Egypt, but a few of them remained in the mountains of Hebron, and Amram thy father remained with them.
>
> 11 And the king of Canaan was victorious over the king of Egypt, and he closed the gates of Egypt.
>
> 12 And he devised an evil device against the children of Israel of afflicting them and he said unto the people of Egypt: 'Behold the people of the children of Israel have increased and multiplied more than we.

EXO.1:8 Now there arose up a new king over Egypt, which knew not Joseph.

> 13 Come and let us deal wisely with them before they become too many, and let us afflict them with slavery before war come upon us and before they too fight against us; else they will join themselves unto our enemies and get them up out of our land, for their hearts and faces are towards the land of Canaan.'

EXO.1:10 Come on, let us deal wisely with them; lest they multiply, and it come to pass, that, when there falls out any war, they join also unto our enemies, and fight against us, and so get them up out of the land.

> 14 And he set over them taskmasters to afflict them with slavery; and they built strong cities for Pharaoh, Pithom, and Raamses and they built all the walls and all the fortifications which had fallen in the cities of Egypt.

EXO.1:11 Therefore they did set over them taskmasters to afflict them with their burdens. And they built for Pharaoh treasure cities, Pithom and Raamses.

> 15 And they made them serve with rigour, and the more they dealt evilly with them, the more they increased and multiplied. And the people of Egypt abominated the children of Israel

EXO.1:13 And the Egyptians made the children of Israel to serve with rigour:

EXO.1:12 But the more they afflicted them, the more they multiplied and grew. And they were grieved because of the children of Israel.

Chapter 47

1 And in the seventh week, in the seventh year, in the forty-seventh jubilee, thy father went forth [2303 A.M. = **Anno Mundi' = years of the world**] from the land of Canaan, and thou was born in the fourth week, in the sixth year thereof, in the [2330 A.M.] forty-eighth jubilee; this was the time of tribulation on the children of Israel.

Comment:1: In this chapter I have included many Bible verses as the stories are very parallel, and yet with slight differences.

2 And Pharaoh, king of Egypt, issued a command regarding them that they should cast all their male children which were born into the river.

EXO.1:22 And Pharaoh charged all his people, saying, Every son that is born ye shall cast into the river, and every daughter ye shall save alive.

3 And they cast them in for seven months until the day that thou was born; and thy mother hid thee for three months, and they told regarding her.

4 And she made an ark for thee, and covered it with pitch and asphalt, and placed it in the flags on the bank of the river, and she placed thee in it seven days, and thy mother came by night and suckled thee, and by day Miriam, thy sister, guarded thee from the birds.

EXO.2:3 And when she could no longer hide him, she took for him an ark of bulrushes, and daubed it with slime and with pitch, and put the child therein; and she laid it in the flags by the river's brink.

5 And in those days Tharmuth, the daughter of Pharaoh, came to bathe in the river, and she heard thy voice crying, and she told her maidens to bring thee forth, and they brought thee unto her.

EXO.2:5 And the daughter of Pharaoh came down to wash herself at the river; and her maidens walked along by the river's side; and when she saw the ark among the flags, she sent her maid to fetch it.

6 And she took thee out of the ark, and she had compassion on thee.

EXO.2:6 And when she had opened it, she saw the child: and, behold, the babe wept. And she had compassion on him, and said, This is one of the Hebrews' children.

7 And thy sister said unto her: 'Shall I go and call unto thee one of the Hebrew women to nurse and suckle this babe for thee'.

EXO.2:7 Then said his sister to Pharaoh's daughter, Shall I go and call to thee a nurse of the Hebrew women, that she may nurse the child for thee?

8 And she said (unto her): 'Go.' And she went and called thy mother Jochebed, and she gave her wages, and she nursed thee.

EXO.2:8 And Pharaoh's daughter said to her, Go. And the maid went and called the child's mother.

EXO.2:9 And Pharaoh's daughter said unto her, Take this child away, and nurse it for me, and I will give thee thy wages. And the women took the child and nursed it.

9 And afterwards, when thou was grown up, they brought thee unto the daughter of Pharaoh, and thou didst become her son, and Amram thy father taught thee writing, and after thou had completed three weeks they brought thee into the royal court.

EXO.2:10 And the child grew, and she brought him unto Pharaoh's daughter, and he became her son. And she called his name Moses: and she said, Because I drew him out of the water.

10 And thou was three weeks of years at court until the time [2351-] when thou didst go forth from the royal court and didst see an Egyptian smiting thy friend who was [2372 A.M.] of the children of Israel, and thou didst slay him and hide him in the sand.

EXO.2:11 And it came to pass in those days, when Moses was grown, that he went out unto his brethren, and looked on their burdens: and he spied an Egyptian smiting an Hebrew, one of his brethren.

EXO.2:12 And he looked this way and that way, and when he saw that there was no man, he slew the Egyptian, and hid him in the sand.

11 And on the second day thou didst and two of the children of Israel striving together, and thou didst say to him who was doing the wrong: 'Why dost thou smite thy brother'.

EXO.2:13 And when he went out the second day, behold, two men of the Hebrews strove together: and he said to him that did the wrong, Wherefore smites thou thy fellow?

12 And he was angry and indignant, and said: 'Who made thee a prince and a judge over us Thinks thou to kill me as thou killed the Egyptian yesterday.'

EXO.2:14 And he said, Who made thee a prince and a judge over us? intendest thou to kill me, as thou killed the Egyptian? And Moses feared, and said, Surely this thing is known.

13 And thou didst fear and flee on account of these words.

Chapter 48
The Angel of the Lord talks to Moses

1 And in the sixth year of the third week of the forty-ninth jubilee thou didst depart and dwell (in [2372 A.M. = **'Anno Mundi' = years of the world**] the land of Midian, five weeks and one year.

Comment:1: 2372 A.M.] This is 2372 years after the Creation of the world. According to Bible charts on my wall in front of me, this date should be later, as it puts the year around 100 years after the death of Joseph. Joseph died at 110 years old. He spent most of his life in Egypt. If Moses came along only 100 years later, after the death of Joseph, then the promise to Abraham about his descendants being in bondage and captivity down in Egypt for 400 years couldn't have been fulfilled. Something about the above date is *too early*. It should read around 1450 BCE or 2500 A.M

C.2 Why this discrepancy in the timeline? Now that is a mystery, that needs to be solved. I will state here for the record however, that although the Bible and Apocryphal books differ slightly as to times and dates and some events, in general the books complement each other wonderfully. The books of Jubilees and Jasher really do fill in the details that are missed out in the Bible. It would also appear that the Septuagint version of the Old testament is much more reliable than the Old Testament in the K.J.V, as you will clearly see later in this chapter.

C.3 N.B In comparing different scriptures, we see that certain stories in the Old Testament in the K,J.V of the Bible are occasionally sadly inaccurate in content, and that their content has actually been changed from the original meaning, as given originally in the Hebrew text. Why is that? How did that happen? I explain these things and answer these questions in detail in the Appendix of this book, as to how that came about.

2 And thou didst return into Egypt in the second week in the second year in the fiftieth jubilee.

3 And thou thyself know what He spoke unto thee on [2410 A.M.] Mount Sinai, and what prince Mastema desired to do with thee when thou was returning into Egypt.

EXO.3:1 Now Moses kept the flock of Jethro his father in law, the priest of Midian: and he led the flock to the backside of the desert, and came to the mountain of God, even to Horeb.

EXO.3:2 And the angel of the LORD appeared unto him in a flame of fire out of the midst of a bush: and he looked, and, behold, the bush burned with fire, and the bush was not consumed.

EXO.3:3 And Moses said, I will now turn aside, and see this great sight, why the bush is not burnt.

EXO.3:4 And when the LORD saw that he turned aside to see, God called unto him out of the midst of the bush, and said, Moses, Moses. And he said, Here am I.

EXO.3:5 And he said, Draw not nigh hither: put off thy shoes from off thy feet, for the place whereon thou standest is holy ground.

EXO.3:6 Moreover he said, I am the God of thy father, the God of Abraham, the God of Isaac, and the God of Jacob. And Moses hid his face; for he was afraid to look upon God.

EXO.3:7 And the LORD said, I have surely seen the affliction of my people which are in Egypt, and have heard their cry by reason of their taskmasters; for I know their sorrows;

EXO.3:8 And I am come down to deliver them out of the hand of the Egyptians, and to bring them up out of that land unto a good land and a large, unto a land flowing with milk and honey; unto the place of the Canaanites, and the Hittites, and the Amorites, and the Perizzites, and the Hivites, and the Jebusites.

EXO.3:9 Now therefore, behold, the cry of the children of Israel is come unto me: and I have also seen the oppression wherewith the Egyptians oppress them.

EXO.3:10 Come now therefore, and I will send thee unto Pharaoh, that thou mayest bring forth my people the children of Israel out of Egypt.

EXO.3:11 And Moses said unto God, Who am I, that I should go unto Pharaoh, and that I should bring forth the children of Israel out of Egypt?

EXO.3:12 And he said, Certainly I will be with thee; and this shall be a token unto thee, that I have sent thee: When thou hast brought forth the people out of Egypt, ye shall serve God upon this mountain.

---

4 Did he not with all his power seek to slay thee and deliver the Egyptians out of thy hand when he saw that thou was sent to execute judgment and vengeance on the Egyptians.

EXO.4:24 And it came to pass by the way in the inn, that the LORD met him, and sought to kill him.

C.4 The Bible states that the LORD met him and sought to slay him, but is that true? According to this Book of Jubilees it was not the LORD or his angel, but it was Mastema or SATAN a fallen angel who tried to kill Moses. I thank

331

God for this book of Jubilees that tells the true story in this case.

C.5 Mastema is another name for **Satan.** What do the last two verses actually mean? '3 *Mastema desired to do with thee when thou was returning into Egypt* **4** *'Did he not with all his power seek to slay thee?'* What did Mastema (Satan) try to do against Moses? Obviously, Satan put up a big fight against Moses, as he didn't want his pet project of the Empire of Egypt destroyed or Satan's power circumvented by the Power of God through his prophet and leader Moses. Egypt was rife with satanic power as evidenced by the priests of Pharaoh being able to turn their staffs into snakes when Moses demonstrated the power of God before Pharaoh in his first meeting with Pharaoh. Many of the plagues that Moses brought forth by the power of God, Satan's high priests could also do the same. I always thought that it was so stupid of Pharaoh's priests to bring more frogs out upon the land just to prove they could make the same curses as Moses. The people were tired of the bug-eyed pests of the burping frogs, so why make even more of them. However, it does illustrate an important point, and that is that Egypt was very in tune with Mastema (Satan) and so Satan tried to stop Moses before he even got started on his mission to deliver the Children of Israel from Egypt.

EPH.6:12 For we wrestle not against flesh and blood, but against principalities, against powers, against the rulers of the darkness of this world, against spiritual wickedness in high places.

EPH.6:13 Wherefore take unto you the whole armour of God, that ye may be able to withstand in the evil day, and having done all, to stand.

C.6 Moses took a stand against Satan and won, but *what exactly was the trial* he had and what *specific battle that he had with Satan 'when thou was returning into Egypt'?*

I just discovered that it has to do with the 'letter of the law' whereby Satan can 'accuse the saints' before God for sins and crimes they have committed whether intentional or unintentional. This story also shows how false religions end up under the jurisdiction of Satan himself who uses the 'letter of the law' to accuse, condemn and judge and even execute people. Mastema (Satan) ends up telling his followers to do many evil things which God Himself never intended. Stephen in the New Testament absolutely nailed this topic of religions which have been overcome by Satan in ACTS 7:

ACT.7:52 Which of the prophets have not your fathers persecuted? and they have slain them which shewed before of the coming of the Just One; of whom ye have been now the betrayers and murderers:

ACT.7:53 Who have received the law by the disposition of angels (Fallen angels) and have not kept it.

C.7 Satan is the Accuser of the saints, and he is also one of the Death angels and executioners of Judgement, when it is permitted by God. The great importance of Jesus having come as the Messiah was to both defeat Satan and to put an end to his reign of terror through using the 'letter of the law' before God. That is, Satan comes into the courts of heaven and accuses Moses of not having fulfilled God's commandment to circumcise his son, which was punishable by death. So Mastema used the law, to try and go and slay Moses as he was on his way to see Pharaoh. The reason why Moses forgot to circumcise his son on the 8th day, was probably because he was distracted by the fact that he had just been given an enormous responsibility by God to go to Pharaoh and to command him to let the Children of Israel go free, or else God's great Judgements would follow.

C.8 One can clearly see here in this Old Testament, in this Jubilees version, how that Satan will try and condemn and destroy God's servants by persuading them that they have 'broken the law' and therefore deserve severe punishment and in the case of 'not circumcising one's child the 8th day Moses supposedly 'deserved to die' according to Mastema's twisted logiC. Here is the actual story:

The King James Version (1611) of the Old Testament:

EXO.4:24 And it came to pass by the way in the inn, that **the** LORD *met him*, and sought to kill him.

C.9 This version in the Bible has been altered from the original text. Think for a moment, why would the Lord slay Moses whom he had just commanded to go to Pharaoh and to deliver the Children of Israel. Is does not make any sense. What did the original text say? We can see more clearly by reading the Septuagint version of Exodus written in 300 BC:

EXODUS LXX 4.24 And it came to pass that the *angel of the Lord* met him in the way in the inn and sought to slay him

C.10 In this Book of Jubilees, it tells the real story as it states that, it was Mastema (Satan) who sought to kill Moses because he hadn't obeyed one tiny law. Here clearly Satan was using the 'letter of the Law' to try and both condemn Moses, and then he himself wanted to be the executioner of the law. Satan is an evil *Fallen angel* who does upon occasion have the power of Death over people, if God allows. So, Mastema was holding the law over Moses head and stating to his wife if you don't immediately circumcise your son then I will kill Moses, because that is my right to execute judgement on all who disobey.

C.11 The following is a wonderful verse about the day will come when Satan will no longer be able to accuse the Saints before God anymore and neither will he have the power to condemn and execute death on the saints anymore:

REV.12:7 And there was war in heaven: Michael and his angels fought against the dragon; and the dragon fought and his angels,

REV.12:8 And prevailed not; neither was their place found any more in heaven.

REV.12:9 And the great dragon was cast out, that old serpent, called the Devil, and Satan, which deceives the whole world: he was cast out into the earth, and his angels were cast out with him.

REV.12:10 And I heard a loud voice saying in heaven, Now is come salvation, and strength, and the kingdom of our God, and the power of his Christ: for the accuser of our brethren is cast down, which accused them before our God day and night.

REV.12:11 And they overcame him by the blood of the Lamb, and by the word of their testimony; and they loved not their lives unto the death.

C.12 Look at the difference between The KJV of The Old Testament & The Septuagint version concerning Zipporah's reaction to this event:

EXO.4:25 Then Zipporah took a sharp stone, and cut off the foreskin of her son, and cast it at his feet, and said, Surely a bloody husband art thou to me.

EXO.4:26 So he let him go: then she said, A bloody husband thou art, because of the circumcision.

C.13 This would make Zipporah to be in direct rebellion against both her husband and God Himself. But is that what was originally written?

EXODUS LXX 4.25 And Sephora having taken a stone cut off the foreskin of her son and fell at his feet and said' The blood the circumcision of my son is staunched

As you can see the whole meaning has been changed in the KJV of the Old Testament. Why is that? Now that is a very big topic!

C.14 In summing up, there have been some stories like this that I read in the KJV of the Old Testament and found the stories odd or seemingly out of context. Now I know why! See the write-up on the KJV of the Old testament in the **APPENDIX.**

5 And I delivered thee out of his hand, and thou didst perform the signs and wonders which thou was sent to perform in Egypt against Pharaoh, and against all his house, and against his servants and his people.

6 And the Lord executed a great vengeance on them for Israel's sake, and smote them through (the plagues of) blood and frogs, lice and dog-flies, and malignant boils breaking forth in blains; and their cattle by death; and by hail-stones, thereby He destroyed everything that grew for them; and by locusts which devoured the residue which had been left by the hail, and by darkness; and (by the death) of the first-born of men and animals, and on all their idols the Lord took vengeance and burned them with fire.

7 And everything was sent through thy hand, that thou should declare (these things) before they were done, and thou didst speak with the king

334

of Egypt before all his servants and before his people

8 And everything took place according to thy words; ten great and terrible judgments came on the land of Egypt that thou might execute vengeance on it for Israel.

EXO.7:20 And Moses and Aaron did so, as the LORD commanded; and he lifted up the rod, and smote the waters that were in the river, in the sight of Pharaoh, and in the sight of his servants; and all the waters that were in the river were turned to blood.

EXO.8:5 And the LORD spake unto Moses, Say unto Aaron, Stretch forth thine hand with thy rod over the streams, over the rivers, and over the ponds, and cause frogs to come up upon the land of Egypt.

EXO.8:16 And the LORD said unto Moses, Say unto Aaron, Stretch out thy rod, and smite the dust of the land, that it may become lice throughout all the land of Egypt.

EXO.8:17 And they did so; for Aaron stretched out his hand with his rod, and smote the dust of the earth, and it became lice in man, and in beast; all the dust of the land became lice throughout all the land of Egypt.

EXO.8:19 Then the magicians said unto Pharaoh, This is the finger of God: and Pharaoh's heart was hardened, and he hearkened not unto them; as the LORD had said.

EXO.8:20 And the LORD said unto Moses, Rise up early in the morning, and stand before Pharaoh; lo, he cometh forth to the water; and say unto him, Thus saith the LORD, Let my people go, that they may serve me.

EXO.8:21 Else, if thou wilt not let my people go, behold, I will send swarms of flies upon thee, and upon thy servants, and upon thy people, and into thy houses: and the houses of the Egyptians shall be full of swarms of flies, and also the ground whereon they are.

EXO.8:24 And the LORD did so; and there came a grievous swarm of flies into the house of Pharaoh, and into his servants' houses, and into all the land of Egypt: the land was corrupted by reason of the swarm of flies.

EXO.8:28 And Pharaoh said, I will let you go, that ye may sacrifice to the LORD your God in the wilderness; only ye shall not go very far away: intreat for me.

EXO.8:29 And Moses said, Behold, I go out from thee, and I will intreat the LORD that the swarms of flies may depart from Pharaoh, from his servants, and from his people, tomorrow: but let not Pharaoh deal deceitfully any more in not letting the people go to sacrifice to the LORD.

EXO.8:32 And Pharaoh hardened his heart at this time also, neither would he let the people go.

EXO.9:6 And the LORD did that thing on the morrow, and all the cattle of Egypt died: but of the cattle of the children of Israel died not one.

EXO.9:10 And they took ashes of the furnace, and stood before Pharaoh; and Moses sprinkled it up toward heaven; and it became a boil breaking forth with blains upon man, and upon beast.

EXO.9:11 And the magicians could not stand before Moses because of the boils; for the boil was upon the magicians, and upon all the Egyptians.

EXO.9:12 And the LORD hardened the heart of Pharaoh, and he hearkened not unto them; as the LORD had spoken unto Moses.

EXO.9:23 And Moses stretched forth his rod toward heaven: and the LORD sent thunder and hail, and the fire ran along upon the ground; and the LORD rained hail upon the land of Egypt.

EXO.9:24 So there was hail, and fire mingled with the hail, very grievous, such as there was none like it in all the land of Egypt since it became a nation.

EXO.9:25 And the hail smote throughout all the land of Egypt all that was in the field, both man and beast; and the hail smote every herb of the field, and brake every tree of the field.

EXO.9:26 Only in the land of Goshen, where the children of Israel were, was there no hail.

EXO.9:35 And the heart of Pharaoh was hardened, neither would he let the children of Israel go; as the LORD had spoken by Moses.

EXO.10:13 And Moses stretched forth his rod over the land of Egypt, and the LORD brought an east wind upon the land all that day, and all that night; and when it was morning, the east wind brought the locusts.

EXO.10:14 And the locust went up over all the land of Egypt, and rested in all the coasts of Egypt: very grievous were they; before them there were no such locusts as they, neither after them shall be such.

EXO.10:15 For they covered the face of the whole earth, so that the land was darkened; and they did eat every herb of the land, and all the fruit of the trees which the hail had left: and there remained not any green thing in the trees, or in the herbs of the field, through all the land of Egypt.

EXO.10:22 And Moses stretched forth his hand toward heaven; and there was a thick darkness in all the land of Egypt three days:

EXO.10:23 They saw not one another, neither rose any from his place for three days: but all the children of Israel had light in their dwellings

EXO.11:4 And Moses said, Thus saith the LORD, About midnight will I go out into the midst of Egypt:

EXO.11:5 And all the firstborn in the land of Egypt shall die, from the first born of Pharaoh that sitteth upon his throne, even unto the firstborn of the maidservant that is behind the mill; and all the firstborn of beasts.

EXO.11:6 And there shall be a great cry throughout all the land of Egypt, such as there was none like it, nor shall be like it anymore.

EXO.11:7 But against any of the children of Israel shall not a dog move his tongue, against man or beast: that ye may know how that the LORD doth put a difference between the Egyptians and Israel.

EXO.11:8 And all these thy servants shall come down unto me, and bow down themselves unto me, saying, Get thee out, and all the people that follow thee: and after that I will go out. And he went out from Pharaoh in a great anger.

EXO.12:29 And it came to pass, that at midnight the LORD smote all the firstborn in the land of Egypt, from the firstborn of Pharaoh that sat on his throne unto the firstborn of the captive that was in the dungeon; and all the firstborn of cattle.

EXO.12:30 And Pharaoh rose up in the night, he, and all his servants, and all the Egyptians; and there was a great cry in Egypt; for there was not a house where there was not one dead.

EXO.12:31 And he called for Moses and Aaron by night, and said, Rise up, and get you forth from among my people, both ye and the children of Israel; and go, serve the LORD, as ye have said.

EXO.12:32 Also take your flocks and your herds, as ye have said, and be gone; and bless me also.

EXO.12:33 And the Egyptians were urgent upon the people, that they might send them out of the land in haste; for they said, We be all dead men.

---

9 And the Lord did everything for Israel's sake, and according to His covenant, which he had ordained with Abraham that He would take vengeance on them as they had brought them by force into bondage.

10 And the prince Mastema stood up against thee and sought to cast thee into the hands of Pharaoh, and he helped the Egyptian sorcerers, and they stood up and wrought before thee the evils indeed we permitted them to work, but the remedies we did not allow to be wrought by their hands.

C.14 What I like especially about this Book of Jubilees is how the workings of God and the supernatural as well as Satan and the spirit world, are brought out much more than in most other books, including the Bible itself. I find that the Jewish Books of both Jubilees and Jasher really fill in a lot of the gaps of things not fully explained in the K.J.V. of the Bible.

C.15 This above verse says a lot! 1) It is stating that Satan personally took a stand against Moses when he challenged Pharaoh. Why? Because Satan is a sort of 'King of the Empires' of mankind. He obviously felt threatened by both Moses and God's power as manifested through Moses and his brother Aaron! 2) It answers the question that I brought up earlier in this very chapter as to why Pharaohs magicians were dumb enough to use their supernatural powers to cause even more frogs to appear? Because Satan himself was there in person directing the sorcerers.3) The angel is telling Moses that God only allowed Satan to do so much damage, but that Satan's sorcerers couldn't heal and undo the evil that they had created, whilst God through Moses could heal!

11 And the Lord smote them with malignant ulcers, and they were not able to stand, for we destroyed them so that they could not perform a single sign.

12 And notwithstanding all (these) signs and wonders the prince Mastema was not put to shame because he took courage and cried to the Egyptians to pursue after thee with all the powers of the Egyptians, with their chariots, and with their horses, and with all the hosts of the peoples of Egypt.

C.16 Mastema is not put to shame yet despite all the miracles which God performed against Pharaoh. He now still had the chance to pursue after the Israelites. Satan is totally blind to reality and can't see his inevitable downfall. The truth be known, God has been countering Satan for thousands of years, and always ends up out-manoeuvring Satan every single time? Why is Satan so blind to this fact - that he cannot win fighting against God, as he is merely a creation of God and not God himself? He is totally insane and the 'truth' in Satan's mind is 'whatever he says it is', at any given moment of time.

13 And I stood between the Egyptians and Israel, and we delivered Israel out of his hand, and out of the hand of his people, and the Lord brought them through the midst of the sea as if it were dry land.

14 And all the peoples whom he brought to pursue after Israel, the Lord our God cast them into the midst of the sea, into the depths of the abyss beneath the children of Israel, even as the people of Egypt had cast their children into the river He took vengeance on 1,000,000 of them, and one thousand strong and energetic men were destroyed on account

of one suckling of the children of thy people which they had thrown into the river.

EXO.14:5 And it was told the king of Egypt that the people fled: and the heart of Pharaoh and of his servants was turned against the people, and they said, Why have we done this, that we have let Israel go from serving us?

EXO.14:6 And he made ready his chariot, and took his people with him:

EXO.14:7 And he took six hundred chosen chariots, and all the chariots of Egypt, and captains over every one of them.

EXO.14:8 And the LORD hardened the heart of Pharaoh king of Egypt, and he pursued after the children of Israel: and the children of Israel went out with an high hand.

EXO.14:9 But the Egyptians pursued after them, all the horses and chariots of Pharaoh, and his horsemen, and his army, and overtook them encamping by the sea, beside Pihahiroth, before Baalzephon.

EXO.14:10 And when Pharaoh drew nigh, the children of Israel lifted up their eyes, and, behold, the Egyptians marched after them; and they were sore afraid: and the children of Israel cried out unto the LORD.

EXO.14:19 And the angel of God, which went before the camp of Israel, removed and went behind them; and the pillar of the cloud went from before their face, and stood behind them:

EXO.14:20 And it came between the camp of the Egyptians and the camp of Israel; and it was a cloud and darkness to them, but it gave light by night to these: so that the one came not near the other all the night.

EXO.14:21 And Moses stretched out his hand over the sea; and the LORD caused the sea to go back by a strong east wind all that night, and made the sea dry land, and the waters were divided.

EXO.14:22 And the children of Israel went into the midst of the sea upon the dry ground: and the waters were a wall unto them on their right hand, and on their left.

EXO.14:23 And the Egyptians pursued, and went in after them to the midst of the sea, even all Pharaoh's horses, his chariots, and his horsemen.

EXO.14:24 And it came to pass, that in the morning watch the LORD looked unto the host of the Egyptians through the pillar of fire and of the cloud, and troubled the host of the Egyptians,

EXO.14:25 And took off their chariot wheels, that they drave them heavily: so that the Egyptians said, Let us flee from the face of Israel; for the LORD fighteth for them against the Egyptians.

EXO.14:26 And the LORD said unto Moses, Stretch out thine hand over the sea, that the waters may come again upon the Egyptians, upon their chariots, and upon their horsemen.

EXO.14:27 And Moses stretched forth his hand over the sea, and the sea returned to his strength when the morning appeared; and the Egyptians fled against it; and the LORD overthrew the Egyptians in the midst of the sea.

EXO.14:28 And the waters returned, and covered the chariots, and the horsemen, and all the host of Pharaoh that came into the sea after them; there remained not so much as one of them.

EXO.14:29 But the children of Israel walked upon dry land in the midst of the sea; and the waters were a wall unto them on their right hand, and on their left.

EXO.14:30 Thus the LORD saved Israel that day out of the hand of the Egyptians; and Israel saw the Egyptians dead upon the seashore.

EXO.14:31 And Israel saw that great work which the LORD did upon the Egyptians: and the people feared the LORD, and believed the LORD, and his servant Moses.

---

15 And on the fourteenth day and on the fifteenth and on the sixteenth and on the seventeenth and on the eighteenth the prince Mastema was bound and imprisoned behind the children of Israel that he might not accuse them.

C.17 '*Prince Mastema was bound and imprisoned behind the children of Israel that he might not accuse them'*.

This reminds of a verse in the Book of Revelations:

REV.12:10 And I heard a loud voice saying in heaven, Now is come salvation, and strength, and the kingdom of our God, and the power of his Christ: for the accuser of our brethren is cast down, which accused them before our God day and night.

REV.20:2 And he laid hold on the dragon, that old serpent, which is the Devil, and Satan, and **bound him** a thousand years,

---

16 And on the nineteenth we let them loose that they might help the Egyptians and pursue the children of Israel.

17 And he hardened their hearts and made them stubborn, and the device was devised by the Lord our God that He might smite the Egyptians and cast them into the sea.

18 And on the fourteenth we bound him that he might not accuse the children of Israel on the day when they asked the Egyptians for

---

vessels and garments, vessels of silver, and vessels of gold, and vessels of bronze, in order to despoil the Egyptians in return for the bondage in which they had forced them to serve.

19 And we did not lead forth the children of Israel from Egypt empty handed.

C.18 Here we see clearly the workings behind the veil of the spirit world, where Satan is bound, imprisoned and restricted, being the 'mad dog' that he is. He is imprisoned by God Himself behind the Israelites who are trapped at the seashore. One day 'mad-dog' Mastema (Satan) will be locked up for good and gotten rid of:

REV.20:1 And I saw an angel come down from heaven, having the key of the bottomless pit and a great chain in his hand.

REV.20:2 And he laid hold on the dragon, that old serpent, which is the Devil, and Satan, and bound him a thousand years,

REV.20:3 And cast him into the bottomless pit, and shut him up, and set a seal upon him, that he should deceive the nations no more, till the thousand years should be fulfilled: and after that he must be loosed a little season.

Chapter 49

1 Remember the commandment which the Lord commanded thee concerning the Passover, that thou should celebrate it in its season on the fourteenth of the first month, that thou should kill it before it is evening, and that they should eat it by night on the evening of the fifteenth from the time of the setting of the sun.

2 For on this night - the beginning of the festival and the beginning of the joy - ye were eating the Passover in Egypt, when all the powers of Mastema had been let loose to slay all the first-born in the land of Egypt, from the first-born of Pharaoh to the first-born of the captive maid-servant in the mill, and to the cattle.

Comment:1: This is interesting as in the Bible it states that it was the 'angel of the Lord' that 'Passed over' the houses of the Egyptians. Here however it is stating that it was Satan and his forces. So, which was it?

EXO.12:29 And it came to pass, that at midnight the LORD smote all the firstborn in the land of Egypt, from the firstborn of Pharaoh that sat on his throne unto the firstborn of the captive that was in the dungeon; and all the firstborn of cattle.

C.2 Satan is certainly one of the 'Angels of Death' or the 'Grim Reaper':

REV.6:8 And I looked and behold a pale horse: and his name that sat on him was Death, and Hell followed with him. And power was given unto them over the fourth part of the earth, to kill with sword, and with hunger, and with death, and with the beasts of the earth.

C.3 Does God upon occasion use the dark side of the spirit world to carry out His will? Yes, he does, as evidenced many times in the Bible. Mastema or Satan was hoping that through Pharaoh he would be able to kill all the first born of Israel as that was Pharaoh's decree. However, God turned Pharaoh's decree against him, and turned it into a self-proclaimed curse upon the Egyptians instead. Satan is a monster who likes to destroy God's creation one way or the other, and he is frequently coming before the throne of God to get permission to 'accuse and condemn and judge people'. Sometimes he is given permission as clearly shown in the story of Job:

JOB.1:6 Now there was a day when the sons of God came to present themselves before the LORD, and Satan came also among them.

JOB.1:7 And the LORD said unto Satan, Whence came thou? Then Satan answered the LORD, and said, From going to and fro in the earth, and from walking up and down in it.

JOB.1:8 And the LORD said unto Satan, Hast thou considered my servant Job, that there is none like him in the earth, a perfect and an upright man, one that fears God, and hates evil?

JOB.1:9 Then Satan answered the LORD, and said, Doth Job fear God for nought?

JOB.1:10 Hast not thou made an hedge about him, and about his house, and about all that he hath on every side? thou hast blessed the work of his hands, and his substance is increased in the land.

JOB.1:11 But put forth thine hand now, and touch all that he hath, and he will curse thee to thy face.

JOB.1:12 And the LORD said unto Satan, Behold, all that he hath is in thy power; only upon himself put not forth thine hand. So Satan went forth from the presence of the LORD.

---

3 And this is the sign which the Lord gave them: Into every house on the lintels of which they saw the blood of a lamb of the first year, into (that) house they should not enter to slay, but should pass by (it), that all those should be saved that were in the house because the sign of the blood was on its lintels.

4 And the powers of the Lord did everything according as the Lord commanded them, and they passed by all the children of Israel, and the plague came not upon them to destroy from amongst them any soul either of cattle, or man, or dog.

5 And the plague was very grievous in Egypt, and there was no house in Egypt where there was not one dead and weeping and lamentation.

6 And all Israel was eating the flesh of the paschal lamb, and drinking the wine, and was lauding, and blessing, and giving thanks to the Lord God of their fathers, and was ready to go forth from under the yoke of Egypt, and from the evil bondage.

C.4 *'Paschal lamb'* It is interesting to note in reading the New Testament that Jesus who is also known as the 'Lamb of God who taketh away all the sins of the world' This phrase was spoken by John the Baptist at the very beginning of Jesus ministry on earth. Three years later he was crucified on the very same weekend that the Jews in Israel were sacrificing the Paschal Lamb. In modern times we know Paschal as meaning Easter. When John the Baptist referred to Jesus as the "Lamb of God who takes away the sin of the world" (John 1:29), the Jews who heard him might have immediately thought of any one of several important sacrifices. Every morning and evening, a lamb was sacrificed in the temple for the sins of the people.

EXO.29:42 This shall be a continual burnt offering throughout your generations at the door of the tabernacle of the congregation before the LORD: where I will meet you, to speak there unto thee.

(For more info see **Exodus 29:38-42**)

C.5 Why is it that in general Jewish Christians no longer hold to all the old laws of the Temple as mentioned above? This is because Christians see that Jesus fulfilled the whole law of sacrifice by sacrificing himself on the cross for the sins of the whole world and there it was no longer necessary to keep the tradition of the Lamb sacrifice as the real Lamb of God had already been slaughtered for the sins of the whole world. Jesus in dying on the cross for the sins of the whole world fulfilled the entire Jewish laws. I would go further and state as it does in the Book of Acts

ACT.7:48 Howbeit the Most High dwelleth not in temples made with hands; as saith the prophet.

---

7 And remember thou this day all the days of thy life and observe it from year to year all the days of thy life, once a year, on its day, according to all the law thereof, and do not adjourn (it) from day to day, or from month to month.

8 For it is an eternal ordinance, and engraven on the heavenly tablets regarding all the children of Israel that they should observe it every year on its day once a year, throughout all their generations; and there is no limit of days, for this is ordained for ever.

9 And the man who is free from uncleanness, and does not come to observe it on occasion of its day, so as to bring an acceptable offering before the Lord, and to eat and to drink before the Lord on the day of its festival, that man who is clean and close at hand shall be cut off: because he offered not the oblation of the Lord in its appointed season, he shall take the guilt upon himself.

10 Let the children of Israel come and observe the Passover on the day of its fixed time, on the fourteenth day of the first month, between the evenings, from the third part of the day to the third part of 1 the night, for two portions of the day are given to the light, and a third part to the evening.

---

11 This is that which the Lord commanded thee that thou should observe it between the evenings.

12 And it is not permissible to slay it during any period of the light, but during the period bordering on the evening, and let them eat it at the time of the evening, until the third part of the night, and whatever is left over of all its flesh from the third part of the night and onwards, let them burn it with fire.

13 And they shall not cook it with water, nor shall they eat it raw, but roast on the fire: they shall eat it with diligence, its head with the inwards thereof and its feet they shall roast with fire, and not break any bone thereof; for of the children of Israel no bone shall be crushed.

14 For this reason the Lord commanded the children of Israel to observe the Passover on the day of its fixed time, and they shall not break a bone thereof; for it is a festival day, and a day commanded, and there may be no passing over from day to day, and month to month, but on the day of its festival let it be observed.

15 And do thou command the children of Israel to observe the Passover throughout their days, every year, once a year on the day of its fixed time, and it shall come for a memorial well pleasing before the Lord, and no plague shall come upon them to slay or to smite in that year in which they celebrate the Passover in its season in every respect according to His command.

16 And they shall not eat it outside the sanctuary of the Lord, but before the sanctuary of the Lord, and all the people of the congregation of Israel shall celebrate it in its appointed season.

17 And every man who has come upon its day shall eat it in the sanctuary of your God before the Lord from twenty years old and upward; for thus is it written and ordained that they should eat it in the sanctuary of the Lord.

18 And when the children of Israel come into the land which they are to possess, into the land of Canaan, and set up the tabernacle of the

> Lord in the midst of the land in one of their tribes until the sanctuary of the Lord has been built in the land, let them come and celebrate the Passover in the midst of the tabernacle of the Lord, and let them slay it before the Lord from year to year.

C.6 After Moses brought the nation of Israel out of Egypt, God commanded Israel to enter the Promised land and go to **Shechem** to pronounce the blessings and the curses of the Mosaic Covenant on the nation **(Deut.27:4)**. Joshua did this, and dividing the nation, "Half of them stood in front of Mount Gerizim and half of them in front of Mount Ebal" **Josh.8:33)**. From Mount Ebal, they shouted the curses if they disobeyed the law, and from Mount Gerizim, they shouted the blessings if they obeyed. And there on Mount Ebal, Joshua built an altar to God, and on a pillar of stones he wrote a copy of the law **(Joshua.8:30-35)**.

> 19 And in the days when the house has been built in the name of the Lord in the land of their inheritance, they shall go there and slay the Passover in the evening, at sunset, at the third part of the day.
>
> 20 And they shall offer its blood on the threshold of the altar, and shall place its fat on the fire which is upon the altar, and they shall eat its flesh roasted with fire in the court of the house which has been sanctified in the name of the Lord.
>
> 21 And they may not celebrate the Passover in their cities, nor in any place save before the tabernacle of the Lord, or before His house where His name hath dwelt; and they shall not go astray from the Lord.
>
> 22 And do thou, Moses, command the children of Israel to observe the ordinances of the Passover as it was commanded unto thee; declare thou unto them every year and the day of its days, and the festival of unleavened bread, that they should eat unleavened bread seven days, (and) that they should observe its festival, and that they bring an oblation every day during those seven days of joy before the Lord on the altar of your God.
>
> 23 For ye celebrated this festival with haste when ye went forth from Egypt till ye entered into the wilderness of Shur; for on the shore of the sea ye completed it.

C.7 SUMMARY: Jesus did away with all the Old laws. How could He do that? Because He was the one who gave the laws in the first place. After Jesus died for the sins of the whole world, it was no longer necessary to have the symbols of the 'coming LAMB OF GOD', as He had already come and died for all of mankind. Today we no longer must worship God in any given temples. Temples and traditions are passed away. Finished. No longer needed. Why? Jesus himself said this in the Story of the Samaritan woman at the well:

JOH.4:20 Our fathers worshipped in this mountain; and ye say, that in Jerusalem is the place where men ought to worship.

JOH.4:21 Jesus saith unto her, Woman, believe me, the hour cometh, when ye shall neither in this mountain, nor yet at Jerusalem, worship the Father.

JOH.4:22 Ye worship ye know not what: we know what we worship: for salvation is of the Jews.

JOH.4:23 But the hour cometh, and now is, when the true worshippers shall worship the Father in spirit and in truth: for the Father seeks such to worship him.

JOH.4:24 God is a Spirit: and they that worship him must worship him in spirit and in truth

C.8 Having said that we no longer need temples: On the other hand, if certain temples help people to get together and worship God, then that is fine. However, none of us are limited any longer to temples. We can worship God any place, and anytime in spirit and in truth.

Chapter 50

1 And after this law I made known to thee the days of the Sabbaths in the desert of Sin[ai], which is between Elim and Sinai.

2 And I told thee of the Sabbaths of the land on Mount Sinai, and I told thee of the jubilee years in the sabbaths of years: but the year thereof have I not told thee till ye enter the land which ye are to possess.

3 And the land also shall keep its sabbaths while they dwell upon it, and they shall know the jubilee year.

4 Wherefore I have ordained for thee the year-weeks and the years and the jubilees: there are forty-nine jubilees from the days of Adam until this day, [2410 A.M. = **'Anno Mundi' = years of the world**] and one week and two years: and there are yet forty years to come (lit. 'distant') for learning the [2450 A.M.] commandments of the Lord, until they pass over into the land of Canaan, crossing the Jordan to the west.

5 And the jubilees shall pass by, until Israel is cleansed from all guilt of fornication, and uncleanness, and pollution, and sin, and error, and dwells with confidence in all the land, and there shall be no more a Satan or any evil one, and the land shall be clean from that time for evermore.

Comment:1: *'No more Satan'*. When does Satan get locked up? When does he finally get permanently eliminated forever?

REV.20:1 And I saw an angel come down from heaven, having the key of the bottomless pit and a great chain in his hand.

REV.20:2 And he laid hold on the dragon, that old serpent, which is the Devil, and Satan, and bound him a thousand years,

REV.20:3 And cast him into the bottomless pit, and shut him up, and set a seal upon him, that he should deceive the nations no more, till the thousand years should be fulfilled: and after that he must be loosed a little season.

REV.20:7 And when the thousand years are expired, Satan shall be loosed out of his prison,

REV.20:8 And shall go out to deceive the nations which are in the four quarters of the earth, Gog, and Magog, to gather them together to battle: the number of whom is as the sand of the sea.

REV.20:9 And they went up on the breadth of the earth, and compassed the camp of the saints about, and the beloved city: and fire came down from God out of heaven and devoured them.

REV.20:10 And the Devil that deceived them was cast into the lake of fire and brimstone, where the beast and the false prophet are, and shall be tormented day and night for ever and ever!

---

6 And behold the commandment regarding the Sabbaths, I have written (them) down for thee and all the judgments of its laws.

7 Six days shalt thou labour, but on the seventh day is the Sabbath of the Lord your God.

8 In it ye shall do no manner of work, ye and your sons, and your menservants and your maidservants, and all your cattle and the sojourner also who is with you.

9 And the man that does any work on it shall die: whoever desecrates that day, whoever lies with (his) wife, or whoever says he will do something on it, that he will set out on a journey thereon in regard to any buying or selling: and whoever draws water thereon which he had not prepared for himself on the sixth day, and whoever takes up any burden to carry it out of his tent or out of his house shall die.

C.2 God created everything in six days, and He rested on the seventh. He expects us to take a day each week to spend especially in His Word and in prayer; but it does not have to be a tradition that it has to be a Sunday (Christians) Saturday (Jews) Friday (Muslims). God is no longer limited by traditions of man or even by his old Mosaic laws, which were done away with and finished with the arrival of the Messiah. According to Jesus, you don't even have to worship God in a Temple anymore:

ACT.7:48 Howbeit the Most High dwelleth not in temples made with hands; as saith the prophet,

ACT.7:49 Heaven is my throne, and earth is my footstool: what house will ye build me? saith the Lord: or what is the place of my rest?

JOH.4:21 Jesus saith unto her, Woman, believe me, the hour cometh, when ye shall neither in this mountain, nor yet at Jerusalem, worship the Father.

JOH.4:23 But the hour cometh, and now is, when the true worshippers shall worship the Father in spirit and in truth: for the Father seeks such to worship him.

JOH.4:24 God is a Spirit: and they that worship him must worship him in spirit and in truth.

C.3 Jesus the Messiah simplified the Laws of Moses down to just two laws:

MAT.22:37 Jesus said unto him, Thou shalt love the Lord thy God with all thy heart, and with all thy soul, and with all thy mind.

MAT.22:38 This is the first and great commandment.

MAT.22:39 And the second is like unto it, Thou shalt love thy neighbour as thyself.

MAT.22:40 On these two commandments hang all the law and the prophets.

C.4 Jesus came to fulfil all the laws of Moses and the prophets

MAT.5:17 Think not that I am come to destroy the law, or the prophets: I am not come to destroy, but to fulfil.

MAT.5:18 For verily I say unto you, Till heaven and earth pass, one jot or one tittle shall in no wise pass from the law, till all be fulfilled.

MAT.5:19 Whosoever therefore shall break one of these least commandments, and shall teach men so, he shall be called the least in the kingdom of heaven: but whosoever shall do and teach them, the same shall be called great in the kingdom of heaven.

C.5 Old laws and traditions were done away with the arrival of the Messiah:

MAT.19:8 He saith unto them, Moses because of the hardness of your hearts suffered you to put away your wives: but from the beginning it was not so.

MAR.7:13 Making the word of God of none effect through your tradition, which ye have delivered: and many such like things do ye.

2CO.3:6 Not of the letter (of the law), but of the spirit: for the letter (of the law) kills, but the spirit giveth life.

---

10 Ye shall do no work whatever on the Sabbath day save what ye have prepared for yourselves on the sixth day, so as to eat, and drink, and rest, and keep Sabbath from all work on that day, and to bless the Lord your God, who has given you a day of festival and a holy day: and a day of the holy kingdom for all Israel is this day among their days for ever.

11 For great is the honour which the Lord has given to Israel that they

---

should eat and drink and be satisfied on this festival day, and rest thereon from all labour which belongs to the labour of the children of men save burning frankincense and bringing oblations and sacrifices before the Lord for days and for Sabbaths.

12 This work alone shall be done on the Sabbath-days in the sanctuary of the Lord your God; that they may atone for Israel with sacrifice continually from day to day for a memorial well-pleasing before the Lord, and that He may receive them always from day to day according as thou hast been commanded.

13 And every man who does any work thereon, or goes a journey, or tills (his) farm, whether in his house or any other place, and whoever lights a fire, or rides on any beast, or travels by ship on the sea, and whoever strikes or kills anything, or slaughters a beast or a bird, or whoever catches an animal or a bird or a fish, or whoever fasts or makes war on the Sabbaths:

14 The man who does any of these things on the Sabbath shall die, so that the children of Israel shall observe the Sabbaths according to the commandments regarding the Sabbaths of the land, as it is written in the tablets, which He gave into my hands that I should write out for thee the laws of the seasons, and the seasons according to the division of their days.

C.6 Anyone not observing the Sabbath shall die? Now that really sounds crazy! What did the apostle Stephen say about some of these so-called laws supposedly given by Moses: According to the Apostle Stephen some of the old restrictive laws of the Jews were not given by God at all but became traditions by which the hierarchy of the Religionists used to keep the people in bondage through fear.

ACT.7:53 Who have received the law by the disposition of angels (fallen angels) and have not kept it.

C.7 To understand the severity of the Laws of Moses, one would have had to have lived in the times of Moses. The Israelites had just come out of the land of the Egyptians, where the Pharaoh could have someone killed 'on a whim'. Israel was coming out of a nation that was entrenched in Satanism, great witchcraft and idolatry, so at that particular time, God had to be very severe with His laws, at least for a season until Israel could learn not to live the ways of the Egyptians or the Canaanites who both were both idol worshippers. As stated in this very chapter verse 5: *'until Israel is cleansed from all*

351

guilt of fornication, and uncleanness, and pollution, and sin, and error, and dwells with confidence in all the land, and there shall be no more a Satan or any evil one, and the land shall be clean from that time for evermore.' The truth be stated only Jesus, the Christ can cleanse us all from our sins. When Jesus died on the cross, he both defeated Satan and did away with the Old Mosaic Laws in paying for the sins of the whole world on the cross.

HEB.10:1 For the law having a shadow of good things to come, and not the very image of the things, can never with those sacrifices which they offered year by year continually make the comers thereunto perfect.

HEB.10:4 For it is not possible that the blood of bulls and of goats should take away sins.

HEB.10:8 Above when he said, Sacrifice and offering and burnt offerings and offering for sin thou would not, neither hadst pleasure therein; which are offered by the law;

HEB.10:10 By the which will we are sanctified through the offering of the body of Jesus Christ once for all.

SALVATION

JOH.3:36 He that believeth on the Son hath everlasting life: and he that believeth not the Son shall not see life; but the wrath of God abides on him.

Finally, I challenge you, that if you have not already prayed to receive Jesus into your heart, so that you can have eternal life, & be guaranteed an eternal place in Heaven, then please do so immediately, to keep you safe from what is soon coming upon the earth!

Revelations 3.20 "Behold, I stand at the door and knock, if any man hears my voice, and open the door, I will come into him and live with him and him with me".

John 3.36. "He who believes on the Son of God **has eternal life**." - That means right now!

1JN.1:9 If we confess our sins, he is faithful and just to forgive us our sins, and to cleanse us from all unrighteousness.

Once saved, you are eternally saved, and here is a very simple prayer to help you to get saved: -

"Dear Jesus,

Please come into my heart, forgive me all my sins, give me eternal life, and fill me with your Holy Spirit. Please help me to love others and to read the Word of God in Jesus name, Amen.

Once you've prayed that little prayer sincerely, then you are guaranteed a wonderful future in Heaven for eternity with your creator and loved ones.

1 John 4.16 "For God is Love"

As I mentioned earlier in this book, your Salvation does not depend on you going to church, and your good works.

Titus 3.5 "Not by works of righteousness which we have done, but according to His mercy he saved us".

Your salvation only depends on receiving Christ as your saviour, not on church or religion!

John 14.6 'I am the Way, the Truth and the Life, no man cometh unto the Father but by me

ACT.4:12 Neither is there salvation in any other: for there is none other name under heaven given among men, whereby we must be saved.

John 3.3 Jesus explained that unless you become as a child you won't even understand the Kingdom of Heaven.

"He that comes unto Me, **I will in no wise cast out»- Jesus**

MORE ON SALVATION: http://www.outofthebottomlesspit.co.uk/418605189

APPENDIX

I CH 3: THE STORY OF THE SERPENT ON EARTH: FROM THE BEGINNING TO THE END.

JASHER 3.17-18 And after the completion of the seven years, which he had completed there, seven years exactly, [**8 A.M. = ANNO MUNDI =YEARS AFTER CREATION**] and in the second month, on the seventeenth day (of the month), the **serpent** came and approached the woman, and the serpent said to the woman, 'Hath God commanded you, saying, 'Ye shall not eat of every tree of the garden?' And she said to it, 'Of all the fruit of the trees of the garden God hath said unto us, Eat; but of the fruit of the tree which is in the midst of the garden God hath said unto us, Ye shall not eat thereof, neither shall ye touch it, lest ye die.'

Comment:1: Here is given information that is not in the Bible in that it specifies the exact date that Satan entered into human life on the earth: *'After seven years, which he had completed there, seven years exactly, [8 A.M.] and in the second month, on the seventeenth day (of the month'*

As one can see from the following Bible verse the *Great Flood* and *Judgement of God* happened on *exactly same day* that *Satan entered human life* and tempted Eve and both Adam and Eve fell, and sin had entered into the pristine life on earth. That is the same day, but 1500 years later:

GEN.7:11 In the six hundredth year of Noah's life, in the *second month*, the seventeenth day of the month, the *same day* were all the *fountains of the great deep broken up*, and the windows of heaven were opened.

C.2 Here we have some new information in this *Book of Jubilees*: Consider, why did Satan enter human life and corrupt Eve on the specific date of: **7** years after Adam and Eve were place in the Garden of Eden: In the **2nd** month and on exactly the **17th** day of the month? We find out in looking at the Genesis story of the Great Flood that it also happened when Noah was exactly **600** years old: in the 2nd month and on the **17th** day of the month.

God is **very exact** when it comes to both **creation** and **numerology** whether Man wants to believe it or not.

Conclusion: Satan originally ruined mankind's relationship to God in bringing *disobedience* and *rebellion* into the physical realm on a **specific date**: God in return brought His great judgements of all the fruit of Evil produced by both Satan, his Fallen Angels and disobedient mankind with the Great Flood of Noah on the **anniversary of the exact same date** that **Evil** first entered the **Garden of Eden**.

C.3 This shows that exact dates, times and seasons *are* important to God, as stated so well in my other book '**Ezdras Insights**':

II EZDRAS 6.1 And he said unto me, 'At the beginning of the **circle** of the earth, before the **portals** of the world were in place, and before the assembled winds blew.

II EZDRAS 6.6 Then I planned these things, and they were made through me and not another, just as the end shall come through Me and not another.

C.4 Looking at Biblical Numerology at the exact age of Noah at the time of the Great Flood i.e. **600** years old: **6** is the number of a man: **60** is an absolute number of creation as in **60** seconds; **60** minutes etc **10** is the number of 'Completion' or of 'The Law'. Noah being exactly 600 at the time of the Great Flood, God was making a statement: 'Because of man's sins judgement is enacted at the **appointed exact time'**.

C.5 Why does it state that the Serpent came into the Garden after Adam and Eve had been in the Garden of Eden for exactly **7** years? 7 is God's number and He obviously gave Adam and Eve 7 years of Grace without being tempted by Evil. This proves that God can withhold Evil from the world if He so wishes, until it is His perfect time for Evil to overcome the world because of the sins of the world.

2 TH.2:7 For the mystery of iniquity doth already work: only he who now lets will let, until he be taken out of the way.

C.6 What is the meaning of *'he who now lets will let'?* This is talking about an angel who 'holds back' the 'flood-tide of iniquity' in the End of Days.

However, there is a time limit to God's mercy and grace. When the world has become as wicked as it was before the Great Flood, then Great Judgements will soon follow, starting with the **Rise of the Anti-Christ**, The **Image of the Beast**, the **Mark of the Beast** during the **Great Tribulation**, followed by the **Wrath of God and Armageddon.**

2 TH.2:8 And then shall that Wicked be revealed, whom the Lord shall consume with the spirit of his mouth, and shall destroy with the brightness of his coming:

2 TH.2:9 Even him, whose coming is after the working of Satan with all power and signs and lying wonders,

2 TH.2:10 And with all deceivableness of unrighteousness in them that perish; because they received not the love of the truth, that they might be saved.

2 TH.2:12 That they all might be damned who believed not the truth but had pleasure in unrighteousness.

2 TH.2:11 And for this cause God shall send them strong delusion, that they should believe a lie*:

C.7 The lie that the Anti-Christ (Possessed by Satan) is god and should be worshipped like an *idol* and all on earth should be branded with his Mark of 666

REV.13:16 And he causes all, both small and great, rich and poor, free and bond, to receive a mark in their right hand, or in their foreheads:

REV.13:17 And that no man might buy or sell, save he that had the mark, or the name of the beast, or the number of his name.

REV.13:18 Here is wisdom. Let him that hath understanding count the number of the beast (666): for it is the number of a man; and his number is Six hundred threescore and six.

REV.19:20 And the beast was taken, and with him the false prophet that wrought miracles before him, with which he deceived them that had received the mark of the beast, and them that worshipped his image. These both were cast alive into a lake of fire burning with brimstone.

REV.19:21 And the remnant were slain with the sword of him that sat upon the horse, which sword proceeded out of his mouth: and all the fowls were filled with their flesh.

REV.20:2 And he laid hold on the dragon, that old serpent, which is the Devil, and Satan, and bound him a thousand years,

REV.20:3 And cast him into the bottomless pit, and shut him up, and set a seal upon him, that he should deceive the nations no more, till the thousand years should be fulfilled: and after that he must be loosed a little season.

REV.20:7 And when the thousand years are expired, Satan shall be loosed out of his prison,

REV.20:8 And shall go out to deceive the nations which are in the four quarters of the earth, Gog, and Magog, to gather them together to battle: the number of whom is as the sand of the sea.

REV.20:9 And they went up on the breadth of the earth, and compassed the camp of the saints about, and the beloved city: and fire came down from God out of heaven and devoured them.

REV.20:10 And the Devil that deceived them was cast into the lake of fire and brimstone, where the beast and the false prophet are, and shall be tormented day and night for ever and ever.

❚❚ CH 4: DOES THE EARTH HAVE A SPIRIT?

GEN.4:11 And now art thou cursed from the earth, which hath **opened her mouth** to receive thy brother's blood from thy hand.

Why is this strange expression used in this verse '**earth opened her mouth**'. That can't possibly be literal, can it? There is another example of this in the Book of Revelations:

REV.12:15 And the serpent cast out of his mouth water as a flood after the woman, that he might cause her to be carried away of the flood.

REV.12:16 And the **earth helped the woman**, and the **earth opened her mouth**, and

swallowed up the flood which the dragon cast out of his mouth.

The above expressions are very strange. They are speaking as if the earth itself is a live entity. I am sure that most of us think it is just very expressive language. But is that all to it, or does the earth itself actually have a spirit?

There are many people on this planet that actually do believe that the earth has a spirit. The ancient Greeks called it Gaia. In the last 'Insights book', that I wrote which was called **Jasher Insights**.

In that book taken from the ancient Jewish book of Jasher it also stated that the Earth is alive and actually helped the children that were born to the Israelites when they were living in Egypt. Pharaoh had order the execution of all the baby boys. It states in the Book of Jasher that the women would go and hide the babies out in the forests or at least away from the cities and that the earth would help and take care of the babies until they were fully grown. Read my book **Jasher Insights Books II** for more on this amazing topiC. Here is a quote from my book **Jasher Insights II**:

JASHER INSIGHTS BOOK II CHAPTER 67 verse 54

54 'And from that day forward, when the time of delivery arrived to those women of Israel who had remained with their husbands, they **went to the field** to bring forth there, and they brought forth in the field, and left their children upon the field and returned home.'

55 'And the Lord who had sworn to their ancestors to multiply them, sent one of his **ministering angels** which are in heaven to **wash each child in water, to anoint and swathe it and to put into its hands two smooth stones from one of which it sucked milk and from the other honey, and he caused its hair to grow to its knees, by which it might cover itself; to comfort it and to cleave to it, through his compassion for it.'**

56 'And when God had compassion over them and had desired to multiply them upon the face of the land, he **ordered his earth to receive them to be preserved therein till the time of their growing up**, after which the **earth opened its mouth** and vomited them forth and they sprouted forth from the city like the herb of the earth, and the grass of the forest, and they returned each to his family and to his father's house, and they remained with them.'

III CH 6: THE 'ABYSS': In the New Testament, the original
Greek word of the Scriptures for Abyss, pronounced *ab-us-sos*, describes a *deep pit* - so deep that it is, in effect, bottomless. I say *in effect* **bottomless** because the Scriptures describe the abyss as being *on earth*, or rather *in the earth.* Since the Bible refers to the **abyss** as a **place where demons are imprisoned**, it would **not then be entirely a physical place** within the earth anyway, since **demons are spirits who can pass through physical barriers. The Abyss** is a **spiritual** *and* **physical place** _within_ the earth.

Depending on the version of the Bible, the original Greek word is variously translated as "Abyss," "The deep," or "The Bottomless pit."

The Abyss Of Demons

Demons feared Jesus not just because He had the power to cast out demons (as did, and do, others e.g. Matthew 10:8 -), by means of the Holy Spirit, to cast them out of someone they possessed, but also because He had the power and authority to sentence them into **The Abyss**.

"Jesus then asked him, "What is your name?" And he said, "Legion"; for many demons had entered him. And they begged Him not to command them to depart into the **abyss**." (**Luke 8:30-31 RSV**) **SOURCE:** http://www.keyway.ca/htm2003/20030424.htm

OTHER ABYSESS

BOOK OF JUBILEES: CH 6 Abysses

5.29 And (on the new moon) in the fourth month the fountains of the great deep were closed and the flood-gates of heaven were restrained; and on the new moon of the seventh month **all the mouths of the *abysses* of the earth were opened,** and the water began to descend into the deep below.

6.28 And on the new moon of the fourth month the **mouths** of the depths of the *abyss* beneath were **closed.**

6.29 And on the new moon of the seventh month all the **mouths** of the *abysses* of the earth were **opened**, and the **waters began to descend into them.**

SEPTUAGINT LXX Genesis 7.11-12 In the six hundredth year of the life of Noah, in the second month, on the twenty seventh day of the month, on this day were all the '**fountains of the *abyss*' broken up**, and the floodgates of heaven were opened. And the rain was upon the earth forty days and forty nights.

C.12 On the 7th month many abysses of the earth were opened, and the Flood waters descended into these 'abysses'. Modern man has no idea about these abysses, and probably wouldn't believe you even if you told him about them, but apparently the **'abysses'** do in fact exist.

Abysses are mentioned in the **Bible** and other **Apocryphal books,** but mostly they are talking about '**THE ABYSS**' or the '**BOTTOMLESS PIT'.**

Here in the **Book of Jubilees** we are told that there are many **abysses** into which the Flood waters from the Great Flood drained out. Such Abysses must be enormous, in order to quickly drain out the excess waters in the oceans until the mountains and land reappeared! Like pulling a giant plug out of an enormous bath!

BOOK OF ENOCH 54.3 And he said unto me, "These are being prepared for the hosts of Azazel, so that they may take them and cast them into the *abyss* of complete condemnation and they shall cover their jaws with rough stones as the Lord of spirits commanded."

5 And I saw a flaming fire and beyond these mountains is a region the end of the earth. There the heavens were completed, and I saw a deep *abyss* with columns of heavenly fire, and among them I saw columns of fire fall which were beyond measure alike towards the height and towards the depth.

IV BACKGROUND TO 'JUBILEES'

The Book of Jubilees, was probably written in the 2nd century B.C.E in Hebrew., and is an account of the Biblical history of the world from Creation to Moses. It is divided into periods ('Jubilees') of 49 years. The Book of Jubilees, or, as it is sometimes called, "the little Genesis," purports to be a revelation given by God to Moses through the medium of an angel ("the Angel of the Presence,"), and containing a history, divided up into jubilee-periods of forty-nine years, from the creation to the coming of Moses.. The Book, which was composed in Hebrew, is divided into fifty chapters, and appears to be complete. (**SOURCE**: http://www.sacred-texts.com/bib/jub/jub02.htm)

V WAS THE BOOK OF JUBILEES PART OF THE CANON?

The **Book of Jubilees**, sometimes called Lesser Genesis (Leptogenesis), is an ancient Jewish religious work of 50 chapters, considered canonical by the Ethiopian Orthodox Church as well as Beta Israel (Ethiopian Jews), where it is known as the Book of Division.

SOURCE: https://www.revolvy.com/page/Book-of-Jubilees

VI VERSIONS AND ORIGINAL LANGUAGE

The Bible agrees with the **Septuagint LXX** except for the ages of the Patriarchs Arphaxad down to Nahor, where the Septuagint has added 100 years to the age of each of the Patriarchs. Why did this happen you may ask? I covered this at length in my book 'Jasher Insights' The only complete version of *Jubilees* is in Ethiopian, although large fragments in Greek, Latin and Syriac are also known. It is believed that it was originally written in Hebrew. If at times one gets the impression that you are reading a first draft of Genesis, you are in good company. R.H. Charles, the translator, a distinguished academic Biblical scholar, concluded that *Jubilees* was a version of the Pentateuch, written in Hebrew, parts of which later became incorporated into the earliest Greek version of the Jewish Bible, the Septuagint. (Source: http://www.sacred-texts.com/bib/jub/index.htm)

VII WHAT DOES THE YEAR OF THE JUBILEE MEAN?

FIND OUT ON MY WEBSITE: http://www.outofthebottomlesspit.co.uk/443919789

VIII ASTRONOMICAL *'TIME'* FAKERY

C.1 According to the Elite who run the planet: the truth is whatever 'they' say that it is! (That was quoting a former U.S.A president , showing how arrogant the elite are!) This is certainly true of science also, which alters the truth to fit the elite's agenda when it suits their purpose: The Elites Goal: *to* destroy all faith in the creator - **by inserting randomness into** all science **and** in fact all the Arts as well. Science today teaches that there is 'no order to things', just randomness and chaos. Supposedly, according to modern science, the whole universe was created 'out of absolutely nothing'. - Poof-Hey-Presto Chango! - Voila!" Even to a small child that sounds crazy! (**Romans 1**):

ROM.1:20 For the invisible things of him from the creation of the world are clearly seen, being understood by the things that are made, even his eternal power and Godhead; so that they are without excuse:

ROM.1:21 Because that, when they knew God, they glorified him not as God, neither were thankful; but became vain in their imaginations, and their foolish heart was darkened.

ROM.1:22 Professing themselves to be wise, they became fools.

According to them, 'Everything just happened by accident'. Their crazy logic however is *not* borne out *by the facts*, as there are many proofs of the Absolute in both the nature as well as in physics, mathematics, astronomy and all the sciences.

1TI.6:20 'O Timothy', keep that which is committed to thy trust, avoiding profane and **vain babblings**, and oppositions of **science** falsely so called:

IX BACKGROUND OF DIFFERENT WAYS OF MEASURING THE LENGTH OF THE YEAR

SOLAR YEAR=365 ¼ Days?

LUNAR YEAR=354 Days?

PROPHETIC YEAR=360 Days?

WHY THE DIFFERENCE IN MEASURING THE LENGTH OF A YEAR, AND IN FACT THE LENGTH OF THE MONTHS ALSO?

C.2 Both in the Book of Enoch and the Bible it states that the sun revolves around the earth and *not* that of the earth around the sun. Although I have noticed that some writers erroneously state that the Book of Enoch gave the Jews their Solar calendar. This is simply not correct. If one takes the time to properly study the Book of Enoch, it states that the sun is revolving around the earth.

C.3 Religionists *in their constant battle to try to please* 'science falsely so called' they often end up compromising their faith in the actual Word of God. So, if science challenges the Bible and suddenly states that the Bible must be wrong, and that in fact the earth revolves around the sun and not the earth around the earth, then the religious system just 'gives in' and compromises instead of standing up for God's Word through his many prophets who all stated that there are 360 days in the year from Pre-Flood times mentioned in the Book of Enoch to the prophets Daniel and John the Revelator.

C.4 We have today the Solar calendar which tells us that there are 365 ¼ days in a year. We also must add one extra day every 4 years which is called a leap year.

X HOW THE SCIENTISTS ALTERED TIME: FROM ROTATIONS OF THE EARTH AND SUN TO AN ATOMIC CLOCK, RELATED TO RADIATION INSTEAD, BY 1967!

C.5 In ancient times before Christ, there used to be what is referred to today as the **prophetic year** containing only **360** days in the year as quoted in both the prophetic books of Daniel and Revelations.

Why did God through His prophets refer to the year as having **360 days**, *unless it was true?*

C.6 In both the **Book of Enoch** and the **Book of Jubilees** it states that there are **364** days to the year, but is it just possible that the **number of the days have been deliberately tampered** with in both the books of Enoch and Jubilees?

In reading the Book of Enoch repeatedly you will see that Enoch also describes the year as having 12 months of 30 days, which is 'The Prophetic Year' equal to 360 days. So why one announcement in the Book of Enoch as to 364 days? It is inconsistent with most of the text.

Again, in this Book of Jubilees it states also 364 days.

My opinion: I think the numbers have indeed been tampered with. Why? As I have stated in '**Enoch Insights**' and '**Jasher Insights**' as well as this book of **Jubilees Insights**, the exact dates of historical events differ slightly between these books upon occasion. Most times and dates are very similar but occasionally one time or day seems out of place. Why is that you may ask? Probably at some time in the past the books, or around 150 years ago when modern science was really starting to take off with Evolution many books were slightly tampered with by those who didn't want the books to remain canonized – in other words discourage most people from reading the books. The original books of **Enoch, Jasher and Jubilees** have incredibly revealing information for those who take the time to study them thoroughly and repeatedly.

C.7 Example: Consider an object rotating around another in a perfect circle. How can we describe this action other than stating the object rotates in a perfect circle of **360** degrees? If one was to therefore put any given number of days in the year, it would be logical to put exactly 360 days to the year which is was used to be called an **Absolute number.**

C.8 If people were to think that there were 360 days in the year it might get them to thinking:

I) that sounds like the number of the degrees in a circle.

II) 360 is divisible by 12. Like 12 months in the year.

III) 360 is also related to the number of minutes and seconds. 60 x 6. Wow 360 is a very special number so maybe there is a God of the absolutes a person may deduce. So, **science as so often guided by Satan or evil spirits** decided they had to **corrupt the concept of Time** itself!

C.9 Why would Science deliberately want to alter the number of days in the year, you might ask? Simple: because if the number is 360 it **proves the existence of God as it is not a random number and it also** it proves **total order** and shows a **reliable constant**. However, the scientists in their desire to *disprove the existence of God* tried to *alter the days to 365 ¼,* but we now have the messy add-on of the leap year. This means that we have to add on a missing day every 4 years. I am sure that is not how God originally created the Time-Sequence.

XI LIES IN SCIENCE: They deliberately **lie about ancient wisdom** and knowledge as though it was ridiculous. They try to ridicule the old wisdom and the old knowledge as though it were all false & mere superstition, and in fact according to them (the modern scientists) are the only ones that really know anything of value, and furthermore they've only found it out lately and are revealing these marvellous truths to you for the first time! The truth is that man has forgotten so much of the ancient science and mathematics which was much more advanced than the sciences of today. As mentioned by Sir Issac newton who was the discoverer of gravity in the 17th century. Author: Or better said 'he re-discoved gravity Modern man is not as smart as he thinks he is. [**SEE ASTRONOMICAL FAKERY**: http://www.peopleofthekeys.com/news/docs/library/Astronomical+Fakery%21]

C.10 I know science tells us that the rotation of the earth is slowing down, but is that TRUE? Isn't the whole universe *created perfectly* and *governed by absolute Maths*, of which the so-called Ancients were aware of.

C.11 Stating that orbits are decaying or that the spinning of the earth is slowing could be just a method of 'controlling the facts'. After all, most people don't understand science that well!

We know from scriptures that there used to be 360 days to the year, which were 12 x 30-day months, and not like modern times with the random length of the months being 31, 30 or 28 days or even 29 as in the case of February in a Leap Year.

Man has really 'messed up the days and times and seasons. It used to be very simple with 360 days to the year; 12 months of exactly 30 days each. 24 hours to each day.

C.12 So how did the 'Powers that be' manage to alter the length of the year?

The 'Powers that be' added the minutes and seconds and set the exact length of the second and minute to fit their 'Altered Calendar', to become the confusion mentioned above of 365 ¼ days to the year etC.

However, in their desire to prove that *'time is random'* they still left traces of their errors.

The fact that every 4 years they still must add on exactly one day to the calendar also shows a *constant*.

XII C.13 With modern science insisting on the Big Bang Theory and no Creator, their whole theory is built on randomness and disorder.

For this reason, anything in nature that proved order and specific constants in mathematics had to be destroyed or altered as the Powers that be didn't want the general public to both believe in order and thus the Creator. This has not only been done in mathematics, but also in every other branch of science, as they did not wish to retain God in their knowledge, they became fools.

ROM.1:20 For the invisible things of him from the creation of the world are clearly seen, being understood by the things that are made, even his eternal power and Godhead; so that they are without excuse:

ROM.1:21 Because that, when they knew God, they glorified him not as God, neither were thankful; but became **vain in their imaginations**, and their foolish heart was darkened.

ROM.1:22 Professing themselves to be wise, they became fools,

ROM.1:23* And changed the glory of the uncorruptible God into an image made like to corruptible man, and to birds, and four-footed beasts, and creeping things.

Romans 1.23 seems to perfectly describe *Evolution*

ROM.1:25 Who *changed the truth of God into a lie* and worshipped and served the creature more than the Creator, who is blessed for ever. Amen.

XIII c.14 There is no chaos & randomness to the universe. The Big Bang has happened only in the scientist's head! I see only perfect order in **God's Creation.**

BOOK OF ENOCH 2.1 Observe ye everything that takes place in the heaven, how they **do not change their orbits**, and the luminaries (stars) which are in the heaven, how they **all arise** and set in order each in his season, and **transgress not against their appointed order.**

Psalm 19.1 'The heavens declare the Glory of God and the firmament shows His Handywork'

Ancient maths stated that the **whole universe** is **governed** by **absolute constants**. These being the following numbers: **7:360:**

C.15 We find that the **orbits of the stars and planets are all governed by these numbers** in detail, including the distance to the sun, and the distance to the moon. The weight of the sun and the moon etC. are all governed by *absolute constants* proving that the whole universe was by Godly design and is not random but exact, and in the Bible it mentions years, months and days and hours. Notice however that both minutes and seconds are a relatively modern invention and could be **randomly set** to a **given standard.** Let's find out where minutes and seconds came from? ' *(* SEE **DAVID FLYNNS** book **'TEMPLE AT THE CENTRE OF TIME'** about ancient constants: *https://www. skywatchtv.com/2017/06/01/late-david-flynns-cydonia-secret-chronicles-mars-analysis-proven-new-findings-suggest-cloudeaters-may-lived-red-planet-long-time/)*

XIV WHERE DID THE CONCEPT OF TIME COME FROM? *The reality is, even though we've decided that there is a need to divide up time, the actual process and the way we go about it has been changing for millennia. The cruel irony is that even though we know we need to measure time, there has never been a consensus on what time really is.'*- It wasn't until about the 14th century, when mechanical clocks were common-place, that a fixed length for an hour became widely accepted.-'

'The idea of using this base 60 system as a means of dividing up the hour was born from the idea of devising a geographical system to mark the Earth's geometry. The Greek astronomer Eratosthenes, who lived between 276-194 B.C., used this sexagesimal system to divide a circle into 60 parts. These lines of latitude were horizontal and ran through well-known places on the Earth at the time. Later, Hipparchus devised longitudinal lines that encom-passed 360 degrees. Even later, the astronomer Claudius Ptolemy expanded on Hipparchus' work and divided each of the 360 degrees of latitude and longitude into 60 equal parts. These parts were further subdivided into 60 smaller parts.'

The first accurately measurable means of defining a second came with the advent of the pendulum. This method was commonly used as a means of counting time in early mechanical clocks. In 1956, the second was defined in terms of the period of revolution of the Earth around the Sun for a particular epoch.

CHANGING TIME FROM ROTATIONS OF THE EARTH, MOON AND SUN

Here is where science falsely so-called high-jacked the time & to be more precise the timing of the second to no longer be related to the revolutions of the earth around the sun (or vice-versa for the geo-centrists)- With the development of the atomic clock, it was decided that it was more practical and accurate to use them as a means to define a second, rather than the revolution of the Earth around the Sun.

(**SOURCE**: http://www.todayifoundout.com/index.php/2011/08/why-we-divide-the-day-into-seconds-minutes-and-hours/)

XV The 360 Day Prophetic Year of the Bible

The biblical-prophetic year consisted of 360 days. Abraham, the father of Israel, continued to use the 360-day year, which was known in his home in Ur of the Chaldees. The Genesis account of the flood in the days of Noah illustrated this 360-day year by recording the 150-day interval till the waters abated from the earth. The 150 days began on the seventeenth day of the second month and ended on the seventeenth day of the seventh month (Genesis 7:11,24 and 8:3-4). In Other words, the five months consisted of thirty days each; therefore, twelve months would equal 360 days (12 x 30 = 360 days).

The book of Esther (1: 4) indicates the same 360-day length of year by recording the six-month-long feast of Xerxes as continuing exactly 180 days.

The Prophet Daniel recorded that the time of the absolute power of the Antichrist over the nations will last three-and -one-half years (Daniel 7:25). John, in the book of Revelation, described this same three-and-one-half year period (Revelation 13:5-7) as consisting of forty-two months of thirty days each, totalling 1260 days (Revelation 11:2-3; 12:6). The biblical writers used *the ancient 360-day biblical year in both the historical and predictive parts of Scripture.*

PROOF

There is conclusive evidence to show that the prophetic year of Scripture is composed of 360 days, or twelve months of 30 days.

The first argument is *historical*. Thus the earliest known month used in

Biblical history was evidently thirty days in length, and twelve such months would give us a 360-day year.

The second argument is *prophetical*…Dan. 9:27 mentions a period of Jewish persecution Since this persecution begins in the "midst" of the Seventieth Week and continues to the "end" of the Week, the period is obviously three and one-half years. Rev. 13:4-7 speaks of the same great political Ruler and his persecution of the Jewish "saints" lasting "forty and two months." Rev. 12:13-14 refers to the same persecution, stating the duration in the exact terms of Dan. 7:25 as "a time and times and half a time"; and this period is further defined in Rev. 12:6 as" a thousand two hundred and three score days." Thus, we have the same period of time variously stated as 3 ½ years, 42 months, or 1260 days. Therefore, it is clear that the length of the year in the Seventy Weeks prophecy is fixed by Scripture itself as exactly 360 days.(1)- (**SOURCE**: http://jewishroots.net/library/prophecy/daniel/daniel-9-24-27/360-day-prophetic-year.html)

CONCLUSIONS:

C.1 What if someone has deliberately altered the time sequence of the length of the days of the years as into the exact number of hours, minutes and seconds?

C.2 What would it look like if we started with 360 days in the year like 360 degrees in the circle and worked backwards? Then how many hours in the day and minutes and seconds. 60 sounds right for seconds and 60 sounds right for minutes but what about the exact length of a second?

C.3 At some time the actual 'second' was altered very slightly to give us 3651/4 days in the year instead of the original 360 given originally by God Himself - in order to seemingly make TIME itself seem to be just random. As mentioned before the scientists who altered the length of a second made a big mistake because we still must alter our years every 4 years or every Leap Year, but we always add the very exact same amount of time In other words, we add **a** constant. The whole universe is made up of 'absolute constants' like **360 and pi and the number 7** proving that God does in fact exist. There is indeed a Creator. http://www.outofthebottomlesspit.co.uk/421607713

XVI - THE BOOK OF REMEDIES

Comment:1: Hezekiah censored the **Book of Remedies,** according to the **Jewish book The Talmud,** which they say probably originally descended from Noah or one of his sons. The book was dictated to Noah by an angel. God told Hezekiah to hide away the **Book of Remedies** as it was causing people in Israel to misuse its knowledge and power. Here is some more information concerning the **Book of Remedies** and why it was banned by Hezekiah, king of Israel around 750 BCE. The following is in my opinion excellent material:

'Despite the protests of Maimonides, the Talmudic sages may indeed be relating to the **pitfalls of medical knowledge**. Elsewhere in rabbinic literature, we find a harsh and unusual statement: "The best of the **doctors** is destined for <u>**Gehenna**</u>" (M. Kiddushin 4:14). Jewish scholars have offered different explanations for this unsympathetic verdict, all of them **limiting the judgment to a certain class of doctors**: doctors who **cause death** when they could save lives (Rashi, 11th century, <u>**France**</u>); doctors who **act in bad faith** (Ri, 12th century, Germany); doctors who **act recklessly and callously** (Ramban); doctors who **pretend to be experts when they are truly ignorant of the profession** (Kalonymus ben Kalonymus, 14th century, Provence) or doctors who act when there are others who have greater expertise than them (Rabbi Simon Duran, 14th-15th centuries, Majorca-Algiers). One commentator, himself a recognized physician, appended this adage to doctors who perform internal operations, perhaps reflecting the state of medical knowledge in his day (Rabbi Isaac Lampronti, 17th-18th centuries, <u>**Italy**</u>). We might offer another possible understanding of this unforgiving declaration. **The best of doctors may be inclined to credit their own acumen for their medical achievements.** Such foolishness, say the sages, leads one from the path of God. The faculties with which we are endowed and the opportunities that befall us, should **not be seen** as the **strength of our own hands**. Rather, it behooves us to remember God and **His role behind the scenes** as the playmaker and facilitator (**Deuteronomy 8:17-18**).

An oft-recounted parable tells of a person drowning at sea; as he struggles in the water gasping for breath he fervently prays to God for salvation. Seemingly out of nowhere a boat sidles up to him and throws a buoy in his direction. The man refuses the assistance proferred: "I am waiting for God to save me!" he calls, and continues to gallantly tread water, praying for redemption through God's mighty hand. A helicopter miraculously flies by and offers the drowning man a rope-ladder to climb out of the clutches of the ocean. Once again the help tendered is rebuffed: "God will save me!" he shouts and continues to valiantly keep afloat, passionately beseeching the Almighty to save him. As his strength wanes and his demise approaches, the man lets out one last heartfelt prayer, and a piece of driftwood slides within reach. Instead of clutching it, the man pushes it aside, thinking: "Surely, God will not forsake me." Alas, the waters finally overtake him, and the man appears in Heaven before God: "Why did You not heed my heartfelt prayers? Where were You in my time of need?" he complains. In a booming voice God responds: "Who do you think sent the boat, the helicopter and the piece of driftwood!?" Seeking medical advice is not folly. The challenge is to recognize that professional medical assistance attained is truly a gift from God. As such, the doctor is a messenger of God, charged with the eminent task of saving lives. But it is not the doctor who heals, nor is it the medicine or ointment; God is the true healer'. (**Source: Ref**: <u>https://www.jpost.com/Jewish-World/Judaism/World-of-the-Sages-Books-of-Remedies</u>])

XVII THE COMPARISON BETWEEN THE K.J.V of the BIBLE AND THE SEPTUAGINT

C.1 In general, I personally prefer to read the Septuagint version of the Old

Testament than the K.J.V. as it tends to have more details. However.

C.2 There is one area, where *the Septuagint and the K.J.V of the Bible seriously disagree,* which has become a point of contention with some.

C.3 Below I first put the Bible Longevity Chart as shown in the KJV of the Bible and in the following page a chart showing what it would look like going by the Septuagint version of the Bible.

C.4 The **K J Version** of the **Old Testament in the Bible** commissioned by King James I of England, (who came to the throne in 1601) was put together in 1611 and involved 70 Old Testament experts working on it.

C.5 The Septuagint or LXX for short, version of the Old Testament was also put together by 70 Jewish Old Testament scholars in around 275 B.C.

So, you might ask: 'What is the difference between them?' That is a very good question.

In general, I would state that the Septuagint is a much more original Old Testament account. The K.J.V was seriously influenced by a Jewish Masoretic sect in 100 AD who tried to alter and rewrite the Septuagint which resulted in the Masoretic Old Testament text from which the King James Bible O.T came into being.

C.6 Although in general I believe the Septuagint to in general being a more accurate account of the ancient Hebrew Old Testament, there is one area of the Septuagint that doesn't seem to add up - literally:

Something doesn't seem right with the Septuagint Longevity Chart and the question is why? Did someone tamper with the timeline and if they did, what was the reason?

Both the Bible and the Apocryphal books of both Jasher and Jubilees agree on the Longevity Timelines. Even the Septuagint agrees with these three other books in the timeline from Adam to Shem. Where the problem arises in the Septuagint is the ages of Shem's son Arphaxad and resultant descendants until Terah the father of Abraham. The Septuagint adds 100 years to each of 8 descendants coming after Shem. (See the chart below.) This would result in the age of the earth no longer being around 6000 years as recording in the Bible and other Apocryphal books but more like 6800 years old. If the Septuagint longevity chart were correct it would mean that many of the stories as given in the Jewish Apocryphal book of Jasher & Jubilees would have to be incorrect. Why? Because according to both the Bible and the Apocryphal books of Jasher and Jubilees Noah and Shem were still alive in Abraham's time, even though Abraham was in fact the 10th generation after Noah as a direct descendent.

C.7 So, who has the Longevity Time Chart correct? Well since there is a general agreement between both the KJV of the Bible and both the Apocryphal books of Jasher and Jubilees, the preponderance of scripture would state that the Bible's Longevity Chart is in fact the correct one.

C.8 Another consideration is the following: When King James of English commissioned 70 experts to put the modern K.J.V. Bible together, *those experts were not under any sort of pressure to comply with certain agendas.* The king simply wanted a good version of both the New and Old Testaments to be combined and made available for all English-speaking peoples.

C.9 However, when the Septuagint was put together in around 300 BC it was put together by 70 Jewish Old testament scholars who were living in Egypt at the time as slaves to the Grecian Empire, which was ruled in the Sleucian south part of a 4 part empire by a Pharaoh who was de-facto a stooge of the Grecian empire.

THE EGYPTIAN EMPIRE.

C.10 Egypt was powerful around 2000BC - 1500 BC and was wrecked by God Himself in the Judgments of the '10 Plagues' at the time of Moses in around 1520 BC.

C.11 Look at today. The Egyptians claim that their ancestors were the makers of the amazing Pyramids and other structures such as the Sphinx. However closer investigation shows that in fact these amazing structures were built further back in time and *before* the Great Flood.

C.12 I propose that Pharaoh, one of the main sponsors of the Septuagint made a simple stipulation to the 70 enslaved Jewish Old Testament scholars. He wanted the writings in the Septuagint to put the time of the Great Flood further back in time, so that Pharoah could continue to *state that the Pyramids were made after the Great Flood* and not before. So, he *had the scholars simply add 800 years to the Longevity chart* by altering the date at which each first children was born to *Shem and then Arphaxad and then Salah, Eber, Peleb, Reu, Serug, Nahor & Terah.* They simply added 100 years to each one of them, which is very odd, and it looks odd on the time-chart for several reasons.

Editor: Here is some interesting info about the Egyptians: The scholars of the present day who write about Egypt are in gross error. They accept so many things concerning the Egyptians as history, science, and learning, which nevertheless have no other foundation than astrology and false visions. They esteem the Egyptians more ancient than they really are, because in those early times they appear to have possessed such knowledge of abstruse and hidden things. But I saw that, even at the coming of Semiramis to Memphis, these people, in their pride had designedly confused their calendar. Their ambition was to take precedence of all nations in point of time. With this end in view, they drew up a number of complicated calendars and royal genealogical tables. By this and frequent changes in their computations, order and true chronology were lost. That this confusion might be firmly established, they perpetuated every error by inscriptions and the erection of great buildings.-

SOURCE: http://alternativegenhist.blogspot.com/2010/12/dating-of-flood-and-creation-of-adam.html

C.13 Consider the following: Just before the Great Flood, God said that He would destroy all of mankind except for Noah and family. He also stated that from now one Mankind would live for only 120 years. Therefore, the Septuagint versions that Arphaxad waited until he was 135 years old before having his firstborn child doesn't seem right, when God had just stated that *man would start to live progressively shorter in years and eventually it would narrow down to only 120 years old.* It was stated in this Book of Jubilees in Abraham's time. Abraham himself still lived to be 175, but it was stated even in his time than soon man would only live to be 120 then 75 years of age and finally only 70. This is exactly what has happened since Abraham's time. King David who lived 1000 years after Abraham only lived to be 70 years of age.

OBS. Since the time of King David 3000 years ago, which was half of the World's History of approximately 6000 Years to date, the length of a man's life has generally stayed around *70 Years on average.*

The exception to that, has been in different Dark Ages & the Industrial Age, when millions of people's lives were cut short by plague and by pollution causing the disease called *consumption (T.B.)*, which also killed so many people during the coal mining age of the 19th century. In fact, just 150 years ago, many people lived very short lives, such as 35 years, due to the heavy industrialization in the world.

XVIII TIME-FRAME OF 7000 YEARS OF WORLD HISTORY

(Approximate dates AC=After Creation)

CREATION AC 0 (±4000 BCE)

ENOCH AC 600

NOAH   AC 1000

ABRAHAM AC 2000

MOSES   AC 2500

DAVID   AC 3000

DANIEL AC 3500

JESUS CHRIST AC 4000

DARK AGES AC 5000

MODERN TIMES AC 6000

2ND COMING OF CHRIST circa AC 6000

MILLENIUM AC 6000-7000AC

GREAT WHITE THRONE JUDGEMENT AC 7000

THE NEW HEAVEN & THE NEW EARTH AC 7000 to ETERNITY

XIX THE AGE OF THE EARTH chart below is the traditional chart, but is it completely accurate?

Please see the modern charts *below*, which point out that the '430 years of the Jews being in Captivity', started with Abraham having a son called Ismael of an Egyptian woman who afflicted his biological son IsaaC. As one can see in the traditional Age of the Earth Timeframe Chart the '430 years of bondage of the Jews' starts with Jacob going down to Egypt. If we take this into consideration and take the date of Jacob entering into Egypt and compare it to the time of Abraham there is a discrepancy of 215 years!

AGE OF THE EARTH CHART (traditional)

Bible Ref.	GENEALOGIES		EARTH'S AGE	ACTUAL DATES
Gen 5.1,2	The creation of Adam		6 days	4160 BCE
Gen 5.3	Creation of Adam to birth of Seth	130 years	130 years	4030 BCE
Gen 5.6	Birth of Seth to the birth of Enos	105 years	235 years	3925 BCE
Gen 5.9	Birth of Enos to birth of Cainan	90 years	325 years	3835 BCE
Gen 5.12	Birth of Cainan to birth of Mahalaleel	70 years	395 years	3765 BCE
Gen 5.15	Birth of Mahalaleel to birth of Jared	65 years	460 years	3700 BCE
Gen 5.18	Birth of Jared to birth of Enoch	162 years	622 years	3538 BCE
Gen 5.21	Birth of Enoch to birth of Methuselah	65 years	687 years	3473 BCE
Gen 5. 25	Birth of Methuselah to b. of Lamech	187 years	874 years	3286 BCE
Gen 5.28-9	Birth of Lamech to birth of Noah	182 years	1056 years	3104 BCE
Gen 7.6	Birth of Noah to birth to the FLOOD	600 years	1656 years	2504 BCE
Gen 11.10	Flood to birth of Arphaxad	2 years	1658 years	2502 BCE
Gen 11.12	Birth of Arphaxad to birth of Salah	35 years	1693 years	2467 BCE
Gen 11.14	Birth of Salah to birth of Eber	30 years	1723 years	2437 BCE
Gen 11.16	Birth of Eber to birth of Peleg	34 years	1757 years	2403 BCE
Gen 11.18	Birth of Peleg to birth of Reu	30 years	1787 years	2372 BCE
Gen 11.20	Birth of Reu to birth of Serug	32 years	1819 years	2341 BCE

Bible Ref.	Description	Years	Cumulative	Date
Gen 11.22	Birth of Serug to birth of Nahor	30 years	1849 years	2311 BCE
Gen 11.24	Birth of Nahor to birth of Terah	29 years	1878 years	2282 BCE
Gen 11.26	Birth of Terah to birth of Abram	70 years	1948 years	2212 BCE
Gen 21.5	Birth of Abram to birth of Isaac	100 years	2048 years	2112 BCE
Gen 25.26	Birth of Isaac to birth of Jacob	60 years	2108 years	2052 BCE
Gen 47.5-12	Birth of Jacob to entering into Egypt	130 years	2238 years	1922 BCE
Ex.12.40,41	Entering Egypt to Exodus	430 years	2668 years	1492 BCE
1 Kg.6.1	Exodus to Solomon's Temple	480 years	3148 years	1012 BCE
BC/AD	1012 BCE to year 0	1012 years	4160 years	0 AC/BCE
	Year 0 to TODAY	2018 years	2018 years	2017 AD

TOTAL YEARS from Creation to today   6178 years ([3] Is this date accurate? We will investigate this in detail)

AGE OF THE EARTH CHART
(Updated)

Bible Ref.	GENEALOGIES		EARTH'S AGE	ACTUAL DATES
Gen 5.1,2	The creation of Adam		6 days	4160 BCE
Gen 5.1,2	The creation of Adam	6 days	3975 BCE	
Gen 5.3	Creation of Adam to birth of Seth	130 years	130 years	BCE
Gen 5.6	Birth of Seth to the birth of Enos	105 years	235 years	BCE
Gen 5.9	Birth of Enos to birth of Cainan	90 years	325 years	BCE
Gen 5.12	Birth of Cainan to birth of Mahalaleel	70 years	395 years	BCE
Gen 5.15	Birth of Mahalaleel to birth of Jared	65 years	460 years	BCE
Gen 5.18	Birth of Jared to birth of Enoch	162 years	622 years	BCE
Gen 5.21	Birth of Enoch to birth of Methuselah	65 years	687 years	BCE
Gen 5. 25	Birth of Methuselah to b. of Lamech	187 years	874 years	BCE
Gen 5.28-9	Birth of Lamech to birth of Noah	182 years	1056 years	BCE
Gen 7.6	Birth of Noah to the FLOOD	600 years	1656 years	BCE
Gen 11.10	Flood to birth of Arphaxad	2 years	1658 years	BCE
Gen 11.12	Birth of Arphaxad to birth of Salah	35 years	1693 years	BCE
Gen 11.14	Birth of Salah to birth of Eber	30 years	1723 years	BCE
Gen 11.16	Birth of Eber to birth of Peleg	34 years	1757 years	BCE
Gen 11.18	Birth of Peleg to birth of Reu	30 years	1787 years	BCE

Gen 11.20	Birth of Reu to birth of Serug	32 years	1819 years	BCE
Gen 11.22	Birth of Serug to birth of Nahor	30 years	1849 years	BCE
Gen 11.24	Birth of Nahor to birth of Terah	29 years	1878 years	BCE
Gen 11.26	Birth of Terah to birth of Abram	70 years	1948 years	BCE
Gen 21.5	Birth of Abram to birth of Isaac	100 years	2048 years	BCE
Gen 25.26	Birth of Isaac to birth of Jacob	60 years	2108 years	BCE
Gen 47.5-12	Birth of Jacob to entering into Egypt	130 years	2238 years	BCE
Ex.12.40,41	Entering Egypt to Exodus	245 years	2483 years	BCE
1 Kg.6.1	Exodus to Solomon's Temple	480 years	2963 years	BCE
BC/AD	1012 BCE to year 0	1012 years	3975 years	0 AC/BCE
	Year 0 to TODAY	2018 years	2018 years	2018 AD
TOTAL YEARS from Creation to today		**5993 years**		

CONCLUSION: Today in 2019, It looks like the world is 5994 years old and not 6178 years old. Now that makes a lot of difference. It has been stated that the Age of the Earth is determined by the days of Creation. One day =1000 years.

YEAR   0 Creation =4000 BC

YEAR 1000 DEATH OF ENOCH & BIRTH OF NOAH = 3000 B.C

YEAR 2000 ABRAHAM= 2000 B.C

YEAR 3000 KING DAVID = 1000 B.C

YEAR 4000 JESUS THE MESSIAH= YEAR 0 A.D

YEAR 5000 DARK AGES =1000 A.D

YEAR 6000 2ND COMING OF CHRIST-RAPTURE-WRATH OF GOD-MILLENIUM STARTS

YEAR 7000 END OF THE GOLDEN AGE- BATTLE OF GOG AND MAGOG - WHITE THRONE JUDGMENT- NEW HEAVEN NEW EARTH

EXPLAINING THE 430 YEARS OF CAPTIVITY OF ABRAHAM'S SEED. Were the Israelites over 400 years in captivity down in Egypt or were they only a much shorter time in Egypt itself. Look at the following chart which explains that the scriptures mention 430 years of Captivity in Egypt. Those 430 years of captivity started with Abraham, and not with Jacob and his sons in Egypt.

Patriarch: Age	Event	Passage	Years from Promise	Years to Exodus
Abraham: 75	God makes the promise to Abraham and he leaves Haran.	*Genesis 12:1–4*	0	430
Abraham: 75-85	God tells Abraham his descendants "will be sojourners in a land that is not theirs and will be servants there and they will be afflicted for 400 years."	*Genesis 15:13*; *Acts 7:6*	0–10	420–430
Abraham: 85	Abraham has lived in Canaan for 10 years and takes Hagar as his wife and she conceives Ishmael.	*Genesis 16:3–4*	10	420
Abraham: 86	Ishmael is born.	*Genesis 16:15–16*	11	419
Abraham: 100 Ishmael: 14	Isaac is born.	*Genesis 21:5*	25	405
Abraham: 105 Isaac: 5 Ishmael: 19	**Isaac is weaned and Ishmael (MOTHER IS EGYPTIAN) mocks/persecutes IsaaC.**	*Genesis 21:8–9*; *Galatians 4:29*	30	400
Abraham: 140 Isaac: 40	Isaac marries Rebekah.	*Genesis 24:1–67*; *25:20*	65	365
Abraham: 160 Isaac: 60	Esau and Jacob are born.	*Genesis 25:26*	85	345
Abraham: 175 Isaac: 75 Jacob: 15	Abraham dies.	*Genesis 25:7*	100	330
Isaac: 151 Jacob: 91	Joseph is born.		176	254
Isaac: 168 Jacob: 108 Joseph: 17	Joseph is sold by his brothers and taken to Egypt.	*Genesis 37*	193	237
Isaac: 180 Jacob: 120 Joseph: 29	Isaac dies.	*Genesis 35: 28–29*	205	225
Jacob: 121 Joseph: 30	Joseph is made second in command by Pharaoh.	*Genesis 41:46*	206	224

Jacob: 130 Joseph: 39	Joseph reveals himself to his brothers two years into the famine with five years left. Jacob meets Pharaoh.	*Genesis 45:4–6* *Genesis 47:9*	215	215

Jacob: 147 Joseph: 56	Jacob dies.	*Genesis 47:28– 49:33*	232	198
Joseph: 110	Joseph dies.	*Genesis 50:26*	286	144
	Only 64 years pass from the time Joseph dies to when Moses is born..	*Exodus 6:16–20*		
Moses: 3 months	Moses is placed in a basket and adopted by Pharaoh's daughter.	*Exodus 2*	350	80
Moses: 80	Moses and Aaron speak to Pharaoh beginning the exodus from Egypt.	*Exodus 7:7*; *Exodus 12:40–41*; *Galatians 3:16–17*	430	0
SOURCE	https://answersingenesis. org/bible-questions/ how-long-were-the-israelites-in-egypt/			

IN CONCLUSION: If the real date of the age of the earth is in fact 5993 years, then the last 7 years of World History could possibly soon be upon us. (Of course this might just be an approximate date if we have not taken some things into consideration - but it is an interesting possibility and would indicate that time is indeed running out!)

That could be turn out to be very important, as Bible prophecy predicts that at the beginning of the Last 7 years of World History, we will see the infamous Anti-Christ (Satan Incarnate) come on the scene, and that he will 'come in peaceably' according to the Book of Daniel. The A.C. will offer to solve the world's problems of wars, religious conflicts and the economic mess that we are in and will introduce a '7 Year Religious Pact' cantered in Jerusalem in Israel. The Anti-Christ will eventually make Jerusalem his Capital. This would mean that the 3rd Temple in Jerusalem must be built very soon, in order for the Anti-Christ to both make Jerusalem his International Capital, and to use the Temple in Jerusalem, in the midst of the '7 Year Religious Pact', to install the 'Image of the Beast', as in 'Revelations 13' fame.

IT COULD BE THAT WE ARE RUNNING OUT OF TIME VERY FAST!

The good news is that after the '7 Years of The Antichrist', Jesus will return and rapture his own children to heaven. Then will come the Marriage Supper of the Lamb, followed by the Battle of Armageddon and the Wrath of God and finally the Golden Age of the Millennium, where all he truly saved saints of Jesus Christ will rule together with Him for 1000 years of peace.

Could it be that 2020 will mark the start of the Last 7 Years until the Earth is exactly 6000-years old? Could 2020 also be the Time/Prophecy marker for the start of the Last 7 Years of World History? Could 2020 bring in the Anti-Christ & his 7 Year Religious Pact with Jews, Moslems and Christians?

According to the Bible, it would be more like 3 ½ years of 'Plastic Peace', as the Anti-Christ deceives the whole world as he consolidates his control over the nations. Then followed by 3 ½ Years of Terror called the Great Tribulation. (For further study See **Daniel 8, 9 & 11; Matthew 24; Revelations 13; 2Thessalonians 2**)

XX NEPHALIM (Fallen angels) & REPHEIM (Giants- The sons of Fallen angels, who made love to human women)

C.1 Why did the particular group of Fallen angels who came after Enoch in around 1100 years after creation become so depraved as to mate with animals and beasts and all kinds of creatures by shape-shifting and becoming as the beasts and birds and fish and insects so as to transmit their **D.N.A** into the resultant offspring?

C.2 If such a thing was even remotely possible, which unfortunately there is plenty of evidence to support this otherwise crazy notion. Why don't most people want to address this crazy idea or questions like it? Plain and simple, because they would be afraid of the ramifications of such an idea and of what it might mean if it could yet happen on our planet in the near future, through sciences like Transhumanism. It is a very scary prospect!

C.3 Mankind has been conditioned for centuries to believe that man is in control of his world & that God doesn't exist. Have a very good and deep look around! Does it really appear that man is in control of this world? Man has been conditioned to live mostly for himself and money or Mammon. Man has willingly allowed himself to become largely mindless and almost totally controlled, as long as he can have success with money and wealth which are totally false gods or Idols to worship. God never intended for humanity to be mindless slaves of the Merchants of this world. Most of those in the West act as if they have forgotten that all of us have a soul which lives forever. Unfortunately, mankind has come to believe all the lies that are being constantly spoon-fed to them by the Elite of the planet and their brainwashing control systems; Their total control of humanity is filtered down through everything from Politics to Economics; Man's Religions to Modern education to the Sciences, to the Medical profession. All are based on the lie of *Evolution* and the Satanic dogma of 'Survival of the Fittest' and 'To the Strongest' in our 'Dog eat dog' world.

BRAINWASHING THE MASSES

C.4 All the main media are constantly spewing out blatant lies and fabrications about our world and other nations. Most people never stop long enough to ask enough of the right questions or to even question the Status Quo. Why is that? The truth be known that even if we wanted to change the above horrendous conditions of our planet of which I have only mentioned a few of the underlying problems, Politics and Revolution cannot change things. Why? Because the underlying problems of our planet are of a spiritual nature. First, we must destroy and get rid of the inherent evil in mankind; and the truth is that only God himself can do that. Only when Jesus as the Messiah returns and locks up Satan and his Fallen angels (Devils) & Giants and other creatures or entities (Demons) and their stooges the corrupt Merchants, rulers and leaders, who rule the earth by evil means & oppression, then all peoples will finally have peace and prosperity. That's what we all look forward to: The Golden age of the coming Millennium.

REBELLION OF SATAN & THE FALLEN ANGELS

C.5 Who is in the background in the negative spirit world always influencing mankind to do mostly evil and to follow his pride? It started with the Rebellion of Satan long before the creation of this physical domain. It was enhanced by the Fallen angels coming to earth some 500 years after the Creation taking the beautiful women as their wives.

C.6 GIANTS AND DEMONS Their sons became giants who unfortunately became monstrous cannibals who devoured mankind. God ordered his angels in heaven according to the Book of Enoch to cause one set of giants to fight against another until they were all destroyed. Once the Giants were largely killed off before the Great Flood, their spirits became what is known as the disembodied spirits of the Giants, which today we call demons. Apparently these disembodied spirits, some hundreds of years before the Great flood communicated from the negative spirit world to their fathers the Fallen Angels or even to other Fallen Angels who were roaming the earth and asked them to find a way to bring them back to the physical plane from the spiritual zone they were in which is on a slightly lower level than he physical plane.

C.7 CHIMERAS/HYBRID CREATURES: So, the Fallen angels started creating CHIMERAS of hundreds of types, by mating with different animals and creating '**hybrid creatures**' which God Himself had not created and thus had no spirit. The demon spirits of the former disembodied Giants could enter into these chimeras and thus the spirits of the giants were able to come back to the physical plane once more. These spirits of the giants were not yet bound up or yet judged. The judgement of them has not yet happened, so they are free to roam and possess people and creatures upon the earth time and time again.

XXI ORIGIN OF THE HYBRID CREATURES & CHIMERAS KNOWN AS THE GIANTS & THE MONSTERS IN THE BOOK OF THE GIANTS

C.1 The Fallen angels discovered that if they could create something which was a hybrid which God himself had not created, then it would be easier for the disembodied spirits of the Giants to enter such creatures. This is when the Fallen angels started to change their form into other animals, beast, birds, fish and then started mating with these animals in order to put their unique Nephilim D.N.A into those creatures. Then the disembodied spirits of the giants would enter these created hybrid creatures and thus the disembodied spirits of the giants could make a come-back by possessing thousands of these Satanic hybrid creatures, known as minotaur, centaurs, mermaids, harpies and thousands of other hybrid creatures.

C.2 When one comes to realize through extensive study about all that I have just mentioned, no wonder that it grieved God at His heart and He ended up wanting to destroy His whole creation with the exception of Noah & his three sons and their wives.

GEN.6:6 And it repented the LORD that he had made man on the earth, and it *grieved him at his heart.*

GEN.6:1 And it came to pass, when men began to multiply on the face of the earth, and daughters were born unto them,

GEN.6:2 That the sons of God saw the daughters of men that they were fair; and they took them wives of all which they chose.

GEN.6:3 And the LORD said, My spirit shall not always strive with man, for that he also is flesh: yet his days shall be an hundred and twenty years.

GEN.6:4 There were giants in the earth in those days; and also after that, when the sons of God came in unto the daughters of men, and they bare children to them, the same became mighty men which were of old, men of renown.

GEN.6:5 And God saw that the wickedness of man was great in the earth, and that every imagination of the thoughts of his heart was only evil continually.

GEN.6:7 And the LORD said, I will destroy man whom I have created from the face of the earth; both man, and beast, and the creeping thing, and the fowls of the air; for it repents me that I have made them.

BOOK OF GIANTS: https://youtu.be/zEW1k0qU8Sg?t=256

CERN, UFO'S, WATCHERS & GIANTS: https://youtu.be/dO7EdBRALqE?t=289

C.3 How big were the ancient Pre-flood Giants? Apparently the skeletons of giants up to 45 feet high and been found and I have also heard of a giant skeleton of 75 feet high. The expert on the Giants is Steve Quayle [www.stevequayle.com] However when you hear of the measurements in some of these ancient Hebrew books it, such as this **Book of Jubilees**, then it would seem that the giants were at one time, hundreds of feet high - known as the **TITANS**. Steve Quayle and Tom Horn talk about this in their book '**The Cloud-eaters'**.

A **GOOGLE-MAP** observer mentioned that he found a giant skull sticking out of the ice in the Antarctic, apparently showing the **skull of a GIANT** skeleton which is **24** feet long in size.

This would make the height of the whole Giant skeleton as around **170 feet high.** I can't verify if the image is true of not, as it just happened.

Here is a LINK to GOOGLEMAP: https://www.dailystar.co.uk/news/weird-news/google-earth-uncovers-giant-skull-20715323

XXII IDOL WORSHIPPING & SORCERY LEADS

TO THE 'MARK OF THE BEAST'

C.1 Why is it wrong to worship graven images? Wow! Now that is a very big topiC. What is an Idol? It is something that people put before worshipping God Himself.

C.2 What do most people today give most of their attention to? Is it not the god Mammon?

Most of their decisions rotate around money worship, and acquiring both money and things, rather than to trust God for their needs as God's Word clearly states.

Ph 4.19 'My God shall supply all of your needs according to His riches in Glory by Christ Jesus'.

C.3 So, Mammon is a very big Idol today. Spiritually speaking, there are demons behind the Idols, so *that excessively doing anything,* then that can become an obsession or an addiction, and is in fact Idol worshipping. It can most definitely be influenced by demons if taken to the extreme, to the point that people are worshipping Idols and the demons behind them even without consciously knowing it. Under these circumstances, unless you are **protected by Salvation through Jesus**, then you could get demon-possessed by one of these demons if you don't watch out!

C.4 Before the Great Flood these demons were physically visible as the giants and demi-gods of old. After they died, they became the 'disembodied spirits of the giants'**,** and have been plaguing mankind ever since from the negative spirit world below.

C.5 Another thing that the nations worship is *war* and the various gods of War and Destruction. Second to War is '*sports* worship'. The U.S.A spends more than half of its national yearly budget on weapons of war which destroy other nations in order to make more money and to control and enslave the nations.

Modern people inadvertently have become Idol worshippers and the worst thing is they don't even realize it!

C.6 Man's Religions are another *idol* where people *put $ billions into useless buildings* which could have been *used to feed the poor of the nations* or to send missionaries out to poorer countries to tell them about Jesus.

God never asked people to build expensive religious buildings. What God said was to take care of others, not waste $ billions that could be used to help millions of less fortunate peoples around the world.

ISA.66:1 Thus saith the LORD, The heaven is my throne, and the earth is my footstool: where is the house that ye build unto me? and where is the place of my rest?

ISA.66:2 For all those things hath mine hand made, and all those things have been, saith the LORD: *but to this man will I look, even to him that is poor and of a contrite spirit, and trembleth at my word.*

God's commandments are few, as Jesus clearly stated in Matthew 22.3-40 & in fact are just two-fold:

1) Thou shalt love the Lord thy God with all thy heart, all thy mind and all thy spirit & all your strength.

2) Thou shalt love they neighbour as thyself

THE IDOL-WORSHIPPING OF ORGANIZED RELIGIONS.

C.7 Why is it wrong to *worship buildings* as in the case of false organized religions such as Christian churches, Jewish synagogues and Moslem Mosques etc? Again, as with the Idol of Mammon worship, it is stated in the Bible 'You cannot worship God and Mammon'. Religious buildings are generally *halls of Mammon worship* and are generally, spiritually dead places. Why? Because *God certainly doesn't live there,* as He never asked for religious buildings in the first place:, icons in the form of famous paintings, statues and other very expensive idols and talismans right inside the churches (Especially the Catholic churches).

ACT.7:48 Howbeit the most High dwelleth not in temples made with hands; as saith the prophet (Isaiah).

Jesus said, 'Give all that thou hast and give it to the poor and come thou and follow Me.

MAT.19:21 Jesus said unto him, If thou wilt be perfect, go and sell that thou hast, and give to the poor, and thou shalt have treasure in heaven: and come and follow me.

MAT.19:22 But when the young man heard that saying, he went away sorrowful: for he had great possessions.

MAT.19:23 Then said Jesus unto his disciples, Verily I say unto you, That a rich man shall hardly enter into the kingdom of heaven.

The truth be known the religions of man are used by the 'Powers that be' to control the masses to keep them subservient to Mammon and not God.

C.8 Today in modern times unbeknownst to most people there are more idols than ever before. Look how much time young people spend on X-Boxes, Play-stations and I-Phones. Not to mention the serious misuse of both drugs and alcohol. With others it is gambling and wasting both time and money. I have mentioned but a few of the idols that people truly worship today!

C.9 In general, I would say that whatever people put before **God has become their Idol!**

SORCERY

C.1 This word is found many times in the Bible.

BOOK OF ENOCH 65.5 'And a command has gone forth from the presence of the Lord concerning those who dwell on the earth that their ruin is accomplished, because they have learnt all the *secrets of the angels*, and all the *violence of the Satans, and all their powers*, the most secret ones, and all the power of those who practice *sorcery,* and the power of *witchcraft*, and the power of those who make *molten images* for the whole earth.'

REV.9:20 And the rest of the men which were not killed by these plagues yet repented not of the works of their hands, that they should not worship devils, and idols of gold, and silver, and brass, and stone, and of wood: which neither can see, nor hear, nor walk:

REV.9:21 Neither repented they of their murders, nor of their *sorceries*, nor of their fornication, nor of their thefts.

REV.21:8 But the fearful, and unbelieving, and the abominable, and murderers, and whoremongers, and **sorcerers**, and **idolaters**, and all **liars**, shall have their part in the lake which burns with fire and brimstone: which is the second death.

C.2 According to the **Apocryphal Book of Wisdom**, those that **practice sorcery** or **dark arts** pretending **to heal people** and **do miracles** with be **tormented** with **horrible apparitions** and even **monsters** which will become real to them because they will be able to actually see them. Afterwards, the **sorcerers are devoured by these same monsters down in hell [Book of WISDOM Chapters 11-13,17-18]**

As the Bible verse states in the **Book of Job** ' I feared a fear and it came upon me'

JOB.3:25 For the thing which I greatly feared is come upon me, and that which I was afraid of is come unto me.

MORE BIBLE VERSES ABOUT SORCERY: WIZARDS & WITCHES

LEVITICUS 19.31- Regard not them that have familiar spirits, neither seek after wizards, to be defiled by them: I [am] the LORD your God.

GAL.5:19 Now the works of the flesh are manifest, which are these; Adultery, fornication, uncleanness, lasciviousness,

GAL.5:20 Idolatry, **witchcraft,** hatred, variance, emulations, wrath, strife, seditions, heresies,

GAL.5:21 Envyings, murders, drunkenness, revellings, and such like: of the which I tell you before, as I have also told you in time past, that they which do such things shall not inherit the kingdom of God.

ISAIAH 8.9 And when they shall say unto you, Seek unto them that have **familiar spirits**, and unto **wizards** that peep, and that mutter: should not a people seek unto their God? for the living to the dead?

ISA.57:4 Against whom do ye sport yourselves? against whom make ye a wide mouth, and draw out the tongue? are ye not children of transgression, a **seed of falsehood**.

ISA.57:5 Enflaming yourselves with idols under every green tree, **slaying the children** in the valleys under the cliffs of the rocks?

ISA.57:9 And thou went to the king with ointment, and didst increase thy perfumes, and didst send thy messengers far off, and didst **debase thyself even unto hell**.

LEVITICUS 20.6 And the soul that turns after such as have **familiar spirits**, and after **wizards**, to go a whoring after them, I will even set my face against that soul, and will cut him off from among his people.

2 CHRON 33.6 And he caused his **children to pass through the fire** in the valley of the son of Hinnom: also he observed times, and used **enchantments**, and used **witchcraft,** and dealt with a **familiar spirit**, and with **wizards**: he wrought much evil in the sight of the LORD, to provoke him to anger.

ACTS 8.9 But there was a certain man, called Simon, which beforetime in the same city used **sorcery**, and **bewitched the people of Samaria**, giving out that himself was some great one:

ACT.8:9 But there was a certain man, called Simon, which beforetime in the same city used sorcery, and bewitched the people of Samaria, giving out that himself was some great one:

ACT.8:11 And to him they had regard, because that of long time he had **bewitched** them with sorceries.

ACT.13:8 But Elymas the **sorcerer** (for so is his name by interpretation) withstood them, seeking to turn away the deputy from the faith.

JER.27:9 Therefore hearken not ye to your prophets, nor to your **diviners**, nor to your dreamers, nor to your **enchanters**, nor to your **sorcerers**, which speak unto you, saying, Ye shall not serve the king of Babylon:

EZEKIEL 13.6-9 They have seen vanity and **lying divination**, saying, The LORD saith: and the LORD hath not sent them: and they have made [others] to hope that they would confirm the word.

I SAM 15.23 For **rebellion** [is as] the sin of **witchcraft**, and stubbornness [is as] iniquity and **idolatry.** Because thou hast rejected the word of the LORD, he hath also rejected thee from [being] king.

DANIEL 2.27 Daniel answered in the presence of the king, and said, The secret which the king hath demanded cannot the wise [men], the astrologers, **the magicians**, the soothsayers, shew unto the king;

ISAIAH 19.3 And the spirit of Egypt shall fail in the midst thereof; and I will destroy the counsel thereof: and they shall seek to the idols, and to the charmers, and to them that have **familiar spirits**, and to the **wizards**.

WITCHES & WIZARDS:

DEU.18:10 There shall not be found among you anyone that makes his son or his daughter to **pass through the fire**, or that uses **divination**, or an observer of times, or an **enchanter,** or a **witch.**

DEU.18:11 Or a **charmer,** or a consulter with familiar spirits, or a **wizard**, or a **necromancer.**

DEU.18:12 For all that do these things are an **abomination** unto the LORD: and because of these abominations the LORD thy God doth drive them out from before thee.

EXO.22:18 Thou shalt not suffer a **witch** to live.

EXO.22:19 Whosoever lies with a **beast** shall surely be put to death.

EXO.22:20 He that sacrifices unto any **god** (Fallen angels, and demons), save unto the LORD only, he shall be utterly destroyed.

THE ULTIMATE WIZARDS WILL BE THE DEVIL-POSSESSED ANTI-CHRIST & THE FALSE PROPHET OF REVELATIONS 13 FAME:

REV.13:11 And I beheld another beast coming up out of the earth; and he had two horns like a lamb, and he spoke as a dragon.

REV.13:12 And he exercises all the power of the first beast before him, and causes the earth and them which dwell therein to **worship the first beast**, whose **deadly wound was healed.**

REV.13:13 And he doeth **great wonders**, so that he makes fire come down from heaven on the earth in the sight of men,

REV.13:14 And **deceives** them that dwell on the earth by the means of those **miracles** which he had power to do in the sight of the beast; saying to them that dwell on the earth, that they should make an image to the beast, which had the wound by a sword, and did live.

REV.13:15 And he had power to give life unto the **image of the beast,** that the image of the beast should both speak, and cause that as many as would not worship the image of the beast **should be killed.**

REV.13:16 And he causes all, both small and great, rich and poor, free and bond, to receive a **mark in their right hand**, or in their **foreheads:**

REV.13:17 And that no man might buy or sell, save he that had the mark, or the name of the beast, or the number of his name.

REV.13:18 Here is wisdom. Let him that hath understanding count the number of the beast: for it is the number of a man; and his number is **Six hundred threescore and six (666)**

2 THESS 2.9 [Even him], whose coming is after the working of **Satan** with all power and signs and lying wonders.

A TERRIBLE FATE AWAITS SATAN, THE FALSE PROPHET AND ALL THOSE WHO RECEIVE AND WORSHIP THE MARK OF THE BEAST:

REV.20:10 And the devil that deceived them was cast into the lake of fire and brimstone, where the beast and the false prophet are, and shall be tormented day and night for ever and ever.

REV.14:9 And the third angel followed them, saying with a loud voice, If any man worship the beast and his image, and receive his mark in his forehead, or in his hand,

REV.14:10 The same shall drink of the wine of the wrath of God, which is poured out without mixture into the cup of his indignation; and he shall be tormented with fire and brimstone in the presence of the holy angels, and in the presence of the Lamb:

REV.14:11 And the smoke of their torment ascends up for ever and ever: and they have no rest day nor night, who worship the beast and his image, and whosoever receives the mark of his name.

REV.20:11 And I saw a great white throne, and him that sat on it, from whose face the earth and the heaven fled away; and there was found no place for them.

REV.20:12 And I saw the dead, small and great, stand before God; and the books were opened: and another book was opened, which is the book of life: and the dead were judged out of those things which were written in the books, according to their works.

REV.20:13 And the sea gave up the dead which were in it; and death and hell delivered up the dead which were in them: and they were judged every man according to their works.

REV.20:14 And death and hell were cast into the lake of fire. This is the second death.

REV.20:15 And whosoever was not found written in the book of life was cast into the lake of fire.

UNIVERSAL RECONCILIATION

C.3 It would appear that eventually, God will forgive and heal all of His original Creation. Even those who are thrown in the **Lake of Fire** which are **Satan, the Anti-Christ, the False prophet, the sorcerers and Satanists**; those who receive the **Mark of the Beast of Revelations 13**, end up **alive** outside the Heavenly City of **Revelations 21-22.**
It would seem, that God's plan is NOT going to be defeated.
All that used to be in perfection will be eventually returned to perfection, after people have been purged from their iniquities. Those thrown into the Lake of Fire will no longer be allowed choices. That has been taken away from them, and they will be forcibly cleansed from all the iniquity which they absorbed in the time of their existence. After cleansing, they will be allowed to come and live peacefully outside of the great Heavenly City, where we, the Lord's people (those saved by Jesus Christ), will take the leaves of the Tree of Life out to them to heal them of their wounds and sicknesses.

REV.22:15 For without are dogs, and **sorcerers**, and whoremongers, and murderers, and idolaters, and whosoever loveth and makes a lie.

REV.22:2 In the midst of the street of it, and on either side of the river, was there the tree of life, which bare twelve manner of fruits, and yielded her fruit every month: and the leaves of the tree were for the healing of the nations.

XXIII DEVOURING BEASTS & MONSTERS

[C.9 from Chapter 1] Scripture is stating here that an entity called **DEATH** causes some people to be **DEVOURED** by the **BEASTS** of the earth. What is this really talking about?

This is a mystery that most people do not understand. What could be **prowling our planet** waiting to **devour people**? What devours mankind?

Many would argue this is talking hypothetically about sickness, but is it?
In **Revelation chapter 6** it is talking about **the HORSEMAN of DEATH; SICKNESS** is mentioned separately from **BEASTS** that devour mankind.

Is there more evidence in the scriptures that God has some kind of BEASTS or MONSTERS which take VENGEANGE on exceedingly WICKED people?

If we read the Septuagint we will find answers:

SEPTUAGUINT version of ISAIAH CH 13.3-5 we come across this strange passage: 'I give command, and I bring them: **GIANTS** are coming to fulfil my **WRATH**, rejoicing and at the same time insulting……. The Lord and His warriors are coming to **DESTROY** all the world'.

We know that the GIANTS were the offspring of the Fallen Angels and human women before the Great Flood. When the giants died in battle, their spirits became the disembodied spirits of the Giants. After the Great Flood they would do harm to mankind mostly indirectly from the hidden realm of the underworld where they were restricted as evidenced in this very **Book of Jubilees chapter 10.1-2.**

A sort of half-way spiritual realm exists between the physical and spiritual. These DEMONS have been trying to find a way back into our physical plane ever since. We know that people can get possessed of demons, but what about a **Demon coming through a Portal** and appearing in person and **DEVOURING** certain people. Is there evidence of this today?

Unfortunately due to the wickedness of mankind, **portals** are indeed **opening more and more frequently,** where these **entities** are somehow coming through and **devouring anybody in the vicinity**, and then **disappearing again back through the portals.**

This has been reported by the **Special security Forces like Delta of the USA** and **Spetnas Special Forces of Russia**.

We are told that these demons come through portals in areas of CONFLICT (Areas of Evil spirits) such as the WARZONES in Syria and recently in Morocco.

Here is a LINK to some very scary recent episodes with dangerous devouring demons:-

9-FOOT ANNUNAKI MONSTERS DEVOUR SECURITY FORCES IN MORROCCO :
https://youtu.be/oANVFwZWQNw?t=300

XXIV ZION

The first mention of Zion in the Bible is 2 Samuel 5:7: "David captured the fortress of Zion—which is the City of David." Zion was originally an ancient Jebusite fortress in the city of Jerusalem. After David's conquest of the fortress, Jerusalem became a possession of Israel. The royal palace was built there, and Zion/Jerusalem became the seat of power in Israel's kingdom.

When Solomon built the temple in Jerusalem, the meaning of *Zion* expanded further to include the temple area (Psalm 2:6; 48:2, 11–12; 132:13). This is the meaning found in the prophecy of Jeremiah 31:6, "Come, let us go up to Zion, to the LORD our God." In the Old Testament *Zion* is used as a name for the city of Jerusalem (Isaiah 40:9), the land of Judah (Jeremiah 31:12), and the nation of Israel as a whole (Zechariah 9:13).

The word *Zion* is also used in a theological or spiritual sense in Scripture.

In the Old Testament *Zion* refers figuratively to Israel as the people of God (Isaiah 60:14). In the New Testament, *Zion* refers to God's spiritual kingdom. We have not come to Mount Sinai, says the apostle, but "to Mount Zion and to the city of the living God, the heavenly Jerusalem" (Hebrews 12:22). Peter, quoting Isaiah 28:16, refers to Christ as the Cornerstone of Zion: "See, I lay a stone in Zion, a chosen and precious cornerstone, and the one who trusts in him will never be put to shame" (1 Peter 2:6).(**SOURCE**: https://www.gotquestions. org/Zion.html)]

XXV

THE KING JAMES VERSION OF THE 'OLD TESTAMENT' WAS WRITTEN IN 1611 COMPARED WITH 'THE SEPTUAGINT' WHICH WAS WRITTEN AROUND 200-300 BCE

In comparing scriptures from the **Old Testament** and with the **SEPTUAGINT LXX**:

C.1 When considering the Old Testament version the K.J.V of the Bible. How accurate is it?

The Books of the Old Testament in the Masoretic text, as shown in the K.J.V. of the Bible have been written in modern, square Hebrew characters without the vowel points. The earliest manuscripts from this time (100 A.D.) are also missing the vowel points. *This points directly to Rabbi Akiba and his group's efforts to promote rabbinical leadership over Scripture.* His group, referred to as the Council of Jamnia, wanted to produce a foundation copy of the Scriptures as the original had been burned by the Romans when Jerusalem and the Temple were destroyed in 70AD. They made a number of *changes in the Scriptures* (which have come down to us as the *Masoretic Text*).'

C.2 It sounds to me, like this guy Rabbi Akiba in 100 A.D was very bitter because of the destruction of Israel in 70 A.D, in the which 100,000 Jews were crucified around Jerusalem alone, and millions of Jews were driven out of the country of Israel in the famous 'Diaspora'. That was a direct fulfilment of a prophecy given by Jesus Himself 40 years earlier.

C.3 Apparently because Israel did get destroyed, this Rabbi Akiba obviously blamed Jesus and Christianity for the destruction of Israel and decided to try and eradicate all mention of Jesus in the Old Testament, by altering the Septuagint (Greek) version of the Old Testament which had been very carefully translated by 72 men from the original Hebrew in 300 B.C.E.. He did this because Christians were using the Septuagint versions of the Old testament, to prove that Jesus was in fact mentioned in the Old Testament as the Messiah and prophesied about hundreds and even thousands of years before

His actual birth on earth. Here are a couple of examples: Isaiah 53 (whole chapter) and Psalm 22:16.

ISA.53:5 But he was *wounded* for our *transgressions*, he was *bruised* for our *iniquities*: the *chastisement* of *our peace* was *upon him*; and with *his stripes we are healed.*

C.4 I can't think of anyone, other than Jesus Christ himself, who could have fulfilled this Old testament verse in Isaiah written over 700 years before the birth of Christ!

PSA.22:16 For dogs have compassed me: the assembly of the wicked have enclosed me: they *pierced my hands and my feet.*

C.5 The discovery of the Dead Sea Scrolls has really exposed this fake Masoretic text by clearly showing that the Septuagint version of the Old Testament is by far the most accurate, and that the Masoretic text had altered many scriptures.

SOURCE: https://theorthodoxlife.wordpress.com/2012/03/12/ masoretic-text-vs-original-hebrew/

C.6 The Masoretic text has a different wording in Deuteronomy 32:43 and Psalm 40:6. In addition chapters 5 and 11 of Genesis have a much-shortened chronology. Therefore, given these and the other variations, it is a simple matter to determine if the text of a Scripture version is following that of the ancient LXX (Septuagint), used by the Apostles and Church fathers, or is following the Masoretic text which came about 400 years later. If the Bible text does not have the full chronology in Genesis 5 & 11, or the full rendering of Deuteronomy 32:43 or the correct wording for Psalm 40:6 (39:6), then it is *not following the ancient text*, but is from the *changed Masoretic text.*

C.7 The Bible is 100% accurate when it comes to the 'New Testament', but concerning the KJV of the Old Testament, which is translated from the Masoretic Text, and therefore some important things were altered, as those who devised the Masoretic text wanted to expunge all references to Jesus as mentioned in the Old Testament, as their position was anti-Christ.

The only solution today in 2020 is for people to read the *Septuagint* versions of the *Old Testament* which was compiled much earlier than the infamous Masoretic text. The Septuagint was put together in around 300 BCE and the Masoretic text around 100 A.D   http://www.ecclesia.org/truth/comparisons. html

C.8 Here is a website which offers the Septuagint Text alongside the King James version which I personally have found very useful: http://ecmarsh.com/ lxx-kjv/

XXVI - MY SIX BOOKS

1) **OUT OF THE BOTTOMLESS PIT:** http://www.outofthebottomlesspit.co.uk/411702511

2) **ENOCH INSIGHTS:** http://www.outofthebottomlesspit.co.uk/418666481

3) **EZDRAS INSIGHTS:** http://www.outofthebottomlesspit.co.uk/420942154

4) **JASHER INSIGHTS I & II:** http://www.outofthebottomlesspit.co.uk/421385649

5) **JUBILEES INSIGHTS:** http://www.outofthebottomlesspit.co.uk/413438217

USEFUL WEBSITE LINKS:

BIBLICAL CREATION: http://www.outofthebottomlesspit.co.uk/421607713

WORD WARRIORS: http://www.outofthebottomlesspit.co.uk/420555449

THE 4 HORSEMEN: http://www.outofthebottomlesspit.co.uk/412514886

HEAVEN: http://www.outofthebottomlesspit.co.uk/412320663

LIFE AFTER DEATH: http://www.outofthebottomlesspit.co.uk/412645521

BOOK OF DANIEL: http://www.outofthebottomlesspit.co.uk/420616689

BOOK OF REVELATION: http://www.outofthebottomlesspit.co.uk/421238965

MARK OF THE BEAST: http://www.outofthebottomlesspit.co.uk/412733219

SIGNS OF THE TIMES: http://www.outofthebottomlesspit.co.uk/413019004

SIGNS: http://www.outofthebottomlesspit.co.uk/418801558

BABYLON THE GREAT: http://www.outofthebottomlesspit.co.uk/412306605

JESUS THE WORD OF GOD -THE MESSIAH:
http://www.outofthebottomlesspit.co.uk/444500140

ABOUT THE AUTHOR: http://www.outofthebottomlesspit.co.uk/413469553

AUTHOR AT AMAZON: www.amazon.com/author/777.7

FACE-BOOK: GROUP: ENOCH INSIGHTS:
https://www.facebook.com/groups/323412114853716/

My website: www.outofthebottomlesspit.co.uk

E-mail: strangetruths@outofthebottomlesspit.co.uk